THE DEVIL AT HIS ELBOW

THE DEVIL AT HIS ELBOW

ALEX MURDAUGH AND THE
FALL OF A SOUTHERN DYNASTY

VALERIE BAUERLEIN

BALLANTINE BOOKS

NEW YORK

Published in the United States by Ballantine Books, an imprint of Random House,
a division of Penguin Random House LLC, New York.

BALLANTINE BOOKS & colophon are registered trademarks
of Penguin Random House LLC.

Hardback ISBN 978-0-593-50058-3
Ebook ISBN 978-0-593-50059-0

Printed in the United States of America on acid-free paper

randomhousebooks.com

4 6 8 9 7 5 3

Map © 2024 by David Lindroth Inc.
Book design by Debbie Glasserman

For Scott, Amelia, and Luke

You can find meanness in the least of creatures, but when God made man the devil was at his elbow. A creature that can do anything.

—CORMAC MCCARTHY, *Blood Meridian*

CONTENTS

AUTHOR'S NOTE

This is a work of nonfiction, based on interviews conducted over several years with more than two hundred sources. Most sources spoke on the record, though some agreed to share information only on background. This held especially true for sources closest to the Murdaughs, given the sensitive nature of the case and the enduring influence of the family. The book is also based on hospital records, newspaper archives, and thousands of pages of court filings, including non-public depositions and exhibits. No scenes or details were invented. The dialogue and quotes are based on published accounts, were witnessed by the author, or were recounted to the author by credible sources. The author attended the six-week trial of Alex Murdaugh in Walterboro, South Carolina, and accompanied the jurors on their visit to Moselle, the hunting estate where Maggie and Paul Murdaugh were killed.

MAJOR CHARACTERS

THE MURDAUGH FAMILY

THE PAST

Randolph Murdaugh Sr. (1887–1940) Alex's great-grandfather; founder of the *Murdaugh* law firm; Fourteenth Judicial Circuit Solicitor, 1920–1940

Etta Harvey Murdaugh (1889–1918) Alex's great-grandmother; Randolph's first wife and mother of Randolph Jr. and Johnny Glenn Murdaugh

Estelle Marvin (1891–1937) Randolph's second wife, a distant cousin

Mary J. Taylor Hoffman (1900–1969) Randolph's third wife, a divorcée

Randolph "Buster" Murdaugh Jr. (1915–1998) Alex's grandfather; partner at the family firm and Fourteenth Judicial Circuit Solicitor, 1940–1986

Johnny Glenn Murdaugh (1918–1987) Alex's uncle; Buster's younger brother

Gladys Marvin Murdaugh (1916–1997) Alex's grandmother; Buster's wife; grew up on Mackay Point Plantation

THE PRESENT

Randolph Murdaugh III (1939–2021) Alex's father; partner at the family firm and Fourteenth Judicial Circuit Solicitor, 1986–2006

Elizabeth "Libby" Alexander Murdaugh (1939–2024) Alex's mother; a longtime educator and school board member

Richard Alexander "Alex" Murdaugh (1968–) Disgraced lawyer, convicted murderer, and serial thief

Margaret "Maggie" Branstetter Murdaugh (1968–2021) Alex's college sweetheart and late wife

Richard Alexander "Buster" Murdaugh Jr. (1996–) Alex and Maggie's older son

Paul Terry Murdaugh (1999–2021) Alex and Maggie's late younger son

Lynn Murdaugh Goettee (1963–) Alex's older sister

Randolph Murdaugh IV (1966–) Alex's older brother and partner in the family firm

John Marvin Murdaugh (1970–) Alex's younger brother and owner of an equipment rental business

ASSOCIATES, OTHER FAMILY, AND FRIENDS

THE PAST

Ruthven Vaux (1913–1983) Buster's mistress, a socialite who accused him of stealing her divorce settlement

Roberts Vaux (1945–) Buster's illegitimate son and onetime assistant solicitor in his office

Edith Thigpen (1912–2000) Bootlegger's wife and key witness in the federal conspiracy case against Buster

Alton Lightsey (1906–1975) Hampton County Sheriff from 1936 to 1951 and Murdaugh ally who came to see Buster as corrupt

Barrett Boulware (1956–2018) Alex's business partner; shrimper, accused drug smuggler, and former owner of Moselle

THE PRESENT

Russell Laffitte Fourth-generation executive at Palmetto State Bank

Cory Fleming Alex's law school roommate and frequent co-counsel

Chris Wilson Alex's best friend and frequent co-counsel

THE THEFTS

Alania Plyler Spohn Older of the two sisters whose mother and brother were killed in a 2005 wreck

Hannah Plyler Younger of the two sisters

Pamela Pinckney Driver in 2009 wreck in which she, her son, and her niece were critically injured

Hakeem Pinckney (1990–2011) Pamela's son, a deaf teenager who was rendered quadriplegic in the wreck and died two years later when his ventilator was left unplugged

Natarsha Thomas Pamela's niece whose eye was badly damaged in the wreck

Arthur Badger Father of six, widowed when his wife was killed in a 2011 crash with a UPS truck

THE DEATHS

THE FALL

Gloria Satterfield (1961–2018) Longtime Murdaugh housekeeper, died three weeks after falling down the steps at Moselle

Brian Harriott Gloria's older son, a vulnerable adult

Tony Satterfield Gloria's younger son, an emergency room technician

Ginger Hadwin Gloria's younger sister and a classmate of Alex Murdaugh

Michael DeWitt Jr. Longtime editor of *The Hampton County Guardian*

THE ROAD

Stephen Smith (1996–2015) Nursing student killed and left in the middle of a country road

Sandy Smith Stephen's mother and advocate for solving his case

Stephanie Smith Stephen's twin sister

THE BOAT WRECK

Mallory Beach (1999–2019) Killed when boat driven by Paul Murdaugh crashed into a bridge

Anthony Cook Mallory's boyfriend and Paul's childhood friend

Connor Cook Anthony's cousin, Paul's friend, and boyfriend of Miley Altman

Miley Altman Mallory's best friend and Connor's girlfriend

Morgan Doughty Mallory's friend and Paul's girlfriend

Renee Beach Mallory's mother

Phillip Beach Mallory's father

Beverly Cook Anthony's mother

Marty Cook Connor's father

Mark Tinsley Beach family lawyer and onetime friend of Alex's

Joe McCulloch Lawyer for Connor

Austin Pritcher Rookie officer for the South Carolina Department of Natural Resources who led the early investigation

THE MURDERS AT MOSELLE

THE INVESTIGATION

Daniel Greene Colleton County sheriff's deputy and first officer on the scene

Laura Rutland Colleton County sheriff's detective and assistant homicide investigator

David Owen South Carolina Law Enforcement Division (SLED) agent and lead homicide investigator

Jeff Croft SLED agent and assistant homicide investigator

Peter Rudofski SLED agent who prepared eighty-eight-page timeline based on digital records

THE PROSECUTION

Alan Wilson S.C. Attorney General, a Republican who attended much of the trial

Creighton Waters Veteran white-collar prosecutor and the lead on the Murdaugh case

John Meadors Veteran violent-crime prosecutor recruited on the eve of the trial

THE DEFENSE

Richard "Dick" Harpootlian State senator, former prosecutor, and long-time criminal defense lawyer

Jim Griffin Former federal prosecutor and white-collar defense lawyer

THE COURTROOM

The Hon. Clifton Newman Judge overseeing all Murdaugh matters

Rebecca "Becky" Hill Colleton County Clerk of Court

'Nette Grant Colleton County Sheriff's Deputy and security for the Murdaugh family

THE KEY WITNESSES

Blanca Turrubiate-Simpson Murdaugh housekeeper and Maggie's confidante

Marian Proctor Maggie's older sister

Mushelle "Shelley" Smith Overnight caretaker for Libby Murdaugh, Alex's mother

Roger "Dale" Davis Fed and cared for the dogs at Moselle

THE JURORS

James McDowell Alternate juror, a witness's brother, added to the panel the last day

Gwen Generette Juror focused on kennel video

Amie Williams Payroll specialist who led the jury in prayer

Craig Moyer Carpenter who paid close attention to Alex's shows of emotion

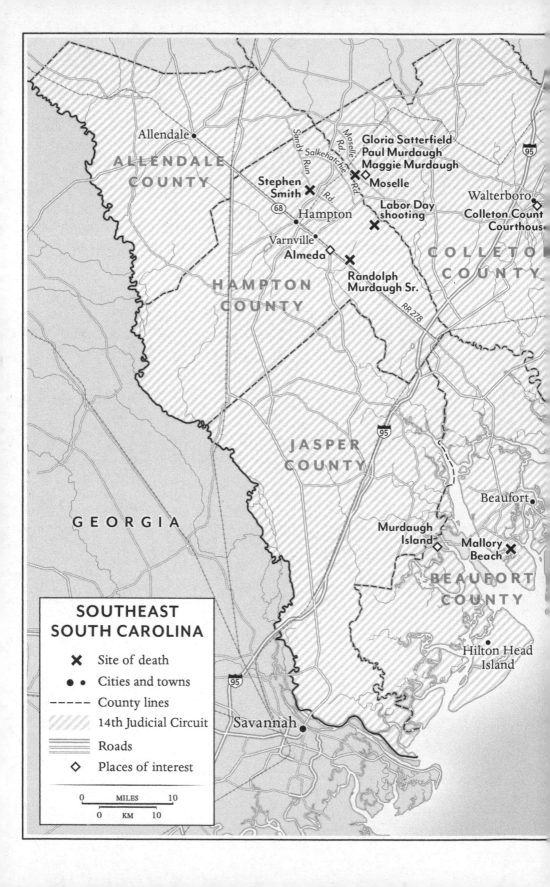

SOUTHEAST
SOUTH CAROLINA

✗ Site of death
• • Cities and towns
- - - - County lines
///// 14th Judicial Circuit
≣≣≣ Roads
◇ Places of interest

0 MILES 10
0 KM 10

ALLENDALE
COUNTY

Allendale •

Stephen
Smith ✗

68 Hampton •

Varnville •
Almeda ◇

HAMPTON
COUNTY

Sandy Run
Salkehatchie
Rd.

Moselle Rd.

Gloria Satterfield
Paul Murdaugh
Maggie Murdaugh
✗ ◇ Moselle

Labor Day
shooting ✗

Randolph
Murdaugh Sr. ✗

RR 278

95

Walterboro ◇
Colleton County
Courthouse

COLLETON
COUNTY

JASPER
COUNTY

GEORGIA

95

Beaufort •

Murdaugh
Island ◇

Mallory
Beach ✗

BEAUFORT
COUNTY

Hilton Head
Island •

95

Savannah •

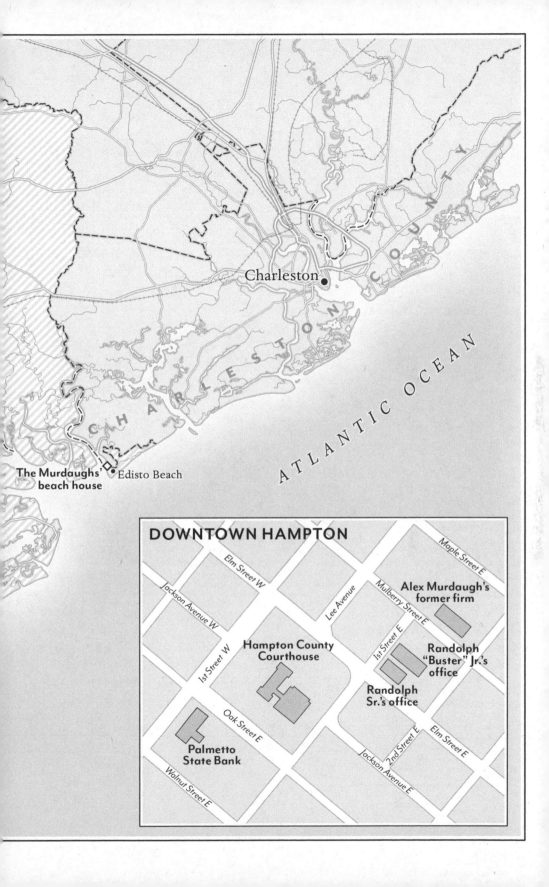

The Murdaughs'
beach house • Edisto Beach

ATLANTIC OCEAN

Charleston

CHARLESTON COUNTY

DOWNTOWN HAMPTON

Maple Street E

Elm Street W

Jackson Avenue W

Lee Avenue

Mulberry Street E

Alex Murdaugh's
former firm

1st Street W

1st Street E

**Hampton County
Courthouse**

**Randolph
"Buster" Jr.'s
office**

**Randolph
Sr.'s office**

Oak Street E

2nd Street E

Elm Street E

**Palmetto
State Bank**

Jackson Avenue E

Walnut Street E

PART ONE

THE PRINCE OF HAMPTON COUNTY

CHAPTER ONE

The accused man sat in the same courtroom where he and his father and grandfather and great-grandfather had accused so many others, sending some to their death for crimes less heinous than the charges he faced. Alex Murdaugh had inherited his forebears' power and prowess and then squandered it, the work of a hundred years washed away in blood. At first, the deputies he'd known as friends exchanged pleasantries when they ferried him to and from jail. Now, several weeks into the trial, they tightened the cuffs a click more than necessary.

In Colleton County, a hardscrabble corner of South Carolina's Lowcountry, the courtroom had always been considered grand, with its mahogany benches and brass chandeliers suspended from a soaring ceiling. It had been designed by the same architect who created the Washington Monument and was crafted to instill a hushed sense of reverence. The front of the courtroom was dominated by a massive dark wood edifice; this was the judge's bench, but the term felt too paltry to describe the structure, which was both imposing and bulletproof. On the wall behind the bench hung the state seal, the motto every child in the state memorized in school: DUM SPIRO SPERO.

While I breathe, I hope.

Portraits of stern-faced court officials, most of them long dead,

gazed down from within gilded frames. One of the paintings, a ren-
dering of Alex's legendary grandfather, had been taken down before
the trial on the order of the judge, who did not want the jury to feel the
old man's eyes upon them as they decided his grandson's fate. In the
portrait's place, a pale rectangle remained on the wall, a hint of missing history.

The judge had been acquainted with Alex's grandfather and had
been a contemporary of Alex's father decades earlier when they were
fellow prosecutors. But it was Alex, the gregarious trial lawyer, whom
the judge knew best. At least, the judge had thought so. After several
weeks of testimony, the judge was no longer sure he had ever known
the man at all.

In the early weeks of the trial, Alex kept up appearances, covering
his shackles with a folded blazer, freshening his breath with Tic Tacs,
trading fist bumps with the bailiffs, arranging for his family to bring
him a John Grisham novel so he'd have something to read in his holding cell. Even on trial for his life, he treated the courtroom as his duchy.
He whispered to his lawyers and smiled at the jurors and stared down
the prosecutors as though he could will them into silence.

Some of the most damning testimony came from those who knew
him best: his family's housekeeper, his wife's sister, another lawyer
who had grown close to Alex and then recoiled after seeing the ruth-
lessness at his friend's core. Once the lawyer understood, he had vowed
to force Alex to a reckoning.

To counter the damage, the defense team showed the jury a video
of Alex's family singing at his birthday party barely a week before their
world ended. Staring at the shimmering footage, Alex began to rock
back and forth, his shoulders jerking, his jaw working furiously, a torrent of motion. Under their voices, his lawyers told him to tone it down.

"This fucking rocking," one muttered during a break. "It's like he's
catatonic."

Then came the morning when Alex took the stand, defying his
legal team's advice. As a veteran trial lawyer, he knew the risks of testifying on his own behalf. But the desire to tell his story was too strong.

He was a Murdaugh. The lawyers in his family had spent decades shaping testimony to suit their needs, rearranging reality not just in court but in every square mile of their territory. It was his right to speak in this courtroom.

He put his hand on the Bible and swore to tell the truth, then settled into the witness box, adjusting the microphone for his height. The wooden chair beneath him creaked.

From an evidence box on the carpet, his lawyer picked up a shotgun.

"On June seventh, 2021, did you take this gun or any gun like it and shoot your son Paul in the chest in the feed room in your property off of Moselle Road?"

"No," Alex said. "I did not."

The lawyer held up the shotgun again.

"Did you take this gun, or any gun like it, and blow your son's brains out on June seventh, or any day, or any time?"

Alex squinted, his jaw working front to back.

"No," he said, more emphatically. "I did not."

The lawyer dropped the gun back into the evidence box with a thud that made spectators jump. Then he picked up a sleek black tactical rifle.

"Did you take a three-hundred-caliber Blackout, such as this, and fire it into your wife Maggie's leg, torso, or any part of her body?"

Alex nodded but said "No, I did not."

"Did you shoot a three-hundred-caliber Blackout into her head, causing her death?"

"I didn't shoot my wife or my son, any time, ever." He nodded again. "I would never intentionally do anything to hurt either one of them, ever."

The lawyer looked at his client. "Do you love Paul?"

"Did I love him? Like no other."

"Do you love Maggie?"

"More than anything."

Alex described that last summer evening with his family, sketching every detail so the jurors could see the picture in their minds. How he and Paul had ridden around the property together in the fading light. How they had inspected fields of corn and sunflowers, looked for signs of wild hogs, and picked up a pistol for a quick round of target prac-tice. How Paul had laughed when Alex couldn't make a sapling stand straight. They had returned to the house at dusk just as Maggie pulled up, he said. Their housekeeper had left them dinner on the stove, cube steak and rice and green beans, and they'd eaten quickly. Afterward Paul had gone down to the kennels to check on one of the dogs, and Maggie had gone with him. Alex said he had taken a nap, then gone to see his mother. When he returned to Moselle, he said, he had found them lying on the ground near the kennels.

As he tried to describe the blood and the stillness of the bodies, Alex began coughing and bobbing his chin toward his chest. For five seconds he was silent, then five seconds more. His face, always ruddy, was now fully flushed. His nose was running.

"It was so bad," he said.

Another long pause, this time lasting nearly a minute. Alex twisted in his seat, seeming to look for something on the floor.

"Can I have some water?"

His lawyer passed him a bottle and Alex took a long drink.

For more than a year after that night, Alex had sworn to police that he had stayed at the house before leaving to check on his mother. Now, in court, he acknowledged that he had in fact joined his wife and son at the kennels for a few minutes before going to his mother's house. Why, his lawyer asked, had he deceived investigators for so long?

Alex paused before answering. He had begun folding into himself.

"Oh," he said finally with a shrug and a sigh, "what a tangled web we weave."

During cross-examination, the lead prosecutor grilled Alex about his pattern of deceit. How he had lied to the first officer to arrive at the scene that night, and then to the captain who arrived soon after, and then to the two detectives who had tried to comfort him, patting his shoulder and offering words of condolence. He had lied to them all and even to his own attorneys about the truth of that night.

Alex stayed calm even as the prosecutor forced him to confirm all the other lies he'd told through the years, to his own family and to his closest friends and the clients who had counted on him. The quadriplegic deaf teenager from whom he had embezzled a million dollars. The young motherless sisters he had left destitute, one of them living out of her car. Had he felt entitled to betray their trust?

"No," Alex said. He had found ways, he said, to live with his sins. He'd told himself he would pay the money back; he was only taking what he deserved; his clients would never miss it.

"To be able to look yourself in the mirror," he said, "you lie to yourself."

The prosecutor wanted to know how Alex had gotten these vulnerable people to trust him. Surely he had looked each of them in the eye as he stole their money.

"Correct?"

The witness had become visibly uncomfortable.

"Answer my question, yes or no," said the prosecutor, "and then you can explain. I'll let you explain all day long."

Alex said he had betrayed many people and regretted it.

The prosecutor cut him off. "I know, Mr. Murdaugh, that you would like for it just to be as simple as that. Just to say, 'Yes, ladies and gentlemen, I stole money,' and have that be the end of it."

Again and again, the prosecutor hammered on Alex's skills as a fabulist. He could lie convincingly and naturally, couldn't he?

"Really that's not for me to judge," Alex said.

"That's true," said the prosecutor. He did not look toward the jury box. There was no need.

The twelve men and women charged with deciding the case studied the face of the accused. They were trying to understand if this man had truly been cold-blooded enough to gun down his wife and son at close range just after dinner on a warm summer evening.

All human beings are flawed and fragile, yes. But the longer Alex testified, the more the jurors wondered if they were in the presence of someone who existed outside expectation and restraint, beyond all boundaries. A man so practiced in pretending that he had become un-knowable.

Some of the jurors suspected he was playing a part with them, too. By now they recognized his tells. His odd habit of nodding yes even as he said no. The extravagance of his explanations, like a child embroidering a story. The endless rocking and weeping.

He cried so hard, so often, that one juror offered a box of tissues. When Alex dabbed his eyes, the jurors seated closest to him, only a few feet away, looked at the crumpled tissues in his hand.

The tissues were dry.

CHAPTER TWO

By the time the trial was over, Alex Murdaugh had revealed himself as a hollow man, capable not just of annihilating his wife and son but of trying to pin the murders on others, defrauding his most vulnerable clients, betraying his law partners and his closest friends, deceiving even his family about almost every aspect of his life. The question that confounded so many was exactly how such a prosperous and respected citizen had come to lay ruin to the lives of everyone around him.

It's impossible to pinpoint the moment Alex Murdaugh's long spiral began. It could have been when he blew out his knee playing football at the University of South Carolina and started taking pills for the pain. Or in the years after, when he started taping little bags of oxycodone under his bed. Some who knew Alex, or believed they did, insisted that his addiction stories were exaggerated, a cover he used to distract attention from his real transgressions. They argue that the downfall began when Alex developed a habit of inventing legal expenses so he could make his clients pay for his family's groceries, vacations, and private school tuition. He'd lost millions in failed land investments during the housing bust, so maybe he'd fallen into a financial hole so deep that he couldn't climb out. It's possible that his work as a personal injury lawyer, dealing daily in the business of death—the more grievous the better—inured him to the suffering of others. Maybe the downfall began the day he first saw his son Paul, barely a teenager, sipping a beer and did not take it from him. Or maybe it was years later, on the foggy night when Paul drunkenly crashed the family's boat out on the marshes, throwing him and two of his friends into the dark water. Within the hour, Alex was racing to the hospital to help his son hide the truth.

The pills, the embezzling, the indulgence of his wayward son—all of these threads braided together to cast Alex into ruin.

Many versed in the history of Hampton County, South Carolina, would point out that the seeds of the fall were planted by three previous generations, besotted with power and stained by bloodshed. Sudden exits had haunted the Murdaughs for more than a century: suspicious accidents, unusual deaths, deaths that were faked, deaths rumored to be murders, death during childbirth, death on the battle-field, death during a quiet night at home, death by musket and shotgun and rifle, death by drowning, death on a dark road, death by stairs. Long before Alex was born, lethal violence was woven into his family's story, along with chicanery and infidelity and enough hubris for several Greek tragedies.

Alex had his secrets. So did his forefathers. Alex's father, grand-father, and great-grandfather could make secrets disappear, and they had taught Alex to embrace the family ethos: To live above the law, you must become the law.

Hampton County, named for a Confederate general who had been one of the South's biggest slave owners, had never recovered from the Civil War, when Sherman's army marched through in two flanks and burned everything in sight. Hampton had been founded as a "white county," one where the vanquished could exist as if the South had never lost, away from the scrutiny of the outside world.

There, among the cypress trees and loblolly pines rising out of the ashes, the Murdaughs carved an isolated empire. For decades the family reigned as the region's chief prosecutors—solicitors, they were called—as well as the Lowcountry's most feared civil litigators, amassing power and wealth through a system of control that served as Alex's true inheritance. Through word and example, his forebears had taught him to tamper with juries and lean on judges and call in favors from governors. Inside Hampton and the other four counties of the state's Fourteenth Judicial Circuit, they decided right and wrong, defined the parameters of justice, and shifted those parameters at will. In those 3,300 square miles, they chose when to set free a violent criminal and when to send someone to the electric chair. Over the decades, external forces had threatened the family's autonomy many times: the railroads, the Depression, the Internal Revenue Service, the Department of Justice. All of them battered the walls of the empire, and all were beaten back. The Murdaughs' authority had endured for so long it seemed inviolable, a way of being, like the Old South itself, with no beginning and no end. The family ruled on until Alex grew old enough to assume his rightful place in the succession.

Then came the day he made the choice to step away.

That decision to turn down the chance to become the circuit's next solicitor might have been the real trigger for Alex's collapse. Afterward, when people asked why, he would grin and say he was too busy making money at the family firm. What Alex didn't say was where much of that money was really coming from.

Alex's fall toppled his family's empire. And it shattered Hampton County's insistence that it was immune to progress.

In the long months before the trial, when he talked about what went wrong, Alex did not wax on about the go-along-to-get-along ways of the small-town South or his family's century of dominance. But if he paused and allowed himself a moment of self-reflection, he might have allowed that the point of no return had arrived on a bright afternoon in the mid-2000s.

The day Alania Plyler, teetering on her crutches, hobbled into his life.

CHAPTER THREE

The young girl lying awake and alone was used to figuring things out for herself. She'd spent weeks in intensive care after that terrible day on the highway, when the SUV spun out and flipped and took her mother and her big brother. Alania Plyler knew even then she needed someone to fight for her in court. Only twelve years old, she wanted a lawyer—a good one.

When she left the hospital after four weeks, Alania moved into a strange house with grandparents she barely knew and an indifferent and alcoholic father who was gone more than he was home. They made room for a hospital bed in the downstairs of the crowded house, and Alania lay there day and night, shifting now and then to relieve the pressure on her crushed shoulder, and on her arm, held together with steel, and on her right leg, broken in two places, and on her mangled left leg. Her body felt like one big cast. Her little sister was her caretaker, feeding her and wheeling her to the bathroom and back. She reminded herself she was not paralyzed. Her injuries, at least most of them, would heal. She believed in miracles.

She closed her eyes and, as she so often did, pictured her mother's face and how it had glowed as she died. Alania knew that the glow was her mother's soul, rising out of the wreckage and ascending to heaven, a last luminous gift from the woman who had been both her mama and her best friend. Whenever she conjured her mother's face, she saw the rest of the car, too. She saw herself trapped in the back seat of the Explorer as it stopped its awful rolling and careened into a stand of pines. Her mother had finally left her father twelve days before, and the TV they'd been returning to him smashed into Alania's left shoulder, pinning her. Her right side was jammed against the door, and the door was lodged against a tree. The front passenger seat collapsed into her lap along with the broken body of her fourteen-year-old brother, Justin. On the other side of the TV, she could hear her eight-year-old sister, Hannah, wriggling.

"Crawl out!" Alania shouted to her. "Run for help!"

Then Alania waited. She could not bear to look at her mother now that the light had left her, nor did she want to look down at her brother. She knew even then that there were things a child should never see. She looked instead out the shattered window, where she could see a flash in the tree branches. It was the fading sunlight reflecting off the CD she'd been listening to on her headphones before the Explorer's tire blew out. In her ears, Usher had been confessing his sins.

Alania and her sister had lost everything that day in July 2005, and while she made a plan for herself and her little sister, she encountered a lawyer who said all the right things. He reassured her over the phone, telling her time and again that what had happened to her family wasn't right. He said he would get justice for her mother and brother, and more money for her and her sister than they could ever spend. On the morning she was scheduled to meet with the lawyer in person for the first time, she walked outside on her crutches and lowered herself into the sedan he had sent just for her and then watched the pines rolling by outside the window as she was ushered a hundred miles into the Low-country.

When she reached the law firm where she was supposed to give her first deposition in the case, her lawyer stepped forward to meet her. He was tall and loud with red hair. Alania noticed that other adults stepped back from him when he got close, like they were scared of him, which gave her a strange sense of comfort. He reminded her of a bulldog. He told her he had a son close to her age. He promised that Alania and Hannah would prevail in the lawsuit he had already filed on the sisters' behalf against the companies responsible for the accident. He said he would make sure Alania and Hannah had a safe place to live, new clothes, and plenty of food. When they were old enough, they'd never have to work unless they wanted to. Alania's mother had worked two jobs, sometimes even a third, selling copies of *The State* newspaper on the side of the road. Money was always on Alania's mind, and the idea of having enough was exhilarating. This lawyer seemed like the type of person who would do exactly what he said he was going to do.

The lawyer told her that he was sure her father was a good man, but he wasn't capable of handling all the legal red tape. He had someone in mind to serve as a conservator for her and Hannah. It was best to have all the paperwork filed in Hampton County, he said, because he knew every single person at the courthouse as well as next door at the bank, and they would make sure it all went smoothly. He had lots of forms to show her and whisked them past her in a flash.

Years later, going through those forms, Alania noticed something strange. On the line for her mailing address, the man had written the address for her grandparents' house, where she and her sister were living. But on the line where it asked why the paperwork was being filed at the courthouse near his office, he had checked the box that said she was a resident of Hampton County.

The lawyer had sworn to protect Alania and her sister. He called her Lainey, the nickname her mother had given her.

"I am going to make this right, Lainey," Mr. Alex said. That's what he'd said she should call him. "You can trust me."

WHEN HE MET Alania Plyler, Alex Murdaugh radiated the confidence of a man at the peak of his career.

On the cusp of forty, he was already one of South Carolina's most powerful trial attorneys, assuming the mantle passed down by his forefathers. His reputation for winning eye-popping verdicts from home-town juries was so established that most of the corporations he sued—or at least, their insurance companies—preferred to settle out of court. He could turn a case worth $100,000 in any other county into a $1 million case in Hampton, just by virtue of who he was. When he wasn't working his caseload, Alex hosted political fundraisers on his family's island compound, offered his counsel to governors and sena-tors, and practiced his homespun charm inside the corridors of the state legislature in Columbia.

On his home turf in Hampton County, Alex was an unstoppable force and an inescapable presence. Walking down the street or into the courthouse, he greeted everyone he saw and often inquired after their mothers and grandmothers. At the Little League fields, where his law firm paid for the uniforms, he beamed at the kids and the umps and the other parents in the stands. Wherever he went, he bestowed small fa-vors upon people who were pleasantly surprised that he remembered them. He tipped generously, always in cash pulled from stacks of bills tossed in the console of his SUV.

He pronounced his name "Ellick Murdick," in the traditional Scot-tish diction that lingered for centuries in the rural South. He liked to call himself Big Daddy, but most friends referred to him as Big Red. At six foot four, he towered over everyone around him, often sidling up to people and slinging an arm around their shoulders. Like many former athletes, he struggled with his weight and often seemed bloated. He had fair skin and bloodshot eyes, his teeth stained from the near-constant pinch of tobacco in his gum. He carried himself like an aging frat boy who had never left the keg party, a red Solo cup of beer or bourbon frequently in hand. Yet he remained surprisingly nimble on his feet and employed his size to dominate, especially in court, where his height conveyed an automatic authority. With his booming laugh and easy sense of humor, he established himself as the center of atten-tion at every pool party and civic luncheon, as if he generated his own gravitational field. He had a knack for reading people, assessing their vulnerabilities, divining what they wanted to hear. Everyone in Hampton knew him, and many nurtured the bone-deep belief that he was a friend they could count on.

He had always been the town's fortunate son. As the schools integrated, a lot of white kids moved to new private schools known as segregation academies. Alex stayed in public school, a man of the people, like his father and grandfather. At Wade Hampton High, he'd been the prom king, the senior voted best all-around and the star quarterback who led the Red Devils to win the regional championship. His adult life seemed bathed in the same amber light. He married Maggie, the blond beauty he claimed to have loved since the moment he first saw her at the University of South Carolina. Maggie had gone to high school in the Philadelphia suburbs and didn't know what to make of the tall country boy, as brash as she was quiet. Alex pursued Maggie until she accepted his invitation to his fraternity formal in Savannah, a Kappa Alpha ball called Old South. Maggie wore a gown straight out of *Gone with the Wind;* Alex wore a gray Confederate uniform. They were wed in a two-hundred-year-old church in downtown Charleston, with the reception at the historic Hibernian Hall, site of the 1860 political convention that was a tipping point for the Civil War. Maggie's sister was her matron of honor; Alex's father was his best man. He promised she would never have to work unless she wanted to.

Alex had only one condition: They had to live in Hampton. Maggie made a beautiful home on Holly Street on the outskirts of town, a two-story white brick house with black shutters and a shaded front porch. They added a pool for their sons, Buster and Paul, who liked to have their baseball and soccer teammates over for parties. Alex coached the boys' teams year after year, just as his father had coached him. Their house sat down a long, wooded driveway across from the Hampton cemetery, where multiple generations of Murdaughs were buried in a family plot guarded by a wrought iron gate.

On weekends, the family would drive an hour southeast to their house on Edisto Island, a shabby-chic beach town of cottages, fishing piers, and hole-in-the-wall bars. Reachable mostly by backroads, Edisto was a haven for the wealthy professional class of rural South Carolina. Alex and Maggie bought the beach house when the boys were just starting school. Their friends would fill their coolers from a commercial ice maker before going out for a day of fishing or, better yet, just tooling around on a boat with some beers. Alex had many boats over the years. In those days, his main boat was named *Bad Boys*.

Maggie devoted her life to her family. Before her marriage, she had briefly worked at the power company, and years later, she and her mother-in-law opened a gift shop called Branches in downtown Hampton, but it had soon closed. Now Maggie focused on Buster and Paul and her husband. She was a smiling and generous hostess. She wore her wealth as lightly as she could in the poor place she lived, carrying her Louis Vuitton purse on vacation but her Coach purse in town. Still, she kept some distance from the friends she made in Hampton, never certain whether they liked her or her last name.

Alex stayed in constant motion. He often worked in his mobile office, a Suburban paid for by the law firm. Always speeding, he was pulled over plenty but rarely ticketed. The one state trooper who dared to ticket him for having an open container of alcohol was mysteriously reassigned two months later, and the ticket was dismissed. Alex kept his grandfather's solicitor's badge face up on the dashboard. When he got pulled over, he'd move the badge to the cupholder, where it was harder to ignore. He even had blue lights installed. A favorite trick was to roll up at a party, lights flashing, making his arrival even more of a spectacle than it already was.

At the law firm, Alex alternated between bursts of intense focus huddled at his desk, and spells leaning against doorways, shooting the breeze until his cellphone rang, which it inevitably did. Sometimes he answered in the hallway, went to his office to talk, and picked up another call on his desk phone, alternating between the two conversations. He tended to be most productive late in the day, working right up to the deadline for filing briefs or responding to defense lawyers. His habits spawned headshakes and sighs from the paralegals who stuck with him. He wrote them $100 checks for minor holidays and

$500 checks for major ones, always with a cheerful "Happy 4th!!" or "Happy Birthday!" in the memo line.

Alania Plyler had been referred to Alex by a lawyer in Columbia who'd helped Alania's father out of a jam. The lawyer knew Alex because everybody knew Alex. Forging relationships was his specialty. One of Alex's mentors, a friend of his father's named Jim Moss, had hired Alex just after law school. When Moss took his protégé for a drink one afternoon, he was stunned by his ability to win over the crowd at the bar. By the time Alex finished clapping shoulders, he had made every single person feel as though he genuinely knew them. And if they ever needed a lawyer, well, he had already slipped them his card.

"Alex was no great student of the law," Moss said. "But he was a good bullshitter. Sometimes that's all you have to be."

Every fall, Alex gave out tickets to friends and colleagues on the fifty-yard line at the University of South Carolina. The Murdaugh tailgate was widely known as the best party in the parking lot, with barbecue, beer, and dozens of Jell-O shots in Gamecock garnet. At the annual convention of trial lawyers, held every August on Hilton Head, the most coveted invitation was to the Murdaugh firm's dinner at the Sea Grass Grille, an island institution with $30 entrées and the best wine list on the island. They'd bring the lawyers and their spouses over on luxury buses. Even though his father and older brother outranked him at the firm, Alex had long since taken over as emcee.

Alex conferred special attention on state troopers, police officers, and sheriff's deputies, some of whose fathers had worked with Alex's father or, better yet, his grandfather. The officers appreciated it when Alex stopped by the station with a cooler jammed with ribeyes. Every summer, at Hampton's Watermelon Festival, the firm raised a tent on the courthouse square with fans, bottled water, and slices of watermelon. At Thanksgiving, Alex doled out turkeys in the firm's parking lot.

The family's largesse was almost as legendary as its influence, but not quite. One Murdaugh or another usually sat on the Hampton

County commission, the school board, and the board of elections. Alex was one of the biggest individual donors in the state, giving $90,000 over a decade to Republicans and Democrats alike. But like his forefathers, Alex was a Democrat and served a decade as the head of the local party, a key position in a predominantly Black community where Democrats still dominated politics. Securing his family's support was the only way to become sheriff or senator or judge. Politicians who sought the Murdaughs' blessing had to accept that they might someday be asked a favor in return. Some of those quid pro quos would be easy. Some would be hard.

WHEN ALEX ENCOUNTERED the Plyler girls in 2005, he had arrived at a turning point in his legal career. In addition to his civil practice, he had been serving for years as an assistant prosecutor, working for his father, who was winding up his tenure as the Fourteenth Circuit's solicitor. Randolph Murdaugh III was the third generation of the family to serve as the circuit's top lawman. After nearly twenty years in office, he was ready to retire, leaving the prestigious and powerful position for his son to claim.

Alex had coveted the job since he was five years old, when he shadowed his father at the courthouse and acted as jury boy, drawing names for the panel. The Hampton County Guardian had covered his visit in a story headlined 4TH GENERATION MURDAUGH IN COURT. For years, Alex had been talking up his plan to run, partly to silence the grumbling of lawyers down in Beaufort, by far the biggest county in the circuit. One Murdaugh or another had been solicitor for more than eighty years, overseeing law enforcement not just in Hampton but throughout the circuit's other four counties. The Beaufort lawyers thought it was time for new blood.

In the months leading to his father's retirement, Alex seemed to be campaigning for the job. Crossing the street from the Hampton courthouse to the sandwich shop, he stopped to glad-hand at each table. The locals took pride in the Murdaughs' historic monopoly on the office, and when they saw Alex, they urged him to keep the power base in Hampton.

"Hey, Bo," they asked him. "What do you say?"

Alex hemmed and hawed. But in the end, he demurred. Duffie Stone, another assistant solicitor and a protégé of Alex's father, was ready to take over. Alex was content to let Stone have the job. If the family's handpicked successor stepped out of line, Alex let it be known that he'd run against him and set things right. It was an empty threat. By New Year's Eve 2005, the day his father's retirement took effect, Alex was already hiding an addiction to opioids. Realistically, there was no way he could prosecute every accused criminal in the Fourteenth Circuit while secretly committing felonies of his own.

Duffie Stone invited Alex to stay on as a volunteer solicitor, granting him his own badge, though he primarily continued to use his grandfather's. Perhaps Alex had convinced himself that a badge was all he needed.

NOW HE WAS free to focus on his lucrative practice at the family firm. In opening arguments in his personal injury cases, Alex would walk up to the jury box and point out the portraits hanging in the courtroom. "That's my daddy," he'd say. "And that's my granddaddy. And that's my great-granddaddy." They'd been fighting for the people for one hundred years, he'd say.

The Murdaughs had a system, built on one simple principle. For decades they had been grooming the county's citizens—people who would one day receive summons for jury duty—to understand that one way to get back at the world, a world that so often looked down on them, was to hit the big guys where it hurt, in their wallets. When their clients cashed their settlement checks, they saw the Murdaughs as their saviors.

In the words of another South Carolina lawyer, "A jury trial is the mechanism for the redistribution of wealth in Hampton County."

With Alania Plyler, Alex had a different kind of redistribution in mind. He saw an opening, and he took it. Then he saw another, and another. Soon he had a system all his own. Alania had no idea what her lawyer was up to. She had almost no choice but to trust him. She and her little sister were grieving and penniless and alone. Mr. Alex was the prince of Hampton County.

CHAPTER FOUR

Pamela Pinckney woke up hours after the crash, her body so shattered she could not move even an inch in her bed in the intensive care unit. Pamela was afraid, not so much for herself as for Hakeem, her nineteen-year-old son, who had been sitting in the back seat of her Ford Explorer when the tire exploded. Pamela had always taken special care of Hakeem, who was deaf. It was crucial to be with him now, because he could read her lips better than anyone else's, and she could always reassure him when he was scared. But Hakeem was confined in a different part of the hospital, and it would be weeks before she would be well enough to be wheeled to him.

That summer day in 2009, the mother and son had been on their way to Family Dollar, the closest thing to a grocery store in Yemassee, a town of less than a thousand people on the southern border of Hampton County. They had spent the morning crabbing on the side of the road. When they got home, Hakeem wanted a bowl of Froot Loops, and they were out of milk. Pamela took Interstate 95, which served as a main street for locals. It was late August, the time of year when the heat was so baked into the asphalt that ladies wore flat shoes so their heels wouldn't get stuck in the parking lot. Pamela brought her daughter and niece along so they could swing by McDonald's on the way. The family had traveled just a few miles on I-95 when her Explorer started to swerve. She tapped the brake and the SUV flipped over and over, then crashed upside down into the metal median, crushing the roof and doors and ejecting all four passengers, none of whom were wearing seatbelts. Pamela was thrown onto the side of the road, where she landed feetfirst, breaking both ankles, her right knee, femur, and shoulder, and her neck. Hakeem was thrown more than a hundred feet and landed on his head.

The wreck shut down the interstate for hours in both directions. Hakeem was airlifted to the hospital in Charleston. Doctors performed surgery on his spinal cord, but it didn't work. The crash left him a quadriplegic.

Pamela had been airlifted to the hospital, too. She'd been there just a few days when Alex Murdaugh came to see her. He was tall and confident and made her feel at ease, even though he was in a suit and she was in a hospital gown with her hair undone, her body immobilized, and screws sticking out of her ankles. Her two front teeth had been knocked out in the crash. Alex sidled up as close to her bed as possible, facing her and looking into her eyes. She told him how she'd heard a loud pop when the tire blew. She told him how Hakeem was her sunshine and a star defender at the school for the deaf in Spartanburg, and how his father was not in the picture anymore. Pamela was a part-time evangelist preacher. She told him she relied on Medicaid and worried whether it would be enough to take care of her son the rest of his life.

In Pamela's eyes, Alex radiated power. In his presence she felt calm, almost optimistic, believing that somehow he was going to make everything okay. He'd handled many of these tire cases and knew exactly what to do. He would represent Hakeem, since his case would be the most complex, and he would get a friend to represent Pamela. When the money came in, and he said it would, he knew a banker who could handle that, too.

There in her hospital bed Pamela signed the paperwork. Over the years to come, she signed whatever he asked, not realizing that one of the forms took away her right to learn what was happening in her case.

Another authorized the transfer of the settlement money into accounts controlled by the banker, not her.

"Whatever you need, I'm here to support you," Mr. Alex said. "You will be like family to me."

THE MURDAUGH LAW firm was an engine that ran on suffering, specializing in personal injury and wrongful death in a place with no shortage of it.

Rural South Carolina had shamefully dangerous roads, thousands of miles unspooling through the swamp with no tax base to support repairs. Poor folks with rusting clunkers and little insurance navigated narrow and crumbling roads with no shoulders. Those same residents often worked in industries like trucking and logging that survived on the workers' willingness to do dangerous work for low pay. The wrecks, the on-the-job injuries, the multiplicity of other woes that defined the lives of so many people in a poor and rural area—all of it was distilled into lawsuits that enriched the firm.

Hampton County had a population of roughly twenty thousand people when Alex's great-grandfather was elected solicitor in 1920. When Alex signed the Pinckneys on as clients in 2009, the population was almost exactly the same. Hardly anyone ever moved away. Hardly anyone ever moved in. The place existed in a state of suspended animation. Hampton had no department store, no Walmart, no bowling alley, not even a Ramada Inn, only a few mom-and-pop motels that had been hanging on since the fifties. The closest mall was in Charleston, more than an hour away. The tallest structures were two smokestacks from a shuttered factory. The only grocery for miles was a Piggly Wiggly that smelled like fried chicken.

Hampton's most impressive public building, its bedrock and its beacon, was the courthouse. The law had always been integral to Hampton's identity, so much so that the town was originally named Hampton Courthouse. More than a century later, the courthouse still occupied its physical and spiritual center. Built in 1878, the ruddy brick Victorian

Italianate building rose above tidy grounds lined with stone benches and war memorials, a popular spot for festivals and outdoor markets and, for decades, lynchings. The big oak with its long sweeping limbs had long since died. But the specter of the hangings lingered whether anyone wanted to think about them or not, and they did not.

The high school, like the county and the town, was named after Wade Hampton, the former Confederate general whose armed militia terrorized freed Blacks after the war. The town's main street was Lee Avenue. A voluntary segregation persisted in the neighborhoods and schools, the barbershops and body shops, the funeral homes and cemeteries. For decades at one doctor's office, many of the older Black patients still used an entrance once reserved for colored only.

Lee Avenue had hummed in the early 1900s with a dress shop, a milliner's shop, and two drugstores. By the early 2000s, most of the storefronts were boarded up. In one block, a trifecta of quick credit companies beckoned.

Get money now!

Weariness hung over Hampton. The most striking exception was on Mulberry Street, near the courthouse, where a bustle of lawyers and paralegals and clients hurried in and out of the new $2 million headquarters of the Murdaugh law firm. The building occupied an entire block. In a downtown reeking of depletion and failure, the Murdaugh building was a fortress, built to last forever.

THE MURDAUGHS SHIED away from taking on clients who had been injured inside the town's plastics factory, long the leading toxic emitter in the state. The family didn't like to sue companies close to home. The preference was to go after big out-of-town corporations. Nobody got mad if they sued an insurance company. The Murdaugh firm's stock in trade had originally been suing railroads. The office on Mulberry Street was known as "the House that CSX built," CSX being the massive corporation that had swallowed the local Charleston & Western Carolina Railway and other regional players.

They became experts in rail safety and policy, from how close was too close to the tracks for a tree branch to how many hours an engineer could work without a break. Just as important, they exploited a quirk in South Carolina law which allowed a personal injury or wrongful death suit to be filed not only where an incident occurred or where a victim lived but anywhere in the state where a defendant did business. That meant if a person was involved in a railroad accident anywhere in South Carolina, they could file suit in Hampton if the railroad went through there, which it did every day.

The Murdaughs almost always won cases filed inside their domain. The firm had leverage with nearly every juror in the five counties of the Fourteenth Judicial Circuit. When they saw who was coming up for jury duty, they could call a relative offering to help clear up a minor charge, or write a letter to a worrisome insurance carrier. They cultivated a reputation for helping people in need, volunteering their services on small stuff like traffic tickets and bill collections so they'd be remembered when the big stuff rolled around.

By the time Alex was signing the Pinckneys and the Plylers as clients, the firm employed experts in several relatively obscure types of product liability: fertilizer, medical equipment, fuel containers. Increasingly, the firm specialized in car crashes. The treads on certain Bridgestone tires had a tendency to separate at high speed. That was especially true with the tires that came standard on Ford Explorers, especially at high speed on hot asphalt, like that in the summertime on Interstate 95.

Throughout the South, the Murdaugh firm was the go-to place for filing lawsuits after these accidents. One of the partners had become a nationally recognized expert on tire safety and was commonly called into cases around the country because of his ability to explain complex engineering concepts in simple terms. The Plyler and Pinckney crashes were exactly the kind of cases the firm was primed to handle. And when Alex set out to quietly defraud those families, he took advantage not just of the clients but of the firm's well-deserved reputation. His standard fee was thirty-five percent of any settlement or jury award, forty if it was a complicated case—enough to earn him a seven-figure income in legitimate income every year. But Alex wanted more.

His scam was surprisingly simple. When the Plylers' and Pinckneys' insurance settlements came in, the funds were deposited into accounts overseen by Russell Laffitte, the local banker he'd lined up as the conservator for both families. When Alex made withdrawals from the clients' funds, the banker looked the other way. Alex often didn't tell the clients the settlement had arrived or the correct amount. He fudged details with the firm, too, billing for experts he never hired, setting aside money for medical bills and later stealing it.

Ultimately, he stole roughly $1 million apiece from the Pinckneys and from the Plylers. Most of the funds could not be paid to Alania and Hannah until they grew up. As minors they had no control of the money, which made it easy for Alex to siphon whatever he wanted.

For years the sisters remained unaware they were being exploited. All they knew was that without their conservator's permission, the cash they needed was out of reach.

When asked to explain his actions later, Alex blamed his addiction. But the amounts he embezzled added up to far more than anyone could spend on oxy. How he spent the rest would become an enduring mystery. Some believed he lost the bulk of it in bad real estate investments. Rumors would circulate that he had buried the cash in PVC pipes.

This much is known: By the time Alex signed the Plylers and the Pinckneys as clients, his spiral had already begun. For years he had been hiding pills and committing penny-ante acts of fraud, padding expense reports and charging personal items to his company card. When Alania Plyler turned to him, he found his first real mark. And on that day in the hospital, when Pamela Pinckney decided to trust him, he found another. But he was just getting started.

Alex contained a multitude of contradictions, all hidden beneath his facade of respectability. He was a family man who used his wife and young children as conversational props to put his targets at ease. He was the son of one of the South's dominant legal dynasties, but also a criminal robbing his most vulnerable clients. For untold years, he had sharpened his talent for deception. He was fundamentally unreadable, a walking mirage, always performing one role or another: devoted husband and father, connected friend, grantor of favors, defender of the downtrodden. One of his favorite turns was a bait-and-switch in which he'd approach someone as if they were his best friend and then hit them up for a favor or deliver an ominous warning.

One sawmill owner remembers how Alex would call a couple of times a year and try to charm the family as he let them know his firm was suing the mill again. "Hey, Bo," he'd start out. "How's the quail hunting out on the farm? How's your mama and them?" Then he'd drop the hammer. "I don't want y'all to worry, but later today you'll get some papers. We're just suing the insurance company."

There was something strangely childlike about the man. His face had the softness of a baby's, and for an adult he showed little willingness to curb his appetites. Along with his drinking and the pills, he had a weakness for strawberry milk and Capri Suns. He never ate breakfast, but he loved to snack on a bowl of cereal in the evening. His favorites were Froot Loops, Frosted Flakes, and Fruity Pebbles, with sugar sprinkled on top for good measure.

His specialty was being nice until he wasn't. He knew how to make threats without saying the threat out loud. He had a volcanic temper, especially when drunk, when he was quick to imagine a slight and throw the first punch. He was the kind of guy who could, in the course of a day, score some pills, cheat on his long-suffering wife, fix three different court cases in three different counties, head to Hampton's Little League fields to coach one of his son's teams, and then host the after-party for players' families.

ALEX'S HOME LIFE appeared idyllic. He was holding forth at poolside cookouts, coaching Buster's baseball team to regional glory, slipping into the woods with both his sons to hunt. Sometimes Paul brought down a dozen ducks in a single day. In the photos with their fresh kill lined up in the bed of a truck, Alex stands beside him, grinning proudly.

Maggie populated her Facebook feed with proof of the family's happiness: pictures of the boys out hunting, decked in camo and gripping shotguns; images of holiday gatherings with candlesticks and Spode china; underwater shots of her and Alex in scuba gear off the Florida Keys, making peace signs with splayed fingers.

The reality was far more complicated. Paul was a source of constant stress. Maggie and Alex had never been able to control him, even when he was little. Some in town whispered that they'd barely tried. It had cost the family some friends over the years, parents who abandoned their desire to be close to the Murdaughs in order to keep their children away from Paul. He was kicked out of his public middle school, an achievement for a Murdaugh in a town where the family ran the school board. He reveled in playing daredevil, climbing onto the roof of the dugout in the middle of his brother's baseball game, distracting the spectators who were too cowed to tell him to get down. His mother and father laughed at his antics, even when he hid in the bushes with a BB gun and shot at the yard men. Who could stop Paul being Paul?

Alex's behavior was not so easily dismissed. Maggie knew, on information and belief (as they said in court), that her husband cheated on her with multiple women. Sometimes she raged. Sometimes she ignored it. But there were always certain women she didn't want him around, knowing his weaknesses. She kept a particularly close eye on him around brunettes, even those among their close friends and extended family.

Alex was forever driving off, coming home late, leaving early the next morning. Keeping track of him was impossible. She soothed herself with cocktails and manicures and shopping and the beach. His drug habit, meanwhile, was increasing exponentially. He'd been prescribed hydrocodone after a series of knee surgeries from 2002 to 2004. As the years passed, he found he could no longer stop. Worse than that, he needed more and more pills to feel anything at the exact time that a federal crackdown on prescriptions made pills hard to get. In 2008 and 2009 he moved almost exclusively to hydrocodone's stronger and longer-lasting cousin, oxycodone.

The first time he took an oxy, its sheer power made him sick. One pill had ten times the dosage of the pills he'd been used to. But soon enough, he was taking an astonishing quantity. Oxy tended to make most of its users sleepy and lethargic, prone to falling asleep in meetings and unable to concentrate. But Alex insisted the drug energized him. Whatever he was doing, he said, the oxy made it more interesting, even long hours behind the wheel of his Suburban. He said he could drive forever on the stuff.

It's unclear how much Maggie understood about all that was happening with her husband. Her Kappa Delta sisters teased her, saying she looked like the perfect politician's wife, but they were not always convinced. Maggie was skilled at deflection and avoidance, but hints of the strain were showing. She was increasingly anxious and scattered. She had a Louis Vuitton wallet but still carried her cash in a Ziploc bag. She was the kind of person, her sister noted, whose checkbook always ended up on the floorboard of her Range Rover.

The addiction, at least, was no family secret. Maggie tended to Alex on the occasions he tried to wean himself off the drugs, shivering on the couch and vomiting for days on end. She would convince herself he'd finally kicked the habit, but still searched the medicine cabinet for stray pill bottles or codeine cough syrup just in case. Paul developed a knack for finding Alex's hidden bottles and baggies of pills, earning himself the nickname "the little detective."

Alex had his oxy habit, but the family's drug of choice was alcohol. Countless social media photos show Alex and Maggie and both their sons drinking cocktails on the boat, riding their property with a beer in a koozie, grinning red-faced through another backyard Lowcountry boil. Paul kept crashing his F-150, picking fights with strangers, yelling at his girlfriend. He had always been aggressive, but alcohol triggered his most volatile instincts. It was another trait he'd inherited from his father. Once, a girl spurned Paul's advances, saying she already had a boyfriend. A few weeks later, when the girl and her boyfriend were at a gas station, Alex and Paul rolled up beside them. Alex got out of the truck and began beating on the hood of the young man's car, shouting "Get out here and fight my boy!"

Alex's life was increasingly chaotic. After a run of bad real estate investments, he was hemorrhaging tens of thousands of dollars a month in interest on loans for land that was all but worthless. His dalliances with women were growing more reckless. He slept with a young bartender who thought she might be pregnant. He had a fling with another lawyer at an out-of-town conference, which ended her marriage. When Maggie found out Alex was exchanging messages with an old flame, she kicked him out of the house. In the end, Alex insisted nothing was going on and Maggie took him back, but her doubts lingered. To an extent she could not have predicted, her fears were well founded. Alex's deceptions were so numerous and so destructive, they constituted a form of violence unto themselves.

Warnings of trouble kept bursting into view. One summer morning in 2009, Alex and Maggie and the boys were at the beach house in Edisto, enjoying a long weekend of boating and grilling with friends. A neighbor back in Hampton called 911 to report seeing smoke billowing out of the Holly Street house. Firefighters put out the flames, but the water and smoke damage were extensive. The investigator, a close friend of Alex's, quickly ruled the fire as arson. Someone, it turned out, had poured diesel fuel throughout the house, then set fire to a backdoor floor mat. Maggie set to work on saving what could be saved and replacing the rest. Alex went to work on the insurance claim. Charges were brought against a contractor who was said to have done some work for the Murdaughs. The man made no public statements and never stood trial. The arson charges were quietly dropped.

After the fire, Alex refinanced the Holly Street house with a no-money-down loan from his friend Russell Laffitte. The loan valued the house at $533,000, far greater than its previous value and six times the median value of homes in Hampton County. He owed another $200,000 on the Edisto house mortgage and more than $1 million on the real estate investments that had gone sideways.

The disconnect between appearance and reality became surreal at the redecorated Holly Street home, where the windows were lined with heavy raw silk drapes and the walls filled with paintings of exotic birds. Inside the house was a faded copy of an old poem, framed in dark wood, titled "The Man in the Glass."

> *When you get what you want in your struggle for self*
> *And the world makes you king for a day*
> *Just go to a mirror and look at yourself*
> *And see what that man has to say . . .*
> *For it isn't your father or mother or wife*
> *Whose judgment upon you must pass,*
> *The fellow whose verdict counts most in your life*
> *Is the one staring back from the glass*

The house was full of mirrors. Years later, in court, Alex would allude to standing in front of one of those mirrors, trying to justify to himself what he was doing.

> *You may fool the whole world down the pathway of years*
> *And get pats on the back as you pass*
> *But your final reward will be heartache and tears*
> *If you've cheated the man in the glass*

There's no way to know whether Alex ever heard the warning in those last lines, or if he did, whether he would have paid attention. He was the scion of a dynasty forged in fraud. Duplicity was his birthright.

PART TWO

MURDAUGH ISLAND

CHAPTER FIVE

RANDOLPH MURDAUGH SR.
(1887–1940)

Past midnight, at a crossing on a dark country road, the dying man waited for the train to take him. At age fifty-three, he'd been sick for years, in and out of the hospital, fighting for time against a feeble heart and poisoned kidneys. He wasn't sure which organ would fail first, but he was tired of waiting to find out.

Randolph Murdaugh Sr. had decided to hurry things up.

It was almost 1 A.M. on July 19, 1940, the height of summer, when the only thing separating hell and Hampton County was a screen door. Earlier in the day, the temperature had climbed past 90 degrees. Even now that the sun was down, the air was still so thick you could touch it, a shroud that beaded on the skin. In this oppressive darkness, Randolph sat in his car at the foot of the tracks, sweat sluicing down his back. The train would be there soon.

Randolph Sr. occupies a hallowed position in Murdaugh lore. Alex's great-grandfather was the first in his family to attend law school at the University of South Carolina and the first to be elected the Fourteenth Circuit's solicitor. He was the founder of the Murdaugh law firm and the architect of the dynasty.

That night, his glory days were behind him. His flagging health had forced him to forgo his last big trial, leaving the case in the hands of his son Randolph Jr.

On that stifling evening, Randolph Sr. had played poker at a friend's house and drunk more whiskey than was advisable. The friend lived in Yemassee, on the line dividing Hampton and Beaufort counties, and when Randolph left, according to the official account, he drove north along Highway 68. The records don't show what kind of car Randolph Sr. was driving, but he had always been a Ford man, typically a black sedan. He had gone about fifteen miles and was near home when he made a sharp right at the desolate Camp Branch crossing, opposite a country cemetery, then drove another ten yards and stopped at the bottom of the incline leading up to and over the tracks. There were no lights or signal arms, not in those days at a crossing to nowhere.

Randolph Sr. had recently suffered a heart attack, but it was his kidneys that rendered him chronically ill. He'd been diagnosed with late stage renal failure, then known as uremic poisoning, a buildup of waste in the blood that, in the days before dialysis and organ transplants, amounted to a slow, inexorable death. As the disease progressed, it made sufferers nauseous and itchy, unable to urinate or unable to stop, with swollen feet and sleeplessness. The heat didn't help.

Randolph had made and lost a fortune on a bet that he could build something lasting in a county with so little. Now he was gambling again, wagering his life for the benefit of his family, including his first grandchild, an infant named Randolph III.

There is no dark like a country backroad at midnight. You can see the stars and moon and little else, no streetlights, no houses or other cars, the only sounds coming from the drone of crickets and the occasional whistle of a distant train. Randolph Sr. knew the train schedule, as did everyone in Hampton County. The long black engine of the Charleston & Western Carolina Railway had already left the Yemassee depot and was speeding toward the Camp Branch crossing. Fully loaded with freight, the train was headed for Augusta and then the wider world—Atlanta, Columbus, places embracing the possibilities of modernity.

The light of the train shone in the distance. When it was less than a hundred yards away, Randolph hit the gas and drove up the grade and stopped, square in the middle of the tracks. Then, in the final seconds of his life, he did a curious thing. He leaned out of the open window into the bright beam of the locomotive's headlight and waved. The train's engineer saw the man and the car on the tracks at the last moment, too late to do anything but strike it at full steam. The impact hurled the automobile some nine hundred feet before the engineer could brake. Randolph's body was found beside the tracks with a broken back and a crushed skull.

At the inquest, the engineer returned to the startling image of Randolph Murdaugh Sr. waving at the train about to run him down. It wasn't the wild gesture of a man trying to avert catastrophe. If anything, the engineer said, the wave was more casual, friendly even, and seemed directed at the train itself. Randolph was saying hello to whatever waited on the other side.

THE CHARLESTON & Western Carolina Railway was the lifeblood of Hampton County. It had taken the railroad to cut a path through the sweetgum and water oak and the black clouds of mosquitoes of the southern coastal plain. Once the railroad was in place, whistle-stop towns sprang up along its routes. The towns grew and split from Beaufort County to form a county of their own, separate from the carpetbaggers and freed slaves of what the white supremacists derided as the Black Republic of Beaufort. With the new county came a county seat, and then a courthouse, and then a phalanx of lawyers who realized the only entity worth suing in their new territory was the railroad. The most cunning of these lawyers was Randolph Sr., and from then on, the Murdaugh family and Hampton County and the railroad were intertwined in an ouroboros, the mythic snake forever eating its own tail.

Randolph lived his whole life on Railroad Avenue in Varnville, the twin town one stop south of Hampton. Trains roared through the family's front yard in a barrage of dust and noise. The tracks ran along a sandy ridge east of the Coosawhatchie River Swamp, a wide, wet barrier that rendered much of the county impassable.

The Murdaugh family moved to Varnville soon after the county was founded in 1878, joining the ruling class of the Confederate old guard. The founding families intermarried, traded favors, and prospered in Varnville, a vast cousinage disguised as a small town. Even before the Civil War, the region that would become Hampton County was a peculiar place, as the soil was not rich enough to grow rice, indigo, or cotton at scale. Some plantations thrived, but far more small farms held comparatively few slaves. Randolph Sr.'s grandfather had owned twenty-three.

Bitterness loomed over Randolph Sr.'s childhood. He had been born in 1887, barely two decades after General Sherman and his troops unleashed what he called "total war" on the Lowcountry. In early 1865, sixty thousand troops marauded in three flanks across the backwoods that would become Hampton County, destroying not just the ordnance and supplies of the depleted military but the food and shelter of civilians, too. To this day, Hampton is known as a "burned" county, stripped of its history as the Union army torched official records, church rolls, and family Bibles.

Randolph's father, Josiah, was a Confederate veteran who'd seen his brother Lazarus killed at the Battle of Petersburg. Josiah fought with an injured leg and impaired sight and was with General Lee at his surrender at Appomattox. Josiah had gone on to make and lose postwar fortunes in cotton, phosphate, and real estate. He was going blind, another loss the family attributed to the war. Randolph's mother, Annie, claimed a distant kinship to Jefferson Davis. Randolph was the youngest of seven siblings, born when his father was fifty-six and his mother was thirty-nine. He was the only one born in Hampton County, the place that would become synonymous with the family name.

Back then, a neighbor was anyone within seven miles, the distance that could be traveled roundtrip on a Sunday. Most families lived on small farms and grew just enough to sustain them. Hampton County was an inland frontier where horses and cattle grazed freely for generations, sometimes straying into neighboring counties and destroying crops. As in the American West, a dispute broke out over whether it was a farmer's obligation to fence livestock out or a rancher's obligation to fence livestock in. Hampton County solved this problem in a way unique in all the South: It built a fence around the entire county, a signal to the outside world to stay away and for those inside to stay put.

"They tried to fence out the twentieth century," says the historian Larry Rowland.

When he was seventeen, Randolph took the train to the University of South Carolina in the capital city of Columbia, a half day's ride and a world away from Hampton County. Randolph was the only student in his class from Hampton or any of the four counties surrounding it, which were predominantly Black, rural, and poor. The university was all white, the result of an 1895 rewriting of the state constitution that rolled back all the Reconstruction-era rights of Blacks and established some of the harshest Jim Crow policies in the Deep South.

At the university, Randolph set the template for the modern Murdaugh man, with a knack for networking and a passion for playing Gamecock football. After earning a degree in history, he enrolled in the USC School of Law. His yearbook bio described him as a legend: "He came here a scrawny 'prep,' he leaves a dignified, grisly [sic] lawyer. In all things he has proven himself faithful and persevering, from biology and third French to football." His motto was recorded as "Whatever thou hast to do, do it now."

He went straight home to Hampton to set up shop in a small wooden building next door to the town's first bank and across the street from the courthouse. He had been home and building his law practice almost two years to the day when his father died.

Josiah's obituary was published in The State, South Carolina's largest newspaper. The writer was not named, but the language closely echoed the ornate rhetoric Randolph would later rely upon before juries and judges. The idealism and yearning almost leap from the page: "We are born of a higher destiny than that of earth," the tribute began. "There is a realm where the sun never fades and where the stars are spread out before us as islands that slumber upon the bosom of the ocean and where the beautiful things that now pass before us as visions will remain in our presence forever."

In Randolph's eyes, his father had assumed his rightful place in that eternal realm. Now it was Randolph's time to make his mark in the world.

Randolph became the Murdaugh patriarch at age twenty-five. Among a dozen lawyers in Hampton, he took pride in never having to hang out a shingle. He was the town's golden boy. If someone needed to sue a seed maker or settle a property dispute or fight the federal government, they knocked on his office door. Randolph had powerful allies, an ease with people of every station, and a reputation for winning.

IN BOTH HIS professional and personal life, Randolph was a man in a hurry. Randolph had married Etta Causey Harvey, the eldest daughter of a country doctor, and scarcely nine months after the wedding, Etta gave birth to Randolph Jr. The young family lived in the house where Randolph grew up. It was a heady time for Hampton, which now had two banks and fifty new streetlights downtown.

Because of the vast size of the judicial circuit, which was larger than Delaware and Rhode Island combined, court was in session just twice a year for a couple of weeks at a time. Every detail of each fall and spring term was front-page news, including the names of the jurors. Spectators filled the courtroom for big cases, and if the seats were full, a jury boy or girl would throw open the window and shout down an account of who said what.

Randolph had started his practice at a fortuitous moment, just after the federal government recognized the danger of rail work, when one in twelve frontline workers—engineers, conductors, firemen, and brakemen—was badly injured in the course of a year and one in thirty-seven such workers was killed. The feds approved a novel type of workers' compensation for the "running trade," a gold mine in the early days of personal injury law. Railroads were dangerous for nonworkers, too, as most crossings had scant grading and no cross arms or flashing lights. Accidents were frequent and violent in Hampton County. A banker was killed and his arm severed while he was crossing the train tracks. A teenager riding between rail cars mangled his leg so badly it had to be amputated. The accident left a mark on Randolph Sr. When the boy fell from the train, he had landed in the Murdaughs' front yard. Randolph was the first to reach him.

Randolph and Etta had been married four years when Etta gave birth to the couple's second son, John Glenn Murdaugh. A little more than two weeks later, Etta died of sepsis.

It seemed the entire world was dying. The Spanish Flu was sweeping continents, claiming as many as fifty million lives. That same year, in the mud of the Argonne Forest in France and the sand of the Gallipoli peninsula in Turkey, the Great War was finally ending, at a loss of another twenty million soldiers and civilians. Randolph had avoided the draft because he had a wife and children, but many of his friends fought in the trenches. Just as the war's survivors were settling back into their lives in Hampton County, Prohibition took hold, creating an illicit market and a host of criminal activity overnight. Suddenly bootleggers were smuggling bottles of whiskey, and mom-and-pop moonshiners were buying telltale amounts of copper pipe, sugar, and Mason jars. Sometimes the lawmen chased them; sometimes they took bribes and looked the other way.

Against this tumultuous backdrop, Randolph entered politics, running for the office of the Fourteenth Circuit's solicitor. A campaign ad proclaimed, "His reputation for being square and giving everyone a clean deal at all times and on every occasion insures the people of the circuit that if he is elected, they will have as their solicitor a competent and fearless officer, and one who cannot be influenced or intimidated by anyone or by [any] means, yet who at all times will be fair, just and impartial."

In a trouncing, Randolph became the chief lawman for a hundred miles. Each county had a sheriff, perhaps a part-time deputy, and a jailer. Some counties had a constable, too, responsible for enforcing liquor laws. But the solicitor was the law.

Randolph worked closely with every officer in the circuit. He was the lone prosecutor but effectively the chief detective, too, showing up at murder scenes and interviewing rape victims. Evidence gathering was rudimentary. Fingerprinting did not exist, leaving the solicitor to assess credibility and vet alibis. Motorcars made traversing the vast circuit less onerous but still a slog. Road construction was haphazard. When drivers reached Hampton County's fence, they had to get out of their cars, open the gate, then get back out on the other side and shut it. Over time, the fence had become an embarrassment. Soon after Randolph took office, it was dismantled.

The new solicitor's comings and goings were noted in newspapers in five counties. Randolph's constituents wanted to know where he stayed, what he ate, and with whom he met. People were especially curious about Randolph's second wife, Estelle Marvin Murdaugh, whom he married discreetly the year after Etta died. Estelle was a distant relation and a comparatively older bride at twenty-eight. She kept a low profile, rarely traveling with him and offering scant fodder for the society pages beyond the occasional bridge game at their home on Railroad Avenue.

It wasn't long before the courthouse janitors dubbed Randolph "Fire and Brimstone." He was barely thirty-three years old when he was elected, but in the courtroom, he was instinctively in command. He projected like a preacher and segued seamlessly from yelling at jurors that they should use their good sense to flattering them for righting the wrongs around them.

Even as he ran the solicitor's office, dispensing justice across the circuit, he continued his lucrative private practice, cementing his reputation as Hampton's most formidable litigator. He operated the levers of power in both civil and criminal courts.

IN MOST PARTS of the country, the Great Depression started in 1929 with the stock market crash. But by then, the Lowcountry had been facing a rolling tragedy for a decade because of the invasion of the boll weevil and the subsequent failure of the local banks, which were al-most entirely dependent on the health of the farming economy.

Randolph and his family scraped by on his solicitor's salary, though it is likely that like other public employees, there were times he was not paid. His private law practice was drying up because no one had money to hire a lawyer. He had land, but so did everybody else, and it was not worth much.

In these times when doing anything, particularly the right thing, was a struggle, Randolph Sr. became increasingly willing to cut cor-ners. A rumor persists to this day that he conspired with the sheriff in the killing of a Black man accused of murder. The motive, allegedly, was to spare Hampton County the expense of jailing and trying the accused. The story was that Randolph and the sheriff took the prisoner fishing in the Savannah River, one county over, and contrived for him to fall into the water, where his body was devoured by alligators.

It's hard to know how much weight to give this account. But at the time, Hampton's citizens saw the story as proof their once upright solicitor was now willing to subvert the law, acting not just as finder of fact but as judge, jury, and executioner, too. It almost didn't matter whether the rumor was true. What mattered was that people be-lieved it.

A clearer indication of the shift in Randolph's moral code was the time the richest man in town shot and killed a highway supervisor be-cause he was angry that the man wouldn't let him drive his Packard on a freshly paved road. Randolph was the prosecutor and his officemate, a sitting state senator, was the defense lawyer. The day the rich man was arrested and released on bail, he made a sizable campaign contri-bution, which was stored in the safe the senator shared with Randolph.

At trial, the man was acquitted after five hours of deliberation. In the weeks that followed, the citizens of Hampton invented a new par-lor game: watching new houses sprout up for nine of the twelve jurors. The jury foreman's house was one of the first in town made of brick, a wanton extravagance and an acknowledgment of the way things worked.

Randolph Sr. could no longer claim the moral high ground. It was understood that the solicitor had been part of the illicit arrangement. Even if he was unaware of the payoffs to the jurors, he could have hardly failed to notice their new houses. The exalted promise of his first campaign—to serve justice with faultless impartiality—was long abandoned.

The rot went much deeper than one case. By the mid-1930s, every Hampton County jury was picked by having a child draw names written on slips of paper inside a box. Some recalled that the box was metal, others said wooden. Whichever was correct, one of the former jury girls later admitted to her family that the box had never held that many names to begin with. Randolph Murdaugh, she said, had made sure of that.

Mr. Fire and Brimstone had picked the jurors he wanted, then put the slips of paper into the box himself.

RANDOLPH SR.'S GREATEST adversary remained the Charleston & Western Carolina Railway. He took two cases against the railroad to the South Carolina Supreme Court, once representing a foreman who'd been demoted to apprentice laborer without notice, and once representing a conductor who'd been fired for "permitting his negro porter to collect tickets and cash fares on his train." Randolph's body had begun to fail him, but he still beat the mighty railroad. Twice.

The health of his second wife was slipping as well. Though she was only forty-six, Estelle was confined to a sanatorium in neighboring Walterboro, where many wealthy women went to give birth. It is not clear whether Estelle was pregnant, but she died six months later. Her death certificate lists the initial contributor of death as prolonged toxemia, a complication of pregnancy now called preeclampsia. The second contributor was midlife arthritis and the third was acute pneumatic fever.

Estelle died at 9 P.M. on a Saturday and was buried at 4 P.M. the following afternoon. Her obituary in the weekly Walterboro paper the following Thursday noted that the solicitor was with his wife when she died. The burial arrangements were grand: "The floral offering was one of the largest and most beautiful, which completely covered the newly made grave."

What the newspaper did not mention was that Randolph had remarried the day before the obit was published. Four days after his second wife died, Randolph Sr. wed his third. The bride was Mary J. Taylor Hoffman, a divorcée fifteen years his junior and the daughter of a state senator. The year before, as Estelle Murdaugh was dying in the sanatorium, Mary had accompanied Randolph on a cruise to Cuba. She had listed her marital status in the ship manifest as divorced. He had listed his as single.

Little is known about Randolph's third marriage. The couple apparently tried to maintain a semblance of a social life, despite Randolph's kidney disease and heart troubles, and were reported to have spent one Christmas Eve at a black tie gala at a mansion in Allendale. Randolph was still considered a local celebrity, though, and when his health grew worse, it was front-page news. SOLICITOR STRICKEN AS COURT OPENS, read a 1939 headline stripped across *The Hampton County Guardian*. Below it, a subhead added: "Randolph Murdaugh, Jr. Takes His Father's Place." By now Randolph Jr., who went by Buster, had graduated from the USC law school and was serving as his father's assistant in the solicitor's office and at the family firm. He was ready to help in any way he could, especially now that Randolph was in and out of hospitals, missing court for weeks at a time.

The case that prompted the breathless headline was a federal civil trial seventy miles northwest in Aiken. Randolph Sr. was defending a wealthy client who had thrown a gun at the back of a salesman, badly injuring him. Right as the trial started, Randolph suffered a heart attack and was rushed to the hospital. At the judge's insistence, Buster took over. It was the first big trial he'd handled without his father. In the end, the jury ruled against the Murdaughs' client, but thanks to Buster's defense, the damages were far less than the injured salesman had demanded.

Buster's victory, though partial, was the first of many. His father would never lead another big case.

IT WAS ALMOST 1 A.M. that sweltering night several months later, in July 1940, when Randolph waited for the up train heading toward Augusta. Perhaps he heard a whistle in the distance. Certainly he would have felt the thrum of the earth as the engine approached.

Suddenly he was pressing the accelerator and climbing onto the tracks, and then the locomotive's beam was flooding the interior of the car, flooding his eyes. Then, at the last second, he gave that casual wave.

The coroner, a protégé of the deceased, was called to investigate. The sheriff, who owed his job to Randolph, came, too. They told reporters there was no immediate indication why Randolph had failed to see the approaching train, but an inquest was set for later that morning. The coroner handpicked a jury to hear witnesses, as was customary in suspicious deaths. By this time, Randolph had been in office twenty years, twice as long as the sheriff and coroner combined, and for as long as most of the jurors could remember.

The jurors were all white men living within ten miles of the crossing. The engineer testified that as the train bore down, he had seen the car parked beside the tracks, as though the driver was waiting for the train to pass. By the time the car lurched up the incline and stopped, it was too late. The jurors, all of whom would have known Randolph personally, ruled his death an accident.

The family sued the railroad for $100,000, equivalent to more than $2 million today and far greater than any previous wrongful death verdict in the state. The newspapers reported that Randolph Murdaugh Sr. had died in a tragic accident. But the people in town knew that made no sense. If he had been headed home, there was no need for him to turn onto a deserted road four miles shy of his house. If it had been an accident, the engineer would not have seen him accelerating onto the tracks. If the car had stalled, he could have jumped out of the way. Instead, he had leaned out the window and waved. Besides, every-one knew Randolph had been deathly ill and deeply broke.

Randolph Sr.'s death was not only a suicide but a suicide designed to perpetrate fraud. If his goal had been merely to end his suffering, there were less traumatic ways. He knew the railroad budgeted settle-ments as part of its operating expenses. Above all, Randolph Sr. knew the railroad would settle to avoid trial, aware that any Hampton jury would side with the deceased local hero.

Choosing a locomotive as the instrument of his death was a gesture of supreme irony. Randolph Sr. had devoted much of his career to suing the railroad on behalf of clients. His suicide was a final trick to outwit an omnipotent nemesis. The railroad had been an inescapable force in Randolph Sr.'s life, and in the end, he both surrendered to that force and exploited it, letting the engine propel him into the beyond and his family into prosperity.

Decades later, when the subject of Randolph's death arose, the Murdaughs made no secret of what had happened. If anyone uttered the word "suicide," they just smiled.

A month after the accident, an election was held for a new solicitor. Buster Murdaugh, then twenty-five, won handily. All at once, Buster was head of the law firm as well as the Fourteenth Circuit's top law-man. By September, Buster was trying cases in front of a new thirty-eight-year-old judge, a future U.S. senator named Strom Thurmond. Like so many others in the courthouse, Thurmond was an old family friend. His father, a former solicitor, had been close to Randolph Sr.

Ultimately the railroad did settle. To this day, the Murdaughs will not disclose the amount. But now Buster had the money and the title and the influence to build an empire.

CHAPTER SIX

After the accident, Pamela Pinckney required seventeen surgeries and two years of physical therapy before she could walk again. She might have healed faster, except she kept skipping her therapy sessions and neglecting to take her meds so she could be with her son. She was still in a wheelchair, unable to place her weight on her broken ankles, so she had to ask her daughter to drive her. But Pamela had to see her boy.

By then Hakeem had been moved to a nursing home on the Georgia state line that catered to the poor and elderly. Even though she lived an hour and a half away, Pamela took to popping in unexpectedly to check on Hakeem. On the way she'd ask her daughter to take her to Walmart to pick up cans of ravioli and Beefaroni, childhood favorites Hakeem preferred to the nursing home gruel, most commonly a gray liquid fed to him through a straw.

Pamela found the nursing home dark and sad, and though she did not know it at the time, it had one of the worst safety records in the South. She had worked as a nursing assistant and had seen how easily patients could be neglected. Hakeem's condition was harrowing enough. He could no longer move his torso or his arms and legs, and he was almost always on a ventilator. Sitting in her wheelchair at the side of his bed, Pamela would pray with him and brush her fingertips across his cheek and tell him how handsome he was. He had always hated to miss church, and in high school he would wait until after Sunday services to make the three-hour trek back to the school for the deaf. By his bedside, Pamela sang his favorite gospel songs, staples of contemporary worship like "God Is Able" and "Miracle Worker."

He'd been given a whistle to blow in an emergency, but one day she found it behind his bed, dusty and forgotten. Another time she discovered her son's bedsheets soggy with urine and as dark as tea, signs that they'd been soiled for hours. Hakeem was supposed to be bathed on Mondays, Wednesdays, and Fridays, but Pamela kept finding dirt between her son's toes. So she and her daughter would give him a sponge bath and change his clothes. She was always sure to rub down any dry skin with oil.

Someone had donated an eye tracking device that allowed Hakeem to communicate simple messages, clicking on letters and words by blinking. Slowly moving his eye around the screen, he kept typing the same message, again and again:

I want to go home.

His desperation made it hard for Pamela to breathe. In his eyes, she could see how afraid he was.

"I'm going to get you home," she told him. "Just give me a little more time."

She told her son how Mr. Alex was working on the lawsuit, pushing for the insurance company to settle. Once the family got that money, she said, she could afford to buy a house that could accommodate a ventilator and all the other equipment Hakeem would need to come home. She was praying for that day to arrive soon.

On October 7, 2011, two years after the accident, Mr. Alex called Pamela with the news that he'd settled Hakeem's case for $10 million. His fee would be $4 million. The rest, he told her, would go to the family. He told her to sit tight because it would take time to sort through the paperwork and get the money in hand. But he promised her it was coming.

Meantime, Alex was living big. Flush with the money he was steal-ing from the Plyler sisters and other clients, he took his family to At-lanta to watch the Gamecocks play in the SEC championship; they stayed at the Ritz-Carlton and drank champagne in the limo ride to the game, with Paul hanging out of the sunroof. He took them to the Ba-hamas for fishing. He bought custom sport coats and monogrammed cummerbunds. Maggie raided the Louis Vuitton store in Atlanta, buy-ing what seemed like one of everything. A favorite was a $3,400 cross-body purse with a thick gold chain.

Word of Alex's golden touch with the insurance companies was spreading. From all over South Carolina, new clients were making pil-grimages to Hampton, ready to sign whatever documents he pushed before them. A recommendation from someone in the courthouse led to his biggest case yet.

ARTHUR BADGER JR. was a widower who had watched his wife die in a car crash. Now he was struggling to raise their six children, all of them living in a mobile home. An investigator from the solicitor's of-fice handed him a piece of paper with the name and number of a law-yer.

Good news, the investigator said. *I've lined up Alex Murdaugh to take your case.*

Arthur had been driving with his wife, Donna, and some friends on a rural road in Allendale County when he started to pass a UPS truck. Suddenly the truck had swerved left, crashing into the passenger side of his Ford Expedition, killing Donna instantly.

Soon, like so many before him, Arthur eagerly signed a stack of forms in Alex's office. He did not realize he had just surrendered the right to represent his own financial interests as well as the rights of his children and his dead wife's estate.

"We're here to help you," the lawyer said.

When the case went to mediation, Alex negotiated a settlement with UPS. It was better that way, he told Arthur, rather than taking the case to trial, where a jury might have found Arthur partially at fault for trying to pass the truck. Alex told Arthur he'd gotten several million dollars for the children from their mother's estate. Most of that money would be deposited in a trust to be disbursed to the children starting when they turned eighteen. Alex also told Arthur he'd arranged for him to receive $370,000, enough money for the family to move into a bigger mobile home.

What Alex did not reveal was that the settlement from UPS's insurance company totaled roughly $8 million, and Arthur was immediately entitled to nearly all of it. Alex also did not tell Arthur he'd secured $1.325 million for himself personally, four times the amount Alex had mentioned. Based on the powers Arthur had signed over to him, Alex set about spending the extra money his client was due, including $152,000 to repay some of what he'd already stolen from the Plyler sisters.

Alex also did not reveal that he had taken nearly $5 million in legitimate fees on the Badger settlements in addition to what he stole.

Through it all, the Badgers struggled to make ends meet. Arthur fell so far behind on his property taxes that the family was threatened with eviction. Arthur hired Alex again to fight the eviction. He also took out a series of short-term, high-interest "lawyer loans" arranged by Alex, putting him on the hook for $50,000 in principal and interest to Palmetto State Bank. For a while, Arthur ignored the flyers that came in the mail offering cash for his children's future settlement payments, a common predatory scheme run by outfits called structured settlement factoring companies. But when he got desperate enough, Arthur sold his youngest children's trust accounts one after another, a total of $2.8 million in future payments, for $200,000 cash.

What choice did he have? "We needed the money," he said.

Alex was adjusting the Murdaugh template. In some ways, his deceptions followed the path laid seventy years before when his great-grandfather allowed the up train to take him down, gambling that his suicide would be ruled an accident. But there was a crucial difference. Randolph Sr. had sacrificed his own life to cheat a rich and ruthless railroad. Alex was stealing millions from poor people to indulge his appetite for private jets and luxury vacations and his endless supply of pills, all of it for himself.

ALANIA AND HANNAH Plyler remained unaware of what their lawyer was doing with their money. The sisters did not realize Alex had stolen from their settlement accounts at the bank, or that he had begun replenishing those amounts with money he was stealing from the Badgers. Ultimately, Alex did repay all of the money he'd taken from the Plyler accounts. But the girls were still minors, and until they reached eighteen, he maintained tight control of their money through his friend at the bank, Russell Laffitte.

The sisters' living situation had been precarious ever since the death of their mother and brother. Soon it grew desperate. For a while they continued staying with their father at his parents' house, but their grief-stricken father was often drunk and angry. Eventually the tension grew so high the girls moved out. They shuttled from the house of one family member to the next, sleeping on couches, carrying whatever they owned in plastic bins and garbage bags. They were receiving their mother's Social Security benefits, roughly $1,000 a month, with most of that money going to whomever they were staying with. The families who were housing them were poor as well, and the arrival of the two sisters often triggered more tensions. Life felt tenuous, as there was no place they called home. Alania later recalled, "Whoever needed the thousand dollars that month the most was where my sister and I ended up living."

The girls' mother and brother were dead, and they had effectively lost their father and grandparents as well. On top of all that, they were being manipulated and cheated by the lawyer and the banker entrusted to protect them, men who mostly existed as voices on the phone. Any time the girls asked for money, they had to go through Laffitte, who made such requests as onerous as possible. When Hannah wanted to visit Disney World with a friend's family—her first true vacation—

Laffitte required the child to bring back receipts for every purchase. Alania, in high school by then, wanted to rent an apartment for her and her sister but couldn't afford to. She had found a part-time job and needed a car to reach both school and the job. She found a used Mercury Capri for $1,750, but when she checked with Laffitte, he pressured her to buy a new Nissan Maxima for $31,000 with a loan from his bank at 18 percent interest. At one point, when Alania's living arrangements became too volatile, she ended up sleeping in the Maxima. When Alania turned seventeen, Russell arranged for another loan so Alania could buy a house for herself and her sister. When the house burned down, she had no insurance for the contents. No one had told her she needed it.

For a long time, Alania believed she and her sister had lost everything in the crash. But then Alex Murdaugh and Russell Laffitte had taken control. "That's when we really lost it all," Alania said. "We lost our mom and our brother and basically traded it in for money. And then they took the money."

All told, the two men stole $1.4 million from the Plylers while Alania kept bouncing checks. Years later, she still struggled to understand the lack of empathy required to commit such a betrayal.

"I can't imagine doing dirty work like that," Alania said. "I don't have the conscience to do that."

ON OCTOBER 11, 2011, Alex was hurrying through the paperwork on the Pinckney settlement, working hard to get his hands on the family's millions, when he heard from Pamela Pinckney. She'd gotten a call from the nursing home.

"Hakeem," someone told her, "has taken a turn for the worse."

Hakeem was taken to the hospital but died a few hours later. For his family, his death was a loss beyond belief. For their lawyer, it was a serious inconvenience.

"Please call me," Alex emailed Russell Laffitte. "911."

The settlement had been reached four days earlier but had not yet been finalized with the court. The $10 million payout had been based on the likelihood that twenty-one-year-old Hakeem would require around-the-clock care for decades to come. It was a sad fact of personal injury law that Hakeem's life was worth far less now that he was dead.

As usual, Alex had a plan. He instructed Laffitte to backdate the documents and submit the paperwork to the court as if nothing had changed. Alex's fee would remain the same. There would be plenty extra to steal.

The ploy worked. The court approved the settlement, and the deal rolled forward. Pamela eventually received a settlement for her own injuries and part of what Hakeem was owed. The paperwork was voluminous but seemed in order. This was a common strategy for Alex—give his clients enough money to placate them and stave off any questions. Pamela's niece received a settlement of $83,000 for injuries to her eye. She promptly bought a car and went about her normal life. She had no way of knowing she was owed a separate $325,000 settlement. Alex stole that $325,000, using $140,000 to pay back Hannah Plyler's account just before she turned eighteen, and passing $100,000 to Russell Laffitte's father, Charlie Laffitte, the chairman of the bank and Alex's godfather. Charlie Laffitte would later say that money was to pay back a loan, but provided no documentation of it. Neither did he report it on his tax return. Lawyers would argue that it was a payment to look the other way as his son and godson used his bank to steal and launder money.

The summer after Hakeem died, Alex chartered a plane to take some friends and his older son, Buster, to Omaha, Nebraska, to watch the USC baseball team play in the College World Series. The Gamecocks played thrillingly, though they lost to the University of Arizona. Buster caught sight of USC's star pitcher on a street corner and posed with him for a picture. On Facebook, Buster joked that it was the future USC Hall of Famer who was starstruck, saying, "Michael Roth wanted to take a picture with me!"

No one knew until much later that the flight to Omaha was paid for by funds stolen from the late Hakeem Pinckney.

Unaware that Alex had been defrauding her family, Pamela Pinckney hired him again to sue the nursing home. Mr. Alex said he'd do anything he could to help her and settled the wrongful death lawsuit out of court. It would be a decade before Pamela learned that Hakeem had died because his ventilator had come unplugged and stayed that way for thirty minutes, leaving him to suffocate. Her lawyer either didn't know what had happened or hadn't bothered to tell her. Pamela wasn't sure which was worse.

ALEX'S CRIMES WERE growing more bold. As the years rolled by with no one questioning him, he began to steal from more and more clients. Initially he stole from one to put money back into the account of another, robbing Peter to pay Paul. But after a while, he was no longer paying anyone back. He was just grabbing as much as he could from as many people as he could, not just from his clients but from his partners and business associates, too, many of them his friends.

"They say you've got two kinds of family, the family you were born with and the family you chose," said one of the lawyers following the case. "Alex stole from both."

By early 2013, when he robbed the Badgers, Alex had embezzled several million dollars. At the same time, he was making even larger amounts in his legitimate fees.

THE MONEY ALEX made in the Badger case—some legitimate, some stolen—was crucial to helping him close the most significant deal of his life: buying a jewel of a property he had long coveted. Moselle, as it was called, was a huge tract of forest and farmland, swamp and timber stands, with more than two miles of frontage on the Salkehatchie River and a stately white home and a long tree-lined driveway. At 1,700 acres, the property was twice the size of Central Park.

Alex wanted to turn Moselle into his family's homestead, much like his parents' homestead at Almeda. But Moselle was bigger, the house was grander, and the claim to Murdaugh history went deep. Moselle was located in Islandton, a small rural community where the Murdaughs had settled after immigrating from Ireland on the eve of the American Revolution. His great-great-grandfather was buried in a family cemetery off a nearby dirt road. Alex wanted to make Moselle the centerpiece of his claim to the family legacy. But first he had to get his hands on it.

For years the property had been owned by Barrett Boulware, a lifelong shrimper who dabbled in land deals. Boulware started as a pinhooker, making lowball offers on land and timber to unsophisticated sellers, often poor Blacks, then selling the assets for a quick profit. He graduated to more sophisticated deals, buying waterfront real estate with as little money down as possible, betting he could subdivide or otherwise make it profitable before the note came due.

Alex had known Boulware all his life. Barrett's father, a lawyer, had represented Alex's grandfather when he was charged with bootlegging back in the 1950s. As a young lawyer himself, Alex had watched Barrett flipping properties and raking in the profits. When Barrett offered to bring him in as a partner on the land deals, Alex had jumped at the chance. Some of the deals had gone sideways, but their friendship remained intact.

Boulware was widely understood to be one of South Carolina's most enterprising drug smugglers. It was not uncommon for shrimpers to be middlemen in the drug trade, with their access to open water, ability to travel from small uninhabited islands to the mainland without raising an eyebrow, and boats big enough to conceal things that need to be hidden. In the 1980s, Boulware had been charged as the kingpin of a pot smuggling ring, caught up in a federal sting investigation called Operation Jackpot, one of the earliest salvoes in the Reagan administration's war on drugs. Boulware had been charged with conspiracy to possess and distribute seventeen tons of pot seized from one of his shrimp boats. The charges were dropped before the case went to trial when the key government witness stepped in front of a car and was killed. A few years later, when Boulware and his wife were pulled over in a traffic stop, police searched their car and found twenty-eight grams of cocaine and seven pounds of marijuana, some of it in his wife's purse. They were convicted but did not serve time.

Alex's legitimate dealings with his old friend were no secret. Whether he also partnered with Boulware in drug smuggling was a subject of ongoing speculation. The rumors had multiplied when Alex and Boulware bought seven islands, all in Beaufort County, ranging from a tenth of an acre to twenty acres. The islands were secluded and unreachable by land, making them ideal for anyone who wanted to unload a shipment on a lonely dock and stash the drugs in the pines.

Boulware and his wife lived at Moselle, in the sparsely inhabited northeastern corner of Hampton County. The property, which stretched just over the Colleton County line, was perfect for hunting and had a fish pond, dog kennels, and a firing range. Boulware and his wife had recently built the 5,200-square-foot house on the southern edge of the property and had planted the live oak trees that led to the front door. Boulware had plenty of room to add a private runway and a hangar. Many assumed Boulware was flying drugs in and out of the property. Why else would a shrimper need his own runway?

Even if the reports were true, Boulware was in danger of losing Moselle. The housing market crash left him squeezed for cash. He faced foreclosure on one of his mortgages and was behind on others. As his business partner and lawyer, Alex was well aware of Boulware's struggles and saw another opening to exploit. Although he was still dealing with financial challenges of his own, he was making the most of the profits from the Badger settlement. Moselle was valued at $1.3 million. Using the stolen funds, plus an elaborate series of trades and five dollars in cash, Alex wrenched Moselle away from his friend in the spring of 2013.

Finally Alex had land, and enough of it to do almost anything he wanted. He had vast swaths of pine woods and miles of river access, even his own runway. With its ties to his family's two centuries of

South Carolina history, Moselle instantly became the crown jewel of his ambitions. Other things were turning his way as well. His profile as one of the state's top trial lawyers was soaring. His pockets bulged with cash, some of it earned legally. Potential clients from near and far sought him out, seeking his magic touch. A whirlwind of enterprise and cunning, he was becoming a legend.

CHAPTER SEVEN

Deep into a summer night, on a lonely stretch of road, a tow truck driver saw something sprawled on the pavement. At first he thought it was a deer that had been hit by a car. Then he got closer and realized it was the body of a young man.

"I see somebody laying out," he told the 911 operator. "It's dark. Somebody's going to hit him."

It was 4 A.M. on July 8, 2015. The driver was on his way to work, crossing the northern edge of Hampton County past farms and timber stands, when his headlights fell on the man's body splayed along the line dividing the two lanes. A bloodstain was already drying around his crushed head.

The driver wasn't sure how to tell the dispatcher where he'd found the body. The road was so isolated, with only an occasional country church here and there, he didn't see any landmarks. He wasn't even sure of the road's official name, just that it was the road to the small town of Crocketville.

Listening to his description, the dispatcher realized the man was talking about Sandy Run Road. "We'll get an officer headed out that way," the dispatcher said.

A sheriff's deputy arrived about forty minutes later, followed by a couple of Highway Patrol troopers a half hour after that. By sunrise, the troopers were putting things together. A search of the area found a yellow Chevrolet Aveo parked on the side of the road roughly three miles away. Inside the car was a wallet containing a driver's license that told them the dead man was a nineteen-year-old local named Stephen Smith. The troopers were not sure what had happened to him. They saw no sign he had been hit by a car. Aside from his fatal head injury, Smith's body did not show the violent disarray of a hit-and-run. His knees had been found resting together, bent neatly at an angle, almost as though someone had posed him. His tennis shoes were on his feet. His cargo shorts were unmarked, his cellphone in his right pocket. Based on Stephen's head wound, the troopers' best theory that morning was that the young man had been shot somewhere else and thrown out in the road.

The coroner called Stephen's mother, Sandy Smith, who headed to the sheriff's office. Stephen was the light of her life, dramatic and fun but also wise beyond his years, forced to face the difficult reality of being an openly gay teen in a small town. Her ex-husband, Joel, Stephen's father, met her at the sheriff's office along with their daughter Stephanie, Stephen's twin. The three of them were waiting in the lobby when Joel's phone rang. It was Randy Murdaugh, Alex's older brother, who also worked in the Murdaugh law firm. Randy had already heard about Stephen's death.

Joel Smith knew the lawyer because he had represented Joel in a workers' compensation claim. As Joel would later tell Sandy, Randy had volunteered that morning to help investigate Stephen's death. The lawyer explained that he was already working with the officers, who needed Stephen's passcodes to get into his devices, including the phone found in his pocket.

"Do you have the code to unlock it?" Joel remembered him asking.

Joel didn't know the code. He thanked Randy for his help but did not know what to think about the Murdaugh family volunteering to assist with the investigation. Even in the first flush of grief, he found the offer puzzling.

Sandy Smith knew the Murdaughs mostly by reputation. She was aware her son had been friends with Buster, Alex and Maggie's older son. The two young men had been opposites in many respects: Stephen was poor and Buster was rich; Stephen was an honor student and Buster got by. But they had played on the same Little League team, coached by Alex and Randolph III.

That morning, trying to understand what had happened, Sandy Smith drove past the crime scene where Stephen's body had been found. A few minutes later, she says, she got a call from Randy Murdaugh.

"Was that you who just drove past?" Sandy remembered him asking.

She hadn't seen Randy by the side of the road, but obviously he'd been there, or someone else at the scene had noticed her and called to tell him. She wondered why. She and her ex-husband had not hired Randy to investigate the case. So, what was he doing?

A few days later, the Smiths started hearing rumors. People were saying Stephen's car had run out of gas; the police had found a rag thrust into the opening of his gas tank. Maybe he'd been by his car, calling on his phone for someone to bring some gas. Maybe he'd been walking down the road toward help. But where would he have been headed? The nearest gas station was miles away. Besides, he'd left his wallet back in his car.

Stephanie could not stop thinking about what her twin brother had been like as a little boy. Back then Stephen had been shy, with a mild stutter. When someone asked him a question, he would whisper in his sister's ear so she could answer for him. Now her brother had been silenced for good. Stephanie retreated into the home where she and Stephen had been living with their father. It wasn't long before old friends came knocking. All of them wanted to tell her what they'd heard about Stephen's death. All had heard the same thing.

"You know who's behind it, don't you?" they told her. "The Murdaugh boys."

. . .

STEPHEN SMITH'S MOTHER could not accept that her son was gone. He had eluded death before, once as a preemie born three months too early, then as a toddler who nearly drowned. It seemed unfathomable that he had survived those ordeals, then grown up and finished high school, only for his body to end up dumped in the middle of a dark country road. Sandy Smith had seen the damage when they pulled back the white sheet and asked her to identify his body. She had been startled by his injuries: the seven-inch gash running below his eyebrow, the hole where the right side of his face used to be.

"The Angel of death has visited again," the family wrote in his obituary. "A Godly life ended on Wednesday morning, July 8, 2015."

Sandy insisted on an open casket. In the days after her son's body was discovered, the rumors persisted. People kept insisting Stephen had been killed by young men he knew, young men he'd gone to high school with, from families far more prominent than his own.

Let them see what they did, she thought. Let them see how they had broken her beautiful child.

The wake was in a small chapel at Hampton's century-old funeral home, just a few blocks down from the Murdaugh law firm on Mulberry. It was a sweltering day, with temperatures still in the midnineties, when family and friends lined up to pay their respects. Joel, Stephen's father, clung to the wall farthest from the body of his son. Sandy stayed by the casket and studied the mourners' faces as they peered inside. Her son was dressed in scrubs, a stethoscope in the pocket, the only way the family knew to honor his desire to become a nurse and then one day a doctor. The mortician had used putty to reconstruct his face and dabbed on makeup to disguise the gash and the deep bruising, but it wasn't enough. In life, Stephen had been modelhandsome, with chiseled cheeks and flawless skin. Now he lay inside the polished wood, his head resting on a velvet pillow, his face discolored and disfigured.

The investigators' theory that Stephen had been shot had been ruled out. The pathologist who performed the autopsy had found no bullet fragments and no other injuries consistent with a shooting; a test for gunshot residue had also come out negative. The pathologist also reported no slash or stab wounds. In her preliminary report, she concluded Stephen died from a hit-and-run. The Highway Patrol troopers who had worked the scene disagreed, reminding the doctor there had been no broken glass or automotive debris in the road or on the shoulder, nor any specks in the open wounds on Stephen's face. His shoulder was dislocated, but otherwise his body was uncannily intact, with no broken bones anywhere other than his face. The biggest tell was that his loosely tied black canvas shoes were still on his feet. Shoes almost always fly off when a body is hit at high impact.

A frustrated investigator at the Highway Patrol went to the pathologist at her office in Charleston and asked her to reconsider. In the trooper's report, he noted that the pathologist was defensive.

The sergeant asked why she'd concluded it was a hit-and-run.

"The body was found in the road," she told him.

"Did you find any glass fragments?" he asked. "Anything to indicate this was a motor vehicle accident?"

"No," she said.

"What do you think could've caused the head wound?" he asked.

"I don't know," she said. "It could've been the mirror of a large pickup truck."

"Could he have been hit by a baseball bat?" the trooper asked.

"That's your job to figure out," the pathologist said, "not mine."

The Hampton County coroner agreed with the Highway Patrol's conclusions, but he couldn't overrule the pathologist's finding. He was an elected official with no medical training, and the pathologist was a veteran doctor, affiliated with the state's major teaching hospital, who had performed hundreds of autopsies. The troopers were working at a considerable disadvantage. Even though they believed Stephen Smith had been murdered, they had almost no expertise in homicide investigation. They thought the case belonged with the South Carolina Law Enforcement Division, better known as SLED, where the detectives knew plenty about solving murders. But once the case was officially declared a hit-and-run, it was the Highway Patrol's jurisdiction.

From the start, it was clear that the case would be especially challenging. The troopers were hearing the same rumors that the case involved the Murdaughs—a legendary Hampton County force that had mastered the art of deflecting unwanted inquiries.

On the first day of their investigation, the troopers interviewed Stephen's family. They learned that their victim had been leading an increasingly complicated life, taking nursing classes at a community college and frequently driving to Hilton Head to meet men he'd met on Craigslist. Sandy Smith didn't flinch from the subject. She thought it likely he had been killed by someone homophobic. Stephen had never hidden his sexuality; from high school onward, he had worn makeup and lipstick, displaying an expertise with cosmetics that surpassed the skills of many of the girls at Wade Hampton High. His sister teased him for always needing five more minutes to leave the house, saying, "I got to look good." But in a deeply conservative county, his boldness had cost him. As a teenager, he had been repeatedly harassed. Sandy told the police the hateful episodes had left him paranoid about his safety. She did not buy the notion that her son had been on his way to buy gas. Why would he have left his wallet in the car? Why not call his father, who lived a few miles away? She also did not think it possible that Stephen would have risked walking along an open road at night. If he'd been heading for a gas station, she said, he would have stayed out of sight, walking through the trees.

The rest of Stephen's family agreed. Sandy and Stephanie both wondered out loud about the men Stephen might have been sleeping with. In the two weeks before he died, Stephen had been unusually secretive. Probably, they said, he'd been seeing someone who didn't want their relationship made public.

The troopers interviewed Stephen's college classmates and tried to track down his Craigslist hookups but got nowhere. They found one older man who claimed to be a boyfriend—Sandy and Stephanie scoffed at the term—but he insisted he'd had nothing to do with Stephen's death. To prove his innocence, the man offered to let the investigators search his phone and give him a lie detector test.

"I'm telling you, man to man, I didn't kill him."

The man said someone had been messing with the battery of Stephen's car. On the night he died, Stephen had called to tell him that a couple of rednecks in a pickup truck had threatened him. The last time he talked to Stephen, at 3:37 A.M., the man heard rumbling in the background, like the whir made by the wide tread of mud tires on an open road. The rumbling, he said, was getting louder.

The troopers tried to confirm what the alleged boyfriend had told them, but had no luck. They heard Stephen had been attacked by some young men coming home from a softball tournament. They pursued rumor after rumor. Almost nobody would talk to them, and when someone did answer questions, they couldn't corroborate anything that mattered. As the days grew into weeks, the investigators realized that even some Hampton County officials appeared to be dodging their calls. Maybe someone had gotten to them. It was also possible, they realized, that threats had not been needed to impose the silence.

Dozens of leads pointed to the Murdaugh family. After Stephen's parents described Randy Murdaugh's unsettling behavior that first morning, the troopers asked the lawyer if what they'd heard was true. Randy acknowledged he had called Joel Smith that morning to express his condolences. But he denied he had offered to represent the family in their son's death or that he asked them for the code for Stephen's phone. He also said he had not visited the crime scene that day when Sandy drove by and he had not called her afterward.

People kept telling the investigators that Randy was talking to possible witnesses, suggesting they pass along various leads to law enforcement.

Again and again, people told the troopers they were messing with the wrong family. Trooper Todd Proctor, the lead investigator, didn't care. He worked out of Charleston, not Hampton County. "I know the Murdaughs are highfalutin'," he said. "And some people say they have a lot of power. That name doesn't mean anything to me."

Officially, the case was still listed as a hit-and-run. But if anyone asked, the trooper would return to his unshakable belief that the pathologist had been wrong. Every one of his colleagues who had worked that morning in June shared his conviction that it was a murder. A lieutenant even went to the sheriff's office and offered to go through the file line by line to prove his case, but the deputy would not even touch the file. It wasn't just the absence of shattered glass on the road, or the shoes that stayed on the victim's feet, or that his body had been found more than a mile from his yellow Aveo. It was that the troopers had found no skid marks and not a single bit of plastic from a broken fender or side mirror. It was that the wallet was in the car, and not in the pocket of a young man supposedly headed for a gas station.

"I can tell you this much," the trooper said. "He didn't get hit by no car."

CHAPTER EIGHT

RANDOLPH "BUSTER" MURDAUGH JR.
(1915-1998)

The bootlegger's wife saw the light-colored Cadillac pull up, sunlight glinting off the ornamental goddess leaning over the hood. The windows gleamed so bright the woman could not see inside, but she already knew who was in the car and what he wanted.

A lawyer in a starched white shirt stepped out of the Cadillac and walked toward the door of the industrial laundry where she was working her shift. She met him up front, her uniform damp with steam.

"I represent the man in the car," he said. "He wants to talk with you."

"No," said the bootlegger's wife. "I'm on the job."

The lawyer reminded her that his client was going on trial in a few days, and the prosecution would be calling her to testify. The client wanted to offer some guidance on what she should tell the jury and what she shouldn't.

The man in the car could get her husband out of prison, the lawyer said. She just needed to say things a certain way.

It was the summer of 1956, and Buster Murdaugh was getting desperate. For years, he had been leading a double life. Since his father had died in the train crash, Buster had served as both solicitor of the Fourteenth Circuit and senior partner in the growing Murdaugh law firm.

On the side, though, he was running South Carolina's biggest bootleg-ging ring. He barely tried to hide it. A dozen law enforcement officers had been on his payroll over the years, especially those who worked in Colleton County, just east of Hampton, which was rural enough to make it easier to hide thousands of stills. No one had dared to chal-lenge the conspiracy until the Justice Department sent agents to ferret out the stills and then charged Buster and dozens of others. Now, as the trial approached, Buster knew he was in trouble, because the case would be heard in federal court, where the Murdaugh name had no sway.

Edith Thigpen Freeman, the laundress Buster came to see that day, had plenty of reasons to sink Buster. Her husband, known as Doc, ran a still near the tiny Colleton County airport, at a place called Jackass Pond. She and her husband paid Buster's men for protection. Edith had discovered that these men had taken advantage of the fact that Doc was illiterate to trick him into paying double. Yet when the feds raided Doc's still and shot him in the gut, his alleged protectors had aban-doned him. He was under guard in a hospital when some of Buster's deputies sneaked into the Freemans' one-room shack and nicked $13,000 in cash from the pocket of Doc's navy peacoat. It was the cou-ple's life savings. Edith knew who the thieves were because later, when she had to beg for cash to pay her husband's medical bills, a deputy had slipped her $500. One of the bills was still marked with her own hand-writing.

Buster recognized how much Edith Freeman could hurt him. She had a little blue spiral notebook she'd kept for her husband, containing the records of his illegal transactions with Buster's men. Now Buster was rolling up with his lawyer in the Cadillac and telling her she could trust him. That night, Edith packed some clothes and checked in to the Francis Marion Hotel, the finest in Charleston, in a room the feds had reserved for her so she could be safe under the protection of U.S. Mar-shals.

The trial started a few days later in the federal courthouse in down-town Charleston, outside Buster's jurisdiction, in front of a judge known for his independence and a jury with only one resident living inside the Fourteenth Circuit. Buster sat at one of the defense tables, wearing a dark blue suit and blue tie. As further proof of his respectability, he had been granted permission to be joined by his wife, Gladys, who wore a brown suit and matching hat with a jaunty feather. Their son, Randolph III, was also in the courtroom, a tall and lanky sixteen-year-old who wore his red hair in a wave across his forehead.

In opening arguments, the U.S. attorney declared the trial "the most important case ever tried in South Carolina. It reaches to the crux of our government and our way of life." Thirty defendants faced eighty counts, but all the talk was about Buster.

"The man with the brains," the lead prosecutor called him. "The man who ran the show."

The case against Buster was compelling but thin, because the solicitor had been careful to put almost nothing on paper. The feds had a deputy who had seen Buster accept a cash bribe in a courthouse corridor. They had the former Hampton County sheriff, who had started out as Buster's friend but had grown appalled by his corruption. But the first witness they called was Edith Freeman, who had written everything down.

As Edith opened the blue notebook and began to read, Buster listened quietly. Either he would leave the courtroom in shackles, or he would find a way to beat this woman and her scribbles.

LIKE A PREACHER'S kid in his father's church, Buster's second home was the courtroom. He had graduated from law school on a Saturday. "The following Monday," he later said, "Daddy handed me an indictment and told me to take over. I've been taking over ever since."

Once he pocketed the railroad settlement from his father's death and became the circuit's top prosecutor at the age of twenty-five, Buster never looked back.

Buster quickly showed he had his own way of doing things, which was brash and loud and theatrical. He puffed cigars and kept a wad of

Red Man in his cheek. In front of juries, he delighted in showing off his aim with the chew, pursing his lips and propelling the brown liquid into a spittoon across the courtroom. When a judge told him no more tobacco in the courtroom, Buster gathered his papers and left. With no solicitor, there could be no proceedings, and court shut down for the day. The judge soon relented.

No matter what courtroom he entered, he was determined to be unforgettable. Juries loved the folksy way he spoke to them and relished his willingness to act out a crime. Once, he traced an imaginary coffin in front of a jury. "This is where Johnny is laying in his grave right now," he said. When the jury came back with a guilty verdict, they avoided stepping inside the invisible box.

Another time, he fell back flat on the courtroom floor and asked a witness to tie a garden hose around his neck and then step on his throat. The witness was a woman who'd been charged as an accomplice. She had come to the courtroom straight from the jail and was wearing a loose-fitting dress and no underwear. When she lifted her foot and put it lightly on his neck, Buster looked up and stopped his narration of the crime.

"It was the only time," one onlooker said, "I've ever seen Buster at a loss for words."

Buster's antics were often entertaining, though equally as often deplorable. When well-connected white men were accused of murder, he repeatedly delayed filing charges, especially in cases in which the victims were Black. Once the hubbub died down, he quietly dropped the charges and allowed the accused to walk free. In one high-profile murder case, he was credibly accused of framing a man by picking up shell casings fired from the dead man's gun and placing them near the gun of the accused. The defendant, who was white, was sentenced to death, but before he could be executed, the South Carolina Supreme Court overturned the conviction based on some of Buster's improprieties and set the man free. More than once, the state supreme court reversed convictions on the grounds that Buster had tainted the jury with hyperbole.

He was always on the hunt for new clients. He sent gifts to every bride and cards to every graduate, knowing some of them would one day need a lawyer. He attended every funeral and was first in every receiving line. The joke was that he wanted to stick a card in the hand of the corpse.

Buster had a small office in the courthouse on the other side of a thin wall from the jury room. When juries retired to deliberate in civil trials, he was known to make boisterous phone calls to his partners at the firm across the street, offering supposedly private reflections on the trial at hand. In one case, he worried that the deliberations were stretching on too long. So, he directed his voice toward the jury room, opening the office window for good measure, and announced that the other side wanted to settle for $150,000.

"It's not enough!" Buster said. "We won't settle for less than $190,000."

The jurors soon returned with a verdict for that exact amount. Buster's "accidental" jury guidance became so routine defense lawyers complained, and the state supreme court banned calls about civil cases from a solicitor's public office. He was manipulative and cunning, quick-witted and ornery, capable of both benevolence and cruelty, mercy and brutality. As one acquaintance put it: "Buster swung a big hammer."

BUSTER'S WIFE, GLADYS, was a spitfire in her own right. Raised on a plantation where her father was a caretaker, she once hid behind the flower bushes during a visit by Wallis Simpson and Edward, the Duke of Windsor. She and Buster were married there under a canopy of moss-covered oaks. They had met in college, and Gladys taught for several years before their children were born. Gladys was sharp-tongued and independent yet steadfast.

Buster was committed to his family, but in keeping with the double standard of the time, he remained an epic carouser with girlfriends in every law practice, government office, and cat house in the Lowcountry.

He met his match in one particular paramour, a Northeastern so-cialite who was a sharpshooter and scratch golfer with a mind as quick as her tongue. Ruthven Vaux came from one of the nation's first fami-lies and was married to Harry Cram, who owned the Foot Point plan-tation in Beaufort County. Ruth met Buster at a luncheon and mentioned she was seeking her release from the U.S. Naval Reserves, where, in the early days of World War II, she had helped train pilots in Florida using a flight simulator. Buster had connections with both U.S. senators and offered to help. Two years after they met, Ruth told Buster she was having his baby.

As the story goes, Buster told one of his fixers to get a gun, hide under Ruth's front porch, and wait for her to come home. Burrowed under the steps, the man had a few sips of whiskey and passed out. Buster would later say, "I would've killed that woman if he hadn't got-ten so drunk."

Having survived the bungled attempt on her life, Ruth gave birth to a son. She named him Roberts Vaux. One day, when Buster was not home, Ruth decided to bring the baby to the Murdaugh house to see his half brother, Randolph III. The maid told her Gladys was in the middle of a bridge game, but Ruth would not leave. Gladys excused herself from the other ladies and stepped out to have a word. The porch was shaded and white, lined by prizewinning camellias Buster trimmed with a penknife. Ruth was dressed as though she came from money, which she did. But if Gladys was unnerved, she didn't show it.

"These boys are brothers," Ruth said. "We need to let them meet."

"They may be brothers," Gladys said, "but please don't ever come here again. Don't let my name, or my son's name, ever come out of your mouth. I wish you the best. Now goodbye."

Gladys did not allow the scandal to wreck her marriage.

"Murdaughs," she often said, "don't divorce."

Despite the acrimony, Ruth maintained a working relationship with Buster for several more years, as Buster represented her in her own inevitable divorce. That professional relationship blew up spectacu-larly, however, when Ruth bumped into her ex-husband, who casually mentioned that he had settled the divorce for $25,000. Ruth was in shock. Buster had told her the settlement was for $15,000, and $4,000 had gone to Buster's fee. Ruth and Buster sued each other. The dispute was messy and petty and mean, described by *The* (Charleston) *News and Courier* as "a maze of complaints, charges, cross-complaints and counter-charges," with "wordage that would smoke up asbestos paper." Since all the Fourteenth Circuit judges knew Buster, the proceedings were moved to the little town of St. Matthews, seventy miles north-west. The day of the hearing, the lawyers announced the matter was settled, with Buster not even bothering to show up. Back home in Hampton County, many whispered that the whole debacle had been staged for Gladys's benefit, Buster's way of showing his wife that the only thing left between him and Ruth was spite.

Buster did little to tamp down rumors about Ruth or any other woman. "It's never a bad thing," he said, "if they're talking about you fucking."

It was known that if Buster liked you, he'd help you any way he could. If he didn't like you, he'd hurt you any way he could. Once, when a lawyer in Columbia got Buster's son Randolph out of a drunk driving charge, Buster thanked him and said, "Remember, if you ever need anybody killed, send them on down to Hampton County."

It was impossible, even then, to nail down how much was true. Woody Gooding, who worked for Buster at the law firm and considered him a close, if complicated, friend, said Buster bragged about the awesome power of tearing up an indictment. "I'm talking about murders that went away," he said. "DUIs are nothing."

Buster didn't mind when people believed the worst of him. "I don't know how many lies have been told about me, but it sure sounds good," he once said. "I don't disagree with anything anybody says about me. As a matter of fact, I sort of encourage it."

BUSTER HAD BEEN in office for a decade when his reign came under siege. First, he faced disbarment. A client filed a lawsuit accusing Buster of stealing as much as $4,000 from a mortgage fund, and as word spread, lawyers began whispering similar tales involving other clients. Reckoning on strength in numbers, the bar associations of Hampton, Beaufort, and Colleton counties asked the state bar to investigate. The hearing was held in the ballroom of the Wade Hampton Hotel in Columbia in September 1949. The bar association's grievance committee called more than seventy witnesses, including legislators and prosecutors, and though the proceedings were secret, the coming and going of these witnesses generated front-page news. The grievance committee deliberated for weeks but in the end announced that the allegations against Buster had been dismissed.

Next came the Internal Revenue Service, which accused Buster of systematically hiding income and exaggerating losses. The investigation dragged on for years. Buster kept no cash receipts, no disbursement book, and no client or case list. If the auditors learned Buster had settled a case, they had to track down the client to find out Buster's fee, if the clients would tell them. Eventually the IRS concluded that Buster owed $23,000 in back taxes and penalties. By the time he lost on appeal in fall 1955, the statute of limitations had expired. The judge determined that Buster had been "grossly negligent" but was responsible for only a fraction of what he owed. Buster had run out the clock.

The third threat, from the U.S. Justice Department, was the gravest, and Edith Freeman was at the center of it. The bootlegging trial started on September 17, 1956. Buster had been running the moonshine operation for so long and with such impunity, it seemed astonishing that anyone was daring to challenge him. Moonshining was a billion-dollar business in the United States during the 1950s. Prohibition was over, but people still wanted to avoid the federal taxes on alcohol, which ran as high as $10.50 a gallon, or roughly $120 today. Buster's duties as solicitor put him in position to control the flow of the liquor and to track the feds. He knew as early as 1951 that the FBI was watching him, searching for the stills under his control and trying to get people to testify against him. If he was worried, he did not show it.

Even so, Buster had been unable to get Edith Freeman to hand over her damning blue notebook.

Just before opening arguments, U.S. District Court judge Walter Hoffman called both sides to his chambers. The judge ran such a tight courtroom that he held lawyers in contempt for infractions as mundane as tardiness. Now he was livid. A witness had come forward alleging jury tampering even before the trial began. And it was not just any witness, but the longtime sheriff of Hampton County.

Sheriff Alton Lightsey had been an ally of Buster's for decades, and of Randolph Sr. before that. When the old man died in the train crash, Lightsey had made the pivotal assessment, publicly at least, that the wreck was an accident. Now Buster and the sheriff had fallen out because Buster had backed Lightsey's opponent in the recent election. The sheriff said he had come to see Buster as a man of low morals and empty words. That morning, in the judge's chambers, the sheriff said Buster had sent someone to his house a few nights before to find out whether he could be persuaded to go easy on Buster.

"We have the jury fixed for mistrial," the sheriff remembered the man telling him. "But we want a clear acquittal."

The defense attorneys denied the accusation, and the judge threatened to jail anyone who approached a juror.

The case was called the Great Colleton County Whiskey Conspiracy. Sheriff Lightsey testified that Buster was the kingpin of the operation. Deputy Riddick Herndon said he'd paid his boss, the Colleton sheriff, a $400 bribe on behalf of a bootlegger and had seen the sheriff slip Buster his share of $200 cash in a courthouse hallway. Buster, he remembered, had chided the sheriff for offering him the bribe in public view.

The government's star witness was Edith Freeman. The showdown between her and Buster felt almost biblical. Edith was a slender middle-aged woman, unassuming, with hardly any connections and a husband who kept cycling in and out of prison. Her desire to take on Buster was either foolish or valiant or both.

Edith told the jury her husband was a bootlegger because he'd failed at everything else, from gas station attendant to bus driver. She said Mr. Murdaugh had promised to represent Doc after the raid in which he was injured, and to bail out his three helpers, young Black men Doc feared might be beaten in prison. Mr. Murdaugh had also promised to investigate the theft of the family's life savings, to bring charges against the federal agent who shot Doc, and even to get back an old family car the feds had seized in the raid.

"I trusted Mr. Murdaugh," she said. "I was perfectly satisfied that Mr. Murdaugh was going to take care of all of it for me."

Eventually, Edith said, she came to feel that Mr. Murdaugh was putting her off, always saying he was close to working everything out. At first it would take a day for him to call her back, then a week, and then he stopped returning her calls. In the end, he broke every promise he had made. When a federal investigator approached her, she said, she'd handed over her notebook and told him all she knew about the sheriff, the deputies, and the prosecutor.

"I didn't have too much respect for any of them," she said. "It's bad enough for Doc to violate the law, but it's worse for them to."

Edith was the first witness. Buster was the last. His performance on the stand could not have been more different from the straightforward testimony of the bootlegger's wife. When the prosecution tried to corner him, Buster used his dual role as solicitor and defense lawyer to defend any action he took. He was especially slippery when the prosecutor reminded him he'd already admitted paying $3,000 to Sheriff Thompson.

"Didn't you say that you and the sheriff were kiting checks to one another for years?" the prosecutor asked.

"No," Buster said. "That money was for investigations carried out for me in a civil case." He added that it was also a thank-you for the sheriff's checking up on Buster's clients. "It is the custom in our area to get someone to take care of a family in need."

The prosecutor reminded Buster that he had protected a man who ran a still for him and had later represented him in court when he was charged with possessing forty-eight gallons of illegal whiskey. The case had gone to the U.S. Supreme Court, with Buster fighting for his client all the way.

"You defended him in federal court," the prosecutor said. "Why didn't you prosecute him in your state court?"

"He wasn't indicted by the grand jury," Buster answered.

"You knew him as a bootlegger, though?"

"I only knew him as a farmer," Buster said.

Though they were weighing a complex web of evidence against dozens of defendants, the jury reached its verdicts in only a few hours. At 9:45 P.M., everyone gathered again in the courtroom. Buster joined his legal team up front, with Randolph III seated nearby. For the first time in weeks, Gladys was nowhere to be seen. She had maintained her composure throughout the trial, but now she was too nervous to stay in the courtroom and had taken refuge in the courthouse lobby.

Judge Hoffman began reading from the verdict sheet, calling the name of each defendant in alphabetical order.

"Guilty . . . guilty . . . guilty . . ."

The judge said the word so many times, it seemed he would never stop. Buster chewed his lip as he waited for his name to be called. In front of the jury, he had displayed righteous confidence. Now that facade fell away. As the judge kept reading, Buster breathed heavily and drew his hand rapidly across his mouth.

The first fifteen defendants had all been found guilty. Then the judge read name number sixteen.

"Murdaugh."

A slight pause.

"Not guilty."

Buster's shoulders collapsed and he appeared to break down. A friend ran downstairs to the lobby to find his wife, who wept at the news.

"I have never had any fear as to the outcome of the indictment presented against me," Buster told reporters. "I thank God that the jury brought in a true verdict insofar as I am concerned."

Insofar as I am concerned.

That five-word flourish revealed so much about Buster, who was so willing to condemn his accomplices as long as he walked away.

Buster was not in court the next morning when Hoffman sentenced the others. When the judge was done, he castigated Buster, calling him grossly unethical and wondering how he could show his face back home. In fact, the solicitor returned home a conquering hero. The leaders of the region's Methodist churches even took out an ad: "May God bless him and his family always."

Buster had fixed the case, just as Judge Hoffman had been warned. Not long after the trial, the Justice Department sent a bulletin to all U.S. attorneys, informing them that witnesses had been intimidated and even bribed.

Though the jurors lived beyond Buster's usual reach, he was not deterred. One lived in Orangeburg, about an hour from Hampton. But this juror had gone to high school with one of Buster's cousins, and a few days before the trial, the cousin had invited him to dinner at Baroody's Steak House. The juror was elected foreman, and once the trial started, he showed an unusual determination to finish it in Buster's favor. As deliberations began, the foreman learned his father was dying. Judge Hoffman offered to release the man to be with his family. But the foreman declined, even though an alternate juror was available to take his place.

The cousin who had invited the foreman to dinner was later charged with jury tampering, but he, too, was acquitted. Buster, meanwhile, was elected to a fifth term. He was still bristling at the temerity of the federal prosecutors who had faulted him for not bringing bootlegging cases in whiskey-soaked Colleton County. One of the first things he did after his acquittal was charge two people with violating the liquor law. One was Riddick Herndon, the deputy who had testified to seeing Buster accept a bribe. The other was Edith Freeman.

Edith's courage had left her with nothing except a misdemeanor conviction and a fine.

BUSTER WORKED AS solicitor for another thirty years. No one ever ran against him again. He had beaten the state bar, the IRS, and the

Justice Department, even though he was guilty of almost everything he'd been accused of and much more.

Old Buster—that's what people had taken to calling him—refused to retire, even after a heart attack and years of failing health. "You can't kill a cur dog," a friend said. Eventually the legislature passed a law forcing solicitors to step down at seventy-two or forfeit their retirement benefits. Before leaving office, he persuaded the governor to appoint his son Randolph III to complete his term. Even then, he kept working alongside his son as an assistant solicitor.

Buster had proved that Murdaughs could fix juries, corrupt sheriffs and judges, cheat on their taxes, steal from clients, play both sides of the law, and define justice however they chose. By his own admission, he had also proved that a Murdaugh could arrange a murder and face no consequences.

CHAPTER NINE

Deep into the fall of 2015, the Highway Patrol troopers were still chasing rumors about the death of Stephen Smith. Most of those rumors pointed to Alex Murdaugh's sons.

People insisted to law enforcement, more than forty times, that Buster or Paul had been involved. The troopers knew Paul had a reputation as the wilder of the two. They drove all over Hampton County trying to nail down Buster's and Paul's whereabouts on the night in question but made little progress. Buster did not return their call. The file does not show whether they reached out to Paul, but he was sixteen, three years younger than his big brother, and the troopers would need a parent's permission to interview him.

The troopers kept searching. They heard that Buster and some friends might have run down Stephen with his truck, and that Buster had sold the truck afterward. They tried tracking down friends who could place Buster or Paul at the softball tournament that night. But the friends proved unreachable, and people said they'd left town.

As time passed, more rumors surfaced. Someone told the investigators a green Jeep had been following Stephen just before he died. Someone else heard the name of a young man—not a Murdaugh— who had struck and killed Stephen. The lead investigator went to the source, but the trail led nowhere. The man said he was passing along his tip because Randy Murdaugh had encouraged him to share what he'd heard with police.

Another tip came from Chris Smith, Stephen's older brother. Someone had approached Chris at work and said he and Buster Murdaugh and some friends had been out smashing mailboxes when they came upon Stephen by the side of the road. Buster had beaten Stephen to death with a baseball bat because he was gay, he said. And Buster had threatened to kill him, too, if he told anyone what he'd seen.

The investigators couldn't corroborate this story, either. Every lead seemed to evaporate.

Stephen Smith's family had little doubt that at least one Murdaugh was involved. Sandy, Stephen's mother, kept returning to how cagey Stephen had been in the weeks before he died. His friends had told her Stephen was hinting about a secret new flame, someone who mattered in Hampton and was hiding his sexuality. Stephen wouldn't give a name.

"If you knew who it was," he said, "you'd be surprised."

ALEX WAS NAMED president of the state trial lawyers' association, the networking and lobbying group founded by his grandfather, that year. He accepted the role at the gala breakfast of the association's annual conference in August 2015. He celebrated with an all-night party in the hospitality suite at the Westin Hilton Head. Nineteen-year-old Buster was there, redheaded and, at six foot two, almost as tall as his father. He was already planning to go to USC law school, just like the Murdaugh men before him. Onlookers remember watching Buster walking through the crowd with an Igloo cooler full of ice on his head, shooing aside some of the most powerful lawyers in the state.

Alex was well liked and well connected, always ready with a wink and a quip, the life of every party, ready to bet a hundred dollars a hole on golf when the other guys might have stuck with ten. Bakari Sellers, the 2014 Democratic candidate for lieutenant governor, thought of Alex as a brother.

At the same time, the dissonance between Alex's two lives was increasing. He was in constant overdrive, working the phone as he drove between home and the office, racing to Beaufort and Columbia and Charleston for countless appointments. He was burning through money as fast as he could get it, with his checking account frequently overdrawn by tens of thousands of dollars. He took Maggie on a private plane to New York City for the wedding of a principal of Forge Consulting, which worked with lawyers at Alex's firm on investing settlement money. It was a rich irony that Alex paid for the trip with stolen client funds laundered through a new dummy account at Bank of America, named "doing business as Forge," a strategy to borrow his friend's corporate name to better shield his thefts from the law firm.

He was stealing millions, almost daring anyone to catch him. And with his acquisition of Moselle, questions were swirling about the runway and the planes. Paul was in high school, inviting friends to party at Moselle every weekend. Privately, he confided to a friend that drug shipments were still landing on the property.

Alex's personal life was splintering as well. He'd always had a penchant for strip clubs; he'd started a brawl at one in law school. His closest friends knew he'd had sex with a sex worker on a boys' night out on Isle of Palms in 2015. But they probably did not know he had visited her multiple times, or that their encounters involved violence. One night, she said, Alex had choked her with a washrag. Another time he pulled her hair so hard it came out in clumps.

Once he'd turned his back on becoming the next solicitor, there was no trace of public service left in the man.

OFFICIALLY STEPHEN SMITH'S case was listed as a hit-and-run. But the pathologist who reached that conclusion had been fired. By that time, she had grown weary of the investigators who questioned her judgment. Before she left, she had told a deputy coroner from Hampton County that if he wanted, he was free to change the cause of death on her report.

Put down whatever you like, she told him.

That October, Stephen's father, Joel, died in his sleep. The doctors suspected cardiac arrest. Sandy and the rest of the family called it a broken heart. He was buried beside his son, in a country cemetery on the same lonely road where Stephen's body had been found.

Months were passing, and the investigators were running in circles. The Highway Patrol sergeant was incredulous that he and his team could be stonewalled by an entire county. "There was very limited information coming in," he'd later say. "And at a certain point in time, where do you go?"

Sandy couldn't let go. She remembered Stephen's shyness as a boy, the way he'd whispered his thoughts to his twin sister, Stephanie, so she could speak for him. Now that her son was gone, Sandy believed the family had to speak for him.

Frustrated by the lack of progress, Sandy kept returning to the scene, hoping to uncover something that had been missed. One day she found a footprint a couple of hundred feet from where her son's body had been found. She told the lead investigator about it, but nothing happened.

She wrote to the FBI asking for help. She wrote to Governor Nikki Haley. She urged anyone who knew the truth to step forward. She acknowledged that some of Hampton's most prominent names were being bandied about but didn't want anyone to let that intimidate them. The worst part, she said, was knowing that those responsible were Stephen's classmates.

"People need to realize that these murderers are still out there and it could be their child next," she said. "I know what his first words were, but I need to know what his last words were. I want to know who took my son from me."

Michael DeWitt Jr., the editor of *The Hampton County Guardian,* had grown up with Alex and his brothers. In middle school he'd taken an English class taught by Libby Murdaugh, Alex's mother. In the years since, he'd been a frequent guest at Randolph III's monthly cookouts at Almeda. The weekly newspaper's office was barely 400 feet from the law firm. The editor had covered Randolph III's retirement, the hundredth anniversary of the firm, even young Buster winning an award in Boy Scouts. But he was hearing the same rumors as everyone else in town and knew there was no way to draw attention to Stephen Smith's killing without blowback. Ultimately DeWitt decided he had enough of the community omertà. Somebody in Hampton held the key to solving Stephen's death, and the editor wanted them to step forward.

In late November, he called his lone reporter into his office. "We're going with a story about Stephen Smith in our Thanksgiving edition," he said, "along with the warm and fuzzy crap we usually put in there. Call Stephen's mother. Ask her to come see us."

The editor published the interview on the front page along with a photo of Sandy Smith holding a glamour shot of Stephen. "I know who killed my son," she said, adding that one of the people involved was a former classmate from a prominent family.

Accompanying the piece was an editorial. The headline declared IT'S TIME TO DO THE RIGHT THING, HAMPTON COUNTY.

Then DeWitt waited. He was gratified when people came up to him in Piggly Wiggly and patted him on the back for having the courage to publish the story. But he was deflated when weeks passed and no one came forward with new information.

The editor stopped going to the Murdaugh cookouts. He no longer felt welcome.

CHAPTER TEN

One winter morning, the Murdaughs' housekeeper was running late. Gloria Satterfield's car had been squealing, so she'd dropped it off at her brother's house for him to tinker with and borrowed her sister's car. She had stopped at McDonald's for some sweet tea, then driven out to Moselle.

Another long day awaited. Paul had entertained friends the night before, and there was sure to be piles of dirty dishes and a scattering of empty beer cans.

It was February 2, 2018. Lawyers and investigators would make a beat-by-beat timeline of what happened next.

Gloria usually reported to work at Moselle by 8 A.M. But that morning, because of her car troubles, she'd arrived closer to 8:30.

Maggie told investigators she was still asleep when her housekeeper arrived. She awoke to the sound of dogs barking. The family had several dogs who were usually clamoring for attention outside. Bubba, a yellow Labrador, was Maggie's favorite, but there was also Blue the Labradoodle and Sassy the short-haired pointer. A young chocolate Lab named Bourbon had been boarding at obedience school, and his return the day before had gotten the other dogs excited.

But the barking Maggie heard had a different edge. The dogs were sounding an alarm. Maggie looked out the bedroom window and saw Gloria sprawled at the bottom of the front-porch steps. Her feet were up on the steps, and her head was down on the brick patio. Even from the window, Maggie said, she could see blood.

She ran downstairs yelling for Paul. Her youngest son had been living at home, taking classes at a commuter school to get his grades up and keeping an eye on his dad, whose health he was worried about. He told the investigators that he, too, had been asleep upstairs that morning. When he raced downstairs, his mother called Alex and then 911.

"My housekeeper has fallen, and her head is bleeding," Maggie told the dispatcher, her voice calm, almost monotone. "I cannot get her up."

GLORIA HAD BEEN with the family for twenty years. When the boys were little, she'd been responsible for much of their raising. As a toddler, Paul had trailed after Gloria, clutching her skirts. He called her GoGo. Gloria told friends she loved Buster and Paul like her own.

The family held on to the house on Holly Street, but as the boys finished high school, they spent more and more time at their massive new homestead. Gloria followed the family to the big white house in the middle of nowhere.

Moselle became a high-end playground. Alex and Maggie threw parties for the boys' friends, setting out beer kegs and renting elaborate inflatable slides. They hosted fundraisers for Democratic candidates for governor and organized dove hunts for law enforcement officers.

Feral as he was, Paul embraced the wildness of the place, the woods teeming with coyotes and bobcats and feral hogs lumbering through the underbrush, the hawks rising above the pines with snakes and rabbits still twisting in their talons. Alligators swam in one of the ponds, and Paul liked to jump in and swim with them, almost daring them to attack.

Paul and Buster hunted as often as they could. One Christmas, Alex and Maggie surprised their sons with expensive rifles. The twin .300 Blackouts were custom semiautomatic weapons built on an AR-15 frame, known for their power and their ability to fire subsonic rounds and their effectiveness at hunting medium-sized game, such as feral hogs. Buster's gun was black; Paul's was tan. They were fearsome and magnificent weapons, built by a cousin of Alex's who happened to be a weapons expert. Each had a night scope and a suppressor, or silencer, sending the price for the pair of guns to $9,200.

Maggie's older sister, Marian, was her closest confidante. They were seven years apart but spoke almost every day, especially as their children grew up. Marian was mother to three Charleston debutantes. They joked about Maggie climbing into the deer stand and reading *Southern Living* while the men hunted. But Marian could not hold her tongue about the Blackouts.

"Maggie, why would you give those boys those guns?"

"They love to shoot hogs," Maggie said.

"I know," Marian said. "It just scares me for the boys to have such dangerous weapons."

Paul was so attached to his rifle that he kept it in his F-150. The following October, he went to a Halloween party and left the truck unlocked, with the Blackout inside. When Paul came back, the gun was gone. Alex and Maggie quickly bought him another one.

CLEANING THE MASTER bedroom one day, Gloria found a Ziploc bag of oxy taped beneath Alex's side of the bed. She was too scared to show it to Maggie, fearing that her boss would suspect her of snooping and maybe fire her. She showed the bag to Paul, who called his grandfather. Maybe he would know what to do.

Gloria tended to tread lightly in a family with such fraught dynamics. She understood that Alex and Maggie were unlikely to help her if she tried to rein in the boys. Once, when Paul was little, he had pulled a kitchen knife from a drawer and pointed it in her direction.

"What are you going to do about it?" he'd said.

The problem had worsened as Buster and Paul grew into teenagers and were recruited into the drunken rituals of their parents' social lives. On Facebook, Buster posted a photo of himself preparing more than fifty Jell-O shots for his parents and their friends for a football tailgate. He was sixteen. Sometimes Alex and Maggie would load the boys in their Sea Hunt and take them to a sandbar in the middle of the Beaufort River, a popular summer hangout where crowds partied on the sand or aboard boats that rocked in the shallows along the shore. Paul, already showing signs of becoming a belligerent drunk, picked fights with grown men. He was thirteen.

Gloria had changed their diapers, picked up their dirty clothes, cleaned their bathrooms, and mopped their floors. Almost every night she cooked the family's dinner before she drove the twenty-five miles back to the mobile home she shared with her own sons. When she returned the next morning, she would find the Murdaughs' dishes still dirty, set aside wherever they'd been eating, often scattered around the living room in front of the TV.

For all of these services, Alex and Maggie offered Gloria no health insurance or paid vacation time. They paid her $10 an hour, always in cash.

IT TOOK TWENTY minutes for the rescue crew to reach Moselle. Alex later told the insurance investigators he had rushed home from the law firm and had arrived as the paramedics were loading Gloria into the ambulance. He followed them to the Colleton Medical Center, the hospital in Walterboro. Doctors there discovered that Gloria's injuries were more severe than they first appeared, so they ordered her airlifted to a trauma center in Charleston. The paramedics turned over her purse to Alex for safekeeping.

Alex got word to Gloria's younger son, Tony, who was a certified nursing assistant in an emergency room and knew enough about head injuries to fear the worst. He was relieved when he finally saw his mother in the intensive care unit. She was alert enough to recognize him, and was even able to give her Social Security number to a woman filling out paperwork. She had a crushed skull, a dozen broken vertebrae, several broken ribs, and a hematoma on her brain, but she could move her arms and legs. Maybe she hadn't had a stroke, as he feared.

Over the next few days, Gloria showed signs of improvement, even sitting up slightly with the help of a physical therapist. But she had underlying health issues, including kidney disease and high blood pressure, plagues of the working poor. She still had the hematoma, and she spiked a fever from an infection. The surgery on her broken ribs took a toll.

A week into her hospitalization, as Gloria reached her fifty-seventh birthday, she was unconscious almost all of the time. Nurses inserted a feeding tube. Tony asked if his mother was brain dead, but the doctor said no.

Maggie came to see Gloria once. Gloria's family was at her side every day, as her fever climbed and her oxygen saturation fell. When her heart stopped, the hospital staff revived her with CPR and put her on a ventilator. Tony held his mother's hand.

"You don't have to hang on for my sake, Mom," he told her. "I talked with God. I know we're gonna be okay."

Gloria started pulling at her mask, as though she was trying to say something. But she couldn't do it. A few hours later, she was gone.

The Murdaughs attended Gloria's funeral at Sandy Run Baptist Church. The program listed Alex and Maggie and the boys as members of the family. After the service, Paul bolted for his truck, his girlfriend, Morgan, trailing behind. Inside the truck, he cried and cried. He had often told Morgan that GoGo had been like a mother to him. He said that even when she got on him about his drinking, he knew she had his best interests at heart. He kept her picture in his wallet.

At the reception, Alex made a beeline for Tony. Alex was saying he was sorry, going on and on about how the dogs had tripped Gloria on the steps. Alex said she'd told him that herself before the ambulance took her away.

"I feel terrible about all this," he said. "Let me help you. I have a plan."

Alex told Tony he had a $500,000 insurance policy on the house at Moselle. He said he could get another lawyer to sue him and that the settlement would cover Gloria's medical bills, the funeral, and maybe $100,000 each for her two sons. Tony and his brother needed that money. They'd been living with Gloria in her mobile home, and the settlement would cover the payments and possibly even buy it out-right. Tony was an ER tech, scrambling to pay off his school loans. His brother, Brian, was making a little more than minimum wage as a stock boy at Piggly Wiggly.

Tony knew Mr. Alex filed lawsuits all the time. He was puzzled, though, by what Alex was telling him about the dogs. That first day in the hospital, when she could still talk, his mother had told the doctor she didn't know what had made her fall.

Alex said he couldn't be Tony's lawyer because it would be a con-flict of interest, but he knew another lawyer to file the suit. His banker friend Russell Laffitte could serve as personal representative in the case, representing the family.

"I'll take care of you," Alex said. "You're like family to me."

ALEX WORKED QUICKLY. Within three weeks of Gloria Satterfield's funeral, he'd met with an adjuster, sent letters to the insurance carrier, and made it clear that the company needed to pay the policy limit or he'd sue them for bad faith. The adjuster was taken aback. It wasn't clear to him that the dogs had anything to do with the housekeeper's death. He thought it likely a judge would consider the case not as a wrongful death suit but as a workers' compensation claim. Alex was saying Gloria had not been scheduled to work that morning and was only there to pick up a check for work she'd done at his mother's house, which defied logic.

In the end, the adjuster caved to Alex's demands, reasoning it wouldn't be worth it to challenge his claim and end up in front of a

Hampton County jury. The adjuster recommended that his insurance company write a check to cut their losses. The payout was key to Alex's plans, because it triggered access to $5 million in umbrella coverage he'd gotten through another company.

Alex had the first half million by the holidays. It was a big Christmas, with quail hunting and Santa hats and spiked punch. Alex's relatives gathered to play Chaos, a Murdaugh family game in which no one really knew or followed the rules. A couple of days later, Alex took Maggie, his sons, and Paul's girlfriend, Morgan, to Charlotte to see the Gamecocks play in the Belk Bowl, with seats on the fifty-yard line.

The Murdaughs were home by New Year's Eve. Paul and Morgan went to a party with some friends, including Morgan's good friend Mallory Beach. It was a happy occasion, the night Mallory became an official couple with Anthony Cook, her longtime crush and one of Paul's best friends. They had a lot to celebrate, and Paul, in particular, had a lot to drink. By the end of the night, he was struggling to stand, talking gibberish and stretching his arms wide with his fingers splayed open. When it was time to go home, he wouldn't let Morgan drive. As they left the party, he careened his truck into a friend's BMW and totaled it.

Alex was summoned to drive the kids home. Alex talked with the parents who owned the BMW and promised to replace the car out of pocket. No need to call the police or the insurance company.

In a matter of weeks, Alex had burned through most of the check he'd received for Gloria's death. The money was intended for her sons, but Alex did not tell them it existed. Nor did he tell them he had already filed the claim with his excess carrier for several million more. He was already making arrangements to hide those funds as well. In the months to come, when Gloria's sons asked him the status of their money, Alex would text a quick update.

> *Been working on the case and made me think about you. Call me anytime I can help.*

Tony Satterfield did call, but Alex didn't always pick up. Tony assumed the lawyer was busy. When more time passed and he still couldn't reach him, Tony used the fax machine at his office to send copies of an ominous hospital bill and an eviction notice.

What does this mean, Tony wrote neatly on a cover letter, *and do I need to do anything?*

Alex never responded. Gloria's home was repossessed.

CHAPTER ELEVEN

RANDOLPH MURDAUGH III
(1939–2021)

The boy did as he was told and listened to the confession. The murderer had poisoned his elderly sister and buried her alive, and now he was in the Colleton County jail admitting all of it to the solicitor and his son.

Randolph Murdaugh III was nine years old. He didn't want to be stuck inside the jail for hours, hearing the details of what this man had done to his ailing and bedridden sister. Dinnertime was approaching, and Randolph wanted to go home. But his father insisted the child stay and listen.

"I gave my sister some strychnine," the killer was saying. "It was as much as could be placed on the end of a knife. I put it in a cup of coffee."

"Why?" asked Buster Murdaugh. "Why did you do that?"

"She had messed up her bed so many times," the man said. "I guess I did it out of pure meanness."

Young Randolph must have blinked. Perhaps he found it hard to breathe. Randolph felt bad for the dead sister and how she had suffered. But he felt for her brother, too. The killer wasn't big and scary, like a monster. He was just an old man, sick and weary and so small. The more he talked, the smaller he became.

Randolph's father had raised him to see the world in absolutes. There were good men and there were bad, and his father's job was to determine which was which and make the bad ones pay. What did it mean, then, for Randolph to feel anything for this husk of a human seated before him, spilling his life away with every word?

Randolph idolized his father. For years the child had trailed him into court after school. On the weekends they would climb into Buster's cluttered station wagon to hunt deer and quail. That Saturday in April when Buster took Randolph to the jail, the two of them had spent the morning casting their lines on the banks of a river. Randolph may have known his father was working on a big case, because the front page of the newspaper was filled with the sordid details. The eighty-year-old woman had disappeared from the falling-down farmhouse she shared with her brother. No one had seen her for days. When sheriff's deputies were dispatched to the house, the old man had been cagey. Deputies found the sister's mattress burning out back, and her dress and shawl tossed among the trees.

Buster himself had discovered the body. He was using his walking stick to poke around a hog pen when he noticed a patch of freshly turned topsoil. Five Black prisoners from a chain gang helped with the search, and he called for them to start digging. As they clawed at the dirt, Buster kept poking his stick until he touched something that didn't belong there. Under a layer of crumpled fertilizer bags and blankets, he saw the emaciated body of the missing sister. She was folded in half. Deputies arrested the brother and took him away.

"Call me when he's ready to confess," the solicitor told them.

The next day, the sheriff tracked down Buster and his son on the riverbank. The suspect wanted to talk, the sheriff said, but only if he could make his statement to Old Buster. The father and son loaded their fishing gear and drove to the jail in Walterboro. Buster told Randolph he needed him to listen and remember what the suspect said. Randolph wanted no part of it, but his father told him that was too bad.

Buster and Randolph made their way to the jail, a hundred-year-old building that resembled a neo-Gothic castle, with crenelated parapets and turrets. Many children are frightened of jails, even riding by them in a car, but this one was particularly imposing, and Randolph knew he was being escorted inside to look a murderer in the face. Buster led his son into the jail's interior, a warren of crumbling walls that smelled of rancid food and flop sweat. White prisoners were crowded on metal cots, Black men on dirty mats. There was a constant clamor of clanging doors and the ramblings of miserable men.

Buster took Randolph inside a room and instructed him to sit. A guard brought the accused forward, and the interrogation began.

"The coroner said your sister weighed barely sixty pounds. I know you killed her but did you starve her, too?"

The man said he had neither killed nor starved his ailing sister. He said he had taken care of her for years as she lost her mind and memory. By the time she died, he said, she was no longer able to do anything for herself and he had the farm to tend.

After hours of dodging Buster's questions, the man finally told the truth. He thought he'd given his sister enough rat poison to kill her, he explained. But when he went to her room the next morning, she was still alive. So he dug the grave out in the hog pen and buried her there, covering her with blankets and dirt.

"Was she dead?" Buster asked.

"Her eyes were shut," the man said, "but she was breathing a little."

When it was over, Buster had both a confession and, in his son, an impeccable witness. If the case went before a jury, it would likely be in the fall, when Randolph would be starting fourth grade.

Randolph told his father he didn't want to be responsible for sending the man to death row or putting him in prison for the rest of his life. Buster told the boy he would make him testify, even if he had to declare him a hostile witness.

"You can just sit in court," he said, "and hold your subpoena."

Decades later, after Randolph succeeded his father as solicitor, he would return to the Colleton County jail many times and bring charges in hundreds of other homicides. When asked about his career, he told people that emulating Buster's example was all he ever wanted.

"I never wanted to be a fireman," he said. "I never wanted to do anything other than practice law."

The truth was, Randolph had not been allowed to consider another life. His conscription into the family business had been ordained from his first breath. Being born a Murdaugh was a life sentence all its own. And part of that life, inevitably, was to become acquainted with death, and the worst of what human beings can do to one another, even those they love.

EACH GENERATION OF Murdaugh men was the same but different. Randolph Sr. had started with shining ideals. Buster had reveled in his sharp-elbowed willingness to construe the law as he chose. Randolph III was the dutiful son who did what was required to keep the dynasty going. He was not a crusader like his grandfather or a bulldog like his father. Randolph III never aspired to be epic. He was recognizably mortal, reassuringly ordinary, wired more like other people. He didn't have the cruel streak that made people fear Buster. Those who knew Randolph remember him as tough but fair, even kind. His joy was his family, and he loved nothing more than being outdoors with Alex and Paul. He only ever used a shotgun, his trusty Bo Whoop, which he got for his high school graduation. For him, hunting wasn't really the point.

A judge who'd watched him in court for twenty years said Randolph's gift was making everyone feel special. After people spoke with him, the judge said, "they would say, 'I may not agree with him, but I sure do like him.'"

Randolph III surrendered to the path laid by his father and grandfather. He was a Murdaugh, after all. When he was sixteen, he drove the family's Ford station wagon through a stop sign in Beaufort and struck another car, badly injuring the driver. He fled the scene. The driver, a well-known local writer and mother of two, was bedridden for six weeks with a broken hip. Beaufort was a small town and she was able to find out who was driving. It turns out her family had known the Murdaughs for decades. She agreed not to sue on the condition that

Randolph III come to her bedside and apologize. No charges were filed, either, as it would have been up to Old Buster to bring them. He went on to play football at USC, mostly warming the defensive bench, and graduate from USC's law school. He was not at the top of his class, but he was a big man on campus. It was preordained that he would return to Hampton to join the firm and serve as an assistant solicitor under his father. Fidelity to the family blueprint guaranteed him almost unlimited power, at least inside Hampton County and the rest of the Fourteenth Circuit. Hampton County remained a desolate place mired in the muck of the past. But inside that blighted landscape, the Murdaughs were the unquestioned sovereigns. To borrow a term from one South Carolina historian, Randolph had been raised to become a master of a small world.

Buster's influence was not restricted to Randolph III. He became close to his second son, too, the child who had been born out of his relationship with Ruth Vaux. When the two boys were young, Ruth had tried to introduce them on the Murdaughs' front porch. Now Roberts Vaux had grown up, and his parents had reached an understanding. Buster's younger son had become a lawyer as well. Roberts and Randolph formed a friendship that lasted the rest of their lives, Randolph even serving as a groomsman in Roberts's wedding. Buster hired Roberts as an assistant solicitor, too, to work alongside Randolph. New employees in the office were warned that the quickest way to be fired was to remark on the resemblance between the two men.

Taking advantage of the peculiarities of South Carolina statutes, the firm continued to thrive by suing the railroads and other big corporations. In the early 2000s, Walmart bought twenty acres of land on Carolina Avenue, including most of the block where Randolph Sr. first built a home a century earlier. But before construction began, Walmart realized its error. Hampton was what legal advocacy groups call "a judicial hellhole," a place where hometown jurors leveled $1 million judgments against big corporations in cases that would get a $100,000 judgment anywhere else in the state. If Walmart opened its doors in Hampton County, the Murdaughs would take them to court for every slip-and-fall in the state. Ultimately, Walmart canceled construction and gave the land to the town for free.

The Murdaughs perpetuated the illusion that they were Hampton's benefactors, fighting for neighbors who had nothing. But their legal chokehold chased away businesses, deprived people of jobs, kept doctors from opening a practice, and made it more expensive to raise families. Because the county's tax base was so depleted, property tax rates rose far higher than in wealthier jurisdictions. Car insurance rates rose as well. The Murdaughs were thriving as the town around them sank.

Randolph III worked a total of fifty-eight years in the solicitor's office and ran unopposed during his twenty-year tenure in the top job. He tried many cases in the same Colleton courtroom where his father's portrait hung in the back. From watching his father in court as a little boy, Randolph had learned to treat the courtroom like a stage. When he delivered closing arguments, he could wrap his words in what a defense attorney called his "fire and brimstone voice," a term similar to the moniker bestowed long ago on his grandfather. Sometimes Randolph wept openly in front of the jury.

During one murder trial, a pathologist was describing the wounds she had found on the victim's torso. Realizing that her testimony was confusing the jurors, Randolph removed his suit jacket, handed the pathologist a red marker, and invited her to step down from the witness chair and draw on his white button-down shirt, showing the jurors exactly what she meant.

"Are you sure, sir?" the pathologist said.

Randolph III smiled and admitted that his wife, Libby, would be mad when he came home with the marked-up shirt.

"But that's okay," he said. "She'll get over it."

Randolph and Libby had met at Wade Hampton High School and been together ever since. Now they were raising four kids, Lynn, Randy, Alex, and John Marvin. Randolph III coached their Little League teams on the same fields where Alex would grow up to coach Buster and Paul. He was a devoted father, but after his strict upbringing, he tended toward leniency, especially as his younger sons reached high

school. At the family's homestead in Almeda, a few miles south of
Hampton, Randolph allowed Alex and the other boys to throw raucous parties where kids got drunk, smoked pot, and built bonfires. One
fall, a bunch gathered at the property to build a class float for the
Homecoming parade featuring a pyramid of beer cans. When they ran
out of beer at a friend's party, one of the Murdaugh boys took the solicitor's car to buy more, reasoning that no cop would pull them over.

Randolph III's circuit consistently had one of the lowest conviction
rates for drunk driving in the state, a scandal he shrugged off. It's not
that people weren't charged, it's that the charges were often dropped
by the solicitor, or nolle prossed. Randolph once signed an affidavit
that he knew every single eligible juror in one of the counties in his
circuit.

"You nolle pros somebody for DUI," a fellow lawyer said, "they're
going to remember it."

By the time Randolph III became solicitor in 1986, bootlegging had
largely been replaced by drug smuggling, especially in the hundreds of
remote islands off Beaufort County's coast. Runways were cleared in
the woods for plane shipments of marijuana bales. Shrimp boats ferried bricks of cocaine from remote inlets. Boats docked late at night on
tiny islands. Randolph III prosecuted drug cases, but he defended them,
too, including accused smugglers in the federal government's Operation Jackpot sting in the early 1980s. He also was rumored to have followed his father's example and worked with the drug runners,
accepting bribes to ignore activity on his turf, even warning crews
when he learned a raid was imminent.

Like his father, Randolph III was a flirt and philanderer. When the
first strip club on Hilton Head Island was set to open, a group of citizens lobbied for tighter regulations and strict enforcement of the laws
governing nudity and alcohol. Randolph III promised to "keep a close
eye" on the matter and made sure he was in attendance at the Gold
Club's opening night. Randolph III once grew so enamored of a paramour, he holed up with her in the condo he kept on Hilton Head,
leaving Libby at home with their four school-aged children.

A week or so later, an obituary published in *The State,* South Carolina's largest newspaper, announced the death of Libby Murdaugh. The obit said she had died at home and included an effusive list of her life's accomplishments, noting she had been a vice president of the Hampton Country Club.

Only one detail was incorrect: Libby was alive.

Libby claimed to have been shocked. The first word she got of the obit, she said, was when a neighbor phoned her in hysterics.

"You're dead!" the neighbor cried.

"Well, obviously I'm not," Libby said.

That morning, Libby made a hasty appearance on local radio station WBHC ("We Built Hampton County") to dispel the rumors and thank friends who had already sent flowers.

Her friends at the Hampton Country Club and at bridge club and at the Methodist church assumed Libby had called in the obit herself. The paragraphs were almost identical to what Libby had submitted for publication years before in her wedding announcement. As for motive, the friends thought Libby had intended the news of her death to shame her husband into returning home, or to flush out his girlfriend. Some wondered if Libby had intended the obit as a veiled threat, suggesting what she might do, either to herself or Randolph, if the man didn't come to his senses.

Embarrassed by the public furor, Randolph's mother put an end to the drama herself. Gladys headed out to Hilton Head, found her son, and, with the help of her yard man as muscle, dragged him back to Hampton to rejoin his family. Having lived for so long with Buster's wandering eye, Gladys would have had no illusions about her boy swearing off other women. But he was a Murdaugh, and she made it clear to both Randolph and Libby that they had no choice but to stay together.

Murdaughs don't divorce. It was one of the rules. There were no exceptions.

· · ·

IN 1998, JOHN Marvin, Randolph III's youngest son, threw a party at Murdaugh Island, a spit of land Old Buster had bought as a family retreat decades before. Some of the guests headed out onto the water in a boat loaded with Miller Light and Bud Light, northbound on the Broad River. As they passed underneath a bridge and into a tricky stretch known as Hazzard Creek, the boat ran aground, jolting the passengers. Whatever they hit was only a fleeting obstruction, and the boat took off as suddenly as it had stopped.

It took a moment for the party to realize someone had been thrown overboard. When the driver turned around, they found the missing passenger walking dazed in knee-deep water, bleeding from his face. They hauled him into the boat and wrapped their shirts around his head to staunch the bleeding, then sped toward a nearby marina. They had not gone far when they saw a boat driven by John Marvin, who was taking another friend for a joy ride. Together they headed toward the marina, where they were met by a sheriff's deputy and an officer from the Department of Natural Resources. In a remarkable display of deference, law enforcement drove John Marvin and the other party guests back to the island. An ambulance took the injured man to a hospital; from there he was airlifted to a trauma center in Savannah.

The investigation was riddled with suspicious lapses from the start. The report from the scene claimed the driver had passed a field sobriety test, but the report showed no evidence of those results. In his report, the DNR officer checked a box noting the crash had occurred during hazardous weather, when in fact the water was calm and the moon was full.

The men from the boat lied about how their friend had injured his head, saying that when he went overboard, he had hit an oyster shoal. The trauma center, though, concluded he'd been run over by the boat.

Because the boat was connected to the Murdaughs, the DNR brought in an officer from another region to oversee the investigation. He was frustrated at every turn and knew the men were lying. Eventually they admitted they'd been drinking on the island and on the boat and had thrown the beer overboard.

Some of the passengers also admitted John Marvin had helped them practice what to say so they could keep their stories straight. It took more than a month before the victim recovered enough to talk with the agent. The only record from the session was a single-paragraph summary revealing nothing of significance. More than a month later, the driver was fined for having too few life preservers.

There's no proof that Randolph III personally sabotaged the investigation. But the Murdaughs had been shutting down scandals for longer than most people could remember. The crash had happened to a boat belonging to Randolph, or at least one acquired in a drug bust by his office, after a party organized by his youngest son on an island bearing the family name. But there is no evidence anyone questioned Randolph about the boat or why it was kept moored for years at his family compound. Before police arrived at the marina, John Marvin had allegedly helped his friends streamline their stories, which turned out to be riddled with omissions and lies.

Randolph would have made it a priority to stay abreast of every detail. The crash exposed his family to the possibility of multiple lawsuits, and it threatened Randolph's political future. John Marvin could have faced charges of obstruction, except that as solicitor, Randolph III had the final say on what charges would or would not be filed. It was his call, always.

RANDOLPH III WAS a civic leader and a public servant who fought for law and order. He was also a rake and a scoundrel. Late at night, he hung out at a house where he and his buddies drank and caroused with women. It wasn't quite a bordello, but it was close, and Randolph could do as he pleased. If even half the smuggling rumors were true, he had made compromises that would have landed other men in prison. In all of it, though, he displayed a moderation that would have been unthinkable to his father.

When Randolph III finally stepped down from the solicitor's office, he already knew Alex had no intention of succeeding him. Randolph must have been shaken by his son's rejection of the office that had been the source of the Murdaughs' power. But he said nothing, at least not publicly. He remained close to Alex and the boys, helping to coach their baseball teams, taking to the field in his own uniform. He joined the family fishing on the boat, duck hunting at Moselle, in the back of a limo at another bowl game. In photos from that time, Randolph often stands just behind Alex, his hand on his son's shoulder.

Randolph made no secret of the fact that Paul was his favorite grandchild. He worried about the boy's drinking and his refusal to grow up even as he started college. He must have noticed Alex's and Maggie's inability to control Paul. Randolph saw Paul's self-destructive streak and did not know how to help calm the boy. The bond between the two of them persisted, though.

What Randolph made of Alex's erratic behavior remains a matter of debate. He was aware of his son's opioid addiction, because Paul had told him about the pills Alex hid under his bed, and he knew about Alex's repeated stints in detox. He was all too aware that his son was sinking deeper into debt. For years, Randolph had tried to help his son climb out of the hole, lending him more than a million dollars over time.

Randolph had his own struggles. Libby's dementia was progressing rapidly. For the moment she had round-the-clock nursing care at the family homeplace in Almeda. Randolph's time was short, too. He was fighting lung cancer and heart disease and shuttling to and from the hospital. He had survived one heart attack but was still eating the deep-fried specials at his favorite meat-and-three dive in Allendale County.

His doctor caught him one day. "You know darn good and well you cannot have fried pork chops, now, don't you?"

The old man laughed. "I'm sorry, Doc. You've got me dead to rights."

In the fall of 2018, just before his eightieth birthday, Randolph accepted the Order of the Palmetto, South Carolina's highest civilian honor. During the ceremony, speakers thanked Randolph for his lifetime of service. One person said Randolph's grandfather was gazing down on him with approval from heaven. A photo taken afterward shows Randolph surrounded by Libby, all four of his children, and all ten of his grandchildren. Paul stands just behind his grandfather, beaming.

"I am a fortunate man," Randolph said. "There is no question about that."

It was only five months later when the old man's phone sounded in the middle of the night. Randolph did not recognize the number but picked up anyway. It was Paul, calling from an ambulance. He had been in another drunken crash, this time on a boat that had been speeding through the marshes. The boat had hit a bridge, and the impact had thrown Paul and some of his friends into the water. One had gone under and had not come back up.

Soon Alex was pulling up outside his father's house, and the two of them were racing toward the emergency room where Paul and three of the other survivors had been taken. They had to get there before anyone asked too many questions. They had to tell Paul and his friends what to say and what not to say.

One boat crash already had disappeared under Randolph's watch, years before. Surely, he and his son could make this one go away, too, if they moved fast enough.

Paul and the others were waiting for them at Beaufort Memorial, the same hospital where the injured man had been taken in the earlier boat crash back in 1998. Two of the officers who'd worked on that case, two decades before, were still with the DNR and were high-ranking enough by now that they would have roles overseeing the investigation, despite their allegiance to the family.

On Murdaugh Island, the echoes went on forever.

PART THREE

THE WILDERNESS

CHAPTER TWELVE

That Saturday evening, before everything went wrong, Paul had been driving one of his father's fishing boats, the seventeen-foot *Sea Hunt*. Paul and Morgan Doughty, his on-again, off-again girlfriend, were with two other young couples, all headed toward an oyster roast on Paukie Island, at a friend's house northeast of Beaufort.

The sun was setting as they headed into the maze of waterways that crisscrossed the Lowcountry, winding through the barrier islands dotting South Carolina's Atlantic coast. In the fading light, the view glowed with primeval beauty. Signposts of modern civilization flickered nearby: seafood restaurants, hotels, a couple of golf courses. But the marshes stood apart, a no-man's-land that had been fought over across four centuries by the Yamasees and the French and the Spaniards and the Scots and the English and then the Confederate and Union armies. In many ways, the lush Spartina grass that stretched toward the horizon still felt untouched. Wrens and finches and purple martins darted above the creeks and inlets; ospreys cruised over the waves, scanning for mullet. Dolphins arced above the water's surface, gray and glistening and then gone. The pluff mud just beneath the surface was spongy and soft, home to all manner of crabs and crawlies, as rich with life as with decay. A briny tang rose into the air as the tide dropped, the brackish water rushing toward the ocean.

By the time Paul and his friends motored past Parris Island and turned into the wide open of the Beaufort River, it was completely dark, and the city lights were glittering in the distance. They would have made better time if they had taken Paul's truck, but he had heard police were mounting DUI checkpoints around Beaufort, and he didn't care to risk it. He'd just gotten out of some underage drinking charges and preferred not to go through the hassle again. He wanted to knock back some beers with his friends that night, preferably six in a row through a funnel. The boat was better, he said. No cops would be waiting on the water.

Morgan, Paul's sometime-girlfriend since eleventh grade, wasn't sure how much longer she could put up with him. His recklessness scared her. When they were first dating, he'd badly burned his arm throwing gas on a blazing barrel of trash just to see what happened. She'd been in the passenger seat in the F-150 a couple of months back when he'd crashed into a ditch, and the memory still shook her. She told people he'd nearly killed her, and his parents had chastised her for trying to call 911. Even worse, Morgan could not stand the things he said when he was drunk, that her father was poor and she was a slut, words that hurt almost as badly as when he hit her.

Paul was nineteen years old, and had just transferred to the University of South Carolina after bringing up his grades at the commuter school. Even if he'd had the grades, he had no desire to go to law school, like his older brother and his father and grandfather and great-grandfather. He could barely get admitted to USC, despite his family's many years as donors and trustees. For now, at least, he was going through the motions, majoring in criminology, which made his friends roll their eyes given his brushes with the law. Sometimes he talked about starting a logging company. All of his dreams led home to Hampton County.

When he was sober, Paul could be kind, which was why Morgan

kept taking him back. He was charming and quick with a joke, the first person their friends would call if they were out of gas or their boat wouldn't start. Morgan loved the way he cared for his grandmother as Libby struggled with her dementia. Paul went to see her at least once a week, holding her hand and coaxing a smile even when she didn't seem certain about who he was. All his friends had seen his sweet side, but just as often, they'd seen his wild side. When Paul was drunk, he would provoke both strangers and friends. Even at five foot seven and 140 pounds, he was willing to take a punch and happy to throw one. He was always eager to steer the boat to a clandestine corner of the big sandbar on the middle of the Beaufort River, where young men met to knock the fire out of each other. Afterward he never bothered to cover his bruises.

When Paul grew especially drunk, he seemed to become someone else. His face grew red, his blue eyes grew as wide as half dollars, and he began to sway and curse. His friends dreaded the emergence of the alter ego they had come to call Timmy. Timmy was a horror show, obnoxious, aggressive, defiantly irresponsible, sure to hijack any evening. In Timmy, the most unpleasant strains of the Murdaugh men rose to the surface: the assumption of entitlement, the brutality barely veneered by charm, the conviction that the family reigned over everything around them. The clearest sign of Timmy's arrival was that Paul would strip off his clothes for no reason, even if others were watching, then splay his fingers wide and spread his arms as though he were flying. He no longer spoke, only screamed.

Earlier in the evening Paul had bought $49 worth of light beer, hard seltzer, and cigarettes at a convenience store. He had skirted the drinking age by using his older brother's ID. Paul was six inches shorter, but he and Buster shared the same curly red hair, a shade so intense it made the Murdaugh boys impossible to miss. The resemblance made it easy for Paul to use his brother's license, so much so that Buster gave up on getting it back and carried his passport instead. Paul was constantly riding on his family's shoulders; he knew no other way.

On the night of the oyster roast, he drove a boat owned by his father while drinking beer obtained with his brother's ID and paid for with his mother's credit card. Later that night, after the oyster roast, he planned to crash with his friends at his grandfather's river house at Murdaugh Island. Sometimes Morgan wondered how he made it through even one minute on his own.

Paul and his friends left the oyster roast after midnight. The adults at the party, including some of their parents, begged them to stay over or take an Uber home, but Paul was not willing to leave the boat behind. They had traveled about halfway back to the island when Paul decided he wanted a nightcap, so he docked at a landing in downtown Beaufort near his favorite dive bar, Luther's Rare & Well Done. The hardwood floors were perpetually sticky; it was part of the bar's charm, along with the late-night classic rock and Chester, the yellow-and-white tomcat who had been rubbing against customers' legs for years. Paul's childhood friend Connor Cook followed him into the bar, reckoning that the chances of getting back in the boat as quickly as possible were better if Paul were not left to his own devices. The rest of the group huddled in their coats and waited in some swings overlooking the river. Inside Luther's, Paul flashed his brother's ID. The bartender didn't question it. She was from Hampton; she knew the Murdaughs.

He used his mother's credit card again to treat himself and Connor to a round of Jägerbombs, heavy and potent pours in red Solo cups. Connor bought a round of Lemon Drops. They downed both sets of drinks in less than twelve minutes, and as they left the bar, Paul scuffled with another customer outside. Paul had bumped into the man, and the man said something, and suddenly Paul kicked over two chairs.

"You want a piece of me?" he said.

Connor pulled his friend away and led him toward the dock so they could all head for the cabin on Murdaugh Island. The group quickly realized it may have been Paul who had gone to the bar, but it was Timmy who came back. Even before they left the dock, his friends tried to stop him from getting behind the wheel. One asked for the keys. Timmy refused.

"Nobody knows this fucking river better than me," he said, stripping off his clothes down to his plaid boxers. "This is my fucking boat, and no one else is driving my fucking boat."

THE NIGHT WAS cool and dark, with almost no moon, and as the temperature dropped, a fog gathered over the water. The boat had no running lights, so Paul studied the GPS, the popcorn trail of white-dot coordinates showing the way home amid the outgoing tide and shifting sands. When Paul lost track of where they were, Connor pointed a flashlight ahead, but it didn't help much. Anthony Cook, Connor's cousin, was so chilled by the hovering damp he put on his raincoat.

Any sober person would have known to navigate through the darkness slowly. But Paul insisted he knew the river and ignored his friends' pleas to slow down. Earlier in the evening, when they'd left the oyster roast, Paul had barely avoided hitting Beaufort's iconic swing bridge. Now it was late and he was even more drunk and unsteady on his feet. He was steering erratically, speeding up, slowing down. He sometimes drove the boat in wide, meandering circles to waste time and annoy his friends.

Eventually the Sea Hunt entered narrow Archers Creek, the cut-through between two rivers, the Beaufort and Broad. Making it that far, in those conditions, was no small feat. Even in the daytime, when it was easier to weave past the submerged mud flats and sandbars, the passage through the creek was shallow and winding. Now it was pitch dark, and the tide was going out, and the walls of high grass on the nearby banks seemed to be crowding inward.

Anthony had had enough.

"Give me the keys or let us out on a dock!" he yelled.

The three young women chimed in. Connor's girlfriend, Miley Altman, yelled that it was not funny, she had to work in the morning. She and Morgan and Mallory all worked at a Beaufort boutique called It's Retail Therapy. Over the roar of the engine, Morgan screamed at Paul, telling him to knock it off. Paul put the throttle on idle and left Connor at the wheel for a moment, then took a few stumbling steps toward Morgan.

"What are you going to do, hit me?" she said. "Like you have all those times before?"

Paul slapped Morgan's face, then spat on her. He was an inch from her face when he yelled "Shut up, you fucking whore!"

The assault was shocking, even to these friends who knew how ugly Timmy could be. Mallory and Miley had encouraged Morgan to leave Paul for good. But they had also supported her when, without fail, she gave him another chance. It was no small thing to leave a Murdaugh.

Miley wrapped Morgan in a blanket and held her while she cried. Connor Cook looked away. Connor and Paul had known each other since before they could remember; Paul still called him by his childhood nickname, Cotton Top. Now, in spite of Miley's pleas that he do something, Connor stayed silent, knowing the only thing more dangerous than Paul drunk and angry was Paul drunk and angry and cornered.

Mallory Beach, Anthony's girlfriend, spoke up to confront Paul directly. She told Paul his driving scared her.

"You're being stupid," she said.

Paul pointed at Mallory and moved toward her as though he was going to get in her face, too, but Anthony, who had two years and six inches on Paul, warned him off.

"Don't make that mistake," Anthony said.

The moment hung in the air, the two young men staring each other down. Finally, Paul backed away and returned to the wheel. Now that he had been challenged, he was in a fury. He slammed the throttle down, the boat going faster and faster until its bow reared at an angle, hurtling up the creek at twenty-nine miles an hour. Miley looked up from comforting Morgan and saw the bridge looming yards ahead and screamed. The boat hit a group of wooden pilings, then rammed into one of the bridge's thick concrete columns before spinning out across the water and lurching to a halt on the rocks along the shore. The impact sent three members of the party careening against the hard surface of the boat and threw the other three, Paul, Anthony, and Mallory, into the cold dark water. Paul sputtered to the surface and fought the current to swim from one barnacle-covered piling to the next until he was close enough to stagger up the soft mud of the creekbank. Anthony soon joined him, and they were all accounted for, except one. No one could find Mallory.

Morgan alternated between calling Mallory's name and crying in pain. Her fingers had been crushed between the boat and the bridge.

"Y'all, there's so much blood, there's so much fucking blood!" she screamed, her voice breaking. "Where the fuck is Mallory?!"

Paul stood on the side of the creek in his boxers, acting as if he was still in charge.

"Calm down," he said. "Everything's going to be okay. I promise. Everything's going to be okay."

He said it over and over. What could he possibly do to make this okay? He wasn't even looking for Mallory. He was just pacing aimlessly in the mud.

Anthony saw red. He grabbed Paul and slammed him on the dirt under the bridge. "Is this what you wanted?"

Anthony jumped back into the creek, fighting the current as he searched for his girlfriend.

It took time to locate a working phone, one that had not died in the course of the evening or gone overboard in the crash. At 2:26 A.M., Connor called 911. His jaw had been broken, and he clutched his face as he spoke to the operator. He had to climb out of the boat and scramble up the bank to make himself heard over Morgan's screaming. He was yelling for Paul to tell him the name of the bridge they'd hit. The phone died in the middle of the call; it was chaos, the whole conversation. In the confusion, the dispatcher sent law enforcement to the wrong place and it was twenty minutes before the first officers arrived. They understood right away that the odds of finding the missing young woman were long and growing longer by the minute. The creek was only seven feet deep but the current was strong, and the fog was de scending so fast they couldn't see to the other side of Archers Creek a few short yards away.

Paramedics arrived and began wrapping the kids in blankets, triaging injuries. Paul's chest and legs were bleeding, scraped by barnacles where he'd clung to the bridge pilings. Anthony had dislocated his shoulder swimming against the current. He was out of the water now, his eyes bloodshot, the red and blue lights of the emergency vehicles playing across his face. Suddenly he turned to Paul and again began screaming at him. It looked to him as though Paul was amused.

"Bo, you fucking smiling like it's fucking funny!" Anthony said. "My fucking girlfriend is gone!"

Anthony was a big guy, and when he lunged at his friend a second time that night, it took a moment for the Beaufort County deputies to pull him off.

"That motherfucker needs to rot in fucking prison! He ain't going to get in no fucking trouble."

The deputies put Anthony in the back seat of a cruiser to let him warm up and cool down. He looked back over at Paul.

"Do you know the name Alex Murdaugh?" he asked the deputy in the front seat. "That's his son. Good luck."

Through it all, Paul was agitated and belligerent, defying the orders of the emergency workers, insisting he was fine when he clearly was not. It took four paramedics and two deputies to wrangle him into an ambulance. He kept trying to climb out, so they restrained him with black straps crisscrossing his chest. They could smell the alcohol not just on his breath, but emanating from his skin. All told, he'd had nineteen drinks.

Connor and Miley climbed into the same ambulance. A deputy joined them to keep an eye on Paul. Morgan insisted on riding in another ambulance because she didn't want to be near her boyfriend. It took forty-five minutes but finally the crews flipped on their lights and headed for Beaufort Memorial Hospital.

When Paul calmed down enough to catch his breath, he started making calls. He had dropped his phone somewhere on the muddy bank of the creek, so he borrowed a phone from one of the EMTs. His first call was to his grandfather, who listened carefully to Paul's account of the wreck. Connor, seated a couple of feet away, heard Randolph Murdaugh III's booming voice ask who had been at the wheel.

"Cotton Top," Paul said. "Cotton Top was driving."

CHAPTER THIRTEEN

Alex Murdaugh got the call at home just after 3 A.M. Within minutes, he was throwing on some khaki pants and a T-shirt, then climbing into his black Suburban. On the way, Alex picked up his father, Randolph III, at the family homeplace at Almeda. Given what had to be done, Alex knew he would need the old man's help.

Inside the Suburban, Alex and his father raced toward Beaufort Memorial. Accustomed to driving fast late at night, Alex pushed toward ninety miles an hour. He was confident no one would question a Murdaugh speeding through Hampton County, but he'd long since had blue lights installed on the SUV just in case. The drive between Hampton and Beaufort requires concentration at any speed, even in the daytime, but now the two-lane road was shrouded in the same fog that had settled over the water. Under normal circumstances, the forty-seven miles between the Murdaugh home and the hospital would have required a little more than an hour. Despite the fog, Alex covered that distance in half that time.

Alex and his father were on their phones, forming a plan. Randolph III called friends in law enforcement. Alex talked with his wife, Maggie, and his older son, Buster, filling them in on what had happened. But the more significant calls were to and from Paul while he was still in the ambulance, speaking on the EMT's phone. Knowing his son, Alex would have understood that no matter what Paul said, he would never have relinquished the steering wheel, not to Connor or anyone else. Murdaughs insisted on control.

As the Suburban approached Beaufort, Alex kept his foot on the gas. If he and his father were going to contain the damage, they had to reach the hospital first, before any of the other parents. Preferably before the police.

THE SUBURBAN PULLED up to the hospital at 3:45 A.M. Alex had alcohol on his breath as he walked through the sliding glass doors. His father was a half step behind him. Alex didn't recognize the security guard at the hospital's check-in counter, but the guard knew his name. Almost every law enforcement officer for a hundred miles knew of the Murdaughs.

He scribbled his initials on the forms he was handed. Yes, he was responsible for his son's care; no, he did not have a copy of his insurance card. He slapped the visitor's sticker on his shirt at an angle, pushed his reading glasses on top of his head, and barreled down the hall. On the outside of his khaki pants he had clipped his grandfather's badge, easily recognizable by the brass solicitor's star. Usually Alex kept the badge on the Suburban's dashboard. He only carried it with him when he knew he'd need it.

Alex and his father found Paul easily in bed 10 of the emergency room. All they had to do was follow the screams. Paul was still naked except for his boxer shorts. He'd kicked off the blanket and was trying to climb out of bed, pulling at the wires to the sensors on his chest and yanking off his blood pressure cuff.

"Y'all should be doing your jobs and looking for my friend!" he yelled. "Fuck you! I'm leaving!"

Though the crash had occurred more than ninety minutes before, Paul was still visibly intoxicated, his slender frame thrashing, his face bright red and mottled with flecks of dirt and debris from being submerged in the water. As Alex and Randolph III walked in, a physician's assistant arrived to evaluate the young man's injuries. She had a doctor and a male nurse as backup; they'd all heard the commotion. Paul's pulse was racing. His blood pressure was 169/111, near heart attack level.

Paul's father and grandfather stepped back outside. Alex walked around the floor and introduced himself to the staff, shaking hands. Randolph III stood by Paul's doorway and watched his favorite grandson buck and roar. The boy had never been able to sit still, never gotten his impulsivity under control.

"What happened?" the physician's assistant asked.

"I don't know," Paul said.

Had Paul been drinking? He wouldn't say.

Where was he hurt?

"I'm fine," he said. "Everything's good."

She asked him a series of routine questions. How would he rate his pain? Zero, he said. Had he recently traveled outside the United States? No. Did he consume alcohol? Yes, socially.

"In the past few weeks, have you felt that you or your family would be better off if you were dead?" she asked.

"No."

The physician's assistant typed in orders for IV fluids, CT scans, and a tetanus shot. She also ordered bloodwork to test for a possible brain injury, given Paul's erratic behavior. The test showed his blood alcohol level as 0.286, more than three times the legal limit, blackout drunk.

"Patient is very intoxicated, eyes are bloodshot," the physician's assistant wrote. "Patient very anxious, abrasions on chest and legs."

As more ER staff entered the room and crowded around his son, Alex watched from the doorway, taking the situation in. The emergency room was laid out in a square, with patient beds on three sides and a nurses' station at the center. Alex squinted to make out the codes on a tracking screen mounted on the wall. The ambulances had brought several of Paul's friends to the hospital. Alex had to find them.

The Beaufort Memorial emergency room was green, white, and

gleaming. Its newness was a testament to the wealth of Beaufort County, a retiree mecca that had grown to ten times the population of Hampton County. Beaufort's coastal prosperity was in stark contrast with the rural poverty of the rest of Murdaugh territory. Alex knew that the Murdaugh name might not invoke the fear here it once had, when Beaufort was as remote and insular a place as the rest of the circuit. But he was confident he could still get his way with a look across the room at almost any law enforcement officer. Even in Beaufort, his name and his grandfather's badge still had a warming effect.

A sheriff's deputy was seated in a chair out in the hall. He rose to introduce himself, hand extended. Alex shook it, put his arm on the deputy's shoulder, and thanked him for keeping an eye on his boy. The man's boss, the sheriff of Beaufort County, had been in office for twenty years and knew the Murdaughs well. Randolph III had backed his candidacy.

Paul would not stop yelling and cursing. The ER's security supervisor came by to check on the clamor and stopped to chat with Alex and Randolph. The three men were deep in small talk when a fish and wildlife officer ducked into Paul's room. Austin Pritcher was a newly minted game warden, following in his father's footsteps after a brief stint in baseball's minor leagues. He wore his black Department of Natural Resources cap pulled low over his eyes, like the pitcher he'd long been. He was the rookie assigned to overnight duty, so the crash was his responsibility until detectives could arrive. He'd just come from Archers Creek, where Anthony Cook had told him Paul had been the one behind the wheel.

Now the officer pressed the point with Paul.

"Who was driving when the boat hit the bridge?" Pritcher asked.

"Why do you need to know who was driving?" Paul said. "That isn't going to help find Mallory. What if it was me who was driving the boat?"

"Was it you who was driving?"

"I definitely was not driving. These are all my best friends."

Pritcher backed out of the room and went down the hall until he reached bed 22, occupied by Connor. When the officer walked into Connor's room, his girlfriend, Miley, was standing by his side. She and Connor had been close since seventh grade. Both had known Paul as long as they could remember; their parents had been friends since their days at Wade Hampton High School.

Miley and Connor already had told the nurse that Paul was driving, but telling law enforcement was something else altogether.

When the officer asked what happened, Miley stayed silent. Connor looked down.

"I don't remember anything but hitting the bridge," he said.

Pritcher studied the two witnesses for a moment. As the nurse came in to numb Connor's broken jaw with lidocaine, he told them he'd come back. He returned to Paul's room to request a formal statement, which, to his surprise, Paul agreed to. He was pulling forms from his clipboard when Alex Murdaugh and his father walked in. Randolph Murdaugh III stood ramrod straight, even at seventy-nine years old, even in the middle of the night. He'd been solicitor before Pritcher was born. He was visibly annoyed.

"Paul will not be giving any statement."

"Mr. Randolph," Pritcher said, calling the old man what so many had called him for decades, "I'm talking to Paul."

"Well, I'm his lawyer starting now, and he isn't giving any statements."

Alex motioned for the officer to join him outside. Randolph watched from the doorway. His eyes were light but it was hard to make out the color, as he was so often squinting, often with mirth but this night disdain. He went by the nickname Handsome, not because he was, but because he could.

Out in the hall, Alex put his hand on Pritcher's shoulder, leaning into him. The officer was tall but Alex Murdaugh was taller. Their fathers had been friends since before Pritcher was born and had finessed many scrapes together over the years.

"You know I can't have my son give any statement in this condition, right?" Alex said. "Do you have any reason to think Paul was driving?"

"That's what I'm trying to figure out," Pritcher said.

Alex's eyes darted to the tracking board, where a light registered a new trauma patient in bed 26: Doughty, M. He patted Pritcher on the back and set off.

Morgan had been crying since she'd set foot in the ambulance, cradling her injured hand in a towel. She'd ridden in a separate ambulance so she could stay away from Paul. She said she never wanted to see him again.

Alex made a beeline for Morgan's door. He'd treated Morgan like his own daughter for four years. She'd vacationed with the family; one Thanksgiving, the Murdaughs had taught her to hunt. Now Morgan heard Mr. Alex's distinctive voice, high-pitched, pinched, and loud, as he came down the hall. He was telling someone he needed to talk with her. He walked into her room without knocking, but his voice trailed off when he saw the nurse tending to her hand, the skin peeling from her fingers.

He backed out of the room and down the hallway, keeping an eye on her door. He tried calling Morgan's mother but she didn't pick up. He'd keep trying. She'd answer eventually.

Morgan asked the nurse to keep Mr. Alex out of her room.

"I just know too much to know better," she said. "He's sketchy. He's good at covering stuff up."

Officer Pritcher tapped on the doorframe. Morgan told him to come in and shut the door.

"I don't want anybody to hear what I am going to say."

Morgan explained how she'd been under the blanket when the crash happened. She said she had heard Miley call out Connor's name just before the crash, which made her wonder if there was a chance Connor had been the one driving the boat. But Morgan doubted it. She told the officer it would have been completely unlike Paul to relinquish the wheel. With her good hand, she wrote out a statement: "We hit the bridge and rode up onto the rocks. Mallory was nowhere to be found."

The charge nurse popped her head in to check on Morgan, who repeated that she didn't want Mr. Alex anywhere near her. The nurse could see why. The young man in bed 10 was among the most arrogant teenagers this nurse had ever dealt with. Now his father was walking around the emergency room as if he owned the place and talking to these young people without their parents present. The nurse couldn't believe it. The Murdaugh name might give him cachet where he was from, but it meant nothing to her. She was from Beaufort and did not care how things were done in Hampton County. In this ER, there were rules.

When the charge nurse walked out, Alex was leaning against the wall outside Morgan's door. He told the nurse he was a lawyer and was looking out for Morgan.

"I have to tell her what to say," he said.

"I'm sorry, she requested no visitors."

"But I'm responsible."

"No. She is an adult and in my ER. I am now responsible for her."

The nurse told Alex to return to his son's room and stay there. To make sure he complied, she followed him down to Paul's room. When he walked inside, the nurse posted a security guard at the door and told him Mr. Murdaugh was not allowed to wander the unit at will. Either he could stay in his son's room or wait in the lobby, but no more barging into other patients' rooms.

If Alex was fazed by the nurse's rebuke, he didn't show it. He radiated a casual calm, as if he was in no hurry, when in fact he was maneuvering as quickly as possible to forestall disaster. Since arriving at the hospital, he had ambled down the halls like a small-town mayor pumping hands with his constituents, smiling and saying hey and patting backs.

Outside Paul's room, Alex greeted the hospital security guard dispatched by the charge nurse to keep an eye on both him and his son. Alex told the guard he was going to the vending machine. Did he need anything? No, the guard said, he was good.

Paul, his girlfriend, Morgan, Connor, and his girlfriend, Miley, were all accounted for at the hospital. Anthony was still down at Archers Creek, pacing the bank as the rescue crews searched for his girlfriend, Mallory. Alex was already in touch with Connor's parents, whom he'd known his whole life. He told them he was at the hospital and had things under control. He did not call Mallory's parents. The Murdaughs and the Beaches did not run in the same circles. Alex said he didn't see what good could come from calling them. Better to let them sleep.

As Alex headed for the vending machine, he caught a break. Rounding a corner, he saw Connor being pushed in a wheelchair to the CT machines. Connor was wearing a white hospital gown and had a gauze bandage taped to his swollen face. Alex stopped in front of the wheelchair and crouched down. Back in the day, Alex had coached Connor, Paul, and Anthony's baseball team, alongside Connor's dad. Many times over the years Alex had bent down to talk to the boy during batting practice, offering advice or an encouraging word, just as he was doing now.

"Everything is going to be all right," Alex said. "Keep your mouth shut. Tell them you don't know who was driving. I've got you."

Connor knew enough to do what he was told. He'd heard rumors about what happened to anyone who crossed the Murdaughs. He didn't know the truth of those stories, but they scared him. His whole life he'd heard people say that any trouble the Murdaughs got into, they got out of. And he'd been friends with Paul long enough to see how the family protected him.

The technician waved Alex off and wheeled Connor down the hall. Alex went to the waiting room and bought a bottle of water from the machine. For a moment he dropped the facade of nonchalance and paced feverishly, rolling the bottle in his hands. He had already called Connor's dad once. Now he called him again. When Marty Cook picked up, he was still on the road, heading for the hospital. Alex told his old friend everything would be okay if they all stuck together. He said he had things under control. Marty had been nervous with the first call and was flat-out scared by the second. What exactly did Alex have under control?

In the reception area Alex called Maggie, who was at home awaiting updates. He said Paul was fine, and he was getting things in order. But there was no word about Mallory Beach.

"I know she's gone, baby," Alex said. "She's gone. Don't worry about her."

The guard at the front desk traded looks with the receptionist. After Alex left, they compared notes. Had they just heard what they thought they'd heard? A triage nurse had overheard the phone exchange, too, and was struck by Alex's detachment.

Back at bed 10, Randolph kept watch at his grandson's bedside. An ER technician came in to request a urine sample for a drug screen. She was young and pretty, and as she handed him the bottle, Paul leered.

"Would you hold it for me?" he asked.

The tech ignored him. When she came back, collected the container, and turned to walk away, he pointed at her behind. "Oh wow, that's nice."

Randolph III had heard enough.

"Shut the fuck up!" he told his grandson.

The old man wandered out into the hallway, muttering "He's drunker than Cooter Brown."

As the hours drifted toward dawn, Alex kept working his phone. He made a dozen phone calls in the ER and had dozens more to make: his lawyer, his insurer, his brother, his dealer.

He waited until the security guard outside Paul's room was gone so he could return to visiting the rooms of Morgan and the other friends. He kept studying the tracking board, waiting until the witnesses were back from X-rays and other tests, then slipping into their rooms to try to talk to them. Morgan was in surgery for two hours to repair her hand; the doctors were hoping to avoid having to amputate her fingers. When she was wheeled back into her room, Alex tried repeatedly to talk with her, but her nurse wouldn't let him in the room. From her bed, Morgan could hear what Mr. Alex was saying in the hall. He kept insisting he was responsible for Morgan.

"She's with me," he said.

Alex's studied calm was rapidly fraying. He was growing more insistent, even blunt. At one point he cornered Officer Pritcher in a corridor and got in his face, gesturing with both his arms.

Pritcher pulled out his phone and called someone at DNR, and when the other person answered, Pritcher talked and listened. Then he asked the other person if they really wanted him to test Connor's sobriety and not Paul's. Was he supposed to write in his report that there was confusion over who had been driving the boat?

The other parents drifted. Miley's mother, Gina Altman, was in the hallway outside her daughter's room when Randolph III approached her. She knew he'd been at the hospital for nearly an hour.

"Is there any word at all on where Mallory is?" she asked, fighting tears. "Have they found anything?"

"Who are you talking about?" Randolph III said.

"Mallory Beach, Mr. Randolph," she said. "I'm talking about Mallory."

He paused. "Oh, I'm pretty sure we know how that's gonna end up," he said.

Miley's mother couldn't believe what she'd just heard.

The charge nurse's attempt to corral Alex was breaking down. He was wandering the emergency room, taking Paul with him once the boy could walk. At 5 A.M., when both Connor's parents and Miley's parents had arrived, the Murdaughs gathered with them inside Connor's room as though they were convening a summit. As Alex spoke, Paul stayed quiet and looked at the floor. Randolph III stood tall with his face of granite. All of the parents were still recovering from the shock of hearing about the crash. Fearing their son was being scapegoated, Marty and Christine Cook were especially upset. The police had been trying to talk to Marty. He wasn't sure what he should say.

"Y'all calm down," Alex told them.

They had to get onto the same page, he said, to prevent one tragedy from turning into two. He reminded them of his family's ties to law enforcement and to judges. Everything would be fine.

"Don't worry about this," he said. "Let me take care of this."

. . .

IN THE HUNDRED years of the family's reign, there had never been a more perfect—or public—demonstration of how the Murdaughs operated. Alex's and Randolph III's methods inside the emergency room were not subtle. They did not conceal their motives. They didn't have to threaten anyone. Their presence alone conveyed menace.

Their goal was to create another kind of fog. They didn't need the young witnesses to lie outright about what had happened on the water. If they all stayed quiet, the authorities would not be able to prove Paul had been behind the wheel at the moment of impact.

One way or another, Alex and his father could not allow the truth to come to light. As prosecutors, both knew Paul's behavior could land him in prison for decades. As trial lawyers, both understood that the family could lose millions of dollars if there was a wrongful death suit. Alex also understood, with a clarity his father could not possess, what would happen to him personally if such a lawsuit was filed. Any good plaintiff's lawyer would subpoena Alex's bank records, his credit card statements, his deposits and withdrawals going back years. The proof of his embezzlements would spill into the open, threatening him with not just financial devastation but prison. There was still a chance Alex could stop these things from happening. He and his father had been lucky to reach the emergency room first. They had the added advantage of their lifelong bonds and the weight of their family name. If they leveraged all of these variables, both Paul and Alex might be able to walk away from the wreckage.

Two inconvenient truths complicated Alex's plan. First, the crash had occurred not in Hampton but Beaufort, where the family's sway had faded. The charge nurse, for one, had felt no trepidation in the presence of Paul's father and had stopped him cold from talking to Morgan Doughty. Other witnesses would soon feel emboldened to push back, too. Second, the Murdaugh empire had been built in secrecy and isolation, far from the eyes of strangers, before cellphones, before body cams for officers and dashboard cams for their cruisers, before hospitals across the country had installed security cameras in every corridor.

Almost everything Alex did that night, from making all those calls on the road to waving both arms in Officer Pritcher's face, was recorded and stored. This digital record did not offer a complete chronicle of the crash and its aftermath. But within hours of Connor's placing the 911 call, the gaps were being filled with sworn statements not just from Morgan and the rest of Paul's friends and their parents, but from the nurses and the doctors and the investigators at the crash site and at the hospital, from the sheriff's deputy tasked with keeping an eye on Paul in the ambulance and the physician's assistant who had been subjected to Paul's rants and curses, and the receptionist and the triage nurse who had overheard Alex's revealing phone comments about the missing Mallory Beach. Even the attractive young tech, the one Paul had insulted when she asked him for a urine sample, would share her recollections. The tech had heard the young Murdaugh loudly admiring her ass as she walked away but had chosen not to turn around and confront him. She had let the crude remark drop, at least until one of the investigators asked for her statement.

The rescue crews were still searching for Mallory Beach, or for her body. Alex was still telling himself he could control what lay ahead.

CHAPTER FOURTEEN

That Sunday morning, the sun rising over the water was so muted by fog that its rise registered mostly as a shift in light from black to gray. At dawn the rescue crews were still having difficulty seeing. Even so, they roused their bosses to summon more boats, divers, and helicopters. Trucks hauled an armament of heavy chains to drag the murky water. Scuba teams sank beneath the surface. Navigators studied tidal charts and maps tracking the currents and the depths to assess whether it was more likely that Mallory Beach had been carried deeper into the marshes or swept toward the ocean.

News of Mallory's disappearance had not yet made it onto the morning broadcasts. Soon her face would be everywhere, in heavy rotation. But in this brief window of anonymity, Paul was allowed to walk freely out of Beaufort Memorial without having been cuffed or charged.

"Am I going to be okay?" he asked his father and grandfather. *Keep your mouth shut,* they told him. *Do as we say.*

Three generations of Murdaugh men stepped out the glass doors of the emergency room and into the chilly damp of that morning. Alex was back on the phone, working the angles, calling in favors. Randolph III's jaw was set. The old man had been looking for the exit and accidentally walked into a storage closet. Someone had chastised him with a sharpness that suggested they did not know to whom they were speaking. Paul shuffled behind his father and grandfather in borrowed blue scrubs and bare feet, wobbling and tentative.

Alex climbed behind the wheel of the Suburban, his father beside him, Paul in back. Paul was at loose ends without his iPhone, which he hadn't seen since the crash. Like his father, Paul was almost always on his phone, his life a daisy chain of calls and texts and attempts at connection, however tenuous. He was not wired for reflection.

Alex pulled out of the parking lot and turned onto the main drag. Hampton County had been Beaufort's country cousin from the days when horses and buggies rumbled from the waterfront mansions of the city to the far-flung farmhouses of the backwoods. Alex followed the same route now. In the Sunday morning stillness, he drove past a Starbucks, a new sushi bar, hotels springing up along the greenway. Then he and his father and son sped across the marshes that had seemed so eerie the night before. Somewhere in that wilderness was Mallory.

As they left the city for the countryside beyond, they crossed a divide between a place that embraced the future and a place stuck in the nineteenth century. Beaufort was small, but it was an island of wealth and progress. The real South, the old South, was rural and poor. The real South was Hampton County.

Soon the road narrowed to two lanes canopied by live oaks shrouded in Spanish moss. The canopy was so thick and the forest on either side so tangled with kudzu that that stretch of road felt like a tunnel where the centuries fell away. The road passed the ruins of Old Sheldon Church, which had been burned in the American Revolution, restored to glory, then burned for good by General Sherman. All that remained was a ruddy shell of arches and pillars, a spot favored by brides and ghosts.

In the thousands of pages of sworn testimony gathered later, not a single word sheds light on what Alex and his father and son talked about while cocooned in their leather-cushioned SUV. Did anyone mention the crash? Did Paul remember Anthony consigning him to hell? While his father drove them across the marshes, had Paul gazed out the window and thought about Mallory alone in the wet and cold?

Paul's father and grandfather had other troubles. Alex knew that at any moment someone in the firm might discover the lengths to which he'd gone to pay his debts and feed his addictions, both to pills and the high life. Randolph III's health was failing fast. His wife was disappearing further into her dementia. Long before the boat crash, Randolph had worried about Paul, his favorite grandson, who seemed oblivious to consequence.

A few miles past the crumbling church, the Murdaughs reached the pine barrens of Hampton County, and then it was a straight shot for thirty miles, with no stop signs or traffic lights, down a highway parallel to the train tracks and lined with Sabal palms. They passed a few scattered churches and businesses: the Golden Crown motel, the Holy Temple Church of the Lord Jesus Christ, and Bertha's Creations, a gift shop whose owner occasionally left a sign on the door announcing she would open late due to her 9 A.M. therapy session. As they drew closer to Hampton, even these proofs of modest viability gave way to a string of long-abandoned buildings, shattered and decrepit, and empty houses with caved-in roofs, consumed by vines. A sign by the road declared:

> YOU ONLY HAVE TO FORGIVE ONCE.
>
> RESENTMENT AND HATE LAST A LIFETIME.

RENEE BEACH'S CELLPHONE woke her a little before 5 A.M. Her mother had heard there was a boat crash involving a Murdaugh boy, the wild one. Was Mallory home? Renee said no, Mallory was spending the night out with Miley. She hung up and called her daughter's phone but it went straight to voicemail. By the time she called her ex-husband, Phillip, she was frantic.

Phillip called Keith Altman, Miley's dad. Mallory and Miley had been best friends almost since they learned to walk. Phillip asked Keith what was happening.

"They're looking for her," Keith said.

"No, God," Phillip said. "Not my child."

The Beaches could not help noticing that none of the Murdaughs—not Paul, not his father—had shown them the common courtesy of a phone call. More striking, they had not been contacted by any of the half dozen law enforcement agencies working the crash. Beverly Cook, Anthony's mom, had offered to give the Beaches' numbers to an officer at the scene, but he had said thank you, no.

"Until we know something for sure, probably not a good idea to make that call," the officer said. "We don't want to create a panic, have them out here causing issues."

There'd been no official word, no knock at the door, no summons to the scene. In any case involving a missing child, standard law enforcement protocol is to contact the parents immediately. Why the silence now? The Beaches had their suspicions.

The Beaches headed to Beaufort, Renee and her mother from the north side of Hampton County, Phillip and his wife from the south. The Beaches met up on the causeway leading to Parris Island just before 7:30 A.M. They approached an officer standing guard by a barrier of yellow police tape at the entrance to the bridge and told him who they were. Renee said she just wanted to see the boat and see the water where her daughter had disappeared. The officer said he was sorry but he had strict orders that no one was allowed past the tape. He understood how worried they must be, he said, but no civilians were allowed at the crash site while the search continued. He had a colleague bring them a case of bottled water.

Mallory's older sister Savannah arrived shortly after her parents. She lived in Beaufort, a recently married dental hygienist. When she reached the causeway, she saw her father facedown on the ground, arms outstretched, sobbing uncontrollably. Savannah had to fight the urge to run back the way she came.

The family quickly found Anthony Cook, Mallory's boyfriend, pacing. Anthony had not left the causeway since the wreck. His dislocated shoulder was wrapped in a makeshift sling. The other young women from the boat, Miley and Morgan, came directly with their parents from the hospital to the causeway. At the Beaches' request, the families all joined hands that Sunday morning. Renee led them in prayer, asking that Mallory be found safe.

Late that morning, the sky cleared enough for a helicopter to begin flying a grid across the water. It was a heavy red Coast Guard MH-65 Dolphin, flying low and slow over the marshes. The crew had been told they were looking for a nineteen-year-old blond woman, five foot nine, 120 pounds, last seen wearing a barn jacket, pink sweater, dark jeans, and suede booties. The search radius was growing by the minute. Mallory had been thrown overboard at high tide. Now the tide was heading out, lowering the water by as much as eight feet. All of these variables made it impossible to know which way Mallory had been borne. A team of divers entered Archers Creek just underneath the bridge, connected by a long guide rope. They would have to wade along the bottom, foot by foot. A fleet of military, law enforcement, and search and rescue boats set out to troll as far into the coves, creeks, and inlets as they could reach.

By midday, two dozen of Mallory's friends and family members clustered in groups along the long causeway. Someone brought coffee and biscuits. Savannah spoke with reporters who trickled in over the course of the day to ask about Mallory. "Everybody loves her, loves being around her," she said. "We are still hoping and praying that we find her alive."

It was impossible trying to depict her little sister in front of the cameras. Mallory was beloved, yes, but like so many college-aged kids, she was not yet fully formed. She was pretty and sweet and kind. She liked dogs and hunting and fishing and hanging out with her friends under the sun. She was devoted to her church. As a girl, she'd written a poem about her faith on a chalkboard in her room:

> Be strong in the Lord and never give up hope.
> He's gonna do great things,
> I already know

After high school, Mallory enrolled at the University of South Carolina but left after a year. The Lowcountry was all she'd ever known. Back home, she focused on having fun and earning a little money, working at the boutique in Beaufort with her best friend, Miley, and their newish friend Morgan. Sometimes people gave them a hard time about their three M names, but they didn't mind. Mallory and Miley had met Morgan in high school and grown close to her at It's Retail Therapy, taking turns modeling $300 ruffled dresses and $200 designer jeans. They were sassy blondes who loved to laugh and go out on the boat and have a drink. Mallory's social media presence was a series of picture-perfect moments on the water: her smiling in a string bikini; a tan hand holding a cold beer bottle; an open cooler filled with beer and ice, topped with a hot-pink sparkly koozie proclaiming her QUEEN OF FUCKING EVERYTHING.

Mallory preferred Paul in small doses, preferably on land, but even so she was a regular on his boat. In May 2018, almost a year before the accident, she had taken a boat ride through those same marshes. Mallory had posted a photo of herself that day making the "hang loose" sign with the thumb and little finger of her left hand, a pink bracelet dangling from her wrist. It was Memorial Day weekend, a favorite time for Mallory and her friends to head for the big sandbar on the Beaufort River. Mallory and the gang had been out there on Memorial Day weekend the year before that, too, when DNR agents showed up and ticketed both Mallory and Paul for underage drinking. Later Paul's ticket was dropped with some help from his father. Mallory's remained, a smudge on her otherwise clean record.

Mallory's relationship with Anthony Cook was different. She had been in love with Anthony for years before he noticed her. She told people she'd had a crush on him since preschool. She was the little girl Anthony played with while his father, a contractor, worked on her parents' house. Mallory was bubbly and silly. Anthony was reserved and serious and as handsome as she was beautiful. He had flirted with her over the years and finally asked her to be his girlfriend on New Year's Eve, just a few weeks prior. Since then, the two had been inseparable.

Mallory had not officially moved in with Anthony at his parents' house, but since New Year's, she'd spent more nights there than not. Anthony's parents adored her and always had. They'd just been waiting for their son to realize who was standing in front of him.

The night of the crash, Mallory had been the one who'd wanted to go out to Murdaugh Island. Anthony wasn't really up for it; just shy of his twenty-first birthday, he was aging out of his hard-partying days. But Mallory gave Anthony her puppy-eyed look until he relented. By the time their group left the oyster roast, though, she was cold and wanted to go home. When Paul and Connor returned from Luther's, she saw Paul swaying and taking off his clothes and splaying his fingers and knew nothing good would come next.

Back on the causeway, more friends were showing up to support the Beaches. Renee thought about her daughter out in the water somewhere. She thought about Mallory driving her beloved Jeep, singing country music at the top of her voice. She remembered the little girl who had written the poem on the chalkboard beside her bed, the poem that was really a prayer. Was Mal on a sandbar somewhere praying now?

Morning blurred into afternoon. The fog finally lifted but rain showers arrived. Most of those on the causeway retreated to their cars to stay dry. Renee stayed put. So did Anthony.

Somewhere in the fever dream of that day, an F-150 truck cruised up the causeway past the clusters of waiting families. Renee had no trouble identifying the two people inside. Randolph Murdaugh III was driving. Maggie Murdaugh was in the passenger seat. They did not stop to speak with any of the parents. They just stared straight ahead as they pulled up to the yellow tape.

The old man rolled down the window and nodded. The officer lifted the tape and waved them through.

As Renee watched the Murdaughs being welcomed into a place off-limits to everyone else, something awoke inside her. During all these hours at Archers Creek, she had been numb with shock. She had told herself she was attending a vigil, waiting for word. But now she realized this was no vigil. It was a crime scene, and the Murdaughs wanted access for a reason. They weren't here to pray for Mallory. They were here to protect Paul.

That's when Renee knew Paul was going to get away with it. She realized that to fight for Mallory, she was going to have to take the Murdaugh family on. For that, she would need the best lawyer she could find. Preferably someone from outside Hampton County.

A s the search for Mallory continued, Alex summoned Connor Cook's father to the red brick fortress on Mulberry Street for an after-hours conversation.

"A private sit-down," Alex called it.

As teenagers, Marty Cook and Alex had won a football champion-ship together on Wade Hampton's football team, with Alex as quarter-back and Marty as running back. Later that year, in the school's yearbook—*The Rebel*—Alex was voted "Wittiest," "Most Athletic," and "Best All Around," and Marty was voted "Most Spirited." Alex had gone on to make his fortune. Marty was making ends meet one con-struction project at a time. Their sons were close friends. But Marty and his wife were not invited to the parties at Moselle.

Even though he and Alex had drifted apart, Marty owed the Murdaughs. More than once, the family had saved him from spending years behind bars. When he was a junior in high school, his girlfriend broke up with him and started dating some college guy. Marty had tracked the guy down and punched him repeatedly, knocking him out and breaking his nose and his jaw. The guy had missed a semester of school. Old Buster Murdaugh, then the solicitor, had agreed to let Marty plead guilty in a pretrial intervention arrangement. The deal was that Marty would stay out of prison if he paid the young man's medical bills and kept out of trouble for five years, at which point the charges would be expunged.

The problem came the next year, when Marty totaled a friend's new Camaro, a graduation present. His friend's family was furious and wanted to press charges to bolster their insurance claim. Marty was looking not only at potential criminal charges, but also other charges from his failure to meet the terms of his plea agreement. Buster Murdaugh cut him another break. No charges were filed in the wreck, and the assault charges from the earlier case were dropped at the five-year mark. Marty went on to get married and start a family and a contracting business. All these years later, he had not forgotten what the Murdaughs had done for him, and he had no doubt that Alex remembered, too.

Marty pulled in to the firm's parking lot after dark. The only other vehicle in the lot was Alex's Suburban. As he got out, Alex made a show of cutting his phone off and leaving it in the SUV.

"I want you to know I'm not recording you."

Alex led Marty into the locked building, empty except for the two of them, and led him up a winding staircase to the second-floor offices of the senior partners. Alex gestured down the open hall. It was a set piece of his, to use the power of the building to instill awe. It worked with clients who were unsophisticated or poor or both, like Alania. In this case, Marty knew that Alex wasn't all that his image projected.

"Pick your room, Marty. Any one you like." He said he didn't want Marty worrying that he was being guided into a room that had been wired.

Marty took no comfort in this assurance, or in the show Alex had made about leaving his phone in his SUV. The fact that Alex was working so hard to put him off guard made Marty even more wary.

They walked into a conference room and turned on the lights. Marty took a seat. Alex leaned against a conference table. Marty recognized Alex's look, the half smile and slight nodding that meant he wanted something. Alex had recommended a lawyer in Beaufort for Marty to contact. Had Marty talked to the lawyer?

Yes, Marty said. The guy had told him to keep his mouth shut.

Alex asked if Marty had spoken to anyone in law enforcement again. *Yes,* Marty said. The DNR had tracked him and Connor down at the hospital in Charleston, where Connor was having surgery on his jaw. Marty said he had told them it wasn't a good time to talk, and that Connor would be too drugged up to give a statement. Marty told Alex he'd do his best to keep putting off the investigators.

"I need to know where y'all stand. Are you going to tell them who was driving?" Alex said. "Because you don't need to say shit."

Alex had always been half a head taller than Marty. On the football field, Alex's height had allowed him to look out over the defensive line and see when Marty was open. Those moments seemed far away now. Alex loomed over his old teammate, still seated in the chair. Alex said they had to keep their stories straight. He said he'd have an easier time making everything go away if Connor was the driver of the boat and not Paul. There'd be less attention from the media, more wiggle room to steer the outcome.

Marty nodded. If it turned out Mallory Beach was dead, he knew Connor might end up in prison, no matter what Alex promised. He'd known the Murdaughs long enough to imagine what could happen if he refused. They were like the Mafia, he told himself, insisting he repay his debts through this gesture of loyalty. They wanted him to sacrifice his own son to save theirs. After all this time, he'd thought he had better standing with the family.

In that dark and empty law office, looking up into his old friend's eyes, Marty realized nobody had any standing with Alex.

THE MURDAUGHS WERE busy all week. Hours after the crash, they'd insisted law enforcement get a warrant to search the *Sea Hunt*. The boat was full of potentially crucial evidence, since it was marked with the blood and fingerprints of the passengers. If investigators could test the blood for DNA and study the fingerprints, they had a better chance of establishing where the six young people on board had been sitting or standing. The bloodstains were likely to be particularly revealing, since they would have occurred right as the boat crashed and in the moments after. If the evidence put Paul at the wheel and Connor in the back of the boat in that instant, it would corroborate the statements Anthony and Morgan and Miley had already given to Officer Pritcher and other investigators, swearing that Paul, not Connor, had been driving when the boat hit the bridge. The clothes Paul had removed earlier in the night were still in the bottom where he'd tossed them, including the pants that held Paul's wallet, with his older brother's ID—the one Paul had used to buy alcohol—tucked inside. Presumably the boat was littered with empty beer cans. An officer at the scene, scanning the creekbank, had found Paul's missing iPhone, which would contain his call and text history and any photos or videos he might have taken out on the water.

As Alex and his father would have known, obtaining a search warrant on a Sunday was not easy. It took twelve hours for investigators to track down a judge and get him to sign the warrant in the parking lot of a big box store.

The Murdaughs' next move was to arrange to be present when the boat was transported from the crash site into the custody of the Department of Natural Resources. The transport didn't happen until late Sunday afternoon; until then the Sea Hunt had remained out on the rocks, exposed to the fog and rain. Once the search warrant was obtained, Alex's brother John Marvin drove one of the family's boat trailers to a ramp near Archers Creek, where DNR officers were waiting. Later, questions would be raised about whether John Marvin might have helped the officers load the *Sea Hunt* onto the trailer and even possibly been allowed to remove items from the boat. John Marvin and the DNR officers denied it, insisting John Marvin had neither asked nor been allowed to touch the boat.

The mere fact that the family was allowed to assist with the boat's transport before it was processed would have been considered an egregious conflict of interest in almost any other jurisdiction. Here in South Carolina's Fourteenth Circuit, where the Murdaughs had been cultivating conflicts of interest for decades, hardly anyone blinked.

Alex and his father had close relationships with most of the high-ranking officers at the law enforcement agencies working the case. The DNR captain overseeing the day-to-day investigation was Capt. Donnie Pritcher, an old friend of Randolph III's. Donnie also happened to be the father of Austin, the officer who had been among the first to show up at the boat crash on Archers Creek and then at Beaufort Memorial. The DNR's lead detective on the case was a regular at the river house on Murdaugh Island. His wife, an aspiring lawyer, had recently finished an internship at the Murdaugh firm. The DNR lieutenant overseeing the scene and briefing the media was a Hampton native who had grown up with the Murdaugh boys and had served as a groomsman in John Marvin's wedding. At the time of the crash, the sergeant overseeing the sheriff office's response was involved in a lawsuit. His lawyer was Alex Murdaugh.

In one way or another, all of these high-ranking officers were beholden to the Murdaughs. Two of the supervisors had also worked the 1998 boat crash. Alex and his father had called many of them in the hours after the crash.

Midway through that first week of the case, evidence was already disappearing. Some had never been collected. A lieutenant at DNR, a woman who had no patience with her good old boy colleagues, learned something that perplexed her. None of the officers at the crash scene had given field sobriety tests to Paul Murdaugh or his friends as they waited for the ambulances. Such tests were standard practice at crash scenes involving alcohol. Why weren't they administered at Archers Creek? She asked young Pritcher why he hadn't tested anyone at the scene.

"No one told me to," he said.

An audio recording of Anthony Cook's statement that night, when he identified Paul Murdaugh as the driver, disappeared from the case file. Officer Pritcher, who conducted the interview, had heard Anthony say Paul Murdaugh had killed his girlfriend, but that assertion did not appear in his written summary of the interview. The report said Anthony wasn't sure who was driving. Like the audio file, Paul's iPhone was missing, too, along with the pants and shirt he'd stripped off, plus his wallet and the ID he'd used. Photos the techs had taken of the boat as it was being fingerprinted could not be found, either. Not to mention eleven DNA samples the techs had gathered on the *Sea Hunt*, including swabs of bloodstains from the passenger side of the boat, where Connor said he'd been standing.

All of it was gone.

CHAPTER SIXTEEN

Out on the causeway, Mallory Beach's father led the families and friends in prayer. Phillip asked them all to join hands, and then he told God it had been too long since Mallory disappeared beneath the surface of the creek for them to cling to any hope of her survival. Deep down, he said, he knew the rescue crews fanned out across the water were searching not for his daughter but for her body. Mallory's spirit, he said, had risen from the marshes to join Jesus in heaven. Phillip prayed for the strength to accept that his baby was gone, and asked God to invest her death with meaning.

"Let some greater good come out of this," he said. "Something big."

The days melted into an agonizing sameness. The Beaches made the long drive to the crash site each morning and the long drive home each night. Anthony Cook celebrated his twenty-first birthday at the crash site, still waiting for his girlfriend's recovery. His mother brought a cake and ice cream. Renee Beach brought balloons.

By now Mallory's face was all over the news. Much of the coverage focused on the question of who had crashed the boat. DNR sources in law enforcement described confusion over the identity of the driver. The counternarrative the Murdaughs had been pushing was taking hold.

The number of well-wishers on the causeway grew exponentially. Church groups distributed box lunches and coolers of drinks and meals donated by local restaurants. Mallory's family and friends brought phone chargers and lawn chairs. Beverly Cook, Anthony's mother, took a leave from work to be at the scene every day. Beverly had known Mallory since she was a little girl, and to her it felt like losing a daughter. Whenever she felt a wave of sadness coming on, Beverly would go sit in her truck to be alone.

One afternoon, she was in the driver's seat watching the helicopter circle overhead and trying to quiet her thoughts enough to pray when she heard the rear passenger door open. She felt someone settling into the seat behind her. She turned and saw Maggie Murdaugh.

Beverly and Maggie had always been friendly, but never friends. Maggie had not been a regular on the causeway. Yet here she was, sliding into Beverly's truck. It felt like a power move. Beverly's hunch was that Maggie was putting on a show, wanting the others on the causeway to see her. *This is about her,* Bev thought, *not me.*

"Beverly, what do you think will happen?" Maggie said. "What if they never find her?"

"I can't even think like that," Beverly said. "They're going to find her."

"But what if they don't?" Maggie said.

They sat in silence for a moment, then Maggie got out. Later that same day, Beverly's son was standing with friends when he became vaguely aware of being watched. Anthony turned around to find Paul standing a few steps away, his red curls underneath a cap.

"You know I love you, don't you?" Paul said.

"I love you, too," Anthony said. "But you need to go."

Since the crash, Paul had exhibited signs of trying to make amends. He seemed to be drowning in guilt. He kept showing up at the causeway, staring awkwardly at his friends as though he wanted to say something but did not have the words. Phillip Beach had prayed with him, asking God to forgive Paul. Both of them had cried. Paul had texted Morgan and told her he was sorry for what he'd done. Morgan said she would pray for him and then had cut off communication. The others from the boat were now ignoring his texts, too. He was alone with his conscience.

Beverly Cook was still replaying her exchange with Maggie in the truck. She fretted over Maggie's raising the possibility that Mallory's body might never be found. It had almost felt as if she was trying to prepare her for that outcome. An awful thought took shape in Beverly's mind. She knew enough about the Murdaugh family to believe they were pulling the strings of the investigation through their contacts in law enforcement. What if an officer who was especially loyal to the Murdaughs found Mallory first?

The same question was occurring to Mallory's parents. It was hard enough bracing themselves for the day a rescue crew returned to shore with Mallory's body. But it would be even worse if the body was never recovered. There would be no closure, but also potentially no accountability. Without a body, any case would become much more difficult to prove. Renee knew it sounded crazy, but only to people who had never dealt with the Murdaughs. As the days passed, she wondered more and more whether some of the rescue crews were searching the marshes not to bring her daughter's body home, but to hide it somewhere it would never be found.

The Beaches decided to organize their own search. On social media and TV, they put out a call for volunteer boaters to expand the search beyond the police perimeter. Dozens of civilians soon fanned out across the water.

Renee Beach was having trouble finding a lawyer. All the attorneys she'd reached out to so far were either close to the Murdaughs or unwilling to cross them. Early that first week, Renee had gotten a call from Randy Murdaugh, Alex's older brother. Randy knew the family because he'd represented Mallory in an insurance dispute over a car wreck. Now Randy told Renee he was so sorry about what had happened. He and his wife had been at the oyster roast with Paul and his friends just before the crash. Then Randy did something startling. If Renee needed legal help, he said, he would be happy to represent her for free. Renee thanked him, demurred, and got off the phone as fast as she could.

The next day, she finally got a good lead. Someone told her about a personal injury lawyer at a small firm in Allendale, one county over from Hampton. The lawyer's name was Mark Tinsley.

Tinsley already knew Alex Murdaugh well and had been involved with him on many cases. At one point Tinsley had considered Alex a friend, but they were no longer close. Tinsley distrusted Alex, even disliked him, but not enough to jeopardize his small firm's peaceful coexistence with its powerhouse neighbor. It was a truce predicated on lawyers staying out of each other's way.

On the afternoon he first spoke to Renee Beach, Tinsley listened as she told him about Mallory disappearing in the boat crash and about her suspicions that the Murdaughs were working to cover up evidence. Tinsley had a daughter close to Mallory's age and couldn't imagine what it would be like if something happened to her. But Tinsley said he wasn't sure he could help, given the complexity of the case and his past relationships with the Murdaugh firm.

Renee begged him to help her anyway. She shared her fear that her daughter's death would be swept under the rug.

"It's like they're above the law," she said. "It's like the law doesn't pertain to them."

Finally, Renee told the lawyer about standing at the causeway and watching the officer wave Randolph's truck past the yellow tape.

"How was it that they were allowed to go down there?" she said. "I mean, this was my daughter that they were searching for."

Something about that moment got to Tinsley. He had become a lawyer because he wanted to help ordinary citizens fighting forces more powerful than themselves. It offended him when people like Alex Murdaugh preyed on those who could not fight back.

He pictured himself out on that causeway, as if it were his own daughter in the water. He wanted to help Renee. He worried about the appearance of impropriety, given his relationships with the Murdaugh firm, so he called another lawyer, a friend at the state agency that regulated the conduct of judges and lawyers. When the ethics lawyer told him he was in the clear, Tinsley told Renee he'd take the case. He knew it would be radioactive. He knew once he took it, he'd have a responsibility to see it through. In the end, he took it because he knew he was the only one who could.

He started making other calls, starting with the DNR's general counsel in Columbia. He ticked off the conflicts between the Murdaughs and the investigators in charge. Tinsley wanted those officers off the case immediately.

"You've got a problem," he said.

When other lawyers from the Murdaugh firm heard how hard Tinsley was pushing, they grew alarmed. Representing the Beaches was one thing. They understood that Mallory's parents needed an advocate. But gunning for Alex Murdaugh seemed foolhardy. Tinsley needed to think hard about the risks he was taking in challenging one of the state's most powerful and feared families. The other lawyers advised him to turn back before it was too late.

"You don't know me very well," Tinsley said.

THE FOLLOWING SUNDAY, one week after the crash, two brothers went out on their fishing boat to search for the missing young woman. It was the younger brother's day off from his job as an intensive care nurse. He and his brother didn't like to think of Mallory—that's what they called her—alone and exposed to the elements. Like the other civilians who had answered the Beaches' call for help, the two of them felt protective of her. Even if Mallory was dead, she was out there somewhere, waiting to be found.

The brothers figured they knew better than anyone where to look. The two of them, both in their fifties, had grown up on the water and had learned the mercurial ways of the Beaufort and Broad rivers, their changing currents and hidden nooks. They had a hunch Mallory was stuck somewhere in the marsh. So they went out on their boat, a 23-foot Hydra-Sport, at low tide, when they could see deeper into the grasses. The younger brother steered the Hydra-Sport north about 500 yards while the older brother stood on the boat's hard roof and scanned through binoculars. They navigated down a tiny inlet, moving slowly to avoid getting stuck. They had been searching for barely ten minutes when the older brother saw a form that looked out of place. It was thirty yards back from the river's shore, on a tiny creek without a name.

"Stop," he said. "I see her."

Mallory's body had drifted five miles north. Her clothes were covered in mud, her hands ravaged by tiny crabs. She was facedown in the muck, her blond hair visible through the grass. If she had floated another hundred yards, she may have been lost forever.

The younger brother called 911. His voice was cracking.

"We think we found her," he said.

That morning, the Beaches had gone to church and prayed for closure. When Renee arrived at the bridge, she saw a man wearing a jacket labeled CORONER and began to cry. Her daughter had been returned from the wilderness. The case could move forward. Renee was glad her lawyer was ready to fight. But she knew it was foolish to hope for justice.

The Beaches were nobody. The Murdaughs were the law.

PART FOUR

SEVEN SHOTS IN THE DARK

CHAPTER SEVENTEEN

Long after Mallory Beach's body was recovered from the marshes, her boyfriend returned again and again to the dark water where she'd disappeared. When Anthony Cook closed his eyes, his dreams plunged him back into Archers Creek. He felt his wet clothes pulling him into the swirling cold. He thrashed against the current, searching for Mallory under the water. Some nights Anthony surfaced. Some nights he didn't. But Mallory was always gone, and when Anthony opened his eyes, he was screaming.

He took pills to help him sleep, but they made the nightmares more vivid, so he stopped. After turning twenty-one out on the causeway, he kept telling himself Mallory would someday find her way home as a birthday surprise. Some nights he made himself stay up, hoping she would materialize. He didn't want to fall asleep anyway, because then he would sink into the cold water again.

Anthony couldn't bear to go in his bedroom, as he'd so often shared it with Mallory, so he began sleeping downstairs on his family's living room couch, clutching a sweater that still carried Mallory's scent. His mother took to sleeping on another couch nearby. When her son woke from the nightmares, Beverly Cook would hold him and try to comfort him. Turning to her faith, Beverly told her son God loved him and loved Mallory, too, and she knew the two of them would be together again in heaven. Beverly saw how much strength Anthony had inside him, even in the midst of his grief, and she found it humbling.

Beverly wished there was some way to escape the shadow the Murdaughs had cast over her family. Born and raised in Hampton, she'd known the Murdaughs all her life. Alex's mother, Libby Murdaugh, had been her middle school English teacher. Later, when she was married and Anthony was growing up, she had worried about her son every time he played with Paul. The two boys were always close, but Beverly warned her son to be careful. If there was ever any trouble, she told him, Paul and his parents would find someone else to blame. Beverly had spent enough time around the Murdaughs to know they had raised Paul to have no respect for authority and no allegiance to others. No matter how close Anthony felt to his friend, Paul would always consider him disposable.

When Anthony was growing up, his mother had worked as a paralegal at the law firm on Mulberry Street. Beverly had spent years observing Alex up close and watched him transform from one persona to the next. With other partners from the firm, he had played the Southern politician, glad-handing and joking. But if one of the secretaries did something Alex didn't like, his eyes would go dark, and he would stare them down.

Out on the causeway, when Alex showed up among the throngs waiting for the rescue crews to find Mallory, Beverly had studied him closely. His performance was a more subdued version of the politician. He approached the Beaches' friends respectfully and put his hand on their shoulder and spoke to them in hushed tones, radiating concern. To Beverly, all of it was feigned. Alex was there because he wanted something. Maybe he was gauging the mood, assessing what people were saying about Paul. Maybe he simply wanted to show that the Murdaughs were still in charge.

In the early mornings, when the house was quiet and Beverly had time to breathe, she wrote down her thoughts. She would open a note on her phone and tap away, letting all of her sorrow and anger and grief pour out. She described her rage against the Murdaughs. She attested to her belief that a part of Anthony had died with Mallory in Archers Creek. She thanked God that her son was still alive nonetheless and admitted to feeling guilty because he had survived and Mallory had not. She thought about all the wreckage the Murdaughs had left in their wake, not just in the boat crash but across decades of arrogance. She had heard about Alex hustling around the ER to coach the boat crash witnesses. She understood that the Murdaughs were trying to obscure the truth. It felt as though they were killing Mallory all over again. As she put it:

Mallory's life & memory should not be lost in this fog that has now been created, even thicker than the fog over the water that very night.

Beverly was aware that someone was already working to cut through the fog. Renee Beach had told Beverly about the lawyer she'd hired, the one who knew the Murdaughs and how they operated in court. From her years as a court reporter, Beverly remembered Mark Tinsley as a bulldog who did not let go. Already, Tinsley had been busy pursuing the truth in the boat crash. He had sued Alex on behalf of Mallory's parents. He had successfully pressured the Department of Natural Resources to remove the investigators who were close to the Murdaughs. Now he was uncovering other discrepancies in the case, demanding action. If anyone could bring Alex down, it was this guy.

THE HUNTER PURSUED his prey across the top of the world. Through rain and snow, he had hiked up and down mountain slopes, ten miles a day, stopping now and then to glass the terrain with his binoculars to find a glimpse of white fur against black shale. He'd run out of food and was so exhausted he could hardly see straight. Even if he did get a target in his sights, he wasn't sure he could hit it anymore. He'd taken a bad fall down the mountain, plunging twenty feet until his backpack snagged on a rock and saved him. The fall had given him a concussion, badly bruised his back, and broken the middle finger of his shooting hand. Now he was hungry and wet and cold and in pain. He had never felt more alive.

On a ten-day vacation from his law practice, Mark Tinsley was hunting in the Mackenzie Mountains of remote northwest Canada, a thousand miles north of Calgary, on the edge of the Arctic Circle. The only way to reach this place had been with chartered planes and then a helicopter and then his own two feet. The mountains were a realm of isolation, so unchanged and untouched across the millennia it was still possible to find the skulls and bones of woolly mammoths jutting from the snow. The nearest roads and towns were hundreds of miles away. When Tinsley walked the ridgeline, nine thousand feet above sea level, he found the silence intoxicating. The wildflowers he passed were both alien and lush, yellow snow buttercups and white mountain avens peeking out from hillsides that had been cut by glaciers when the world was new. With his otherwise useless phone, Tinsley snapped pictures of purple moss campion and orange sunburst lichens growing along the crystalline stream where he set up camp. He hadn't been able to sleep much, though, because it was high summer, and this far north the sun lit the sky all day and night. He passed the hours after midnight staring out the flap of his tent, watching the caribou graze in the valley below.

Tinsley hunted big game at least three times a year, whenever he could tear himself away from his cases. He stalked moose in the Yukon, slept on rocky hills on the Mexican border in search of mule deer, tracked grizzlies across remote Alaskan islands. On this trip he was hunting Dall sheep, a species coveted for the curved horns of the rams. The horns were ridged with rings, each marking another summer of the ram's life, and if the animal was old enough, its horns curled up to three feet long. The rams were big, some weighing 180 pounds, and strong enough to crush a human skull. Some had been known to push wolves off cliffs. They were also extremely elusive. Tinsley had searched for days until he finally spied a small group on a distant slope. He hiked for hours to get within range, then lowered himself prone to the ground and set his rifle scope on one of the rams, 500 yards away.

Through the scope he studied the ram's horns, counting the rings to confirm it had lived a long life. He scanned the ground around the animal's feet, making sure it wasn't perched too close to a precipice. To him it would have felt disrespectful, knocking a king of the mountains into a free fall. He preferred that the animal die where it stood.

Tinsley raised the sight to the ram's chest and steeled himself, doing his best to ignore the ache in his hand and the throbbing in his back. Everything he had endured to reach this moment was its own reward. He took a deep breath, exhaled slightly, then held the exhalation and squeezed the trigger. A half second later, the ram fell. Tinsley stood up and hiked toward his prize. He did not feel triumphant. He felt grateful.

Many trial lawyers are hunters, known in both their personal and professional lives for their willingness to draw blood. Some lawyers boast about their killer instinct. Some go so far as to decorate their offices in a predator motif, adorning the shelves with statuettes of lions and sharks. Others display their favorite guns in shiny cases or cover the floor in front of their desk with the thick black fur of a bear they'd shot.

For Tinsley, hunting was a way of life. When he wasn't on a prop plane to some remote location with a tent and a rifle on his back, Tinsley hunted on his own thousand acres at home. Those hunts were less about joy than stewardship, a culling of the animal population to keep the system in balance. But there was no denying he loved it. At the end of a workday, he'd crouch quietly in a deer stand, clad head to toe in camo, cradling a longbow or a rifle. As he waited for a target to appear, he'd proofread legal briefs on his phone. He once took aim at a buck out of his bedroom window when he couldn't get downstairs in time. He trained his Weimaraner and his Boykin spaniel to track the smell of blood without eating the fallen turkeys or ducks. Tinsley cooked what he killed, perfecting his recipes for pulled pork tacos made from wild hog and sous-vide elk with vegetables from his garden. His home was given over to his vanquished prey: a stuffed nine-foot brown bear fighting a white wolf in the living room; deer heads mounted by the dozen in his man cave; and a leopard in the home gym poised to pounce from behind the elliptical machine. He hated the word "trophies." It sounded cheap and reduced what had been a sacred experience to an inert and transactional thing. To him, the taxidermied specimens were proof that magnificent animals exist and that there's beauty and good in the world, even when we can't see it.

Now Tinsley was pursuing Alex Murdaugh, and he found it exhilarating. The two of them had been close once, but not anymore. At age forty-eight, Tinsley had been around long enough to have worked with both Alex and his father. He remembered Randolph III as a reasonable man who would do you a favor. He wasn't greedy, and he wasn't a crusader.

"Randolph wouldn't hit two licks at a snake," Tinsley said. "He didn't give a tinker's dam about money or anything else."

Alex was slippery. Tinsley had seen the proof. He loathed Alex's good-old-boy routine, the way he was always working an angle. He suspected Alex had fixed a jury in a medical malpractice case Tinsley had tried in Hampton. At another trial, Alex had suggested to Tinsley that they plant a microphone in the jury room. Tinsley had laughed until he realized Alex wasn't joking.

Tinsley saw Alex traveling on private planes, buying up land, picking up the check at fancy group dinners. Alex was loud and loose in a crowd, a wizard at reading a room. One time he had watched Alex weeping during a closing argument in front of a jury, holding his face in his hand. When he sat back down at the plaintiff's table, Alex had leaned backward over the rail and turned to Tinsley with a grin, saying, "Hey, Bo, you don't think that was too much, do you?"

Tinsley considered Alex a scoundrel and a blowhard. But he had never suspected him of straight-out theft until Alex boxed him out of a million-dollar fee in a case both were involved in. Until that moment they had been close colleagues, even friends. Tinsley's three-lawyer practice in Allendale County had a fraction of the caseload of the sixteen-lawyer Murdaugh firm, but the firms had worked so many cases together that Tinsley had his own security pass to the office on Mulberry Street, allowing him to come and go at all hours.

Their social lives had intertwined as well. Tinsley had invited Alex and his sons to fish on his boat at Edisto and helped Paul reel in a redfish. Tinsley still had a snapshot from that day—Paul, ten years old and barefoot, beaming as he posed with a fish nearly as long as he was tall. Tinsley knew Paul had been a handful, but he also remembered the boy's awkward eagerness to fit in with the adults. As a father of a teenage daughter, Tinsley understood that parenting was a never-ending challenge. But when he began looking into the boat crash, he was stunned at how Alex and Maggie had surrendered to their youngest son's most destructive tendencies, encouraging him to drink and then rescuing him from whatever trouble followed.

"Paul was treated like a wild animal," he said. "If you let them be feral, they will be."

To Tinsley, it was clear that Paul's recklessness had led directly to the death of Mallory Beach. But his parents' indulgence had made the two of them even more culpable. He had collected photos and videos from social media that showed Paul swigging alcohol his parents had provided for him. In one video, Alex and Maggie watched as Paul stumbled through a game of beer pong. Another showed Alex sitting shirtless on the side of a boat while Morgan Doughty poured liquor down Paul's throat. After the boat crash, Maggie had taken down many of the most shocking posts. But by then it was too late. Tinsley had already harvested the most damning photos and videos as evidence. If the case went to trial, he wanted the jury to see the ways Alex and Maggie had nurtured their son's worst instincts, leading him to drunkenly crash one truck after another before finally driving the family's boat into the bridge at Archers Creek.

Tinsley had the blood alcohol results from the hospital and the statements from Paul's friends and from the doctors and nurses, all testifying to Paul's belligerence that night. He had the video footage of Alex Murdaugh prowling the ER. Tinsley was building a case that would make the Murdaughs desperate to settle. He wasn't just trying to hold the family accountable for the death of Mallory Beach. Bit by bit, he was collecting the evidence that they had hidden the truth and pinned the blame on someone else.

He had a mantra, cribbed from the pop psychologist Jordan Peterson: "A harmless man is not a good man. A good man is a very, very dangerous man who has that under voluntary control."

In court, Tinsley was a formidable but complex opponent. He could be empathetic, and he could be ruthless. From his earliest years of practicing law, he had sought inspiration in *A Civil Action*, a nonfiction bestseller about a crusading plaintiff's attorney who risks everything to represent families who are convinced that two corporate giants have poisoned their town's water supply. Like Jan Schlichtmann, the lawyer in the book, Tinsley made a ritual of wearing a gray suit on the first day of trial, as though he were girding himself in armor. On days he wasn't in court, underneath his jacket, he sheathed a sparkling knife with a handle made of hippopotamus ivory.

Tinsley was drawn to both the suit and the blade. The law, for all its decorum and rules, was an inherently savage profession. He cared deeply about the ideal of justice and the social order the law is designed to uphold. But his cases weren't abstractions to be debated in a symposium. He was fighting for real people whose lives had been broken in the most brutal ways. Their loved ones had been killed. Their homes had been foreclosed upon, their belongings repossessed. Some had been hurt so badly they could no longer walk or speak. Politesse was not enough. He had to be willing to scrap and claw.

"Mark Tinsley," said another lawyer, "will suck the marrow right out of your bones."

When Tinsley heard this, he considered engraving the warning on his business card. Tinsley specialized in winning huge payouts for his clients. In personal injury law, that was how justice was defined: Who was at fault, and how much should they pay? The vast majority of cases settled before reaching a jury. Tinsley's job, almost every time, was to build such a fearsome case that the other side would yield as quickly as possible.

Another lawyer who had tangled with Tinsley said he lived by a code so rigid it might as well have been cut into stone by Hammurabi. He had a hard time sitting still and devoured his meals like a demon. His office was such a whirlwind of documents and folders and legal pads scribbled with notes that he was embarrassed to let others see it. Like many litigators, Tinsley was mercurial and impatient. At home he could be quiet, even meditative. But when he was on the clock, he savored a fight.

Once, after a particularly brash takedown of an insurance company executive, Tinsley asked for a favor: Could he take a photo?

"At home," he told the man, "I have this wall with pictures of all the shit I've killed on it. And since I just killed you, I'd like to put your picture on it."

TWO MONTHS AFTER the boat crash, on what would've been Mallory Beach's twentieth birthday, Paul Murdaugh was charged in criminal court.

His father's and grandfather's hardball tactics had bought time and muddled the picture. Even so, Paul faced three felony counts. One, equivalent to manslaughter, was for boating under the influence causing a death. The other two were for boating under the influence causing great bodily injury, one for Connor Cook's jaw and the other for Morgan Doughty's hand. Combined, they carried a potential penalty of seventy-five years in prison.

That May, the charges were formally read in a hearing at the Beaufort County Courthouse. Paul wore a plaid button-down shirt and a navy blazer that made him look like a boy dressed up for church. His parents sat behind him. Maggie fought tears. Alex turned in his seat to shake hands with reporters. Paul was flanked by two of the most powerful defense lawyers in the state: Jim Griffin, who typically represented hospitals on major malpractice claims, and Dick Harpootlian, a Democratic state senator long known as a South Carolina power broker. That day, they demonstrated their ability to arrange special treatment.

The judge set a $50,000 personal recognizance bond, meaning the Murdaughs would have to pay only if Paul missed court. Paul was allowed to move freely around the Lowcountry with no ankle monitor and no alcohol testing, even though he was underage. After bond was set, a bailiff carrying handcuffs approached Paul to take him to the jail for processing. Paul's eyes darted to Griffin and Harpootlian for help. Lawyers for both sides waved the bailiff away; they'd already reached a deal to avoid Paul being escorted behind bars, sparing him the strip search and the mandatory orange jumpsuit. Paul was fingerprinted there with an old-fashioned wooden kit. They took his mug shot in the hallway with an iPhone.

Moments before, under the eyes of the judge, Paul had struck a somber attitude. Now his mouth curled with a hint of a smirk.

CHAPTER EIGHTEEN

A few days after his son was formally charged, Alex returned to the same courthouse to commit his most audacious theft yet.

Once again, he pulled it off by arranging a favor. An old law school friend had become a circuit court judge in Beaufort County with the Murdaughs' help. Alex told the judge he had a big settlement coming that he needed to file quietly. It was the second insurance payout in Gloria Satterfield's death. If reporters heard the news, it would invite more scrutiny on top of the publicity over the boat wreck, and Paul and Maggie were going through so much already. Alex confided to the judge that the settlement filings would disclose details about his insurance policies. He didn't want those details public amid the Beach family's wrongful death suit.

What the judge did not know was that Alex had no intention of sharing a penny of the settlement with Gloria's sons. To make that possible, he had duped her into handling the whole thing in secret, away from open court. The Satterfields' lawyer preferred to keep the settlement quiet, too. His name was Cory Fleming, and he'd been Alex's law school roommate and young Buster's godfather. The judge signed an order approving the settlement in a private meeting in her chambers. The order was given no docket number and Alex's name was removed from the caption used for tracking. No assistant clerk was there to make sure the document was filed in the official record. Alex assured the judge he would walk it down to the clerk's office himself. He may have headed in that direction down the hall, but the document was never filed.

Officially, the settlement never happened.

Alex had already stolen and spent $505,000 from the first Satterfield claim. Now Nautilus Insurance Company had approved a blockbuster payout on his umbrella policy for Moselle. The settlement was for $3.8 million. Alex took $2.96 million, and much of the rest went into Fleming's pocket as his fee. Gloria's sons got nothing.

Alex tore through the millions quickly. He spent $75,000 on a GMC Yukon. He cut checks to his drug dealer for $200,000. He paid off six-figure loans from the bank, from one of his law partners, and from his father, Randolph III, who had stood by his son through all his money trouble. Alex paid down $7,000 in credit card debt. And he paid $500,000 to retain the two high-powered lawyers to keep Paul out of prison.

Whatever was left of the Satterfields' money, Alex knew it would not be enough to make his own crimes disappear. If he wanted to stay out of prison too, he needed to shut down the lawsuit Mark Tinsley had filed on behalf of Mallory Beach's parents. Alex knew Tinsley well enough to recognize that no favor could induce him to let the case fade away. Tinsley was obviously determined to nail down what happened on the water as well as how much Alex could afford to pay in settlement. If Tinsley got his hands on any accurate accounting of Alex's assets and finances, all the millions he'd stolen from the Satterfields and the Plylers and the Pinckneys and dozens of others would come tumbling into the sunlight.

The man had to be stopped.

THAT FEBRUARY, WHEN Renee Beach asked Tinsley to help her take down the Murdaughs, his life was at an inflection point. He had come home from hunting caribou in the Yukon on his fifteenth wedding anniversary to find his house empty, even the horses gone from their stables. That was how he discovered his wife was leaving him and moving to Columbia with their daughter. He hadn't seen his daughter for months. She wasn't even returning his calls.

He was eating alone in a restaurant when he heard a woman seated nearby complaining about her teenage daughter, how messy her room was and how she was going to punish her. It took everything he had not to confront the woman. Didn't she know that the most important thing in her life was preserving that relationship with her child? The day might come, he knew, when the woman would do anything to speak with her daughter one more time. When Renee Beach first called Tinsley, the rescue crews were still searching for Mallory in the marshes. Tinsley's mind had immediately gone to his daughter's long silence and how much it hurt every day not to hear her voice.

The impending divorce had left Tinsley with extra time for the boat wreck case. It gave him a focus for his pent-up emotion. He couldn't bring Mallory back, but he could make the Murdaughs pay for what they'd done.

Tinsley's firm was located across the street from the county courthouse in Allendale. It was a devastated community, even poorer and more isolated than Hampton. There was nothing to do there, no place to go. He got his hair cut in Charleston, did his grocery shopping in Hampton, and ate dinner at home. He didn't mind. He had an aptitude for isolation, and his practice was thriving. As he often put it: "I'm the king of the middle of nowhere."

When he took the Beach case, Tinsley's friends at the Murdaugh law firm gave him their blessing. Perhaps they expected him to go easy. They may even have thought he would be open to a quick and amicable resolution. Tinsley proved them wrong. He anticipated Alex's signature moves—the stonewalling, the foot-dragging, the backstage meddling.

"I knew the playbook," Tinsley said.

He was not surprised when Renee Beach told him DNR had offered the Murdaughs special accommodations. He had personally witnessed how far law enforcement would go to help Alex. He remembered a judicial conference in Beaufort at which Tinsley, Alex, and other lawyers drank too much to contemplate the finer points of the law. On the ride home, Tinsley had passed out in a ball in the back seat of Alex's Suburban, and when he woke up, the car was stopped and Alex was on the phone with 911 dispatchers. He was so drunk he'd gotten lost on roads he'd driven his whole life. Two state troopers arrived in short order to escort Alex Murdaugh home.

ONCE HE AGREED to represent the Beaches, Tinsley filed a torrent of lawsuits against not only Alex Murdaugh but also his father, Randolph III, and the family trust, which owned Murdaugh Island as well as the convenience store that had supplied Paul and his underage friends with alcohol. Tinsley initially filed the wrongful death claim in Beaufort, where the accident had occurred and where the Murdaughs held less sway. But ultimately, he refiled the case in the heart of the family's empire, Hampton County. The case was damning enough, the lawyer believed, that the family would have to settle even on their home turf, a humiliating outcome. If Alex tried to fix the jury or sabotage the case, Tinsley planned to file a separate lawsuit in Beaufort, this time naming Maggie and Paul as defendants. Tinsley knew this would rattle Alex; in an earlier attempt to shield his assets, he had named Maggie sole owner of much of the couple's property. If Tinsley went after her, he could go after Moselle, the empire's crown jewel.

Tinsley applied pressure on every front, including in the media. "How much would you want to be paid to wait on a causeway for seven days as they look for your daughter?" he told a reporter from Hilton Head's newspaper. "Anyone who contributed to causing this, we are pursuing."

In those first months, Tinsley set out to settle with some of the other defendants in the case. The first to settle were the least wealthy ones, including the school principal who had hosted the oyster roast where Paul and his friends had drunk that evening and the mom-and-pop owners of Luther's Rare & Well Done, the bar where Paul had downed the shots before the crash. Tinsley said he'd settle for the limits of these parties' insurance policies if they met his aggressive three-week deadline for sealing the deal. They did, offering up their insurance coverage of $1.5 million. Randolph III and the trust settled, too, with a combined $1.5 million in coverage.

Tinsley was building momentum. He was also clearing his schedule to concentrate on pressuring the Murdaughs. One of his first moves was to file a motion asking Alex's lawyers to turn over the details of his insurance policies. When they delayed, Tinsley filed more motions. Only later would Tinsley learn that Alex's main insurer had dropped him after the massive Satterfield claim.

The requests were routine, but Alex blatantly ignored the deadlines, causing Tinsley to file more motions and restart the clock, only to delay again. After months of these tactics, Alex had barely acknowledged even owning the boat involved in the crash.

The Beaches had hoped for a quick resolution in both the criminal and civil cases. They had no desire to see Paul in prison, but they wanted him to apologize and take responsibility for Mallory's death, and a financial settlement was only fair. But as the months dragged on with Alex meddling in the investigation and stonewalling the lawsuit, the Beaches soured on reconciliation. More and more, they wanted a pound of flesh, with Paul serving time and Alex paying out of pocket. Phillip Beach, whose favorite pastime had been hunting with Mallory, told Tinsley the Murdaughs were not giving his daughter the respect they would show a dead animal.

The Beaches' outrage fueled their lawyer's determination to put Alex in a corner. Tinsley wanted him to be afraid. Only then would he surrender. The insurer finally said that Alex could offer $500,000 from his policy on his boat. Danny Henderson, Alex's law partner and personal attorney, said Alex was strapped for cash but might be able to cobble together an additional $1 million of his own money. Tinsley told him that was a pittance and nowhere near enough to settle the case. He wouldn't accept less than $10 million.

The message struck a nerve. Late that summer, at the annual meeting of the South Carolina Association of Justice in Hilton Head, Tinsley was talking with another lawyer when Alex charged him from across the room. Alex was five inches taller than Tinsley and much louder. He jabbed a finger in Tinsley's face.

"Hey, Bo," Alex said. "What's this I'm hearing about what you've been saying? I thought we were friends."

Tinsley met his gaze.

"Alex, we are friends," he said. "But if you think I can't burn your house down, you're wrong. I'm not taking your insurance money. You need to settle this case."

That night at dinner, Alex crisscrossed the room, chatting up every other lawyer but Tinsley. Alex wanted Tinsley to see how much the other alphas looked up to him. He wanted Tinsley to feel small.

Tinsley smiled. Alex's crude display was not a sign of power, but of fear. He had seen such behavior in the wild. He and his prey were circling on the savanna, sizing each other up.

IN HAMPTON, THE whispers grew louder. No one had failed to notice that three locals with connections to the Murdaughs—first Stephen Smith, then Gloria Satterfield, now Mallory Beach—had died under suspicious circumstances. People were drawing connections, formulating theories, deciding enough was enough.

Soon the town was picking sides. Either people were ready to challenge the Murdaughs, or they were closing ranks in solidarity. The us-versus-them mentality bubbled into public view when the old-guard organizers of the Watermelon Festival announced just weeks after Mallory's death that they'd chosen Randolph III to be grand marshal. The Watermelon Festival was the longest-running festival in the state and the town's claim to fame, with watermelons emblazoned on everything from the water tower to park benches. The organizers defended their choice in coded language:

"The Murdaughs and their firm," they said, "do a lot for the town."

The other side wasn't having it. A cousin of Stephen Smith started an online petition requesting Randolph III be replaced as marshal. "Given the well-publicized and very current controversy surrounding Randolph Murdaugh III and his family," the petition declared, "it is inappropriate to have him serve as Grand Marshal of this year's Hampton County Watermelon Festival."

A supporter wrote: "Justice for Mallory and Stephen. Stop letting this family get away with everything."

Randolph III carried out his duties as watermelon marshal. But the Murdaughs' hold on the town was slipping.

Some were saying the unthinkable out loud. When Connor Cook gave his deposition in the boat case, he alluded to rumors that Paul had pushed Gloria Satterfield down the porch steps at Moselle and had helped dump Stephen Smith's body in the middle of the road. In both cases, Connor noted, nothing had happened to Paul or any member of his family.

"Anything they get in, they get out of," Connor said. "I've always been told that."

CHAPTER NINETEEN

Maggie had always been lonely in Hampton, but now, with all the rumors swirling, she was miserable. When she shopped at the Piggly Wiggly, she was greeted with pointed stares. One day at the hardware store, someone hissed as she passed.

"There goes Maggie Murder."

Soon she was doing her grocery shopping in Walterboro, a half hour's drive away, where almost no one knew her.

One day she was pacing in the kitchen when the housekeeper walked in. Blanca knew that look. Maggie had something to confide.

"Let me make a pot of coffee," she said, "and we'll sit down."

Blanca Turrubiate-Simpson had been cleaning house at Moselle since Gloria Satterfield died. Blanca had known the family for years. She was bilingual, speaking Spanish as well as English, and had translated for Alex and other lawyers at the firm. Before that, she'd been in the Navy, worked as a prison guard, and dabbled in real estate. She had a calm about her that made people open up. She and Maggie had become friends a decade before. Back then, when the two of them saw each other driving around town, they would wave and pull their cars into a parking lot to catch up. Blanca began helping around the house, and after Gloria's death, she had been happy to step in full-time. Blanca's kids were grown, and she liked to stay busy. She saw no stigma in cleaning bathrooms and mopping floors.

"It's an honest job," she said.

In truth, Blanca was much more than the Murdaughs' housekeeper. She was the constant who helped them through their days. She ran errands and cashed checks and often cooked dinner. Whenever she could, Blanca helped Maggie keep up with the boys. She called them "my Buster" and "my Paul." She had no trouble scolding Paul when he deserved it, but her generosity softened whatever she said. She didn't mind picking up the family's clothes and dishes, even their guns. Sometimes the boys would leave their Blackouts in the golf cart; sometimes she found the rifles in the backs of the trucks they insisted on naming. One truck they called Dolly, another White Boy. Blanca accepted all of it, even the times when Maggie made cracks about Mexicans. None of it fazed her.

Now she and Maggie were closer than ever. The two women were both in their fifties. Both had grown up somewhere else and had married local boys who insisted on staying in this lonely and incestuous place. They shared a sense of never quite belonging. Blanca had moved to Hampton in the mid-1990s when there was still a pool that was whites-only by tradition. Her parents were Mexican and she had married a Black man, and she had always felt at a remove in a culture where the races remained so segregated. Maggie worried that people befriended her because they wanted to cozy up to the Murdaughs. Her suspicions became darker after the boat wreck at Archers Creek, when she sensed that her supposed friends mostly reached out so they could get fodder for gossip about her family.

That morning, Maggie poured them both a cup of coffee and led Blanca to the room where the family kept their guns and then closed the door, which was odd. Alex was asleep in the bedroom on the other side of the house. He had been having trouble sleeping ever since the boat crash and was usually in bed until midmorning, even on weekdays. Blanca often cleaned the couple's room last, giving Alex his space.

Maggie told Blanca she had finally gotten Alex to sit still long enough to have a conversation. She had told him she wanted to settle the lawsuit with the Beaches, but he insisted it was impossible. Alex had told her the Beaches' lawyer was demanding $30 million.

Maggie began to cry.

"We don't have that kind of money, Blanca. We just don't."

If it were up to her, Maggie said, she'd give the Beaches everything they had. She'd have no problem selling Moselle and starting over, if they could put this awful case behind them.

"I just want it gone."

Blanca nodded. She understood the power of quiet attention. Sometimes what people needed most was just a friend who would listen.

Maggie told Blanca she suspected Alex was not telling the truth about their finances. She could hear the stress in her husband's voice whenever he talked about the boat crash case. But she didn't know what to believe. She just wanted him to sit with her for ten minutes and fill in the blanks, instead of leaving her to piece the clues together on her own.

"He doesn't tell me everything," she told Blanca. "I think we're in trouble."

IF MAGGIE HAD talked to Mark Tinsley, he could have enlightened her on a few crucial details.

To begin with, her husband was telling her an outrageous lie about the negotiations in the boat lawsuit. Tinsley and the Beaches were pushing for a settlement of $10 million, not $30 million.

Tinsley didn't know the numbers Alex was spinning, but he knew his former friend was hiding something. The case had dragged on for one full year and halfway into the next, and Alex was still refusing to provide the most basic details of his finances. Clearly there was something in his life that he could not stomach being discovered. Tinsley grew more determined to ferret it out.

The Beach case had become Tinsley's grail, an all-consuming quest that gave him purpose and direction at a time when everything else felt off-kilter. His marriage had collapsed. His daughter's sixteenth birthday had come and gone without her answering his calls. She would be off to college soon, and he worried he might lose her for good. Tinsley felt perpetually exhausted, his body aching down to his bones. He wondered if this was what depression felt like.

Whatever energy he had left, he spent preparing for the court-ordered mediation in the boat case. Despite Alex's refusal to share his financials, Tinsley saw the mediation as his best shot at settling. But first he had to gather the evidence to show Alex and his lawyers what would happen if they took the case in front of a jury. Tinsley hired a videographer to pull together an emotional video about Mallory's life to use as leverage in mediation. He tested his arguments in front of mock juries, sharing social media photos that showed Alex and Maggie drinking at parties with Paul when he was in high school. Tinsley told the mock juries how Paul had tried to cast the blame for the accident on Connor Cook, his friend since childhood. No amount of money would bring Mallory back, Tinsley said, but he asked the mock jurors to consider what value they would place on her life if they were sitting on a real jury. Over and over, they returned verdicts in the tens of millions of dollars, sometimes the hundreds of millions.

By the time Tinsley walked into the mediation in September 2020, he had more than enough ammunition. Only a fool would refuse to settle, and Alex was many things, but no fool. The hearing was held at a neutral law firm, with Mallory's parents and Tinsley in one conference room and the Murdaughs and their lawyers in another. The mediator, a white-collar lawyer appointed by the judge, shuttled back and forth to try to broker an agreement. Always theatrical, Alex opened the negotiations with his pants pockets turned inside out.

"You can't get any money from me," he told the mediator, "because I don't have any. I'm broke."

When the mediator reported Alex's claim to the Beaches and their lawyer, Tinsley exploded.

"That's bullshit!" he said. "He can't possibly be broke."

The mediation stretched on for more than eight hours, but Alex would not budge. By the end of the day, Tinsley was more convinced than ever that Alex was guarding a secret. The two lawyers handled exactly the same kinds of personal injury cases, which allowed Tinsley to calculate how much Alex was making from each case. He attended every roster call in the Hampton County Courthouse and knew that half of the lawsuits were Alex's. Tinsley also knew Alex was settling many more cases outside the courthouse, usually taking a fee of forty percent.

"The only way he could be broke," Tinsley said, "is if he's hiding money."

Tinsley filed a motion to compel, asking the judge to force Alex to turn over everything from his tax returns to his 401(k) balances. Tinsley specifically asked for Alex's bank account numbers, a signal that he planned to subpoena the bank. It was a classic move for a plaintiff's lawyer: get under the defendant's skin by demanding something he didn't want you to have. But in the close-knit circles Alex and Tinsley traveled in, it was a declaration of war.

Alex's colleagues called Tinsley's senior law partner and demanded to know what the hell was going on. A mutual friend asked Tinsley to please stand down. Tinsley knew that going after Alex's own money, not just his insurance coverage, meant the entire Murdaugh firm might turn on him. So be it. Alex was playing games with a dead girl's family. The stakes had grown too high. Turning back was no longer possible. The case, he said, had acquired its own gravity.

"It's like trying to stop the rain."

ALEX HAD DONE his best to protect Paul, but all of the lawyer's disappearing skills had not managed to stave off the criminal charges and the strong possibility of a long prison sentence. Now Tinsley's crusade threatened to trigger criminal charges against Alex and send him to prison, too. If Alex had been able to pay the settlement through insurance, he could have made the case go away. But that was no longer an option, given that he'd bastardized his umbrella policy to seize the nearly $4 million claim in Gloria Satterfield's death and his insurance company had dropped him. Now he no longer had adequate coverage when he actually needed it. A great reckoning was coming at the worst possible time, when the Murdaughs were uncharacteristically vulnerable.

The family's woes multiplied by the day. Randolph III was in and out of the hospital with lung cancer and a weakening heart. Libby's dementia had advanced to the point where she needed around-the-clock care. As if that weren't enough, Alex and Maggie's older son, Buster, had been kicked out of the University of South Carolina's law school for plagiarism. Buster's expulsion was devastating, and not just because of the humiliation: If Buster didn't become a lawyer like the four generations of Murdaughs before him, the family's legal dynasty would die. Alex hired a fixer named Butch Bowers to lean on the law school to take Buster back. Bowers was one of the best-connected lawyers in the state, with a specialty in representing Republican politicians on ethics charges, including Nikki Haley and Donald Trump. He had a close relationship with the head of USC's law school. Alex offered him $60,000 to get Buster back into school, half when he accepted the assignment and half when he got Buster reenrolled. The first $30,000 payment was made soon after Alex stole the first Satterfield settlement, making it likely that Alex used blood money meant for Gloria's sons to buy his own son's way out of a lie.

Paul's life, always unstable, had become a rolling calamity. Out on bond, he partied as if nothing had changed. He was still inviting people to Moselle to hunt and drink and play pool. But he had lost the friendships that mattered most. Connor and Anthony no longer spoke to him. Morgan wanted nothing to do with him. He couldn't set foot in Hampton without risking stares from strangers. One of Alex's law partners urged Alex to get his son counseling and make him lay off the booze. A former sorority sister of Maggie's gave the same advice.

He may have been better at hiding it, but Alex was at least as out of control as his son. He was burning through $275,000 a month, with tens of thousands of dollars going to his drug dealer. He'd promised his family he'd given up the pills, but that was another lie. Paul, always known in the family as the little detective, constantly searched for evidence that his father was still using. Finally, Alex and Paul reached a détente. Once the boat crash litigation was behind them, Alex agreed to go to rehab.

Alex and Maggie tried to project stability, but they were coming apart. The two of them rarely slept under the same roof. Alex lived at Moselle while Maggie stayed away, even announcing on Facebook that she'd moved to their house on Edisto Island. She had never gotten used to Moselle and the depth of the darkness there at night. Alex refused to install security cameras, and with the boys off at college most of the time, Maggie felt vulnerable.

In fact, Maggie had never been grounded in a place. Her family had moved around when she was a child because of her father's job with a chemical company. She'd gone to elementary school in North Carolina and high school in suburban Philadelphia, and she'd transferred her sophomore year in college to the University of South Carolina, where she met Alex. Her accent was unidentifiable, sometimes taking on a slight Southern drawl when speaking with her kids, more often flat and even when talking with others. If she felt at home anywhere, it was Edisto. The house was bright and airy, with off-white walls, bright floral couches, and an open living space encircled by windows, a welcome contrast to the heart-of-pine walls and custom leather couches at Moselle. She usually brought the family's eight-year-old yellow Lab, Bubba, to the beach with her for company. The Murdaughs typically kept four to six dogs, most of them tracking dogs who lived in the outdoor kennels and were fed once a day to keep them lean. But Bubba was Maggie's dog, sweet, loyal, and eager to please. He was more of a pet than a hunting dog.

Like many people in times of crisis, Maggie had made her world small, keeping in touch with few friends and confiding in fewer. She found solace in nice things and spent thousands of dollars on Golden Goose sneakers and Christian Louboutin sandals. She drove a new black Mercedes SUV, her present to herself the previous Christmas. For years, she had dieted to keep her weight down, joining support groups and trying new exercise regimens one after another. For the time being, she had given up and sought solace in comfort food and white wine. She got her nails done often, sometimes in her pajamas if she was going to her favorite salon. In a photo from this time period, Maggie stands between her adult sons, arms around their waists. She has her blond hair pulled back, showing her favorite diamond studs, three carats apiece, and is wearing a smile, but it is strained. Her dark eyes are glassy. She has her weight on her back leg and her front knee bent, a pose that women strike because it tends to be slimming. In the picture she's wearing a minidress; she'd liked it so much, she owned three. The dress was Lilly Pulitzer, the uniform of affluent Southern women, blue with a white crosshatched pattern and white piping around the neck, framing her face. She was still beautiful, though she didn't see herself that way. When she saw the picture, she folded up the dress and gave it to Blanca, saying she hated looking like she was wearing a muu-muu.

Almost every day, Maggie talked with Blanca at the house or called her late at night just to chat.

"You up?" she'd say.

"Well, I answered the phone, didn't I?"

And off Maggie would go, sharing the latest bit of news Blanca might have missed. Maggie also spoke on the phone with her sister sometimes several times a day, but she could not share everything. She'd told her sister about Alex's pills when he first went to detox but had not told her he'd started up again, or maybe never stopped. She knew Blanca already knew about the pills because she was always finding little baggies in Alex's pockets and leaving them in a red cup in the laundry room cabinet where she put loose change. But they didn't talk about the open secret of the drugs. Nor did Maggie confess how often the bank account was overdrawn.

One afternoon at Moselle, they were talking about Blanca's kids, who were teens and young adults embarking on their own lives. Blanca was venting about how they always seemed to need money for new clothes or car repairs or help with their cellphone bills, expensive things their parents had to stretch to cover.

Maggie studied her.

"Blanca, are you happy?"

Blanca hesitated. She'd had her ups and downs over the years. Her mother had died when she was eight, and she had been raised by an alcoholic father. She'd served a few fitful years in the military. She'd endured the scrutiny of raising mixed-race children in a small Southern town. Now she and her husband were strapped financially. Every day they struggled to make ends meet, but through it all they had each other.

"Yes," Blanca said. "I am happy. I'm finally happy in my life."

Maggie's face was pinched. She told Blanca that she felt depressed, as if everything and everyone was against her. Blanca took her hand. "When you go out that door," she said, "hold your head up high. Put a smile on your face. Don't let any of these fools around here see you crying. Don't give them that."

There was only so much comfort Blanca could offer. The roots of Maggie's sadness went too deep. On paper, she and Alex were rich. They had their dream house here at Moselle and the surrounding acres of woods and fields, all of it stretching in every direction beneath the dome of the sky, and they had the beach house at Edisto, and expensive cars to drive them wherever they wanted, and boats that they could steer out onto the endless waves. They had friends and family who loved them, and a name that meant something, and a family legacy built to last forever. But beneath all these blessings was an emptiness. They had everything, and they had nothing.

Maggie felt it—the boredom beneath the surface, the sadness seeping into every minute of every day. She was caught in a web of secrets and lies not of her making. She had abandoned hope of a career when she married Alex, and now she was stuck. Her life's work had been her family, but it was not clear what she had to show for it. She could no longer smooth over her sons' problems or trust a word her husband said.

She had been a Murdaugh long enough to know what the wives who preceded her had endured. She had heard the insistence, passed down through the generations, that Murdaughs don't divorce. She'd told Morgan Doughty a more sinister interpretation of the fake obit story. Maggie said she'd been told that Mrs. Libby had been making noise about leaving her husband. Maggie had always heard that Randolph III had called the death notice in as a warning.

CHAPTER TWENTY

The fifth anniversary of Stephen Smith's death had come and gone with little fanfare. The Hampton newspaper's plea to the community for information had gone unanswered. When the troopers returned to town to chase even the faintest of leads, they attracted unwanted attention. The sergeant overseeing the investigation could barely cross the county line before his cellphone would ring.

"Hey, I see you're here in Hampton County," someone from the sheriff's office would say. "What are you here for? Do you need any assistance?"

To the sergeant, the warning was clear enough: *You don't belong here.* On the road, he kept an eye on his rearview mirror to see if he was being followed. "I've never had a case that I felt was shrouded in so much secrecy," he said. "It was a disaster from the start."

Stephanie, Stephen's twin sister, suspected she was being followed, too. She was pulled over time and again by one law enforcement officer in particular. Greg Alexander was the police chief of Yemassee, a small town at the southern edge of Hampton County. Alexander's family had been close to the Murdaughs for generations; they had even helped the chief get acquitted on charges of stealing as much as $10,000 during traffic stops. As best as Stephanie could tell, Chief Alexander was keeping an eye on her, and after a while, she came to appreciate the attention. They became an item. Before long, Stephanie was pregnant with Alexander's baby, tying the Smith, Alexander, and Murdaugh families together for good.

Gloria Satterfield's sons were still waiting for the insurance money Alex had promised them. Brian, who had a developmental disability, had been evicted from his late mother's mobile home and was living with extended family. It had been three years since their mother's death and two years since Alex had pocketed their settlement money. Whenever Tony texted Alex, he got a bare-bones response, if Alex took the time to answer at all.

Hey man, Tony wrote one day. *How is the case going, just curious. Finally getting some movement,* Alex replied. *Still a ways to go.*

The pace of Alex's thefts was accelerating. He had gone from borrowing from his clients' accounts to taking part of their settlements to stealing all their money outright. He was not picky about his victims. He stole from a law enforcement officer, keeping $125,000 meant to settle a workers' compensation claim. He stole $150,000 from a childhood friend injured in a car crash. And he stole from his friend and mentor Barrett Boulware, taking a $75,000 insurance payment while Boulware was destitute and on his deathbed, forced to borrow money so his wife could stay in a hotel during a last-ditch hospital stay.

AFTER MONTHS OF feeling run down, Mark Tinsley knew he was sick. Fearing it was serious, he avoided going to the doctor. He had too much going on to slow down. By the time he went in for tests, his PSA, or prostate-specific antigen level, was 13.2, more than three times the high end of the normal range. He was diagnosed with stage 4 prostate cancer.

His options were grim. The conservative route would be a radical prostatectomy, a surgery to remove the prostate gland, which carries the risk of incontinence or impotence or both. The aggressive route would be an experimental treatment of massive doses of radiation delivered by implanted seeds followed by months of hormone therapy. He opted for the more radical choice and decamped to a clinic in Sarasota for four months. Staring death in the face brought a certain clarity. Tinsley wanted to spend the second half of his life fully alive. He adopted a new philosophy, cribbed from a meme he saw online: *We have two lives. The one we live before we realize we only have one life and the one we live after.*

In Florida, as he entered months of cancer treatment, he was away from the distractions of home and the pull to tend his garden or hunt his land. He homed in on two goals: to get better and to get Alex.

In taking depositions from DNR agents at the scene, he had become convinced Alex had orchestrated a cover-up. Tinsley worked up a PowerPoint presentation summarizing the problems in the investigation. Eleven DNA samples had disappeared, as well as the set of photographs documenting the collection of fingerprints from the boat. Also missing was the initial interview with Anthony Cook, Mallory's boyfriend, in which he'd said Paul was driving.

After one particularly confounding deposition, in which a DNR investigator failed to recall the most basic facts about the crash, Tinsley reached his limit. He called the general counsel for SLED and the office of South Carolina's attorney general.

"Where the fuck is the DNA evidence? The photos? The audio recording of Anthony Cook?"

SLED was paying attention. A few weeks later, his contact in Columbia called back.

"We will be opening an investigation into the eight-hundred-pound gorilla of whatever the fuck happened here," the contact said.

Soon Tinsley was on a video conference with nine other lawyers, several SLED agents, and an investigator for the state grand jury, which oversees public corruption cases. He delivered his PowerPoint that detailed the discrepancies in the boat wreck case.

"How could this be?" one lawyer asked.

"Maybe this is just shoddy police work," Tinsley said.

"There's no way it's this shoddy," she replied.

While Tinsley was in Sarasota, the grand jury issued a flurry of subpoenas. The judge who authorized them told people the unthinkable was finally happening. South Carolina's attorney general was going after the Murdaughs.

FOR THE MURDAUGHS, the first days of the summer of 2021 were a swirl of parties, as Alex and Maggie doubled down on the patterns that had caused them so much grief. They returned to the water to drink and carouse. Maggie was out one day when she texted a friend that Buster had cut his feet on some barnacles as they tried to dock the boat.

Send me a pina colada, she wrote. *A strong one.*

Paul was ticketed for equipment violations while boating in Charleston. He was at the helm of the same boat at Edisto when a DNR officer approached. Paul had been drinking and was heading for open water with a boat full of people. The officer escorted him back to the dock.

"Don't you think you'd have learned by now?" he asked.

Paul called his father, as he always did. Alex asked him to pass the phone to the officer. A few minutes later, the officer went away.

It had been more than two years since the crash and Paul was still out on bond. The pandemic had slowed the courts to a standstill and the Murdaugh defense team was still maneuvering for further delays. They insisted Paul was not the driver and refused to consider a plea deal. Fighting the charges was particularly important to Maggie, who had become convinced her son wasn't driving and had done nothing wrong.

Maggie kept up appearances as she worried over the men in her life. She was calling pharmacy after pharmacy to get an eczema prescription sorted out for Buster and fretting over his return to law school. She was keeping close tabs on Paul and trying to find him an appointment with a heart specialist because his blood pressure was out of control and his feet were so puffy he couldn't put on his shoes. Alex was not sleeping and more frenetic than usual. He was also using again, a fact she'd been reluctant to face until she'd found another stash. She googled the color and markings of each pill she found, in the increasingly familiar ritual of coming to terms with his lies. From the beach house, the little detective texted his father:

When you get here we have to talk, he wrote. *Mom found several bags of pills in your computer bag.*

Alex texted Maggie.

I am very sorry that I do this to all of you. I love you.

She did not answer.

TINSLEY WAS NEARING the end of his treatment in Sarasota. His daughter had come to visit, a rapprochement he considered evidence that good could come from suffering. She invited him to her high school graduation and he planned to be well enough to go. He was going to hot yoga classes after each radiation treatment. He had taken up spearfishing off the pier nearest the clinic, diving with a mask and snorkel and firing a speargun underwater at striped sheepshead. Later he'd panfry the fish for dinner in his rented condo. Sometimes he dialed in to video depositions from a pier by the water. He didn't want the cancer to slow the Beach case, which had already dragged on longer than any family should have to bear.

The judge was losing patience, too. He set a hearing on Tinsley's motion to compel for June 10, and in letters to both sides, he made it clear he was inclined to grant it. Alex was cornered. If he didn't comply, he was likely to be found in contempt of court and sent to jail until he handed over his financial records.

Alex was trying to raise cash by applying for a second mortgage on the Edisto house. But like Moselle, the beach house was in Maggie's name, and she was reluctant to give her blessing to the loan. She didn't refuse outright, but she seemed always to have a reason she couldn't meet with the appraiser.

Alex's firm was starting to ask questions. Alex had worked a personal injury case with Chris Wilson, one of his best friends from law school. The settlement award was $5.5 million, with $792,000 going to Alex and the law firm as his share of the fee. Alex's paralegal had received a separate check for expenses but not the check for the fee, which was unusual, as the checks typically arrived together. On the eve of Memorial Day weekend, she emailed her counterpart at the other firm, saying they needed to sort it out.

That weekend was Alex's fifty-third birthday. He spent it at Edisto with family and friends, including Wilson, whose family had a house nearby. Maggie threw a classic Lowcountry boil of shrimp, corn, and red potatoes. One of the guests recorded a video of a red-cheeked Paul walking toward his father with a drink in one hand and a sheet cake in the other, the rainbow-colored candles flickering in the breeze. Maggie was behind her son, looking on while the crowd sang "Happy Birthday, dear Re-ed" to the guest of honor. Alex blew out the candles midsong and raised his arms in victory.

CHAPTER TWENTY-ONE

The end of May blurred into the beginning of June.

The paralegals at Alex's and Chris Wilson's law firms compared notes on the missing check but couldn't sort out what had happened. Alex's paralegal kept popping her head into his office for a word, but her boss stayed on the phone. At one point, he put his hand over the phone and told her he never got the fee, then shooed her away.

That Friday was June 4. Unable to get answers from Alex, his paralegal reluctantly looped in Jeanne Seckinger, the firm's chief financial officer. Jeanne had known Alex since high school. Several weeks prior, she had chided him for trying to hide some of his income by putting it in Maggie's name. Such deceptions, she told him, were illegal, and the firm wanted no part of it. The unaccountable discrepancy with the $792,000 check was potentially far more serious. Attorneys' fees were to be paid directly to the firm and, after the deduction of overhead expenses, divvied up at the end of the year based on how much business each partner had generated. If the paralegal's suspicions were correct, and Alex had bypassed the firm and been paid directly, it amounted to theft.

Alex spent Friday night at the hospital sleeping on a recliner beside his father, whose breathing grew more labored each day. On Saturday, he and Maggie went to a baseball tournament in Columbia with Chris Wilson and his wife. Alex seemed uncomfortable the whole time and stayed in their hotel room with nausea, muscle pain, and anxiety, hallmark symptoms of opioid withdrawal.

Paul was in Charleston crashing on a friend's couch and partying at a beachfront bar. He'd enlisted Blanca to stay late at Moselle to wash his clothes for the weekend. Blanca had a certain way she liked to do laundry. She poured half a cap of Downy fabric softener in with the Arm & Hammer Cool Breeze laundry detergent, then added another half cap in the rinse cycle. She put a Kirkland dryer sheet from Costco in the dryer and pulled the clothes out right away to hang or fold. Her mother had been a seamstress, and she took great pride in the handling of garments.

"Come on, Ms. B, you can help me out," Paul said.

She relented. She had a soft spot for Paul.

THAT MONDAY, JUNE 7, was just another day filled with errands and appointments and the minutiae that define a family's life. But it was also a day like no other, playing out like a preordained dream.

The minor events that marked those hours would later be reconstructed in a minute-by-minute timeline to be dissected and debated in court, with the prosecution and the defense offering contradictory theories on what those details revealed. A series of texts that went unanswered, a hint of hesitation in a phone call, a seemingly placid conversation in a field near sunset—all of it would become imbued with mystery.

Alex slept in again at Moselle. His time was running out. His own paralegal was pressing him on the missing check. And in three days, he was scheduled to be in court, turning in a detailed accounting of his assets and net worth. Once that happened, Tinsley would see right through Alex's numbers. Even worse, Alex's own lawyer was a partner at the firm who knew what every lawyer there made, down to the penny. He would immediately recognize discrepancies in his income.

Alex got up and dressed a little before noon, once it became clear his phone was not going to stop blowing up with texts about appointments he was missing. On his way out, he saw Blanca. She had already been at work for several hours; she'd even stopped at the Piggly Wiggly on the way in because Maggie had asked her to get a couple of boxes of Capri Suns.

Blanca hardly needed reminding. She understood the family's habits better than anyone else and tried to keep the refrigerator stocked with Alex's favorite flavors of the children's juice drink, Orange Pineapple Tango and Mountain Cooler. She watched Alex rising late every morning, stress written on his face. She washed Paul's clothes, staying late so he could go out partying again. Maggie had told her about Paul getting stopped out on the water a few days before, the boat filled with friends and alcohol, the DNR officer suggesting it was finally time for Paul to stop. Maggie had also told Blanca that Paul had called his father and made the DNR officer go away. The patterns just kept repeating. Paul would never stop.

As Alex headed out the door, Blanca noticed he looked rumpled, as though he'd slept in his clothes. She was worried about his pill use. She'd grown accustomed to finding pills in his pants pockets and in stray baggies. But on his bedside table recently, she'd found a bottle of painkillers prescribed to Randolph Murdaugh III, palliative drugs to ease his last days.

She stopped him and stood on her tiptoes to fix his collar, which was poking out of the top of his blazer. Blanca would later remember, first with the police and then with the prosecutors, that Alex was wearing a polo shirt in a teal she and Maggie both loved, a color they jokingly called seafoam after one of the paint colors Maggie considered using at the Edisto house.

"I'm tired, B," Alex said.

"I know you are," Blanca said.

BY THE TIME Alex showed up at the firm's office on Mulberry Street, it was almost 1 P.M. His paralegal alerted Jeanne Seckinger that he had arrived, and the CFO gathered her paperwork on the missing fee and walked upstairs. It was no small feat to confront the lawyer whose great-grandfather had founded the firm and whose father and grandfather had led the firm from the Depression into the new millennium.

Jeanne had been rehearsing how she would ask the awful questions. She had recognized Alex as a bullshit artist way back in high school but had come to understand that Alex's most chaotic behaviors were strategic.

Alex was leaning on a file cabinet outside his office. When he saw Jeanne, he gave her a dirty look, the likes of which she'd never seen.

"What do you need from me now?"

They walked into his office. Jeanne closed the door.

"I have reason to believe that you received those missing fees," she said. "I'm just trying to do my job. I wouldn't be doing my job if I didn't ask you about them."

Alex was telling her it was all a misunderstanding when his phone rang. It was his brother Randy, calling to say their father was headed back to the hospital. He was having trouble breathing. Randy said it was almost certainly the end.

The mood in the office instantly shifted. Jeanne loved Mr. Randolph. She hugged Alex and let the matter of the missing check drop.

Alex called Maggie, who was in Charleston for a doctor's appointment. She'd been having trouble with her teeth and her stomach and was always off to one specialist or another. He told her his dad's health had taken a turn and asked her to come back to Moselle. Paul was coming home, too.

Maggie was torn. She didn't want to go to Moselle. A crew was at the house in Edisto, working on the remodeling. She got her sister, Marian, on the phone and asked her what to do.

"Mr. Randolph is not doing well," Maggie said. "Alex really wants me to come home."

Her sister knew that Alex and his father were unusually close. Marian understood Maggie's hesitation but told her she might regret it if she didn't make one last trip to say goodbye.

"That's what you should probably do," Marian said.

Maggie reached out to Blanca next. She asked her to make dinner before she left Moselle.

A little later, Blanca texted to let Maggie know the dinner was made and waiting on the stove. She also said she was praying for her, Alex, and Mr. Randolph.

Maggie thanked her. Then, a little over two hours after he'd asked her to come home, Maggie texted Alex her answer.

I will be home to see u in a few hours.

Back in Hampton, Jeanne Seckinger was at her desk when her phone rang. Alex was asking for his 401(k) balance and said he needed it for a hearing in the boat case later that week. Jeanne was caught off guard. Why was he worrying about his 401(k)? Hadn't he left for the hospital to see his father hours ago? She told him she'd get back to him.

PAUL WAS AT his summer job, working for his uncle John Marvin at his equipment rental business in Okatie. Paul was close to his uncle and seemed to do well with the customers. Since the shop was an hour south of Hampton, not everyone who came in the door knew who he was. Lately, Paul had found comfort in anonymity.

When Alex called Paul and asked him to come home to Moselle, Paul agreed. He delayed his departure slightly, though, so his uncle could get back to town to swap vehicles. John Marvin had driven Randolph III's sedan to the hospital in Savannah and wanted Paul to drop the car back at Almeda. With some time on his hands, Paul stopped by Murdaugh Island, his great-grandfather's old fishing camp. The island had been Paul's happy place, at least up until the boat wreck. It is not clear what he did at the island that day, but his phone records would show he stayed for forty minutes. After learning Randolph III was close to dying, Paul might have simply needed a moment to gather himself, soaking up the sun and the breeze wafting over the water.

Alex had told his son that once he got to Moselle, the two of them needed to check on the dove field. Alex and Paul had planted hundreds of sunflowers, painstakingly spacing them in rows. The sunflowers were a big deal to Paul because they attracted doves, one of his favorite species to hunt. But something had gone wrong. The caretaker was new and apparently had oversprayed the flowers, killing them. Alex said they should ride the property and sort out how to replant. Dove hunting season was coming, and the sunflowers needed time to grow.

ALEX GOT TO Moselle first, rolling up in his Suburban at 6:43 P.M. He'd been flooded with messages from family and friends who'd heard his father was back in the hospital. One woman, a former client who liked to share passages from the Bible, texted him late that afternoon. The woman did not seem to know the news about Alex's father. She simply chose that day to share some verses from Ezekiel.

> *The End Is Now Upon You,* her message began. *At that time, people will realize that money cannot save them from the coming calamity.*

Alex went into the house. A few minutes later, Paul arrived and the two of them went out to ride the property and survey the damage to the sunflowers. They called and texted the groundskeeper to come help, but it was his day off and he didn't respond.

As the sun was getting low, Alex and Paul stopped by a stand of fruit trees at a corner of the property called Sawtooth Oaks. One of the trees was dying, a source of mirth for Paul and frustration for his father, who tried and failed to make it stand up straight before it flopped over. They crossed Moselle Road to the far side of the property and went target shooting with a pistol.

Maggie had stopped for a pedicure, so she was the last to arrive, pulling up to the house in the Mercedes just as Alex and Paul wrapped up their tour. The three of them went into the house for dinner. Blanca had made Paul's favorite meal, the cube steak he called "steakburger." Paul ate quickly and apart from his parents, who sat in their usual spots on the leather sectional in the living room. The TV was on, as it always was at Moselle. What the two of them talked about is unknown. Paul had texted them both a picture of his swollen feet. Did they talk about their youngest son's health, or about all the other troubles in his life? Had Maggie asked Alex whether he was using again?

The couple ate in less than fifteen minutes. By then it was dusk and the sky was darkening. Maggie and Paul went down to the kennels together to check on the dogs. Paul was taking care of a friend's dog, a chocolate Lab puppy named Cash, who had something wrong with his tail. Paul stepped into Cash's kennel to take a photo of the tail so his friend could show the vet. Maggie watched the dogs run and play. Bubba had to mark every tree. Sometimes he'd prance back to her, bearing a treasure. That night, it was prey.

"Hey, he's got a bird in his mouth!" Maggie said. "It's a guinea!"

"It's a chicken," Paul said under his breath.

Paul's phone was almost always in his hand, and that night was no different. He used it so much, the battery was typically dead by the end of the day. He was carrying on multiple text conversations, including one with a friend seeking a movie recommendation. Paul suggested the latest remake of *A Star Is Born*, but the friend wasn't interested.

No I need something happy. Don't like watching sad movies.

Neither Paul nor his parents went to the hospital to see Randolph III. Instead, Alex got back in the Suburban and headed for Almeda to check on his mom.

At 9:46 P.M., on the way back, he called Maggie's phone. There was no answer. He called Paul's phone, but no answer.

At 9:47 P.M., he texted Maggie.

Call me babe.

Paul's friend Rogan Gibson, the owner of the Lab puppy, was expecting a picture of Cash's tail. Rogan called Paul at 9:29 P.M. When Paul didn't pick up, he texted Maggie a few minutes later. Still no response.

At 9:57 P.M., the friend called Paul again.

No answer.

A minute later, he sent Paul a one-word text.

Yo.

AT 10:06 P.M., the dispatcher at the Hampton County sheriff's office answered a 911 call. On the end of the line was a man's voice. He was speaking high and fast.

"This is Alex Murdaugh at 4147 Moselle Road. I need the police and an ambulance immediately. My wife and my child have been shot badly."

"Okay," the dispatcher said. "You said 4147 Moselle Road in Islandton?"

"Yes, sir," Alex said. "Please hurry."

Checking the address, the dispatcher realized the call was actually coming from Colleton County, just across the Hampton County line. She transferred Alex to Colleton's dispatch center. The new dispatcher asked him to repeat the address, and he did.

"I've been up to it now," said Alex. "It's bad."

"Okay, how did they shoot—did they shoot themselves?"

Alex gasped. "Oh no. Hell no."

"Okay, and are they breathing?"

"No ma'am."

"Are they in a vehicle?"

"No ma'am, they're on the ground at my kennels . . . She's shot in the head, and he's shot really bad."

The dispatcher could hear Alex crying now. She asked where his son had been shot.

"Ma'am, I don't know but he has blood everywhere."

More gasping.

"I see brain, I can see his brain."

More crying, and then Alex described Maggie's condition. "She's facedown. I tried to turn her a little bit, but she's got a hole in her head."

The dispatcher asked if Paul showed any signs of breathing.

Neither his son nor wife was breathing, Alex said.

"Help me."

CHAPTER TWENTY-TWO

Sergeant Daniel Greene was four hours into his twelve-hour shift when the call went out. He knew it would take every bit of twenty minutes to get from downtown Walterboro out to Islandton, so he flipped on his lights and siren and took off. Greene didn't know whether the shooting victims he was racing toward were alive or dead. He didn't even know the name of the man who'd phoned in the distress call. The night was so dark and the property so isolated that even watching his GPS, the sergeant missed the driveway for 4147 Moselle Road and had to turn around.

Greene drove up the dirt drive and parked just shy of a long set of kennels. With his flashlight, he could see a tall man with red hair standing on the far side. He surmised it was the father who'd made the call. The sergeant walked toward the man, taking the worn gravel pathway between the kennels and a shed. On his left he saw the body of a young man, facedown on a concrete pad, surrounded by water and blood. The young man's brain appeared to be lying at his feet. A few paces ahead lay the body of a woman, slumped facedown on the grass, the ground around her dark with blood.

Greene radioed dispatch and gave the code confirming the presence of two victims, a white female and a white male.

"Whiskey Fox, Whiskey Mike," he said. "Both gunshot wounds to the head."

The redheaded man walked toward him with his arms raised. He was gesturing toward a black Suburban with its driver's door open and hazard lights on. He told the sergeant that after finding the bodies, he'd hurried back to the house to get a shotgun.

"It's in your vehicle?" the sergeant asked.

"It's leaning up against the side of my car."

"You have any guns on you at all?"

"No, sir."

The man was wearing a white T-shirt and dark green cargo shorts. On the pocket of the T-shirt, a logo read BLACK SHEEP, HAMPTON, S.C.

The sergeant approached the man, lifted his shirt, and shone his flashlight along the waistband of his shorts.

"I don't have anything," the man said.

The sergeant pointed toward the bodies. "This is your wife and son?"

"Yes, sir. My wife and son."

The man turned away and bent over, his hands on his knees. He was breathing heavily.

"It's bad," he said, walking back toward the sergeant. "It's bad. I checked the pulses."

The sergeant turned his flashlight toward the shotgun leaning against the SUV. The man took a few steps away from Greene then walked back.

"This is a long story," he said, his voice rushed. "My son was in a boat wreck, oh, a few months back." He sniffled loudly. "He's been getting threats. Most of it's been benign stuff we didn't take serious. He's been getting, like, punched . . ."

The man's voice broke. "I know that somebody . . . I know that's what it is."

That's when it dawned on Greene whom he was talking to. He hadn't recognized the address, but he knew about the boat crash. This had to be Alex Murdaugh.

"When did you get home?" the sergeant said, trying to take him back to the beginning. "Right when you called, or did you go to the house first?"

"I came to the house first," Alex said. "My mom has late-stages Alzheimer's and my dad is in the hospital."

"Okay . . ."

"I left, I don't know what time, I can go back on my phone and tell you the exact times . . ."

Alex was wondering about the ambulance.

"Can they hurry?" he said.

Behind them, the dogs barked. The only other sound was the droning of crickets.

Alex was pacing as he talked, edging closer and closer to the shotgun leaning against the SUV. He seemed distraught, even erratic. Greene didn't want him picking up the shotgun and turning it on himself. The sergeant walked over to the shotgun, pulled on his gloves, and picked it up.

"That is loaded," Alex said. "You might want to unload it."

"Is this the only firearm with you?"

"I'm ninety-nine percent sure that it is," Alex said.

"Wait right here for me for a sec, okay?" Greene walked the gun back to his patrol car, passing the bodies on his way there and back. He had worked dozens of violent scenes, but this one appeared to be particularly gruesome. By the time Greene got back, Alex was on the phone with his brother Randy. He held the phone away from his ear to speak to the sergeant.

"They are dead, aren't they," he said to Greene. It sounded less like a question than a realization.

"Yes, sir, that's what it looks like."

Alex walked away again, wailing to his brother.

By now more deputies were arriving and paramedics were hurrying to the bodies.

Greene tried again to gather basic facts. When was the last time Alex had seen his wife and son?

"Um, it was earlier tonight. I don't know the exact time . . . I was probably gone an hour and a half from my mom's, and I saw them about forty-five minutes before that."

"Okay."

"I rode around with Paul for two hours this afternoon in the pickup truck."

"That's your son Paul?" Greene asked, pointing where Alex was looking.

Alex nodded. "Is somebody gonna check 'em?"

"Yes, sir, they've already checked them."

"It's official that they're dead?"

"Yes, sir, that's what it looks like."

Alex lifted the bottom of his shirt to wipe his face. "I'm sorry," he said. He exhaled. "I'm very sorry. I've got to call her parents."

"What's her name?"

"Her name is Maggie Murdaugh. Margaret Branstetter Murdaugh."

More officers were showing up. As one approached, Alex looked up and said, "How you doing?" Greene continued with his questions.

"And what's your son's first name?"

"Paul Terry Murdaugh."

Alex kept his eyes fixed on his son's body. "What are they doing, covering them up?"

The sergeant looked behind him with alarm. The fire rescue battalion chief seemed to be shaking open a large sheet.

"Tell them they don't need to do that," Greene told his deputy. "Preserve all the evidence we can."

The battalion chief lived a few miles away. He had known the Murdaughs all his life. He told the deputy he was making a judgment call to cover the bodies out of deference to the family, some of whom were on the way. He would not allow them to see Paul's brain, detached and lying in a watery red mess by his ankles. He would not have them see Miss Maggie with her short dress askew. He would not let them see the hole in the back of her head, which was split open like a coin purse.

"We're going to cover them up," the battalion chief said. "That's it."

The sheets were a garish pink, but that was all the paramedics had in the truck. Behind them, nearly all the dogs were lying in their kennels, resting their heads on their paws. Only one stood at alert, watching as they worked. It was Bubba, Maggie's favorite.

LIGHTNING FLASHED IN the distance. Red and blue light from the cruisers and emergency vehicles flickered across the scene. The sheriff radioed for a deputy to run by the office and fetch the event tent so they could cover Maggie's body. The night was hot and sticky, 79 degrees even as it approached 11 P.M.

The deputies assessed the scene. Two different guns had been used to shoot the victims. The plastic wadding of a shotgun shell was visible beside Paul's body; the distinctive shell casings of a .300-caliber Blackout tactical rifle were scattered around Maggie's. Neither type of gun was anywhere in sight. To rule out a murder-suicide, two deputies lifted the sheet and rolled Paul's body slightly to ensure there was no gun underneath. The deputies saw no sign of an ambush, no footprints leading to or from the dense woods, no obvious defense wounds or signs of a struggle. There were tire tracks everywhere but not enough vehicles to account for them, just Alex's Suburban, a farm truck parked on the far side of the hangar, and a dusty four-wheeler with a flat tire that did not appear to have been moved recently.

At one point, a deputy tested Alex's hands for gunshot residue, a routine step in a homicide investigation. Alex agreed readily; the deputy had been a witness in a drug case Alex had recently prosecuted. The deputy took each of Alex's bare hands in his gloved ones as he swabbed them. Alex's hands, he noticed, were not shaking.

The coroner arrived a few minutes after 11 P.M. He was a paramedic, not a doctor, but had been the elected coroner for nearly thirty years and took pride in his ability to estimate time of death. He lifted the sheet covering Paul and put his hand under his armpit, gauging the warmth of his body and whether any stiffness had set in. He did the same with Maggie. He estimated they'd both died around 9 P.M., an hour or so before the 911 call. He did not check their temperature with a rectal thermometer. With so many people watching, he thought it unseemly.

Detective Laura Rutland was among the last of the sheriff's office contingent to arrive. She was good with words, so she'd been asked to draw up a search warrant and track down a sleeping magistrate for a signature. By the time she reached Moselle, it was a little after midnight.

"Do you know the name Alex Murdaugh?" her captain asked.

Rutland had grown up two counties away and had stayed home for a while with her three young children. She'd worked for the sheriff's office for barely a year. The name meant nothing to her.

"Congratulations," the captain said. "That makes you the lead on this."

The captain walked Rutland over to meet the agent who'd be assisting her from SLED, which had been called in because of the complexity of the case. SLED agents commonly supported local law enforcement in the fourteen counties of the Lowcountry, particularly on homicides with multiple victims or cases that posed conflicts of interest for the locals. Rutland was meeting her partner that night for the first time. His name was David Owen.

WHEN THE CALL came in, Owen had been asleep at home in suburban Charleston. He got up and dressed quickly. He'd been doing police work for twenty years and had long since grown accustomed to being woken in the middle of the night. It was the nature of the job. On the ninety-minute drive to Moselle, he had worked the phone, trying to gather as much information as he could. The information he'd been given initially was that Paul Murdaugh, the kid from the boat wreck, and his girlfriend had been shot. But on the drive, he checked in with the office secretary, who was from Hampton.

"That's strange," she said. "I didn't think Paul had a girlfriend right now."

Owen lived in a city of one hundred fifty thousand. He had neighbors whose names he didn't know. Just how small a town was Hampton if his secretary knew offhand the current relationship status of a twenty-two-year-old kid?

The detective found a parking place among all the cars along Moselle Road. By the time he made his way to the shed, he was already wiping his face in the muggy heat. Owen had spent the early part of his career in the crime scene unit, photographing dead bodies, handling evidence, and scanning for fingerprints and footprints. He could tell right away that this scene was a mess. The ideal crime scene was contained indoors. This one was outdoors and sprawling. A light rain was falling off and on, possibly diluting evidence or even washing it away. Moselle was so remote that SLED's crime scene technicians were just arriving from Columbia two hours after the 911 call. The ground around the kennels was gravel, dirt, and wet grass, making it almost impossible to clearly identify tire tracks or footprints. The darkness was so heavy, it was difficult to spot shell casings and stray bullets. It did not help that the bodies had been covered with sheets, potentially altering evidence.

Making matters worse, the scene was crawling with people—not just law enforcement but a dozen civilians milling outside the police tape. Randy, Alex's older brother, was there, along with several of the firm's partners. John Marvin, Alex's younger brother, was there, too, talking to sheriff's deputies who already knew him, and was accompanied by Greg Alexander, the Yemassee police chief who was a friend of the Murdaughs. Chief Alexander had no jurisdiction on this property, so it wasn't clear why he was there. As a police officer, Alexander would have understood that a crowd would make it more difficult to protect evidence. Another complication was that so many of the officers were friends or acquaintances of the Murdaughs. These relationships were already affecting the processing of the scene. It wasn't just Greg Alexander. It was the fire battalion chief who had covered the bodies, and the coroner who had been reluctant to use the rectal thermometer, and the sheriff who was briefing his friend, one of Alex's law partners.

Owen shook hands with Deputy Rutland, and the two of them walked around the scene's perimeter. The smell was overwhelming, particularly near the son's body. His feet were just inside the feed room, and he had fallen on the concrete pad outside it. There were bits of skull on the feed room's ceiling, hair on the doorframe, and blood spattered on the walls. The two investigators were able to see bullet holes in the window at the back of the tiny room. About thirty feet away was the mother's body, encircled by blood and dotted by shell casings in a spiraling ring. They could see well enough beneath the sheet to understand that her head was split open by a gunshot that appeared to have been delivered execution-style.

The detectives joined a circle with the deputies who'd been first to arrive. Together they listened to the 911 call to understand when Alex arrived home and what he saw, as those details were often most revealing in the moments just after the trauma of discovery. They listened to Sergeant Greene describe his first interaction with Alex and the way he'd stopped midsentence to say "How you doing?" to another deputy. They talked through scenarios. Given the presence of ammunition from two guns, they raised the possibility of two different shooters. Owen and Rutland were about to break off to talk with Alex when the captain overseeing the scene piped up. He wasn't eager to say anything, since he'd known the Murdaughs all his life. But he said he was getting a strange vibe from Alex.

When the captain arrived, Alex had told him he'd retrieved Paul's phone from his back pocket and fiddled with it, checking for something. But before he could say what he was doing with the phone, Alex had suddenly stopped talking. It also struck the captain as odd that Alex was not showing any anger. The family and friends of homicide victims commonly vented their grief at police, asking why officers were standing around when they could be out chasing the killers. But Alex wasn't lashing out.

"I'm telling you," the captain said, "don't overlook this guy."

. . .

JUST BEFORE OWEN and Rutland talked with Alex, Owen's supervisor pulled him aside. He told him there was more going on here than he could say at the moment, but Alex Murdaugh had been on SLED's radar for a while for a different reason. It had to do with the boat wreck. The sheriff and SLED's top brass had agreed that since Alex mentioned the boat wreck first thing in the 911 call, it would be best for SLED to take over the double homicide. That made Owen the lead investigator. It was not ideal, catching a case several hours old, with key decisions already made and evidence getting colder by the moment. But it was the job.

Roles reversed, Agent Owen and Detective Rutland walked to the field behind the shed, where Alex was talking with his brother Randy and several other men. Alex had a wad of tobacco in his mouth. One of the men identified himself as Danny Henderson, Alex's personal attorney. He said Alex would agree to an interview as long as he sat in. By now the rain had picked up, so Agent Owen led them out to Moselle Road to sit in his work vehicle, a Dodge Durango. Owen settled in the driver's seat with Alex beside him in the passenger seat. Henderson and Rutland sat in the back. When the doors closed and they were all huddled in the confines of the brightly lit and air-conditioned SUV, Owen handed Alex his business card. The agent clipped his body camera to the rearview mirror, angled it toward Alex, then pressed Record.

CHAPTER TWENTY-THREE

"Just start at the top," Agent Owen said. "Take your time."

Alex began talking about when he returned to Moselle and found the bodies. "I pulled up and I could see them and, you know, I knew something was bad. I ran out. I knew it was really bad. My boy over there, I could see it was . . ."

Alex sniffed loudly. He was hunched toward the door. His eyes were dark, looking out at the night. He started to sob. Both Rutland and his lawyer reached out almost simultaneously to squeeze his shoulder.

"I'm sorry, Mr. Murdaugh," Rutland said.

"I could see his brain on the sidewalk," he said, his voice rising. "I ran over to Maggie . . . Actually, I think I tried to turn Paul over first. You know, I tried to turn him over and I don't know, I figured it out. His cellphone popped out of his pocket. I started trying to do something with it, thinking maybe, but then I put it back down really quickly . . . Then I went to my wife, and I mean, I could see . . ."

Alex looked down, his expression impossible to read.

"Did you touch Maggie at all?" Owen asked.

"I did. I touched them both . . . I tried to take . . . I tried to take their pulse on both of them . . ."

Then he called 911, he said, and then he called his brothers, Randy and John Marvin. Then he called Rogan Gibson, the friend who owned Cash, the chocolate Lab with the injured tail. Alex called and texted Rogan repeatedly that night, telling detectives Rogan lived close by and was practically family.

Alex explained how his father was in the hospital and his mother was at home with Alzheimer's. He said he'd gone to Almeda to check on her. When he came home to Moselle, Maggie and Paul weren't up at the house.

Owen asked what had made Alex come down to the kennels. On his way back to Moselle, he said, he'd texted Maggie but she hadn't responded. When he reached the house, it was empty, so he assumed Maggie and Paul were down at the kennels.

"Had Maggie and Paul been arguing over anything?" Owen asked.

"No," Alex said.

"What was their relationship like?"

"Wonderful."

"How about yours and Maggie's?" Owen asked.

"Wonderful," Alex said. He paused a beat. "I mean, I'm sure we had little things here and there, but we had a wonderful marriage, wonderful relationship."

"And yours and Paul's relationship?"

"As good as it could be."

"Have you been having any problems out here? Trespassers, or people breaking in?"

"None that I know of," Alex said. The only thing that came to mind, he said, was the boat wreck. There had been a lot of negative publicity about Paul's arrest and charges, he said, and strangers had been making vile comments online. Paul didn't tell him everything, he said, but he knew his son had been punched and attacked several times. Owen asked for specific names or instances but Alex couldn't give any. Instead, he told Owen the names of some friends Paul had recently been hanging out with.

Alex still had the chewing tobacco in his mouth. He asked to open the door, then leaned out and spat for a long moment, then settled back in his seat.

Owen asked who else the detectives should be talking to.

Alex paused. "This is such a stupid thing, I'm even embarrassed to say it. But it just didn't make any sense."

He said he'd hired a new groundskeeper who wasn't working out. Alex said the new guy had killed the sunflowers in the dove field and he and Paul had been out there trying to salvage the flowers.

Then he shared an odd detail. The other day, he said, the grounds-keeper had told Paul a story about getting in a fight in high school. "He got in a fight with some Black guys," Alex said. "And an FBI undercover team observed him fighting those guys and put him on an undercover team with three Navy SEALs, and that their job was to kill radical Black Panthers. They did that from Myrtle Beach to Savannah." Alex said he didn't think the groundskeeper had killed Paul and Maggie. But he couldn't help noticing that the man had been off that day.

"What's his name?" Owen asked.

"C. B. Rowe," Alex said. "I sent him a message to text me earlier today about the sunflowers, and he called me back when I was on the way to my mom's house."

"Did you talk to him at that time?"

Only briefly, Alex said, because he was on the other line. "I told him I'd call him back tomorrow, see him in the morning."

"What was his demeanor or attitude?" Owen asked.

"I mean, it seemed normal," Alex said. Owen took down Rowe's contact information and said he'd follow up. Again, the detective asked for the names of anyone harassing Paul. Alex said he couldn't think of any, though he was sure Paul had been getting attacked, even getting a black eye recently in Charleston. Paul was a real man's man, he said. Were it not for the pending criminal charges, his son would have fought back.

"I've never been prouder of him than the way he has handled the pressures and the adversity," Alex said, still speaking of his son in the present tense. "Paul is a wonderful, wonderful, wonderful kid. He can do almost anything. He gets along with almost anybody."

That evening, Alex said, he and Paul had ridden the property together, and then after dinner, he had fallen asleep. "I laid down, took a nap on the couch, probably, I don't know, twenty-five to thirty minutes. I got up. I called Maggie. Didn't get an answer. And I left to go to my mom's."

Maggie had talked about going with him to Almeda, he said. But when he woke up from his nap, she wasn't in the house anymore. He thought he'd texted her, but she hadn't responded. Usually, she was good about answering the phone.

"So that was odd," Alex said. "But it wasn't that big a deal."

From the back seat, Rutland asked, "About what time was that?"

"What time was what?" Alex said. His voice took on a slight edge.

"You sent her a text message?" Rutland reminded him.

Alex pulled out his phone and scrolled through his history. He had texted Maggie at 9:08, saying he was on his way to Almeda to check on his mother. He had texted her again at 9:47, as he pulled out of the driveway at his mother's place and headed back to Moselle. And then he'd tried to call Paul.

"I mean, my calls are right here."

Alex opened the door again and spat, though this time he stayed turned away from detectives a few beats longer. Then he settled back in.

"Can I have a piece of gum?"

"Yes, sir," Owen said, and offered him a piece from a pack in the console. "Anybody else want some gum?"

Alex next asked for water. He seemed subdued, as if all the activity of the day had caught up with him. The interview was winding down.

"Do you have any other children?" Owen asked.

"I do," Alex replied. "A twenty-four-year-old."

"What's his name?"

"He goes by Buster."

Owen was walking Alex through the next steps in the investigation when the phone rang. Buster had arrived from his girlfriend's house in Rock Hill, three hours west.

"Don't let him come up here," Alex said to the caller. "I think we're about done."

CHAPTER TWENTY-FOUR

The magistrate's warrant authorized the officers to search the house. But sheriff's deputies had identified the crime scene as the kennels, a decision Agent Owen didn't question. SLED had a longtime working relationship with Colleton County, including a stint where Agent Owen's lieutenant had filled in as sheriff for a year. He figured if the deputies who were first on scene thought the house had anything to do with the murders, they would have locked it down.

He gave Alex a few minutes alone with Buster, then he and Detective Rutland headed to the house to take Alex's clothes into evidence. The house was roughly 250 yards from the kennels, up a long dirt road. Owen knocked on the door, and a man who identified himself as one of Alex's law partners let them in, through the foyer and into the main living area, where people were gathering and talking quietly. A handful of people were in the kitchen, appearing to put away pots and dishes. Owen told Alex he needed to collect his clothing, then waited in the doorway of the master bedroom while Alex changed. He put the cargo shorts in one brown bag, the white shirt in another, and his brightly colored tennis shoes in yet another. As Owen glanced around the house, he saw no evidence of a scuffle. Nothing seemed out of place.

After turning over the evidence bags to the SLED crime scene technicians, he went to brief his supervisors. They called his attention to the side of the kennels, to a stack of stray bins, including an animal travel crate. On top of the crate lay a chicken. It appeared to be dead.

Owen put on a pair of gloves and went over to inspect the chicken carcass. It was still warm to the touch.

"That chicken has a story to tell," he said. "By God, I wish we could hear it."

The dogs had mostly quieted and were lying in pens. Bubba was closest to the feed room, just a few steps from the chicken. He was still paying attention to the investigators' every move.

"I know this is going to sound crazy," Owen said, "but we need a dog whisperer."

His lieutenant and captain both gave him the side-eye, but Owen was serious.

"I'm telling you, that dog knows what happened."

THE SUN ROSE with Agent Owen still at the kennels. He had watched the crime scene technicians gather evidence; he had ordered background checks on the family employees; he had stood by while the coroner peeled back the damp pink sheets to photograph the bodies. Paul had been wearing light shorts and a black T-shirt. On the back of the shirt in red capital letters was written WHAM BAM THANK YOU MA'AM.

Paul's phone had been placed neatly on the back of his shorts. Using gloves, Owen picked up the phone and tried to power it on so he could put it in airplane mode. But the phone was dead. He put it into an evidence bag and locked it in his Durango.

When the coroner turned over Paul's body, Owen could see that the young man's smooth face was intact, almost unmarred, but flattened like a mask. The back of his head was completely gone. Behind him, the interior of the feed room was a slaughterhouse, with blood and fluids spattered on the walls and red hair plastered to the top of the door. In the early light of dawn, the detectives watched the coroner and an assistant carefully remove Paul's body and place his brain in a bucket.

Maggie's body had been found twelve paces away. She appeared to have fallen to her knees, then forward on her face. Her arms were stretched out on either side of her body. She was facing the feed room. She was wearing a short light pink summer dress. She had been shot five times. One of the bullets had gone straight through her wrist. It had exploded her tennis bracelet and sprinkled the ground beside her body with tiny diamonds.

Owen watched the coroner remove Maggie's body as well. After the van with the bodies left, Owen stepped back to survey the scene, moving the puzzle pieces around in his mind. It was always difficult to know, in the first hours of an investigation, which details mattered. Near the kennels, there was an upside-down cooler on the ground. It was surrounded by empty beer cans. Had someone dumped it in a hurry? At the kennels, there was water pooling on the concrete pad near the feed room. It had been raining on and off, but the kennels were covered. Was the water from the hose used to rinse out the pens? If so, when was it sprayed and why?

The investigators thought they knew what types of guns killed Maggie and Paul, but they had not yet found the murder weapons. Based on Alex's account and the dishes in the kitchen, they felt confident Maggie and Paul had eaten dinner at the house. But they did not know how or when the mother and son had gone down to the kennels. They couldn't tell if they'd tried to defend themselves; the autopsy reports wouldn't be complete for several days. They'd interviewed several people at that point. But none of the pieces were fitting.

Owen was a career law enforcement officer. He'd started out at a small-town police force out of high school, then moved up to a sheriff's office, then eventually joined SLED. He married a woman ten years older; they were overjoyed when, after several years of uncertainty, she had given birth to twin boys. By middle school, the boys had grown into talented athletes and the family's schedule was a blur of football practices and out-of-town baseball tournaments. Being a father had been Owen's deepest hope, so closely held he'd rarely articulated it, even to himself. At work he was stoic and gave away nothing. But at home, with his boys, he grinned so big his eyes disappeared.

The double homicide scene was the most disorganized Owen had ever seen. Nothing about it made sense. He had a hunch Paul had been ambushed in the feed room. Owen was equally confident Maggie had been shot second. If Paul had seen his mother shot, he would not have cowered in the feed room. He would have run to stop the killer. Maggie had died with her body facing Paul. Owen felt sure she'd been running toward her son.

AT DAYBREAK, WHEN the groundskeeper showed up for his daily shift, he seemed unaware that two members of the Murdaugh family were dead.

Agent Owen made a beeline for C. B. Rowe, knowing he was the only person Alex named as suspicious. Rowe was already well known to agents in SLED's Walterboro office, where Owen was based. He was a former high school teacher who had been investigated by SLED and convicted years earlier of sexual battery for a relationship with a student. Owen led Rowe out to his Durango for an interview and they spent more than an hour going over Rowe's dealings with the Murdaughs and his whereabouts before and after the murders. Based on a cursory glance at Rowe's phone, Owen was satisfied that Rowe had probably been away from Moselle. He told Rowe he'd follow up and let him go about his day.

As soon as the interview was over, Rowe texted Alex, who had left for Almeda with Buster.

> Alex for the last hour I have been interrogated by sled about the activities here, he wrote. It was[n't] until the end that they told me what happened. I am so sorry for your loss and my prayers are with you and your family. If you need anything from me let me know.

Alex did not let on that he'd told SLED about Rowe's outlandish vigilante claim, or that he'd been dissatisfied with Rowe's work.

Thank u CB, he texted back. *We will talk but We need to get the grounds clean--drive and yard for visitors if u can start on that.*

THERE WAS NO garbage pickup out in the country. So that Tuesday morning, Roger Dale Davis—the man who cared for the Murdaugh family's dogs—was loading trash in his truck to take to the dump when the phone rang. It was C. B. Rowe.

"You need to get down here," the groundskeeper said. "SLED wants to talk to you. Miss Maggie and Paul have been murdered."

"You kidding me?" Davis asked. When Rowe assured him he was not, Davis put aside the bags. "I'll be up there in a minute."

Davis lived a little over a mile down Moselle Road. He'd been taking care of the Murdaughs' dogs every morning and evening for four years. When he got to the kennels, it was feeding time, and the dogs were barking.

Davis greeted Agent Owen and asked if they could talk once he'd fed the dogs. After making sure the crime scene techs were done with the kennels, Owen told him to go ahead. The ten dog pens, Davis realized instantly, were a mess. Some of the dog beds were on the top of the pens, where they didn't belong. Even more striking, several of the dogs were in the wrong pens. The hose was all kinked up and he hadn't left it that way. He'd run it all the way out so it could dry then wrapped it neatly, like always.

Once Davis fed the dogs, they settled down. He and Owen walked back out to the Durango. Davis told the investigator that the previous day he'd followed his usual routine, feeding the dogs and changing their water and spraying out their pens around 7 A.M. He'd repeated the process at 4 P.M., though in the afternoon he only fed Bubba and the other dogs the family treated like pets. The working dogs ate once a day. Davis said the process had taken about forty-five minutes. Davis said he'd gone home, showered, and retired to his recliner. He hadn't gotten up until bedtime. He said he hadn't noticed anything out of the ordinary the day before, but now plenty was off. In addition to the pooled water and haphazardly wound hose, he was also struck by the fact that the family's black work truck had been parked behind the shed. It hadn't been there when Davis had left the previous afternoon.

He also couldn't figure out who would have put Bubba in the wrong pen. The only person he would have expected to fool with the dogs was Miss Maggie. He knew that she often came down to the kennels to let the dogs run. She loved those dogs, he said, especially Bubba. She'd never have put the yellow Lab in the pen next to the feed room. It was not where he belonged.

EARLY THAT MORNING, the crime scene techs took down the yellow tape. Sheriff's deputies towed Alex's Suburban to the impound lot.

SLED's decision to clear the scene so quickly would later become a major issue in court. Owen and the other investigators would be accused of rushing. Some would ask why the house itself was not sealed off and processed for evidence. Others would wonder why SLED and the Colleton County sheriff's department had allowed so many civilians to wander the property, possibly contaminating the scene.

David Owen found the critiques irritating. When the 911 call came in, the scene was thought to be confined to the kennels. By the time any officers realized the house might be worth searching, dozens of people had walked through those rooms.

In any case, Alex's statements had given the detectives a great deal to think about. Agent Owen thought it possible that Alex's theory was right and the killings had been retribution for the boat crash case. It was also possible that two people had committed the murders. As Owen headed home to get some rest, he kept scanning the crime scene in his mind. It was strange, all the things the investigators had not found—no guns, no sign of a struggle, no tire tracks that suggested anyone fleeing in a getaway car.

Several things about Alex's story did not feel right to Owen. To begin with, Alex had given two different explanations for how he had ended up holding Paul's phone. He had told the captain he'd reached into his son's pocket to pull it out. But in the Durango, with the two detectives, he'd said the phone had popped out of Paul's pocket. Either way, it made no sense that he'd picked up the phone at all. As a prosecutor, Alex would have known not to touch evidence at a crime scene.

As Detective Rutland headed back to the office, she was thinking about Alex's clothes, the ones bagged and ready to be entered into evidence. During the interview, watching from the back seat, Rutland had noticed how clean the clothes seemed, even Alex's white T-shirt. It didn't add up. Alex had told the detectives he had checked both Paul's and Maggie's pulse and had even tried turning over Paul's body. So why were Alex's shirt and shorts pristine? How had he managed to walk on blood-soaked ground and touch the bodies without getting blood on his shoes or clothes?

Detective Rutland had picked up on something else. At home, with her three kids, she was constantly doing laundry. And in the Durango, what she smelled coming from Alex was the scent of freshly washed clothes.

PART FIVE

BLACK BOX

CHAPTER TWENTY-FIVE

Blanca was getting ready to go to work at Moselle that Tuesday morning when Alex called. His voice, normally so brash, sounded shaky.

"B, they're gone," he said. "They're gone."

"What do you mean?" she said. Maggie and Paul were supposed to have stayed over at Moselle. "Did Maggie go back to Edisto?"

"No, B," he said. "They're dead."

She dropped the phone. Her husband picked it up and listened. "Alex and Buster are at Almeda," her husband told her.

"Tell him I'll be right there," Blanca said.

At Almeda, she found herself in a crush of family. Blanca hugged Alex. He was sobbing, talking about Paul's wounds.

"They did him so bad," he said. "They did him so bad."

Alex had come to Almeda to try for a few hours of sleep, but it hadn't worked. He was too distraught, he said, plus his phone was blowing up with texts and calls. It wouldn't be long before people started coming by Moselle with food. He asked Blanca if she would mind going over there.

"I just want the house to look the way Maggie would like for it to look," he said. "Straighten it up the way she would like it. You knew her best."

Blanca said she would. Alex told her to use the formal driveway rather than the back entrance because SLED would still be at the kennels.

Blanca drove the twenty minutes to Moselle in a daze. When she pulled up to the house around 7:30 A.M., she saw Maggie's black Mercedes out front. The golf cart was there, too, but parked at an angle off to the side rather than next to the charger. Blanca walked up the brick steps and turned her key in the lock. It was a hot morning, already 80 degrees, but as she stepped through the door, she felt a wave of cold.

It was dark and she made no move to turn on the lights. She walked through the open foyer and veered right toward the kitchen, where she normally started her day. Right away she noticed there were things out of place, as though the house had been tidied up hastily. Blanca walked to the laundry room, her unofficial office. On the floor by the door, she noticed a pair of Maggie's pajamas, the white-and-lilac ones that Buster's girlfriend had given her for Christmas. They were laid out neatly with a folded pair of her underwear on top. Why? Maggie wouldn't have left them there, and certainly not paired with underwear. Maggie didn't wear panties at night.

Blanca stayed in the laundry room for a long while, numb with grief and unmoored by the strangeness of the house. Until that day, she'd known it as well as her own.

BY MIDMORNING, ALEX'S law partners began to congregate at Moselle. They gathered in the gun room, which served as the den, with a TV and recliners on one side, exercise equipment on another, and a pool table with a heavy cover in the middle of the room. Along one wood-paneled wall, two dozen long guns stood in a rack. Alex's partners wore khakis or shorts and short-sleeved shirts, because they had closed the firm for the day. It was impossible to work amid such tragedy. Besides, they needed to figure out security for the firm's fifty em-

ployees and for the Murdaugh family. What if the killer came for Alex
and Buster next?

John Marvin, the only one of the three Murdaugh brothers who
wasn't a lawyer, felt out of place as the partners plotted next steps. He
needed something to do. After overhearing their musings about Maggie's missing phone, he tracked down Buster, who'd just arrived. Did
Buster have one of those tracking apps? Buster did. He opened the
Find My Friends app and handed the phone to John Marvin, who
pressed "Maggie."

"Holy shit," John Marvin said. "There it is."

The dot representing Maggie's phone showed it nearby, out along
Moselle Road. John Marvin took Buster's phone to the shed and handed
it to one of the SLED agents.

"If y'all want to," he said, "let's go get it."

The SLED agent told him to sit tight. The technology team would
be there soon. John Marvin tried to stay pleasant, though he was fum-
ing. Why wouldn't they take the time to walk with him and find the
phone?

The second wave of law enforcement was rolling in. Even though
he had no official role with the solicitor's office, John Marvin still knew
most officers in the region. He was hunting and fishing buddies with
many of them. He spotted some people he knew, including investigators for the Fourteenth Circuit solicitor's office. John Marvin walked
over and told them what he'd told SLED, that he thought he'd found
Maggie's phone. The men got in one of the investigators' cars. In
about three-quarters of a mile, they reached the spot where the phone
was pinging. From the side of the road, they could see a black iPhone
in the deep grass between a cow pasture and some woods. They called
SLED to pick it up for processing. John Marvin got the password from
Alex and gave it to SLED, and just like that, the phone was open.

John Marvin had stayed at Moselle until 3 A.M. and returned just
before 8 A.M. He didn't want to go back to the house and sit around the
gun room any longer. He made a call to see if it was okay for him to go
to the kennels. The crime scene techs were done. SLED said it was fine.

When John Marvin got to the kennels, he saw little trace of Maggie's death. She'd fallen in the grass, and after her body was removed, someone had covered the spot with dirt, so no blood was visible. But when John Marvin walked toward the feed room where Paul's body had been found, he was horrified.

John Marvin had been close to Paul. They had bonded over their shared sense that, as non-lawyers, they were the family's black sheep. Some even called Paul "Little John Marvin." Now, as John Marvin looked into the feed room, he saw the awful evidence of his favorite nephew's death: bloodstains, strands of red hair, bits of bone, brain matter. On the concrete lay a skull fragment the size of a baseball. John Marvin didn't want Buster or Alex or anyone else to see such things. Later, when he recounted this moment in court, he would say he was seized with the need to do something. So he grabbed a rag and started to clean. Within a few moments, he was overwhelmed. Crying, he called his oldest brother, Randy.

"You need to stop," Randy told him. "Seriously. It's not healthy."

Randy said they would find a professional cleaner. One of the partners was already making calls.

John Marvin hung up, but he couldn't stop. As he later recalled, he began talking to Paul in his mind.

"I love you, Paul. I promise you I'm going to find out who did this to you."

It wasn't long before Randy called back with more bad news. The doctors had done all they could for their father, Randy said. They were sending him home under hospice care. In her dementia, Mrs. Libby was unlikely to fully grasp what was happening, but at least she and her husband would be together.

SHERIFF'S DEPUTIES WERE canvassing neighbors from one end of Moselle Road to the other. The houses were spread out; if anyone had heard shots, they hadn't thought anything of it. No one reported any burglaries. Some neighbors had surveillance systems or doorbell cameras, but the footage was either too far from the road or too dark to tell even the make or model of passing cars. There were no reports of squealing tires or anything else suspicious.

SLED agents met up with Rogan Gibson, the friend of Paul's that Alex had tried to reach by phone or text five times between 10:21 and 10:30 P.M. the night before. Rogan told the agents about Cash, his puppy with the injured tail. He said he'd spoken with Paul over the phone that Monday night at the kennels. Paul had promised to take a video of Cash's tail but never sent one. Maggie and Alex had been at the kennels, too.

"What makes you say that?" asked one of the agents.

"I heard Alex and Maggie talking in the background," Rogan said.

"Are you sure?"

"Well, I'm ninety percent sure," Rogan said.

The agents downloaded texts and a list of calls from Rogan's phone. They told him they'd be in touch.

AT MOSELLE, THE SLED agents proceeded cautiously. The house was full of family and friends. Alex was in and out. In the dark and confusion of the night before, they'd focused on the kennels as the crime scene and only belatedly realized that they needed to search the house, too. A female agent who lived in Hampton and knew the family told Alex's brothers that she needed to go room to room but would take off her radio and badge to be discreet. John Marvin and one of the law partners accompanied her as she walked through each of the four bedrooms and three and a half bathrooms, peeking under beds and opening cabinets and checking the attic where Maggie stored bins of her beloved Christmas decorations. The agent told them she was mostly looking for guns. As far as they could tell, she did not see anything out of the ordinary.

In the gun room, agents were looking for a .300 Blackout and a 12-gauge shotgun, having determined the type of ammunition used to kill Maggie and Paul. They set aside several guns on the pool table.

The agent overseeing the search saw he'd missed a call from his boss. He stepped outside to call him back, using the side door off the gun room.

The agent was standing on the landing at the bottom of the steps when he noticed some weathered shell casings. He knew weapons and ammo; he'd been a firearms instructor and had an extensive gun collection. The spent casings looked like the ones found around Maggie's body. He walked inside and asked one of his colleagues to step out with him. When they got to the landing, the agent turned his back to the house and squatted, saying, "I'm going to see if I can just discreetly pick these up."

The agent used a gloved hand to pick up the casings one at a time. He dropped each one into the separate finger of a blue rubber glove held by his colleague. The casings had clearly been outside for a while, but when the agent rubbed off the dirt coating one end, he could read the label, "S&B 300." It was the same type of ammunition found at the kennels. The agent knew that those cartridges were expensive in the best of times and had been especially hard to come by during the pandemic.

Back inside, he sorted through the Murdaughs' ammunition, which was kept haphazardly in bins. The agent found two boxes of S&B 300. One was open.

After the search of the house, the agents started on the bags of household garbage. They worked outdoors, down by the shed. One investigator sorted through old envelopes and junk mail coated in tobacco juice from a spit cup. She recoiled when her gloved hand hit something squishy.

"Oh, gross," she said. "Spaghetti."

The second bag was more promising. There was a credit card statement with one expenditure circled: $1,021.10 at the Gucci store in Charleston. There were also two empty boxes of ammunition for a 12-gauge shotgun.

In the end, SLED seized two boxes of ammunition, one .300-caliber Blackout rifle, and three shotguns. They had their doubts, though, that any of these were the murder weapons, given how clean they were and how casually they were stowed in the gun room.

ALEX'S LAW PARTNERS were doing some investigating of their own. Ronnie Crosby, one of the senior partners, knew the investigators had not been able to find two of Paul's favorite guns, his .300-caliber Blackout rifle and a shotgun with a camouflage pattern on the grip. They'd searched the rest of the house and property with no luck. Crosby frequently hunted with Paul and knew the young man almost always kept those guns with him, usually in the cab of his white F-150 truck. On the Friday before the murders, Paul had dropped off the truck at a repair shop in downtown Hampton.

The truck was still at the shop. Crosby knew the place well. He was friends with the owner, Jimmy Butler, and took his own family's cars there for service. With Jimmy's permission, Crosby went to the shop and checked Paul's truck, but all the lawyer found was a pistol and a few shotgun shells.

Crosby looked up at surveillance cameras mounted above the shop's front counter. He knew there were other cameras covering the garage and outside lot. Maybe, he thought, Paul had been driving with the guns but had taken them out of the truck when he left.

"What time did he come in?" the lawyer asked. "You still have that footage?"

Together, he and Butler fast-forwarded through the security feeds until they found the footage of Paul at the shop. They saw him drive in and drop off the truck. They saw him leave. But he had taken no guns with him.

Crosby was beginning to think Paul's missing shotgun and Blackout were the murder weapons. The killer or killers, he thought, must have taken them from the house or somewhere else on the property and then used them to gun down Maggie and Paul.

Though Crosby didn't know it, Agent Owen and the other detectives had reached the same conclusion. They were working on the assumption the killer or killers had taken the guns with them and either hidden them or gotten rid of them, possibly throwing them into a nearby river or swamp.

MARK TINSLEY HAD gotten the call at 1:30 A.M. on the night of the murders that Maggie and Paul had been killed. By the morning, he had accepted that the killings would be the end of any claim against Alex Murdaugh in the boat wreck case. He called Mallory Beach's parents and told them their lawsuit against Alex was over. A huge part of being a personal injury lawyer was understanding human emotion. No jury, he said, would return a verdict against a man whose wife and son had been murdered.

That afternoon, the judge canceled the June 10 hearing on Tinsley's motion to compel Alex's financials. Tinsley released a statement on behalf of the Beach family: "Having suffered the devastating loss of their own daughter, the family prays that the Murdaughs can find some level of peace from this tragic loss."

Tinsley felt racked with guilt. It seemed that all the news stories were questioning whether the murders had something to do with the boat wreck. Tinsley was asking the same thing. That Monday afternoon, in the hours before Paul and Maggie were killed, the lawyer had gotten a call from a stranger who was irate after having seen Paul out drinking and boating. "I hope that little redheaded son-of-a-bitch gets what's coming to him," the stranger had said.

After the shootings, Tinsley wondered whether someone had taken it upon themselves to put a stop to Paul's behavior. He gave the man's contact information to SLED, but nothing came of it. The man lived two counties away and had a solid alibi. But Tinsley couldn't shake the worry that something he'd done had gotten Paul and his mother killed.

AGENT OWEN CALLED John Marvin and updated him on the investigation. They needed to arrange proper interviews with Alex and other family members. In his experience, Owen said, people tended to have a memory reset a few days after a traumatic event. They recalled different details and thought of possible additional leads. Follow-up interviews would also give the agents a chance to ask the family about specifics they'd uncovered so far. They agreed to meet the next afternoon at Greenfield, John Marvin's hunting lodge near Almeda.

The week overflowed with loss. As the family reeled from the shock of the murders, they braced for the death of Randolph III. The patriarch was at Almeda now, hanging on while friends stopped by to say goodbye, including some friends in law enforcement. Randolph had been such a towering presence in Hampton County for so many years that it was difficult to envision the place without him.

One of Randolph's visitors that week was his half brother, Roberts Vaux, the son Buster had fathered out of wedlock with Ruth Vaux. Tabor Vaux, Roberts's son and law partner, drove his father out to Almeda. The visit was a short one. Mrs. Libby did not recognize Roberts, but she let him and his son hug her just the same. Randolph, known for so long as Handsome, appeared skeletal, propped in a chair, his breathing labored in spite of his oxygen mask. As nonchalantly as he could, Tabor checked the tube and the cord of his oxygen machine to make sure there wasn't something blocking the flow of air.

Speech had become difficult for Randolph, and although he was overcome with emotion, he said little to his only brother. He expressed no fear of his own death, which had stalked him for years. He said nothing about Alex's problems, though he knew about the pills because Paul had told him, and he knew about the money because Alex had asked for another $600,000 loan barely a week before. Roberts and Tabor expressed their condolences on the deaths of Maggie and Paul, and although they did not linger on the subject, the murders were clearly on the old man's mind.

As the visitors prepared to leave, Randolph reached out and grasped the lapel of Roberts's jacket to pull him close.

"What has become of this family?" Randolph said.

CHAPTER TWENTY-SIX

The obituaries, published in *The Hampton County Guardian*, were masterpieces of the unsaid. No mention of murder, or drunken accidents, or criminal charges, or civil lawsuits.

Paul and Maggie, the obits said, had entered into eternal rest.

Maggie had a heart of pure generosity, and loved welcoming friends and family into her home on any given occasion. She adored her family, and cherished spending time on the boat with her two sons. She will be remembered as a 'second mom' to her sons' many friends. She made the most out of every situation, and lived each and every day to the fullest.

Her son's obit offered a more selective interpretation:

Paul never met a stranger, and had an abundance of friends. He was always eager to lend a helping hand to anyone in need. No one was more loving and genuine than Paul, and because of this, his personality was one-of-a-kind.

The obits were accompanied by a photo of mother and son, taken before Maggie's niece's debutante ball. Maggie beamed in a black gown and dark brown fur, her blond hair shining in a half updo, standing beside Paul, who wore a black tuxedo, a custom bow tie, and his usual crooked grin.

JOHN MARVIN'S HUNTING LODGE was a few minutes' drive from Almeda, where Alex and Buster had been staying. Alex, his brothers, his surviving son, and some of his law partners met there that Thursday morning. They needed to plan the funeral, but the bodies were being autopsied and would not be ready in time. They decided they'd proceed with the ceremony and bury the remains later in a service just for family. Alex insisted the wake be held at Moselle. Maggie, he said, would've wanted it that way.

Once they talked through the funeral schedule, Alex and the group prepped for interviews with SLED scheduled at John Marvin's place that afternoon. Jim Griffin, who'd represented Paul in the boat wreck, had cut his vacation short to join them. John Marvin wanted him there in case things turned confrontational. Alex told the others he had gone to work a little late on the morning of the murders and had a more or less uneventful day. This assertion must have seemed curious to some of the partners, since Alex had been confronted that afternoon about the missing $792,000. No one corrected him, though.

Just before SLED was set to arrive, a friend brought Randolph III over for a visit. He was so frail, with his oxygen tank rolling beside him, he was unable to say much of anything. Randolph looked around at his three sons and his grandson and his law partners, nearly all local boys who'd been handpicked and groomed to lead the firm his grandfather had founded. The crossing where Randolph Sr. had died was only a few miles south of this house. So many other losses had followed over the decades, and now they were preparing to bury Maggie and Paul. As the old man looked at the faces surrounding him, tears fell into his oxygen mask.

A few minutes later, Randolph III said his goodbyes. Moments after he left, a phalanx of law enforcement sedans and SUVs pulled up the winding driveway.

John Marvin stood at his open front door, watching David Owen and Laura Rutland and the other investigators approach. There were at least a dozen of them, far more than anyone expected. If John Marvin felt any surprise, though, he kept it off his face.

"Come inside," John Marvin said. "Have a drink of water. It's hot."

ALEX FOLDED INTO the front seat of Agent Owen's Dodge Durango for the second time. He was accompanied by Jim Griffin, who got into the back seat behind Owen. Alex's face was red from the heat, and Owen was mopping sweat from his forehead, even though the vehicle's air-conditioning was purring. Alex seemed impatient. Again, he was chewing tobacco.

Agent Owen asked to take Alex's phone so a tech could download the contents while they talked. While he was gone, Alex directed his attention to another SLED agent sitting behind him, Jeff Croft.

"Where you from, sir?" he asked Croft.

Barnwell, the agent said.

Alex's face brightened. "I got some cousins in Barnwell."

Casually, Alex probed to see if he and the agent moved in overlapping circles.

"You know Big John Bedingfield, don't you," said Alex.

Croft nodded. Big John and his son, he said, had grown up together. It was Big John who had built the .300 Blackouts for the boys.

"That's my cousin," said Alex. "And Sweet Caroline?"

Back and forth the two men went, making small talk. Alex grinned and patted his knee. By the time Agent Owen returned, the mood inside the Durango was relaxed, maybe even genial.

Owen and Agent Croft remained low-key. They had no desire for their subject to shut down. Even so, Owen was determined to return to the discrepancies in Alex's initial statements. Most pressing was his insistence that he had not joined Maggie and Paul at the kennels after dinner. This contradicted what Rogan Gibson, the Murdaughs' longtime neighbor, had told SLED about hearing Alex's voice on the phone when Paul called him. The investigators believed Rogan. He knew what Alex's voice sounded like and had no apparent reason to lie. He'd told the agents he thought of Alex as a second father.

Agent Owen didn't know what to make of the contradiction. It was possible Alex had been so distraught his memory had gotten jumbled. Or maybe he was lying for reasons Owen didn't yet know. Owen was not ready to consider the possibility that a pillar of the community had slaughtered his wife and son. Everyone agreed Alex was especially close to Paul. It seemed impossible that he would kill the person he loved most.

Owen led Alex through the day and night of the murder. Again, Alex described a routine day at the firm, then riding at Moselle with Paul, sunflowers and target practice. He digressed to talk about Paul rigging his Blackout with attachments, including a scope light. After dinner, when Maggie went to the kennels, he said he'd stayed in the house. He thought he might have heard a car pull up outside. A little later, he said, when he left the house to head for Almeda to check on his mom, he saw a feral cat running away from his Suburban.

Alex paused now and then to open the Durango's door and spit tobacco juice. He talked again about people threatening Paul over the boat crash, but he could offer no specifics or names.

"I mean, I have no idea."

Alex talked about what a fine young man Paul had been. Owen asked Alex what his biggest issue with his son had been.

"Irresponsibility."

The agent turned to Alex's relationship with Maggie. Alex assured him they'd had a strong marriage.

"As good as it could possibly be," he said. "We really didn't argue about anything much. We didn't have much to argue about."

Alex bent over in his seat and began to sob. "I'm sorry. She was a wonderful girl and a wonderful wife and she was a great mother."

Alex asked how the investigation was going. Owen told him the police had interviewed close to a hundred people. He was willing to say that the remote location of Moselle made it unlikely someone had chanced upon Maggie and Paul at random.

"Do y'all have any good clues?" Alex said.

Owen stared straight ahead through the windshield. "We're looking at every angle," he said, "trying to figure out what fits."

Agent Croft returned to the essential question.

"So, the last time you saw Paul and Maggie was when y'all were eating supper?"

Alex nodded and began to cry again.

"It's just so bad. They did him so bad. And he was such a good boy, too."

Agent Owen was avoiding eye contact, trying to keep his demeanor neutral. Inwardly, though, he felt something turn. Alex had just told the agents, for the second time in this interview, that he had not gone to the kennels after dinner.

That son of a bitch is lying to me, Owen told himself. There could only be two reasons why. Alex did it, or he was covering for whoever did.

CHAPTER TWENTY-SEVEN

Alex and his brothers were wrapping up their interviews when they got word from Almeda to come quick. Their father was drawing his last breaths.

They jumped in a car and sped off, tires spinning in the long dirt drive. Almeda was only a few minutes away, but by the time the brothers arrived, Randolph Murdaugh III was gone.

The question the old man had asked the night before, on his final night on earth, hung over all of them. Something had gone wrong with this family. For generations, the Murdaughs had been the keepers of order. Now everything around them was chaos.

The double homicide had ballooned into a national story. Some reports chronicled how the Murdaughs had ruled their corner of the state for more than a century. Some enticed with whispers about the other suspicious deaths possibly connected to the family—Stephen Smith and Gloria Satterfield and especially Mallory Beach.

SLED had released a statement after the killing of Maggie and Paul saying there was no danger to the public, but the assurance raised more questions than it answered. If there was no risk, did it mean the police had found who did it? SLED declined to comment further. The lack of information only stoked the public's appetite. Two Murdaugh podcasts sprang up on the same day, along with multiple Reddit threads and Facebook pages on which amateur sleuths picked apart the case.

A flood of interview requests poured in, straining the patience of all those in the Murdaugh orbit. News organizations were calling at all hours, staking out the law firm, prowling Moselle Road to catch a glimpse of the murder scene. Locals resented the reporters descending on their quiet downtown and accosting people on the street.

The family decided to give one interview to keep the hordes at bay. Randy reluctantly agreed to participate. He had always been an introvert, as quiet and rational as Alex was loud and impulsive. He had never sought to be the solicitor; that had always been Alex's dream. He was happier training his prizewinning hunting dogs and working behind the scenes on cases.

John Marvin and Randy invited ABC to the same hunting lodge where they'd hosted SLED and sat down with *Good Morning America*'s Eva Pilgrim, who grew up in South Carolina. They felt they'd get the fairest shake from someone who knew them.

During the segment, the brothers sat together, their shoulders practically touching. Randy's cheeks looked hollow. John Marvin kept crying. Pilgrim asked how Alex was doing.

"He's upright and he looks strong and making his way," John Marvin said, "then he just breaks down. It's just, I mean, it's tough for us."

After a pause, Randy spoke up, his voice low and even. "It changes you as a family," he said. "I can't imagine the horror that my brother is experiencing."

The brothers bristled when Pilgrim asked about the Murdaughs' power and influence.

"Do you feel like some of the perception of your family has been wrong?"

"Yes," Randy said. "You see words like 'dynasty' used, and 'power.' And I don't know exactly how people use those words, but we're just regular people. We're hurting just like they would be hurting if this had happened to them."

. . .

THE POLICE WERE still hunting for the murder weapons. Divers were dropping below the surface of the Little Salkehatchie River, the swampy stream meandering the territory between Moselle and Almeda. Deputies and detectives on all-terrain vehicles were crisscrossing the woods and fields of Moselle.

The missing weapons added to the challenges facing David Owen and the other investigators: the disarray of the original scene, the possible contamination of the evidence, the failure to lock down the house and process it thoroughly.

The first hours after the 911 call had been confounding and confusing. At first, the deputies weren't even sure what kind of case they were investigating. They had been so worried it was a murder-suicide, they had lifted Paul's mangled body to make sure he hadn't fallen on a gun. Then they'd had to consider the possibility that Alex might have stumbled on what he believed was a murder-suicide and decided to protect his dead son's reputation by taking the shotgun from Paul's hands. When the coroner rolled Paul's body onto its back, it was obvious Paul had been shot twice, ruling out suicide but increasing the likelihood there had been multiple shooters using multiple guns, an even thornier issue.

Then there was the change in command a few hours in, with SLED taking over from the Colleton County sheriff's office because of conflicts of interest, including that some of the deputies had worked on criminal cases Alex had prosecuted.

Another conflict clouded the investigation, this one so serious it threatened to sabotage the case. The solicitor for the Fourteenth Circuit, who would ultimately decide what to do with whatever evidence the detectives collected, was still Duffie Stone, Randolph III's hand-picked successor. Stone had been the circuit's top prosecutor for fifteen years. Stone had made it clear he was not giving up jurisdiction. He insisted he could be impartial.

Stone's refusal to step aside was further proof of the challenges of investigating one of the state's most well-connected families. In private, some members of law enforcement called the Murdaughs "the Lowcountry Mafia." SLED had recently investigated two of the family's closest associates, both of them public officials indicted on corruption charges. Andrew Strickland, Colleton County's former sheriff, had accepted a plea deal that sent him to prison. Greg Alexander, the police chief of Yemassee, had been acquitted after Alex and Randolph III sat behind him in court, installing themselves in the front row where the jury could not miss their familiar faces, a move straight out of *The Godfather*.

It had not escaped Owen's attention that on the night of the murders, Chief Alexander had been among the throng at Moselle, even though it lay miles outside his jurisdiction. Perhaps it had been a statement of loyalty.

The investigators were now studying the contents of both Maggie's and Alex's phones, building a timeline of their respective movements on the night in question. They had Paul's phone, too, but could not unlock it.

So far, they had nothing to confirm Alex's suggestion that the murders might be connected to outrage over the boat wreck. More to the point, they had no evidence placing anyone outside the family on the property that night. They had checked out anyone who might have a grudge against the Murdaughs, but so far, no evidence tied any of them to the murders.

For now, the detectives had only one name on their list, and it was Alex Murdaugh. Crime scene investigators had detected gunshot residue on his left hand, his shirt, and his shorts, but it was impossible to read much into it, since he said he'd been holding a shotgun just before police arrived. Plus, Alex had told SLED that he had fired one round from a pistol while target shooting with Paul. The claim seemed unlikely, based on the type of other shell casings out at the range, but it was impossible to refute.

It didn't surprise the detectives that Alex's behavior and statements had raised questions. In many domestic homicides, the killer turned out to be the husband or the person who had called in the death. And after interviewing him twice, Agent Owen was sure Alex was hiding something. Owen wondered if Alex was being blackmailed. Maybe the killers had threatened him and the rest of his family if he went to the police with the truth.

The investigators considered asking a judge to grant another search warrant, not just for Moselle but for the house at Almeda where Alex had visited his mother. But they decided it was too risky, as another warrant would have alerted Alex that SLED had him in its sights. Better to keep Alex talking.

Agent Owen thought about his own boys and the way his love for them defined him and gave him purpose. He packed their lunches, took them to orthodontist appointments, and planned his life around their practices and games. The notion of a father gunning down his son was unimaginable to him.

Other investigators were having less difficulty making that leap. Deputy Rutland was stuck on how clean Alex's clothes had been that night, the lack of blood on his white shirt or his shoes. Rutland thought it almost certain Alex had changed before police arrived. Why would he do that unless he was the killer?

Agent Croft, who had sat behind Alex in the Durango during the second interview, had no doubts. Croft and Owen had repeatedly watched the dashcam video of that session. Every time, they were struck by how casually Alex lied. The two detectives noticed a pattern. Whenever the agents' questions keyed in on the kennels, Alex broke down. To Croft, the witness wasn't succumbing to grief. He was attempting to distract them.

There was one more thing. When Alex had talked about the severity of Paul's wounds, he'd broken down and said, "They did him so bad." At least, that's how Owen had heard it. But Croft had heard it differently. To his ears, Alex had said:

"I did him so bad."

CHAPTER TWENTY-EIGHT

Hundreds of people crowded into the Hampton cemetery for Maggie and Paul's funeral. The guests included out-of-town cousins, childhood friends, former clients, and fellow lawyers, all parked along the grassy road, some directly across from the Holly Street house where Alex and Maggie had raised the boys. The family plot was ringed by iron gates and marked with a marble slab embellished with carved roses, the final resting place of the men who had started it all, Randolph Sr. and Old Buster. Temporary markers showed where Maggie and Paul's remains would be buried once their autopsies were complete.

In his eulogy, Ronnie Crosby described Paul as a sweet and funny young man who left clothes lying around at houses across the state. Liz Murdaugh said her sister-in-law and nephew shared a devotion to their family and were well lived and well loved. She thanked young Buster for his strength in the wake of devastating loss and told Alex she'd been in awe of his "almost inhuman devotion" to Maggie.

The day was so hot and the air so heavy that four people had to be treated by paramedics. After an hour, the skies opened. The deluge toppled flower arrangements, ruined church shoes, and soaked black dresses to the skin. The mourners rushed to their cars, cutting the service short.

The rain cleared in time for the wake at Moselle. Guests poured brown liquor drinks and piled fried chicken and barbecue on their plates. Some of the mourners whispered about how eerie it felt to be gathered so close to the murder scene. They wondered if it was safe to be there with the killer still on the loose. The most persistent whisper was about the blond woman in the shortest skirt and highest heels, known around town as Alex's longtime mistress. Maggie's friends were shocked that the woman had posted a selfie from the cemetery. Now she was striding around Moselle.

Maggie's sister, Marian Proctor, had barely seen Alex that week, he'd been so barraged by friends and family. She hugged him and asked if there was any word on the investigation. Alex told her the police had no leads but he had a partial theory.

"I think whoever did it," he said, "had thought about it for a long time."

Blanca appeared on the upstairs balcony. Years before, she and Maggie had made a pact. Whoever died first, the other would sing at the funeral. Blanca had been scheduled to sing "Amazing Grace" at the graveside, but the rain had driven everyone away. Now she looked out over the mourners and resolved herself against tears, singing the lyrics she had rehearsed with Maggie so long ago inside this very house:

> *Through many dangers, toils and snares*
> *I have already come*
> *'Tis grace that brought me safe thus far*
> *And grace will lead me home*

Blanca knew, better than almost anyone else, the toils and snares that had troubled Maggie. As Blanca sang, she imagined her friend's face. She didn't know who had murdered Maggie and Paul, but she hoped God's grace had finally allowed them peace.

. . .

THE MURDAUGHS RETURNED to the Hampton cemetery that Sunday, three days after the first funeral. The hearse carrying Randolph's coffin was followed by a curving procession of patrol cars from every law enforcement agency in the Fourteenth Circuit. Close to two hundred mourners gathered around the family plot, where Randolph was buried alongside his father and grandfather.

The sweep of the loss declared itself in the three new graves. The mourners understood they were witnessing the end of a dynasty.

The speakers at Randolph III's funeral talked about his love of his grandchildren, the way he told each of them they were his favorite, all the times he fished and hunted with Buster and Paul. They talked about the day he won the Order of the Palmetto, about his gift for making people feel special, about his love of drinking and smoking and chocolate, about the way he had advised other trial lawyers never to assume they were smarter than the jury.

"Goodbye, my loyal friend," said Donnie Myers, another veteran prosecutor. "Goodbye, my brother."

Libby, Randolph's wife of sixty years, attended the funeral despite her dementia. She'd been told her husband had died. But afterward, she seemed to forget he was gone. Some saw that as a mercy.

THE MOURNERS GATHERED for a reception at Almeda. White tents dotted the lawn, shielding the guests from the summer sun. Libby stayed inside in her hospital bed by the window, her caregiver Shelley Smith in the recliner by her. Shelley had worked for the family for several years, watching over Mrs. Libby four nights a week, making sure she was fed and safe and taking her meds. Most nights, they watched the Game Show Network, Mrs. Libby's favorite.

As the reception wound down, Alex came into the house to check on his mother. Alex and Shelley had gone to school together but Alex didn't usually say much to her beyond hello. But this evening he noted he hadn't seen Shelley since the night of the murders.

< Randolph Murdaugh Sr. was the first of the Murdaugh men to serve as solicitor, or lead prosecutor, for South Carolina's Fourteenth Judicial Circuit, from 1920–1940. He built this home in 1916 in the small town of Varnville, where he raised his family.

^ Randolph "Buster" Murdaugh Jr. took over as solicitor at age twenty-five. He solidified the family's power and wielded it relentlessly over the course of his reign, which stretched from 1940 to 1986, or Roosevelt to Reagan.

< Randolph Murdaugh III was more laid back than his forebears and largely content to let the Murdaugh machine run itself. He served as solicitor from 1986 to 2006 and continued as a volunteer assistant solicitor along with one of his sons, Richard Alexander "Alex" Murdaugh.

A Murdaugh family photo, as it was introduced by the defense as evidence at trial. Alex and his wife, Margaret "Maggie" Branstetter Murdaugh, and their two sons, Richard Alexander "Buster" Murdaugh Jr. (left) and Paul Terry Murdaugh (second from left), lived a glamorous lifestyle, at least on the surface. This photo was taken in spring 2021, just weeks before Maggie and Paul were killed. >

^ The house built by Randolph Murdaugh Sr. was the homeplace for the Murdaughs for more than a century. Buster Murdaugh raised his children there, too, and his son Randolph III moved the house out to family property at Almeda in the year 2000. Alex went to Almeda to check on his mother the night of the murders and establish an alibi.

The Murdaugh law firm's headquarters on Mulberry Street in Hampton is the grandest building in the county. It is across the street from where Randolph Sr. founded the firm in 1910 and a few hundred yards from the courthouse. It is now the Parker Law Group. >

< Portraits of the Murdaugh men hang in several courthouses in the five counties of the Fourteenth Judicial Circuit, including in Hampton County, seen here, from left to right, Randolph III, Buster, and Randolph Sr. A judge removed a portrait of Old Buster from the main courtroom in the Colleton County courthouse to ensure that Alex could get a fair trial.

< Sandy Smith with her son, Stephen, who was killed in 2015.

Stephen Smith's body was found in the middle of Sandy Run Road, a deserted stretch connecting Hampton and the farming community of Crocketville. The road was originally paved with clay in 1916 with contributions from civic leaders, including Randolph Murdaugh Sr. >

Gloria Satterfield was the Murdaugh housekeeper for twenty years and helped raise Buster and Paul. Gloria fell down the front steps at Moselle, hit her head, and died in the hospital three weeks later. Alex told her sons that he felt responsible because she'd been startled by the family dogs and said he planned to sue himself so they would get some money for bills from an insurance settlement. ∨

^ Mallory Beach was nineteen years old when she went on a date with her boyfriend and two other couples to an oyster roast near Beaufort, S.C. The couples were traveling home by boat to spend the night on Murdaugh Island when a drunken Paul Murdaugh crashed into the Archers Creek bridge, killing Mallory.

< The seventeen-foot boat was beached beside the bridge for more than twelve hours because Alex Murdaugh would not give permission for a police search. Investigators eventually took DNA samples and clothing as evidence from the boat but it subsequently disappeared.

Two months after the wreck, the South Carolina Law Enforcement Division, or SLED, charged twenty-year-old Paul Murdaugh with boating under the influence causing death, a felony punishable by decades in prison. >

^ The Murdaugh property known as Moselle is a sprawling and wooded 1,700 acres. The main house (top right) is about 250 yards down a dirt road from an equipment shed (lower center, silver roof) and an old airplane hangar (lower left, red roof) that the family used as a workshop. Across from the hangar was a long narrow run of covered dog kennels.

Alex Murdaugh, seen here in police body cam footage, called 911 on the night of June 7, 2021, to say that Maggie and Paul had been shot. He told Colleton County Sheriff's Sergeant Daniel Greene, the first officer on the scene, that he had not seen them for more than two hours prior to finding their bodies. >

< At the defense's request, the jury visited Moselle at the end of testimony. The author represented print media as the pool reporter. She is standing in the spot where Maggie fell when she was shot, twelve steps from the concrete pad outside the kennel feed room where Paul fell, marked by Court TV videographer Steven Gresham.

Mark Tinsley is a lawyer at a small firm in Allendale, S.C., roughly twenty minutes' drive from Hampton. He knew when he agreed to sue Alex for the wrongful death of Mallory Beach that he would be burning bridges with his former friend and with the powerful Murdaugh firm. He said he took the case because he was the only lawyer around who could: "I knew the playbook." >

< Alex Murdaugh was tried on double-murder charges in early 2023 at the Colleton County Courthouse in Walterboro, S.C. The courthouse was designed in 1820 by Charleston architect Robert Mills, who designed many iconic public structures, including the Washington Monument.

Judge Clifton Newman was tapped by the chief justice of the state supreme court to oversee the Murdaugh criminal cases, which included the two murder charges as well as roughly a hundred financial charges. Newman, a twenty-year veteran of the bench, was known for his calm demeanor and his insistence on order in the courtroom. >

< Buster Murdaugh was in the courtroom every day, sitting behind his father. About halfway through the trial, the judge forced Buster and other family members to move back several rows after they broke courtroom rules on interaction with Alex.

^ SLED Agent David Owen was the lead investigator in the case. His mother died the day before he testified. He was questioned by veteran prosecutor John Meadors about key pieces of evidence, including the clean pair of cargo shorts Alex was wearing when deputies arrived.

Crime scene expert Kenneth Kinsey maintained that the killer was crouched below Paul when he fired the second fatal shotgun blast. Kinsey demonstrated the trajectory with a dowel rod held to the temple of lead prosecutor Creighton Waters. >

< Prosecutors introduced multiple guns belonging to the Murdaugh family to show that they had thoroughly searched the property for the missing murder weapons. At one point, defense lawyer Dick Harpootlian brandished a .300 Blackout rifle in the tight confines of the historic courtroom, seeming to aim at the prosecution table. "Tempting," he said.

^ Jurors said the two days that Alex Murdaugh took the stand were the most important of the six-week trial. Alex showed emotion throughout his testimony, though several jurors said they only ever saw snot and no tears.

^ Alex wore a sport coat every day of the trial until the morning after the verdict was read. He was wearing a prison jumpsuit and showed no emotion as Judge Newman sentenced him to two sentences of life in prison.

"I was here, what, thirty to forty minutes that night?" she remembered Alex asking.

Shelley was thrown off guard.

"No," she said. "I think it was more like fifteen to twenty minutes."

Alex said he thought for sure it was longer. Switching subjects, he asked how Shelley was liking her other job at a local elementary school, where she worked in the cafeteria. He said he knew it was hard sitting up through the nights with his mother and then going to school in the morning.

"When do you sleep, Shelley?" he asked.

"Oh," she said, "I catnap here and there."

He looked at Shelley. If she wanted a different job at the school, he said, he had friends who could make that happen.

She said she was fine. But Alex wasn't done.

"I heard you're getting married," he said.

Shelley nodded. Yes, she said, she was scheduled to remarry that fall.

"Just let me know what you need," he said. "I know weddings can be expensive."

Shelley was rattled. Once he left, she called her brother, a local police officer, and told him what had happened. Her brother told her to do what their mother always told them, which was to tell the truth, even if it hurts.

The next time she saw Alex was two days later. It was near dawn, toward the end of her shift, when he knocked on the door. She was startled, because he never came by that early. He was carrying what looked like a blue tarp balled up in his arms, and he walked past her with it and went up the stairs, toward a part of the house no one had used for years.

She heard Mr. Alex come back downstairs and thought he'd gone, when out of the corner of her eye she saw Mr. Randolph's truck puttering around the property. She looked out the window but couldn't see exactly what was happening because the catering equipment was still parked outside. As best she could tell, Alex appeared to be driving back to the smokehouse. A few minutes later, he drove away in a black truck. She'd never seen him drive anything but the Suburban.

A little later, when Shelley left, she saw a large blue raincoat laid across a rocking chair, the one Mrs. Libby got for her retirement. It must have been a raincoat, not a tarp, that Alex had carried upstairs.

When she came back the next evening, the raincoat was gone.

ON JUNE 25, Alex and Buster announced a $100,000 reward for information leading to an arrest and conviction.

"Now is the time to bring justice for Maggie and Paul," they said in a statement.

Beverly Cook already thought she knew who was responsible. From the moment she heard about Maggie and Paul's deaths, Beverly had no doubt that Alex had killed them. A few days later she had an even more horrifying thought: Alex was setting up her son to take the fall.

Anthony had called her in a panic one day from his job site with the utility company. His foreman had come over to where he was working on a power line, thirty feet above the ground in the bucket of a cherry picker. In front of the crew, the foreman had called up to Anthony and told him to come down. Some investigators from SLED wanted to talk to him. They were still pursuing Alex's theory that the murders were connected to the boat crash. Anthony called Beverly right away.

"Mom," he said, "they want my DNA."

Anthony had not seen Paul since Mallory Beach's funeral, partly out of deference to the legal proceedings and partly because it was too painful. But the two young men had been close before, even mulling semi-serious plans to start a logging business out at Moselle. Many nights, Anthony and Paul had drunk beer and shot pool in the gun room and gone out on the golf cart hunting hogs. Anthony had no doubt his DNA would be all over the place, particularly on the guns.

Beverly was incensed. Like the other passengers on the boat and their families, Anthony had already given the detectives his alibi for the night of the murders. He'd spent the evening with his parents, who had confirmed it. Now the agents were humiliating him on the job and sending him into another anxious spiral.

The next day, Anthony told his boss he needed to work on the ground for a while. He did not feel safe in the box on a hot line with his mind somewhere else.

THE MURDERS HAD a ripple effect. An anonymous report, spreading rapidly through the news coverage, alleged that SLED had opened an investigation into Alex's role in covering up his son's culpability in Mallory's death. In fact, this was true, but SLED wasn't ready to say so.

Sandy Smith heard rumors that SLED would be looking into Stephen's death at long last, too, nearly six years after his body was found in the road. Reporters kept knocking on her door as late as 1:30 A.M. and sending her little dog, Mercedes, into a panic. One day, a couple of SLED agents showed up, asking her for a DNA swab. Given Sandy's animosity toward the Murdaughs, the agents said, they had to eliminate her as a suspect in Paul's and Maggie's murders. It was a slap in the face.

Todd Proctor, the former Highway Patrol trooper who'd led the initial investigation into Stephen's death, used the attention on the murders to speak freely about Stephen's case. In an interview with Fox News, the trooper repeated his long-held contention that Stephen had not died in a hit-and-run.

"It looked like it was more staged," Proctor said. "Like possibly the body had been placed in the roadway."

A few days later, SLED announced an investigation into Stephen's death based on information uncovered in the double homicide case. The agency said nothing about what had triggered the investigation. Social media rushed to fill in the blanks, repeating rumors about the presence of a Murdaugh's name in Stephen's little black book. There were other reports, unconfirmed by SLED, that in the early hours after

Stephen's body was found in the road, one of the Murdaughs' trucks had been taken to a body shop for repairs.

Gloria Satterfield's family kept seeing her name pop up in the coverage and didn't know what to think. Her son Tony was surprised when his uncles showed him a FITSNews.com article about a settlement in the case for $505,000.

In late June, Tony called Alex. Tony said he was sad to hear about Maggie and Paul and quickly got to the reason for his call. Was there any word on a settlement in his mother's death?

Alex thanked him for his kindness and said the good news was that the insurer was close to settling the case. Again, he failed to mention that he'd already received and burned through two settlements totaling $4.3 million.

"Don't worry," he told Tony. "I expect we'll settle this by the end of the year."

CHAPTER TWENTY-NINE

Weeks were slipping by. The police still had no leads on anyone who might want to hurt Maggie and Paul. They had dragged the Salkehatchie River and searched across every acre at Moselle by foot, four-wheeler, and drone, and still could not find the missing murder weapons. Nothing was breaking their way.

John Marvin had helped them recover Maggie's cellphone from the deep grass off Moselle Road. Working with the texts, emails, and calls from that phone, the investigators were building a timeline of what Maggie had been doing in the hours before the murders. They could not account for how her phone had ended up a mile or so away, discarded in the grass. The investigators hoped the phone's GPS data might offer some answers. But when they tried to download the data, they discovered they were too late. Downloading phone data is a finicky business, with phone cracking software struggling to keep pace with encryption technology. By the time SLED hacked into the GPS history on Maggie's phone, the phone's software had overwritten the data from June 7 to make way for more recent information. All that the GPS data showed was that the phone was at SLED headquarters.

The investigators had Paul's iPhone but couldn't unlock it. As Alex and others had explained, Paul had been so secretive he hadn't shared his passcode with anyone, as far as they knew. He hadn't synched the phone to the iCloud, either, which meant they had no way of accessing his call log, or his texts, or his emails or photos or videos, all of which could have told them a great deal not just about his movements on the night of the murder but also about anyone he'd been planning to see that night, anyone who might have been angry with him, anyone who might have been threatening him. Now the investigators were stuck. They knew that if they kept guessing at Paul's code and getting it wrong, the phone would lock them out and might even erase the data inside.

At the start of Alex's second interview with SLED, he had allowed them to download the contents of his own phone, including the GPS data on his movements. After studying his texts and calls and the GPS data, they were building a minute-by-minute timeline of what he had been doing that night. But there were gaps in the timeline during which the phone's contents did not conclusively establish his whereabouts. They knew he had in fact driven to Almeda in his Suburban to check on his mother, but they could not determine precisely when and at what speed. Most Suburbans had a black box that recorded the vehicle's movements via the OnStar telematics system. But when the police checked with General Motors to access the data, their contact told them it was not possible. Alex's Suburban was so new that the company's encryption tools were unable to retrieve the information.

Crime scene techs had searched Maggie's Mercedes but had found no blood or DNA evidence. The sheriff's deputies had seen one significant item that gave them pause: Maggie's wedding ring, tucked in between the door and the driver's seat. But they didn't know what to make of it. Did Maggie always wear her ring? If so, its discovery under the seat might have suggested discord that contradicted Alex's rosy description of the marriage. It was also possible that Maggie sometimes removed the ring, maybe to get her nails done, and had hidden it under her seat while she was inside the salon. She'd gotten a pedicure late on the afternoon of the murder, but there was no evidence of anyone working on her fingernails, nothing that might have prompted her to remove the ring.

SLED still had found nothing pointing to anyone other than Alex, but they had zero physical evidence linking him to the crime. Owen and Croft had left the second interview convinced that Alex had lied to them about his movements that night, but afterward, when they studied the GPS data from his phone, it contained nothing proving their suspicions that he'd gone down to the kennels; as best they could tell, his phone had stayed at the house until Alex left for Almeda. His admission that he'd been frustrated with Paul's recklessness—combined with the obvious tensions of the boat wreck case—left no doubt that the rest of the family's home life was far from perfect as well. Croft believed Alex had accidentally admitted to killing Paul, but when Owen reviewed the interview video again, he still thought he heard Alex saying "They did him so bad," not "I did him so bad."

Something was off. But Owen and Croft knew they still did not have the proof to officially label Alex as a suspect, and they were careful to avoid using that word. They just kept grinding away.

They sent out a flurry of search warrants, including to Snapchat, seeking subscriber information for Paul 9499, Paul's username. In early July, Snapchat responded with a batch of files. Among them was a six-second video Paul sent out an hour or so before he died. Such snaps typically disappear once they're watched, but Paul had saved this one to his memories. Paul had shot the video while he and his father were riding around Moselle at dusk. Alex is standing in a tilled field, fiddling with what appeared to be a dying fruit tree. Paul is laughing.

Alex was wearing a light blue shirt, khaki pants, and loafers, not the white T-shirt, cargo shorts, and pink running shoes he'd had on when the first deputies arrived at the scene. Clearly, he had changed. But when? And why?

Agent Owen and his colleagues watched and rewatched all the other videos they had, searching for clues they might have missed. They pored over the dash cam footage of the interviews with Alex in Owen's Durango and the body cam footage from investigators in the hours after the murders, when they'd searched the kennels and looked through the house. They were watching the film from Agent Croft's body cam when they noticed something strange. Croft had been walk-ing through the house's gun room, joining the initial search for the murder weapons, when his camera caught a small object resting on top of a filing cabinet next to the room's gun rack. It was an empty Capri Sun, with its straw still sticking out of the shiny pouch. On the front of the pouch was a promo for *PAW Patrol,* an animated kids' show about superhero dogs fighting crime.

They froze the video to study their discovery more closely. By now SLED agents had read Maggie's texts and had interviewed Blanca, the Murdaughs' housekeeper. They knew that the only Capri Suns in the house were the two boxes she had bought for Alex on the morning of the murders. But Blanca said Alex had slept late, then immediately left for work, which meant he'd had no time to drink one that morning. He'd been at the office all afternoon and had returned home early in the evening, just before Paul joined him to ride around the property. Alex had said he'd spent the early evening roaming Moselle with Paul; the GPS activity on his iPhone bore that out. That meant he'd probably opened the Capri Sun sometime after dinner. When he was done, he'd left it next to the gun rack.

Was it possible that Alex had actually been sipping a Capri Sun as he grabbed the guns and headed down to the kennels? The notion seemed almost too bizarre to contemplate—a father sipping a sweet children's drink through a straw just before slaughtering his wife and son. But by now the investigators had learned that in this case anything was pos-sible.

IN THE WAKE of the killings, Alex was showered in sympathy. His friends and family fretted over his safety and his health. Clients brought him homemade meals and colleagues picked up his workload. Jeanne Seckinger stopped asking about the missing $792,000, figuring it could wait until things settled down.

During the lull in scrutiny, Alex went to work ginning up the missing money Jeanne had been after him about. He borrowed $250,000 from his managing partner, Johnny Parker, who never turned him down, knowing Alex would have plenty of money to repay him when the firm paid out bonuses at the end of the year. Even though Alex had a subprime credit score and owed Palmetto State Bank millions of dollars, he persuaded his childhood friend Russell Laffitte, the bank's chief executive, to sign off on another $750,000 line of credit, this time off the books. Alex used $400,000 to pay down his overdrawn checking account. He used the loan from Parker and the rest of the line of credit to wire $600,000 to Chris Wilson's law firm. He told Chris he had screwed up the way he had invested the original fee in an annuity and couldn't pay it all back outright. He asked his best friend to front the missing $192,000 until Randolph III's will and Maggie's were sorted out. Then he'd have plenty of cash.

It was all tidied up by mid-July. Chris emailed the Murdaugh firm to say he had the money after all and would be glad to send it over. What Alex didn't mention was that he was still cutting dozens of checks to his drug dealer, Curtis Eddie Smith, whose nickname was Cousin Eddie. All told, Alex paid $305,000 to Cousin Eddie that summer and wrote a $5,000 check to his friend Greg Alexander, the Yemassee police chief who'd shown up so inexplicably at the murder scene.

Alex and Buster were living with Maggie's parents in Summerville, about an hour east of Hampton. Alex had always been close to his in-laws, but in the wake of the murders he clung tight to them, making a show of putting flowers on Maggie's grave and crying at the mention of their daughter's name. At his friends' urging, he carried on with at least a semblance of a social life. He went to a fishing tournament in Edisto, a water festival in Beaufort, and a July Fourth celebration thrown by one of his law partners. Alex often brought Buster with him to the family's house in Edisto, the two of them boating from one party to another.

In late July, he and Buster joined Maggie's family in Key West, staying with them at her sister Marian's house. Marian fretted about Alex and Buster's safety and urged Alex to hire a bodyguard. If it was true that the attack had been some kind of retribution for the boat crash, wouldn't the killer or killers want other members of the family dead, too? But Alex saw no need to hire any protection. He kept his focus on clearing Paul's name and making sure Buster got back into law school as soon as possible.

The contradiction nagged at Marian. Everyone around Alex was concerned for both his and Buster's safety. But as far as she could tell, he didn't seem afraid at all.

BEFORE HE LEFT for Key West, Alex had called Agent Owen to ask if he could get his golf clubs out of the Suburban. Buster had also been asking about some of the guns seized from the house, including his own .300 Blackout. He wanted them back.

Owen said the Suburban was inoperable, since the car's computer system had been removed. But he said Alex could swing by the office before he left and retrieve his clubs and any clothing that had been in the car. The family's guns, Owen said, needed to remain in custody. Alex asked for an update on the case when he came by, but Owen had to dash to an interview. They arranged to talk once Alex returned from Key West.

In spite of the lack of new developments, the murders continued to dominate the news. An issue of *People* magazine featured the case on its cover. "PERFECT" FAMILY, SHOCKING MURDERS, read the headline, which was accompanied by a glamour shot of the Murdaughs, with Maggie in a ball gown, flanked by Paul on one side and Alex and Buster on the other, all three of the men in tuxedos. A yellow circle was over-laid on the photo, with a subhead reading, "DID SOMEONE TAKE JUSTICE INTO THEIR OWN HANDS?"

The issue was still on the stands on August 11, when Alex met with Agent Owen at the SLED office in Walterboro. Alex was accompanied by Cory Fleming, his law school classmate and associate on many big cases, including the Satterfield settlement. Owen escorted the two men to a small conference room where they settled around a table, making small talk. Owen lamented that the air-conditioning had gone out at his house and they all commiserated about the August heat.

Owen thanked them for coming in. Before he answered any of their questions, he said there were some things he needed to ask Alex first.

"Wait a minute," Fleming said. "Hold on. Maybe I'm mistaken, but I thought we were coming here so you can update him."

"I intend to," Owen said. "The update is, I'm doing the investigation, and I have some questions I need answers to."

Fleming pointed his finger at Owen.

"I need you to answer this question," he said, enunciating each word carefully. "Are you asking him questions to further your investigation? Or are you asking him questions because you think that he's a suspect?"

"I am asking these questions to further my investigation."

Fleming raised his voice. "Then does that mean you're not asking him questions as a suspect?" he said. "I'm not comfortable with you asking him questions as a suspect."

Owen had to resist the urge to come across the table at Fleming, matching the lawyer's combativeness with his own. Owen took a beat and slowly leaned back in his chair.

"Let me respond to your question," Owen said. "I told Alex this when we first met. Any homicide investigation, you start with the closest person, and/or the person who found the deceased. In both cases, that's Alex. Everybody stays in that investigation until we can get them out. And right now, because of the questions I have I need explanations for, I cannot get Alex out."

Alex nodded multiple times, saying that he understood. Fleming sat back in his chair, seemingly placated. "That's a reasonable statement," he said.

Fleming explained he was worried that SLED might have believed everything they read on the internet. There were so many wild rumors. "Everybody in the United States of America has an opinion on this case," Fleming said. But he said because he knew everybody involved, he knew it was all a bunch of bullshit.

Owen said he was trying to tune out the noise and focus on the facts. He ran Alex through the timeline of his whereabouts on June 7. Again, Alex explained that he'd ridden around with Paul for a couple of hours, met up with Maggie at the house for dinner, taken a nap while Maggie and Paul went down to the kennels, and then gone to visit his mom at Almeda for forty-five minutes to an hour.

Alex began to cry. *Maggie wasn't supposed to come home that night*, he said. "I've since found out that she was worried about me, and me worrying about my dad, and so she came home."

Owen knew that was a lie. Maggie's sister, Marian, and the housekeeper, Blanca, had both said Alex had asked Maggie to return to Moselle. Seeing her show up would not have been a surprise.

By now Owen understood that Alex was lying about several details. But he saw no advantage in focusing on this one right now. His goal was to prove who had killed Paul and Maggie, and with the questions he needed to ask, he believed this interview would probably be his last conversation with Alex. If Owen lost his focus or his cool, the session would be over. He remained calm even as he asked Alex about the Snapchat video Paul had recorded on his phone, the one that showed Alex fiddling with the leaning sapling.

"You were wearing khaki pants and a dress shirt," the investigator said. "When I met you that night, you were in shorts and a T-shirt. At one point in the evening, did you change clothes?"

What time had the video been shot, Alex asked. He said he assumed he would have already changed into his shorts.

Owen said the video appeared to have been taken around dusk, between 7:30 P.M. and 8 P.M.

"I guess I changed when I got back to the house," Alex said.

Owen turned to what Rogan Gibson kept saying, that he felt sure he'd heard Alex's voice in the background when he'd talked with Paul that night at the kennels. Owen asked Alex why Rogan would be mistaken about that, given he'd spent his entire life around Alex.

Alex said Rogan had already asked him if he'd been at the kennels. "He said he thought it was me."

"Was it you?"

"At nine o'clock?" Alex said. "No, sir. Not if my times are right."

Fleming interrupted to pass along an offer from Alex's brother Randy. The Murdaughs knew everyone in town, from richest to poorest, and they'd like to ask all their contacts to put feelers out, maybe get people talking. Owen had already spoken with Randy about the offer and said SLED couldn't sanction that type of off-the-books investigation.

Owen asked Alex if he had questions for him. Alex asked whether Maggie or Paul had been shot first and whether either of them had seen the other die. Owen said those questions were impossible to answer. Alex asked if they had suffered. Owen said he felt sure they hadn't suffered long. The investigator promised that he and Alex were the two people most invested in knowing what had happened.

The interview had ranged from logistics and small talk to confrontation and retreat. Alex wrapped up his questions by asking Owen to talk to Maggie's parents, as they were eager for an update. Owen said he would.

Owen paused and took a breath. He sat back from the table, his back straight and hands on his knees, facing Alex head-on. Then he said what he expected would be the last words he'd ever speak to Alex.

"Did you kill Maggie?" he said.

If Alex was angry, he didn't show it. He didn't raise his voice or stomp away. He remained seated, arms folded and legs crossed.

"Did I kill my wife?" Alex said. "No, David."

"Do you know who did?"

"No, I do not know who did it," Alex said.

"Did you kill Paul?"

"No, I did not kill Paul."

"Do you know who did?"

"No, sir, I do not know who did," Alex said. "Do you think I killed Maggie?"

Owen held his hands palms up and repeatedly moved one up and one down, as though he were balancing a scale.

"I have to go where the evidence and the facts take me."

"Do you think I killed Paul?"

"I don't have anything that points me to anybody else," Owen said.

"So does that mean that I am a suspect?"

Owen said he had to put his beliefs aside and go with the facts. Maggie and Paul had been killed with family guns, he pointed out. Shell casings from the missing Blackout, found near the house, matched the casings of the shells that had killed Maggie. Finally, the investigator noted that no one else's DNA had been found at the murder scene.

"Well," said Alex, "I understand."

With that, the interview was over. In an hour, Alex had gone from a grieving husband to the sole suspect in the brutal murders of his wife and son.

CHAPTER THIRTY

By the end of summer, Alex was staying in Hampton at a guest house behind his law partner Johnny Parker's house. He asked Blanca to come to the house and talk with him, which was rare. He never sat still long enough to talk.

Blanca met him at the house and sat down on the couch in the small living room. Alex remained standing, pacing.

"I got a bad feeling," he said. "Something's not right."

He said there was a video of him taken the evening Maggie and Paul were killed. Blanca didn't know what he was talking about and didn't say anything.

"You remember that Vinnie Vines shirt," he said. "You know I was wearing that shirt that day."

Blanca was thrown off guard. She felt that Alex was pressuring her to say something that wasn't true. She clearly remembered that on the morning of June 7, he'd had on a blue polo shirt under his sport coat, because she'd fixed his collar as he left for work. He had not been wearing the button-up Columbia shirt that they joked was Vineyard Vines. She hadn't seen it for months.

Blanca didn't say anything. Alex let it drop. After so many years, maybe he had learned she wasn't someone to be pushed around.

. . .

HIS SENSE THAT the tide was turning against him was well founded. He knew he was the only suspect in the murders. He knew SLED was retracing his every step. Now the investigators were asking him about the clothes he'd been wearing, especially the pants and shirt he'd had on in the Snapchat video, only a short time before the murders. And they knew that by the time the police arrived, he'd been wearing something else.

After months of stagnation, the case was finally gaining momentum. Duffie Stone, the solicitor who had initially refused to relinquish jurisdiction, quietly turned over control of the homicide case to state prosecutors. For months, Stone had brushed off the attorney general's pleas and the public outcry over his conflict of interest with the Murdaugh family. But once SLED briefed him on the most recent interview with Alex, Stone's position became untenable.

With the criminal charges against Paul dropped in the boat case, Mark Tinsley tried to keep the pressure on SLED not to forget its investigation into Alex's attempted cover-up in the emergency room. Connor Cook's lawyer, Joe McCulloch—an old hand who knew a good stunt when he saw one—filed a hundred-page motion asking the judge in the boat crash case to let him take additional depositions from the DNR agents on the scene at Archers Creek. McCulloch understood that the judge would almost certainly not grant his motion. But he also knew that reporters were closely following every new document filed in the case. Even if his motion died in court, its contents would draw more attention to all the ways Alex had tried to hide his son's responsibility for the crash.

A few weeks later, as the investigators dug deeper into the murder case, DNR released hundreds of pages of documents and several videos from the boat crash investigations. Internet sleuths scoured all of it, posting their theories about what had really happened on the night of the crash. They marked up photos of the boat, circling bloodstains they took as indications that Connor was on the passenger's side at the time of the crash. They used Morgan Doughty's and Connor Cook's depositions to make a timeline of Paul's previous drunken wrecks. They built string maps resembling the ones on the walls in TV cop shows, showing the relationships between the investigators and the Murdaughs.

The revelations—about the family and the ways they hid their secrets—were piling up.

THE MURDAUGHS WERE not accustomed to being under siege. It did not sit well. At the encouragement of the partners at the family firm, all of the Murdaugh men—Alex, Randy IV, John Marvin, and Buster—attended the annual trial lawyers' association convention in Hilton Head two months after the murders. John Marvin and Buster weren't lawyers. But when all four of them stepped under the lights at the high-profile event, their presence conveyed a message. It didn't matter if the national media was digging into the family's connection to a string of suspicious deaths or if commentators were openly knocking the family for acting like entitled noblemen running a manor. Come what may, the Murdaughs were not cowed.

Late one evening, after meetings and happy hour and dinner, a group of trial lawyers and some of their wives gathered at the hotel bar. McCulloch, Connor's lawyer, was chatting with the others when he looked up and saw a phalanx of Murdaugh men coming down the hallway, with onlookers stepping aside like the parting of the Red Sea.

McCulloch kept talking, trying to ignore Alex and his entourage. After a few minutes, one of his friends pulled him aside and told him to look out because Buster was circling him. Even more disconcerting, the younger man was muttering, "Why is he doing this to us?"

McCulloch looked up and saw Buster staring at him. *Like a hyena sizing up his prey,* McCulloch thought.

Eager to avoid a scene, Joe and his wife headed back to their suite.

The intimidation tactics did not silence the gossip. In the halls and in the quiet corners of the conference, all the talk was about Alex. Only a couple of years before, Alex had served as the association's president. Now he was a walking scandal.

People could easily see the toll the summer had taken on him. He had lost at least forty pounds and was a shadow of his former self, at least physically. But he held court by the swimming pool, a drink always in his hand, Buster at his side.

Tinsley had stayed home that year. It struck him as unseemly to mix and mingle so soon after the murders of Maggie and Paul. But lawyers kept texting him pictures of Alex going table to table shaking hands at the Red Fish grill. He was told that Alex alternated between acting as if nothing had happened and bursting into tears when talking about Paul.

Alex's partners understood that he was taking medication to help him sleep and control his anxiety. His behavior had grown so erratic that his friend Chris Wilson wondered whether Alex might try to kill himself. Alex's financial struggles made it all the worse. Alex still owed Chris $192,000, which was more than Chris could afford to lose. As much as it pained him to admit it, Chris needed something in writing about the debt or else he'd never be able to make a claim against Alex's estate. Wilson buttonholed his friend, scribbled out a promissory note on a legal pad, and asked Alex to sign it. Alex said he understood his friend's concerns and signed the scrap of paper, promising to pay Wilson back within sixty days.

At the law firm, Jeanne Seckinger had been glad to see the $792,000 fee show up in July. *Better late than never,* she thought. But she and Annette Griswold, Alex's paralegal, both still feared Alex was keeping something from them. He was almost never in the office anymore. When he came in, he tended to sit at his desk reading sympathy cards for an hour before calling it a day.

On the Thursday before Labor Day weekend, Annette couldn't find a file in the cabinet and assumed it was somewhere in the clutter on Alex's desk, the black hole that sucked in so many missing things. Alex didn't like her in his office, but Annette needed the file, especially with the holiday weekend approaching. She found the folder on top of the pile on his desk. She opened it, and a check fluttered out, like a feather softly sinking to the ground.

Annette felt as if she was in a movie scene. When she picked up what had fluttered to the ground, she saw it was a canceled check for the missing $792,000, endorsed and deposited by Alex back in March. A burst of hurt surged through Annette, followed by anger. She felt strangely vindicated that she had been right. He'd been lying to her all along.

She went back to her desk and called Jeanne.

"I just found something," Annette said.

"Oh, shit," Jeanne said. "What did you find? Come on over."

Annette went to Jeanne's office and flipped the check in her direction.

"That's one of the fee checks that doesn't exist."

Jeanne sat back in her chair. She had already been pulling records and had suspicions about missing fees in at least two of Alex's other cases, maybe more. Now, with this new evidence from Annette, she accelerated her search and was alarmed to find check after check made out to an entity called "doing business as Forge." It appeared to mimic Forge Consulting, a business used by the Murdaugh firm for investing client settlement money and attorney fees. The checks to the fake Forge account had all been endorsed by Alex and deposited in a Bank of America account. There was no legitimate reason for him to have done this. Client settlement money and attorney fees were required to be routed through the firm for legal, tax, and accounting purposes. The only reason to bypass the firm would be to hide money so Alex could steal it.

Within hours, she was ready to take the evidence she'd found to some of the top partners, including the firm treasurer and Alex's personal lawyer. That evening, Jeanne met with all of them at a partner's plantation home. Ronnie Crosby, the senior partner who'd eulogized Paul, arrived as the others were coming to grips with the awful truth.

"You're going to need a drink," said Danny Henderson, the partner who'd sat with Alex in Agent Owen's patrol car the night of the homicides. "Maybe more than one."

Crosby flipped through the canceled checks. Some were for fees that should have gone to the firm to be distributed among the partners, some were for settlements that should have gone to clients. Already they had discovered millions of dollars in stolen funds. They had no idea how much more they'd find.

"We have to fire Alex," Crosby said. "He can no longer practice with us."

They called Randy, Alex's older brother, and broke the news to him. He, too, agreed they had no choice but to fire Alex.

The next morning, Randy and the other partners summoned Alex to a private home, away from the office. When they confronted him, he did not protest his innocence. Alex told them he'd had a pill problem for twenty years and needed to go to detox. He asked for a leave of absence so he could keep his health benefits.

His request was denied. Randy, appointed as the heavy, told Alex he could resign or be fired. There could be no alternative. He had done egregious damage to the firm's reputation and its future. When all of these financial crimes spilled into public view, there was no telling whether the firm would survive.

Alex said he understood. He told his brother and his closest colleagues, who'd dropped everything to care for him in the wake of the killings, that he had been waiting for this day.

"I always knew I was going to get caught eventually," he said. "I'm just surprised it took y'all so long."

THAT AFTERNOON, ALEX retreated to Murdaugh Island, the river house on the Chechessee, the family retreat for generations.

The next morning, he called his lawyer Jim Griffin and asked him to come over. It was urgent. Griffin took his boat from remote Daufuskie Island north to the river house. He'd gotten to know Alex because he'd represented Paul on the criminal charges in the boat wreck, the culmination of that tragic evening more than two years prior, an evening that had begun on that same island.

Alex told his lawyer he'd been fired for stealing client money. He told him he had a long-standing opioid addiction and had been buying pills illegally for decades. Griffin assured him he would stick by him. Griffin had a tendency to become deeply invested in his clients, staying in touch with some for years after their cases were resolved. Griffin also had a personal understanding of the devastation that could be wreaked by addiction, as his late mother had been an alcoholic and his brother had been suspended from practicing law after a long-running addiction to drugs and alcohol ruined his career.

At Griffin's urging, Alex reached out to his contact at the detox facility he'd been to in suburban Atlanta a few Christmases back. He made plans to go the following Monday. He called Blanca to send a photo of his insurance card, which was in a drawer in the kitchen at Moselle. Once Griffin had left, Alex also called his dealer, Cousin Eddie. Alex had handed over his pills the day before to his brother Randy, keeping only enough to stave off withdrawals. But it was not enough, because he could feel the shaking and anxiety coming on, early symptoms of dope sickness. He'd need more if he was going to make it to Monday.

Alex missed several calls that morning from his friend Chris Wilson, who'd been told the night before by one of the law partners that Alex had been fired. When Alex finally picked up, Wilson said he was heading south from Columbia because he needed to hear from Alex face-to-face what was going on. Alex said he'd meet him at Almeda at noon.

Wilson got to the house first and waited out by the road, just over the train tracks. When Alex pulled in to the driveway, Wilson followed him up to the house and faced him on the porch. Wilson, shorter by a few inches, had been content to be in his friend's shadow for the better part of thirty years. Now he got in Alex's face.

"What the fuck is going on?"

Alex broke down, grabbing some paper towels to wipe his face. Alex said he'd had a drug problem for years and had supported his habit by stealing money from his clients, his law partners, even his family and friends, including Wilson.

"How did I not see this?" Wilson said. "How long has this been going on?"

Alex paused. He said he was really good at covering things up.

"It's been going on for a long time," he said. "I shit you up. I shit a lot of people up."

Chris resisted the urge to hit Alex, whom he'd loved like a brother. Instead, he stormed off.

LESS THAN TWO hours later, a man called Hampton County 911.

"Where's your emergency?" the dispatcher said.

"I'm on Salkehatchie Road," the caller said. "By the church."

"What church? What church are you talking about?"

"I don't know the name of it," he said. "With the red roof."

In a county known for its rural backroads, Salkehatchie was unusually desolate, lined by trees and farmland with few landmarks.

"What's going on?" the dispatcher asked the caller.

"I got a flat tire, and I stopped, and somebody stopped to help me," he said. "When I turned my back, they tried to shoot me."

"Ohhh, okay," the dispatcher said. It was early afternoon on a cloudless summer Saturday. Anyone who'd ever driven Salkehatchie Road knew it was rare to see a passing car, much less a drive-by shooting. "Were you shot?"

"Yes," he said. "But I mean, I'm okay . . ."

"Did they actually shoot you, or they tried to shoot you?"

"They shot me, but . . ."

"Do you need EMS?" the dispatcher said.

"Well, I mean yes, I can't drive," the caller said. "I can't see and I'm bleeding a lot."

"What part of your body?" she asked.

"I'm not sure," he said. "Somewhere on my head."

"What's your name?"

"Alex Murdaugh."

There was a long pause. "Alex Murdaugh?"

"Yes, ma'am."

"Okay. Can you give me a description of the person that shot you or shot at you?"

"It was a white fella," Alex said. "He was a fair amount younger than me. Really, really short hair."

One woman driving by the scene had seen him waving his arms, trying to flag her down. She had no idea it was Alex Murdaugh, but to her the whole thing looked fishy, so she kept driving. Another motorist was willing to stop, though, and agreed to take him to a nearby field where a helicopter was on its way to airlift him to a hospital.

As so often with Alex, the moment swirled with questions. His story about the shooting felt off from the start. It was extremely unlikely that an assassin would ambush him on such a remote stretch of road. He'd been driving Maggie's Mercedes. If someone had opened fire on him, why were there no bullet holes in the vehicle? Even the details of his rescue were confounding. Alex had called 911 at 1:34 P.M. The medevac helicopter had been dispatched nine minutes later. But for some reason the Hampton County sheriff's office had not been sent until 1:55 P.M. Why had the deputies not been dispatched until twenty-one minutes after the initial call?

The helicopter flew Alex to Memorial Health hospital in Savannah, where doctors confirmed he had been shot in the head. The wounds were superficial, though, and once his head was cleaned up and bandaged, Alex was able to talk to the investigators. He told them he'd been driving the Mercedes along Salkehatchie Road when he noticed the low tire pressure indicator light pop up on his dash. When he got out to check the tires, he said, a blue pickup truck had stopped. The driver, he said, had asked if Alex was having car trouble and had then shot him. Alex described his assailant to a sketch artist. Following Alex's directions, she drew a young man with dark eyes and tanned skin. He wore a pensive expression. He had short brown hair and a trim goatee. At even a glance he bore a striking resemblance to Anthony Cook.

CHAPTER THIRTY-ONE

The Labor Day weekend shooting catapulted the Murdaugh saga to a whole new level of crazy. Alex's travails, and the string of suspicious deaths connected to his name, had already sparked months of sensational headlines in media around the world. Now that someone had allegedly tried to kill him, too, a flood of new coverage renewed the possibility of a vendetta against the Murdaughs. People were speculating whether he had been shot by the same person who had gunned down Paul and Maggie.

Marian Proctor, Maggie's sister, took the possibility seriously enough that she was terrified for Buster's safety. Could someone finally hire a bodyguard for him and his father? But many others were instantly skeptical of the whole account. When one of Alex's lawyers called a colleague to report what had happened, the other lawyer scoffed.

"Oh my god," he said. "The jackass has shot himself."

Agent Owen and other investigators from SLED were already considering that theory. On the afternoon of the shooting, Owen had joined the other investigators at the scene. Almost immediately, he had been buttonholed by Alex's brother Randy and another partner at the firm. The two of them told the agent how they'd just found out Alex had been caught stealing large sums of money from clients and from the firm itself, how he'd tearfully confessed to his addiction, and how he'd been fired barely twenty-four hours before he made the 911 call from the side of the road.

Owen was beside himself. The week Maggie and Paul had been killed, the investigator had asked the firm repeatedly whether there was anything in Alex's life, professionally or personally, that might make somebody want to harm his family. SLED had later interviewed Randy and John Marvin and asked if their brother was harboring any secrets, if he had any issues at work, any problems with drinking or drugs, any trouble at home. All of them—the law partners, Randy, and John Marvin—had assured the investigators that other than the tensions from the boat crash case, they knew of nothing out of the ordinary in Alex's life.

Now, standing on this lonely stretch of road where Alex said some random stranger had shot him, Owen pressed Randy and the other partner. Why hadn't they told him about the missing money?

As Owen recalls it, the lawyers hedged. In all fairness, they pointed out, Alex had promised that the $792,000 in question was sitting in another firm's trust account. Technically, they said, the money hadn't really been missing.

"If it's almost a million dollars and you don't know where it is?" Owen said. "That's missing."

That's when it dawned on the detective why it was taking so long to make a case. All along, as he'd investigated Paul's and Maggie's murders, he had been struggling to get the truth from Alex. Now it was clear that others had been withholding key details. The law firm had been searching for the $792,000 since early June. Only hours before Paul and Maggie were gunned down, the firm's CFO had confronted Alex over the missing check. Weeks later, as more evidence of Alex's financial crimes was discovered, no one from the firm had shared that with SLED, either. They hadn't told the authorities about Alex's opioid habit. Any of these revelations would have helped Owen immensely.

Even now, Alex's brother and the other partner were quibbling over the definition of "missing."

At last Owen realized Alex was not the only one obscuring the truth.

FROM THE START of the case, Alex had insisted the murders were almost certainly tied to the boat crash. Now, as investigators questioned him in the hospital, he had offered up a drawing that was a dead ringer for Anthony Cook.

Beverly Cook, Anthony's mother, had long suspected Alex was trying to frame her son for Paul's and Maggie's murders. When Beverly saw the sketch of the roadside shooting suspect, she was sure that Alex was making another try at setting Anthony up.

The investigators, it turned out, had little interest in questioning Anthony Cook or anyone else connected to the boat wreck. Even before he left the hospital, Alex's story about the mystery shooter was falling apart. One of the nurses assigned to Alex had complained that the patient had tried to pressure her into lending him her cellphone, just as Paul had gotten one of the EMTs to hand over his phone in the ambulance after the boat crash. It was a time-tested Murdaugh move, pressing for favors when the stakes were high. When the nurse refused, even after he offered money, Alex tried again with another staff member. SLED had discovered that Alex had repeatedly called Cousin Eddie, who they quickly learned was one of Alex's drug dealers. The Tuesday after the roadside shooting, investigators searched Cousin Eddie's house in Walterboro and found a little ledger of drug deals.

They filed a subpoena for Cousin Eddie's phone records and bank records and confirmed that Alex had been writing him hundreds of thousands of dollars in checks over the years. In the three months since the murders, the pace had accelerated, with Alex sending him checks for more than $100,000. The investigators also reviewed the surveillance footage from the church near where Alex said he was shot. A blue Chevy pickup truck passed by within seconds of the Mercedes.

A few minutes later, the truck went back the other way. It was the same make and model as Cousin Eddie's.

Cousin Eddie told investigators a remarkable story. He said Alex had asked to meet him at a funeral home in Varnville that afternoon and to follow him somewhere, though he didn't say why. Eddie trailed him out to a desolate stretch of Salkehatchie Road, about eight miles from Moselle. Alex got out of the car and was waving a pistol around, explaining that he was so despondent after being fired from his firm that he wanted to die. Eddie wasn't actually sure of Alex's intentions, but he knew he was talking crazy. Eddie said he grabbed the gun, trying to wrest it away, and during the struggle it fired. Alex fell to the ground. Seeing Alex bleeding, Eddie panicked and ran from the car with the pistol in his hand. Then he said he drove away, throwing the gun out the window.

Alex was released from the hospital after a few days and driven by his brothers to the detox facility outside Atlanta. Investigators were trying to set a time to come down for an interview to confront Alex with everything they'd learned. Before they could get there, Dick Harpootlian and Jim Griffin set up a conference call, saying Alex was willing to talk if they did it by phone and agreed to some ground rules.

"We don't want to talk about what happened at Moselle," Harpootlian said.

Finances, either, he said. Only the roadside shooting.

A sheepish Alex admitted he'd been lying about the attempted murder. He confirmed Eddie's account and said he had decided it was best to arrange for his death so Buster would receive his life insurance money, which he said was $10 million. This explanation was another fiction. Alex never had a life insurance policy. That meant if he had been trying to arrange his own death, there would have been no financial benefit for his surviving son.

The only possible motive for making this claim was to wrap himself in the mantle of the selfless father willing to do anything to help his surviving son. Owen wondered if it was a repetition of the same pattern that might have played out at Moselle: When confronted with evidence of his misdeeds, Alex had resorted to violence to take drastic measures to change the subject.

SLED did not arrest him immediately. Working with Alex's lawyers, the agency allowed him to finish his detox regimen and be driven home in a few days by Buster.

Via a publicist, Alex released a statement to *The Hampton County Guardian:*

> The murders of my wife and son have caused an incredibly difficult time in my life. I have made a lot of decisions that I truly regret. I'm resigning from my law firm and entering rehab after a long battle that has been exacerbated by these murders. I am immensely sorry to everyone I've hurt including my family, friends and colleagues. I ask for prayers as I rehabilitate myself and my relationships.

Even by Murdaugh standards, the statement was notable for what it left out. Alex had been forced to resign or else be fired. His statement alluded only vaguely to his addiction and made no mention of why he had left the firm other than to acknowledge some unspecified decisions that he regretted, a far cry from admitting he'd stolen approximately $11 million from his clients and the firm. Whatever mistakes Alex had committed, his statement made it sound as though they might have been caused by his grief over the murders of his wife and son and by opioid addiction.

This was deflection of the highest order. By the time of the murders, Alex had been stealing from his most vulnerable clients for more than a decade. The question that Agent Owen and the other investigators were trying to figure out now was what role the possibility of losing everything in the boat crash case—and being exposed as a craven thief—might have played in the murders. Had Alex killed his family to assume the role of the grieving family man, thereby short-circuiting the boat crash case and his firm's determination to solve the mystery of the missing money?

Agent Owen found it difficult to imagine the mindset of anyone so devoid of human emotion that he'd slaughter his wife and son just to escape going to prison. But after the flood of revelations about Alex's secret life, Owen saw an abundance of evidence that Alex might be a sociopath who relentlessly manipulated other people even if it meant destroying them. Particularly telling, Owen thought, was Alex's willingness to deploy the sympathy card whenever it served him. Jeanne Seckinger, pushing for answers on the missing $792,000, had backed off the moment Alex told her his father was dying. Later that night, he had repeatedly brought up his father's failing health and his mother's dementia as the investigators questioned him about the murders. Although he had shown bursts of grief and shock, some of his behavior had been odd, like the way he'd casually greeted one of the deputies while standing a few feet from the bloodstained bodies. And now he was pretending to have attempted his own death so he could provide for Buster with a nonexistent insurance payout.

Then there was the pattern of Alex's emotional outbursts. As Owen studied the videos of his interviews with Alex, it solidified the investigator's initial impression that Alex was consistently breaking down and sobbing whenever the questioning veered toward something potentially incriminating. He had repeated the pattern through the first two interviews. But in August, when Owen finally informed him he was the sole suspect, Alex had displayed an almost eerie calm, referring to the agent by his first name and fixing him with a cool and collected stare as he denied killing Paul or Maggie. It seemed that Alex dropped the tears because by then he knew it was too late.

MONTHS BEFORE, WHEN his friends at the Murdaugh firm had asked Mark Tinsley to stop pressuring Alex in the boat crash case, Tinsley had warned them that what was coming could not be stopped. Now the rain that Tinsley had predicted was falling in cascading waves.

After the shock of the roadside shooting wore off, Alex's public reputation quickly disintegrated. The sympathy others had felt for him after the murders was now transformed into hostility and suspicion. Two days after the shooting, the law firm announced that Alex had misappropriated funds, and *The New York Times* quoted an anonymous source saying the amount of missing money was in the millions. As the news spread of Alex's financial crimes and his lies about the roadside shooting, the Fourteenth Circuit solicitor's office announced it was barring him from prosecuting cases. Two days later, the South Carolina Supreme Court suspended him from practicing law altogether.

Gloria Satterfield's sons filed a lawsuit against Alex, Russell Laffitte, and Cory Fleming, pointing out that not a penny of the millions of dollars in insurance payments for their mother's death had ever been paid to them. Connor Cook sued both Alex and Buster, alleging that Alex and others had orchestrated a campaign to blame Connor for the crash.

Dick Harpootlian and Jim Griffin, Alex's lawyers, put out a statement insisting Alex was fully cooperating with SLED's investigations into the roadside shooting and the murders of his wife and son. Alex had recently left the detox facility in Atlanta and begun rehab treatment at a facility in Orlando.

Alex was not without fault, the lawyers wrote, but he was just one of many whose lives had been devastated by opioid addiction. The statement may have earned their client another dose of sympathy among the public, but it did not stop the parade of indictments that was coming for Alex.

The day after his attorneys spoke out on his behalf, Alex turned himself in to SLED on charges of insurance fraud and falsifying a police report stemming from the roadside shooting. After he was booked, Alex paid a $20,000 personal recognizance bond and then returned to rehab.

In mid-October, when Alex was released from his rehab treatment in Orlando, police arrested him and returned him to South Carolina to face charges related to his financial frauds. Alex entered the courtroom in a jumpsuit and mask, his shoulders hunched. At the defense table, he turned and scanned the crowd. No one from his family was there.

The judge denied him bond pending a psychiatric evaluation. It was a blow Alex had not expected. White-collar defendants were almost always freed on bond, even Bernie Madoff. He told his family he felt persecuted, singled out. *Not to worry,* though, he said. He could take it. Harpootlian was shocked that Murdaugh hardly seemed to mind jail. He was the first white-collar defendant he'd ever had who wasn't clamoring to make bond.

Multiple lawyers, led by Tinsley, were teaming up to file a cluster of motions to prevent Alex or Buster from disposing of any assets without a judge's permission. When Alex's brother Randy filed suit to reclaim almost $50,000 that he had recently lent to Alex to pay for rehab, a judge signed an emergency order to halt the repayment. Johnny Parker, the firm's managing partner, filed a similar lawsuit to reclaim the balance of the $500,000 that Parker had lent to Alex. Again, an emergency order stopped the repayment. At Tinsley's request, a state judge ordered Alex's assets to be frozen and controlled by court-appointed receivers, an extreme measure usually reserved for corporate bankruptcies.

The body blows kept landing, seemingly every day.

After reviewing the psychiatric evaluation, the judge denied Alex bond for a second time. Hours later, Alex's lawyers filed for a writ of habeas corpus with South Carolina's supreme court, arguing that the state did not have the right to jail their client indefinitely. In their petition, the defense attorneys noted that the psychiatrist who had examined their client had diagnosed him with severe opioid disorder and had recommended he continue undergoing treatment at a residential facility for an additional eight to ten weeks. The psychiatrist, the lawyers said, had also recommended that Alex receive grief therapy and treatment for trauma. She had not found Alex to be a danger to himself or others. Eventually, the supreme court granted the petition, ruling that Alex did have a right to be released after posting bail. A different judge then set his bond for $7 million, requiring that it be paid in full rather than the more customary ten percent. Unable to come up with that amount, Alex remained in custody.

At the bond hearing, Alex told the judge that he regretted his actions, though he was careful not to specify which ones, and that he knew he had hurt people he cared about. He said he had been sober from his opiate addiction for ninety-eight days, and he was thinking more clearly.

"I knew that this news was going to humiliate me," he said, referring to his financial crimes. "Humiliate my son, who's trying to be a lawyer . . . and deserves none of what he's gotten. I knew it would humiliate mine and Maggie's family, who's very proud of me, my family's legacy, which I know I've tarnished badly."

He told the judge that since the murders, he had tried to maintain a close relationship with Buster. But when he was charged in the roadside shooting, he had feared the shock of it would alienate his son.

"All of this was crushing to me," he explained. "I was in a very bad place due to the withdrawals. I made a terrible decision that I regret, that I'm sorry about and frankly that I'm embarrassed about."

A barrage of new charges was announced in November, when a state grand jury indicted Alex on twenty-seven counts for stealing a total of $4.8 million from clients in five counties. A few weeks later, the grand jury indicted him on twenty-one more counts for stealing another $1.3 million from multiple victims.

In the middle of all the indictments, the law firm announced it was changing its name, removing "Murdaugh" from the firm's stationery. His younger brother shared the news in a jailhouse phone call.

"The law firm has dissolved," John Marvin said. "They're re-forming under a new name . . . Just because of all the negative publicity, and all of the stuff they're going through."

Alex took this in.

"What is the new name?" he asked.

"It's going to be operated under the Parker Law Group."

"The what?"

Three generations of Murdaughs had devoted a century to building a legal dynasty. Now, in a little more than ten years, Alex had burned the whole thing down.

BY THE SPRING of 2022, David Owen no longer had any difficulty believing that Alex alone had killed Maggie and Paul. The scale and nature of Alex's financial crimes, along with his willingness to allegedly stage his own murder, only confirmed the investigator's suspicions that this man was a chameleon, capable of anything. There had been such a terrible intimacy to the thefts. He had drawn Alania Plyler and his other victims close and promised to help them and then taken everything. Robbing a motherless girl like Alania or a quadriplegic young man like Hakeem Pinckney required an emotional brutality that was hard to fathom. It wasn't the same as murdering someone, but it was close. And Alex had shown that brutality again and again, always covering it with empty promises and good-old-boy charm.

Agent Owen could not yet prove that Alex had killed his wife and son. He was convinced that Alex had lied from the start about what happened the night of the murders, but knew he did not have evidence that would hold up in court. Alex was a cunning lawyer from a family that had mastered the art of manipulating the system. He was also being represented by two of the savviest defense lawyers in the state. If SLED didn't have the hard evidence to back up murder charges, Harpootlian and Griffin would shred their case and probably sue for wrongful prosecution.

Owen needed something more. The investigators had interviewed Shelley Smith, the woman who spent her nights caring for Alex's ailing mother. Shelley had told them about Alex's strange visit at dawn, when she saw him holding something balled up in his arms. The investigators had found a full body raincoat, meant for kayaking, in a wad in a plastic bin in a junk closet upstairs. The interior of the raincoat was covered with gunshot residue. It was damning circumstantial evidence, but far short of the murder weapons themselves, which investigators believed had once been wrapped inside.

Owen had sent off the white T-shirt that Alex had been wearing when the deputies arrived the night of the murders, after a preliminary test showed it tested positive for microscopic droplets of blood. He and his team were still searching the waters around Moselle and Almeda, hoping to find the murder weapons. Maybe they would get lucky and divine the passcode for Paul's phone and discover something damning there. Owen, knowing his own code was his birthday, had suggested they try Paul's of April 14, 1999, but the tech experts had declined, arguing that they didn't want to waste one of the few passcode attempts the iPhone allowed before automatically erasing the phone. The data from inside the Suburban's state-of-the-art black box remained encrypted.

The investigators, meanwhile, were encountering resistance from the locals who knew Alex Murdaugh best. The hostility to the investigation was not subtle. Some witnesses, after granting interviews to SLED, were being called snitches. Other potential witnesses were simply staying quiet in the shadows.

Owen wasn't just trying to retrieve the contents of Paul's phone, or whatever data had been recorded inside the Suburban. For months now, he and his team had been trying and failing to crack the black box that was Hampton County.

CHAPTER THIRTY-TWO

I n his decades as a lawyer, Alex had figured out how to work angles, cut side deals, bend the rules. Now, stuck behind bars, he remained true to those habits.

Alex was housed in the Richland County jail on the outskirts of Columbia. Early on he got in a fight over equipment at the jail gym. His scraped knuckles and blackened eye were visible at one of his bond hearings and prompted endless online speculation. In a jailhouse phone call, he complained to his older brother about getting moved to a medical unit for his own protection. He told his brother Randy that his lawyers were worried he'd get shivved. "That's what they call it in the pokey when somebody sticks you with a knife."

"Are there people there that have some reason to have animosity towards you?" Randy asked.

Alex said the only reason was the publicity about his case and the talk about his being a prosecutor. Someone might want to gut him for fifteen minutes of fame. He had assured his lawyers he'd be fine. "I told Jim and Dick that I used to be a pretty bad dude," Alex said. "I'm kind of soft now, but I think I can take most of the people in this medical ward."

In jail, as in the outside world, Alex seemed to live on the phone.

Talking with his son Buster, Alex bragged about his mastery of the jail's barter economy. He'd been gambling with his fellow prisoners, and one weekend he had correctly picked the winners in nine out of eleven NFL games. His winnings had been a feast from the commissary: "six soups, four beef sticks, and a bunch of crackers."

"Canteen is the commerce," he told Buster. "It's the trade."

To wheel and deal in the jail, he needed as much currency as possible. He found an easy hustle. After his family members deposited the maximum of $60 a week in his commissary account, he'd have them put an additional $60 in another inmate's account, with that man keeping $15 as his cut and passing the rest on to Alex.

Buster wasn't sure what to say.

"It just looks a little weird," he said. He hoped his dad wasn't making problems for himself, doing anything illegal.

"I'm not," Alex said. "I promise you that's not the case."

Getting in the game, he said, was the only way to survive the monotony and the jail's abysmal food. He'd read all the Pat Conroy and John Grisham books his family had sent him. He'd bribed a one-legged trusty named Charlie for access to the remote for the TV.

"I can watch more than one channel," Alex said. "Cost me a honey bun, three packs of Pop-Tarts, a deck of cards, and a bag of ramen noodle soup."

Before his arrest, Alex had arranged for Buster to be allowed to return to law school at USC, giving him a second chance after he'd been kicked out for plagiarism. The law school had invited Buster to reenroll for the spring 2022 semester. But as the new term approached, it wasn't clear that the deal would hold, given the disgrace now attached to the Murdaugh name. But Alex was not ready to give up.

On the afternoon of December 31, 2021, he got on the jailhouse phone with Jim Griffin and asked him to call Butch Bowers, the well-connected lawyer who had been the family's point man on Buster's readmittance. Classes started the following Wednesday and Buster had not heard whether he would be reinstated.

Bowers, an adviser to multiple governors, explained to Griffin that the law school dean had been traveling and hard to reach. But they had finally spoken and agreed it would be best to hold off on letting Buster return, at least for the moment, given the circumstances of Buster's expulsion and his father's incarceration.

Alex was pissed.

He called Buster, who was at Murdaugh Island with his uncles Randy and John Marvin. Buster was waiting for friends to arrive for New Year's Eve. Alex said there was a wrinkle, and he wasn't sure how the law school could put him off at this late date. He'd paid Butch $60,000 to get Buster back into law school. Alex urged Buster to call Butch right away.

Buster's voice was flat. "I ain't dealing with this today."

"I don't know how they revoke an admission," Alex said. "Do you want to pressure them for you to start this spring in five days?"

"No," Buster said.

"Without a doubt?" Alex said.

"Yes."

"Because I think he might can do that."

"I'm not mentally prepared," Buster said. "I'm not ready to go now. They fucked all that up for me."

"I know you're frustrated," Alex said. "I feel like it's all my fault."

Buster paused. His grades had been abysmal, even before the plagiarism. "No, not entirely," he said. "I share some blame in this."

Alex's next call was to John Marvin. John Marvin asked what he could do to help get Buster back into law school.

Alex, sitting in an orange jumpsuit at the county jail on New Year's Eve, facing dozens of criminal charges, said he was considering legal action, but the reality was that on the Friday of a holiday weekend, they'd have to be ready to file something first thing Monday to force the law school's hand. Alex was willing to do it but didn't think they could beat the clock.

IN JANUARY, THE state grand jury indicted Alex on twenty-three new counts for stealing another $2.27 million. That same month, a judge denied Alex's request to lower his bond, and then some reporters submitted FOIA requests for Alex's jailhouse conversations with Buster and others, and then his lawyers sued the guy in charge of the jail, demanding that no more of their client's phone transcripts be released to the press or the public.

In March, Alex relinquished his rights to Maggie's estate, clearing her assets to be inherited solely by Buster. Two days later, he was accused of violating an agreement forbidding him from moving the family's money around. A week after that, Alex was indicted on a new conspiracy charge and three counts of making a false statement or misrepresentation in connection with his financial transactions.

Owen watched the total number of charges climbing toward a hundred and wondered what it would take to finally add two counts of murder. His team was still searching for the murder weapons, and he was still waiting for the final results of the blood tests with the white T-shirt. The tech guys had not yet been able to unlock Paul's phone so they had sent the phone to an expert at the Charleston police department. But the guy in Charleston couldn't crack the code, either, so he reached out to a contact in the Secret Service.

Charleston police were preparing to share the phone with the Secret Service when the contact asked if anyone had tried the most obvious codes: Paul's birth date, the street number on the house at Moselle, something Paul would have had no trouble remembering.

"People are creatures of habit," the Secret Service agent said.

They tried the birthday first, entering 0414. The phone unlocked immediately. They had had it in their possession for more than ten months, ever since they'd found it on top of Paul's backside at the crime scene, and had never tried the most obvious four digits.

They quickly found a video from 8:44 P.M. on the night of the murders. Paul had shot the video at the kennels when he was checking on Cash, the puppy with the injured tail.

The video, only fifty seconds, opens on Cash wagging his tail inside his kennel as Paul opens the gate. In the light of the phone, Cash's eyes glow yellow and then red. Paul tells Cash to get back as he focuses the phone's camera on the puppy's tail. He's trying to get a good shot of the wound, but Cash is so happy to see him, he won't hold still.

"Quit, Cash, quit!" says Paul. "It's okay . . . Shit. Hold still. It's all right."

Crickets can be heard in the background. Out of the camera's view, Maggie exclaims that her dog Bubba has a bird in his mouth.

"Bubba," says an exasperated voice in the background. It's Alex, watching on.

"It's a guinea," says Maggie.

Paul corrects her, almost laughing.

"It's a chicken," he says.

Alex calls to the dog repeatedly.

"C'mere, Bubba! C'mere!"

Finally, Paul gets hold of Cash's tail to show the wound. Then the video ends.

Paul had told Rogan Gibson, Cash's owner, that he'd be shooting a video that night to let him see how the puppy was doing. But Paul had never gotten the chance to send that video. All this time, it had been inside the phone, waiting for someone to watch it.

On its face, the video was just a glimpse of a young man on a summer night checking on a dog. But in light of Alex's repeated insistence that he had not gone down to the kennels, it changed everything. It proved Alex was lying. In court, the jury would hear Alex's voice, a few feet away from his wife and son, minutes before their deaths.

CHAPTER THIRTY-THREE

Agent Owen and the other investigators had no intention of arresting Alex immediately. They needed the state prosecutors to empanel another grand jury, this one in Colleton County. The statewide grand jury that had indicted Alex on all the financial charges was not permitted by law to consider homicides. The SLED team didn't mind waiting. They needed to tie up other loose ends, including Cousin Eddie. The police thought it might be a good time to see if Eddie would testify. Maybe he knew more than he'd already told them.

Curtis Eddie Smith was a tricky witness for the state. He'd shown a tenuous relationship with the truth, having told several versions of the roadside shooting story. He'd deleted calls and texts and lied about whether he'd sold drugs to Alex. The frequency of Alex's checks to him dramatically increased after the homicides, leading detectives to wonder if the increased payments were blackmail. The state had charged him with running a check cashing scheme to launder money for Alex, cashing more than four hundred checks in relatively small amounts totaling $2.4 million. The state had also charged him with insurance fraud for his role in the Labor Day weekend shooting.

He was also half Murdaugh, a descendant of Lazarus Murdaugh, the secessionist firebrand who was the brother of Alex's great-great-grandfather Josiah. That's why Alex called him Cousin Eddie.

The prosecutors were considering making a deal with Eddie in exchange for his cooperation as a witness, on the condition that he tell the truth. SLED called Eddie in for an interview and a polygraph exam. The polygraph examiner asked what he knew about the murders. Eddie insisted he had been nowhere near Moselle.

"I was thirty-five miles away," he said. "Ain't no way in hell anybody can put me there."

He said his girlfriend would vouch that they had sex and then hung out with two friends. They'd installed a number four fuel injector on a Peterbilt truck and had stayed until approximately nine-thirty, roughly half an hour after the murders were committed.

The examiner said he was ready to start the polygraph. He had Eddie sit in an armless chair, facing a blank wall of the conference room. The examiner strapped a blood pressure cuff around Eddie's arm, a breathing monitor around his chest, and sensors to his fingertips.

"Did you shoot either of those people at that property on Moselle Road?"

The white line flowing smoothly along the bottom of the examiner's laptop, tracking Eddie's biometrics, spiked to nearly the top of the screen.

"Did you shoot either of those people at that property on Moselle Road last June?"

Eddie said no, but the line spiked again.

"Were you present when either of those people were shot at that property on Moselle Road?"

A third spike.

The examiner asked Eddie why his responses about the night of the murders indicated deception.

"I was nowhere near," Eddie said. "I couldn't have been there. I couldn't have flew there and got there fast enough."

The examiner paused.

"It does look like you've got some direct knowledge or some participation," he said. "I think you're leaving something out."

Eddie raised his voice, his words coming out in a rush. "There ain't no way shape or form nobody can put me there," he said. "I was not there."

Afterward, when the investigators looked into Eddie's alibi, his girl-friend and the other friends all confirmed they had been with him until after the murders occurred. The data inside Eddie's phone backed up his account as well, showing him at the house the entire evening. Owen and the others concluded that Eddie might not have taken part in the murders or witnessed them firsthand, but he was hiding something. At 6:24 P.M. on June 8, the day after the murders, he'd sent Alex a mystifying three-word text:

at fishing hole.

Had Eddie and Alex actually met up that evening, and if so, where and what for? Had Eddie been getting rid of something? The investigators didn't think Eddie was telling the truth about the roadside shooting, either, or about why Alex started writing him big checks after the homicides. They wondered again if Eddie was blackmailing Alex, or maybe getting paid for cleaning up the murder scene before the first deputies arrived. They also thought it possible that on the day of the roadside shooting, Alex had intended to shoot Eddie, creating a fall guy for the murders at Moselle.

Eddie did not seem willing or able to tell them the truth, which made him a risky witness in the murder case. Any plea deal was a non-starter, they told him. It was better to keep pushing forward on their own.

CHAPTER THIRTY-FOUR

Mother's Day was May 8. That weekend, Alex was working the phones again from inside the jail. He was trying to arrange a call with his ailing mother. He encouraged Buster to text Maggie's mother and sister and wish them a happy Mother's Day on his behalf. He also reminded Buster to put flowers on Maggie's grave.

"And I want you to put some for me, too," he said. "She'd like that."

ON JUNE 7, the anniversary of the murders came and went. Maggie's family was restless, impatient to know why the case was dragging on. Agent Owen felt for them but could only hint at progress. SLED was working hard to keep the new evidence under wraps until the case went in front of the grand jury.

That same month, the state announced it would exhume Gloria Satterfield's body. The South Carolina Supreme Court, meanwhile, disbarred Alex for stealing $4.3 million from the Satterfield estate.

Two days later, the Colleton County grand jury indicted Alex in the murders of Maggie and Paul.

Because Alex was already in jail, there was no formal arrest, no mug shot, no perp walk. His lawyers put out a statement declaring their client's innocence:

> Alex wants his family, friends and everyone to know that he did not have anything to do with the murders of Maggie and Paul. He loved them more than anything in the world. It was very clear from day one that law enforcement and the Attorney General prematurely concluded that Alex was responsible for the murder of his wife and son. But we know that Alex did not have any motive whatsoever to murder them.

The arraignment was six days later. Alex had the right to waive his appearance, like any other criminal defendant. But knowing that news organizations from around the country would be there, he insisted on seizing his moment in front of the cameras.

The hearing was held in Colleton County's main courtroom, native turf for Alex, as it had been for his father and his grandfather. Buster's portrait, still hanging on the back wall, watched Alex as the bailiffs escorted him forward. Buster had once ordered the killings of his pregnant lover and his unborn child. Now here stood his grandson, accused of worse.

As a young boy, Alex had studied his grandfather holding sway in front of juries across the circuit. Buster had taught the boy a few things about the mechanics of performance in this solemn and sacred space. Buster had shown Alex how to manifest himself as the human embodiment of justice, the public servant seeking vengeance against the wicked. But that wasn't the role required today. As Alex took a seat between his lawyers, he wrapped himself in the aura of an innocent man hounded and harried by the state, fighting for his life even as he mourned the deaths of his wife and son.

Alex had chosen to wear a white linen shirt, khaki pants, and loafers he'd borrowed from Jim Griffin's son. Alex had lost so much weight since the murders that he no longer fit into his own clothes. But he knew it was crucial that he not enter the courtroom in an orange jail-house jumpsuit like any other defendant.

His lawyers had filed for a speedy trial. The sooner the state's shoddy case went before a jury, they said, the sooner their client would be acquitted.

"What say you, Richard Alex Murdaugh?" asked a prosecutor. "Are you guilty or not guilty of the felonies wherein you stand indicted?"

"Not guilty," Alex said, standing straight and tall.

"How do you wish to be tried?"

"By God and my country."

PART SIX

RAIN

One summer morning, not long after the arraignment, the prosecution team made a pilgrimage to Moselle. In the year since the murders, the property had acquired an iconic notoriety. Its brick entry gates had appeared on countless magazine covers. Crews working on several documentaries had already sent drones equipped with video to shoot the long sweeping front drive lined with live oak trees. Outsiders described Moselle as a hunting property or a sprawling estate, and it was both less and more than those things. The property was vast and the house was grand, but the shed and kennels were modest and compact, running right up against each other. The prosecutors had studied the police photos, but they wanted to see the crime scene firsthand.

Agent Owen led the prosecutors across the property, guiding them from the house down to the kennels. By then Moselle had been sold to a neighbor, but for the moment it was in the possession of a receiver overseeing Alex's assets until the sale worked its way through the courts. Blanca and her husband, caretakers in the first months after the crime, had long since moved away.

For the moment, the property was a no-man's-land. The grass was overgrown and thick with weeds. The house was vacant and still, as though it were holding its breath. Down at the kennels, there were no clucking chickens or barking dogs. Blanca had adopted Bubba, Cash had been returned to his owner, and the other animals had been sent to new homes. The shed, located next to the kennels, was empty of all the mowers and other heavy equipment the Murdaughs had kept there. The shed had once served as the property's airplane hangar during the days when Barrett Boulware owned Moselle. The old landing strip had become the road leading to the house.

Walking the grounds, the prosecution team absorbed the layout of the property in a way that wasn't possible on paper. The kennels were approximately 250 yards from the main house. It would not have been easy to see the kennels from the house, but one of the prosecutors gauged the distance and thought if Alex had been inside napping when the murders occurred, he would almost certainly have heard two shotgun blasts followed by five shots from an assault rifle.

Agent Owen was struck by how different the place looked from the night of the murders. The crime scene tape and tent were gone, along with the dozens of onlookers who had tramped around in the rain and the mud. This time it was daylight and the lawmen and women were alone. The only evidence of the murders Owen could find were a nick from a bullet on the side of a quail pen and other holes from shotgun pellets in the window at the back of the feed room. Owen felt a heaviness in the air, though, a weight that pressed against his chest.

He walked over to the spot where Maggie had fallen. No grass remained, just sand and small rocks, from where a cleaning crew had dug to remove the blood. In the middle of the dirt he saw a lone white wildflower. *That's Maggie,* he told himself.

He crossed the cement slab to the spot where Paul had died. It was shocking how close the killer must have been standing when he pulled the trigger. One of the paralegals pointed out a red vine growing through the cracks in the cement. This time the investigator said the quiet part out loud.

"That's Paul."

. . .

THE PROSECUTION HAD no illusions about the challenges ahead. Alex's showmanship at the arraignment had reminded them that they were staking their careers on a circumstantial case against a prominent opponent who had long ago mastered the art of bending justice to his will. If the prosecutors lost, the blowback would be catastrophic.

Creighton Waters, the lead prosecutor, did not care. At fifty-two, Waters was a veteran lawyer who relished the bruising fight ahead. Waters ran the statewide grand jury division and typically brought public corruption or financial fraud cases, complex prosecutions that had prepared him well for this case. He had a reputation for being tenacious and thorough and had already sought ninety financial and drug trafficking charges against Alex. Waters had only prosecuted one homicide case in his career, but to him, it didn't matter. In his mind, this was a white-collar case that had culminated in two murders.

The range and depth of Alex's transgressions insulted the chief prosecutor, who saw Alex's depravity as an affront to the credibility of the legal profession. Waters's father was a well-regarded white-collar defense lawyer, his mother a women's studies professor. Waters had split the difference as a career public servant in the attorney general's office, earning an annual salary that was one-tenth of Alex Murdaugh's. Waters found no greater motivation than taking down powerful people who had gone to rot. He and Alex had attended USC's law school at the same time. The two of them had never crossed paths on campus; Creighton had been a first-year student as Alex entered his third year. Even so, Waters felt as though he'd known men like Alex his entire career: the crooked officials, the dirty cops filling their pockets with bribes, the swindlers in their Gucci loafers. But none of the others he'd prosecuted had gunned down his wife and son.

Determined as he was to bring Alex to justice, Waters recognized the holes in the state's case. The investigators had still not been able to find the missing guns. They had chased rumors of trouble in Alex and Maggie's marriage but had found no one who could verify it. Some of their witnesses were reluctant to testify, having been intimidated by allies loyal to the Murdaughs. Others refused to talk at all, not wanting to cross a family that still held so much sway.

A Highway Patrol lieutenant who'd lost his workers' compensation to Alex's thieving had expressed fear over speaking out against a Murdaugh. "Would I be surprised if he or somebody related to him showed up at my house with a gun?" the trooper said in one of Alex's bond hearings. "Absolutely not."

Alex's family was sticking by him. His brothers had been appointed to represent his financial interests and, by extension, their own, particularly any claim on the siblings' shared inheritance from their father of more than $16 million. Maggie's parents remained resolute, too, professing certainty that the man they loved like their own son might have made some mistakes but would have never killed Maggie and Paul. Alex had gone to great lengths to remain in their good graces, even making sure they knew he had arranged from jail for the Mother's Day flowers to be placed on Maggie's grave.

The state's strongest piece of evidence was without a doubt the kennel video. They also had a report from a blood spatter expert who had identified blood spatter on Alex's Black Sheep T-shirt, drops invisible to the naked eye. Agent Owen and his bosses at SLED asked both Alex's immediate family and Maggie's to come to headquarters for a briefing on the case before they turned over the evidence against Alex to the defense team.

Some of the family members cried when they heard Paul's and Maggie's voices on the kennel video, but they remained unconvinced of Alex's guilt. His siblings swore they heard a fourth voice, clinging to the belief that someone else was there, too. Just because Alex's voice had been on the tape did not prove him a murderer.

"I don't believe you," Maggie's father told Agent Owen. "You need to go out and find who killed my daughter and grandson."

Marian Proctor, Maggie's sister, remained silent out of deference to her parents. But the video fed a gnawing fear that had begun with the revelations that spilled out on Labor Day, when Marian realized her brother-in-law's entire career had been a lie. Alex had told her more than once that he had not been down at the kennels, and now she knew that was a lie, too. She could not stop thinking about an offhand remark Alex had made to her at Moselle in the days after the shootings.

"I think whoever did it," he'd said, "had thought about it for a long time."

DICK HARPOOTLIAN HAD been a household name in South Carolina decades before he took on Alex Murdaugh as a client. Like many defense lawyers, he'd cut his teeth as a solicitor. He'd sent the notorious serial killer Pee Wee Gaskins to death row. In a thwarted attempt to delay his execution, Gaskins had been accused of trying to have Harpootlian's then three-year-old daughter kidnapped. Harpootlian said the scheme proved Gaskins was a "mad dog" who needed to be put down.

While solicitor, Harpootlian had been a contemporary of Buster Murdaugh's and admired the older man's ability to gin up controversy and shrug off criticism. The two of them were kindred spirits who both accepted that right and wrong were not always black and white. Soon after Harpootlian left the solicitor's office and opened his defense practice, he got a call from Old Buster about one of Dick's cases. Harpootlian was representing a Black sailor who'd gotten into a shoving match with some locals at a Varnville bar. In the melee that followed, the sailor had gotten into a car and hit one of the locals. It wasn't clear whether the sailor had veered to hit the man or the man had jumped in front of him, but the injuries had been fatal.

"Mr. Harpootlian," Buster said, "I've got the judge here in two weeks. Be here that Monday at two-thirty P.M. and your boy can plead to involuntary manslaughter with no probation. He's got to pay the funeral bills, though."

It was an offer that seemed too good to refuse, a plea deal instead of a murder trial in front of a Hampton jury. The only problem was that Harpootlian was already scheduled to give a speech on the other side of the state that Monday morning. He decided to charter a plane so he could arrive at the hearing on time and had his secretary call the solicitor's secretary back to see about getting a taxi from the airport.

When Harpootlian landed at the tiny Hampton airport, which had no commercial flights then or ever, a young man was waiting for him, leaning against an old station wagon filled with fishing gear. He was tall and redheaded and introduced himself as Randolph Murdaugh IV, or Randy, Buster's grandson and Alex's older brother. When they walked into the courtroom, Buster stopped in the middle of addressing the judge and turned to face them.

"Judge, the big-city lawyer who wanted me to send a taxi cab to the Hampton airport is here," Buster said. The courtroom erupted in laughter. The client made the plea and it was a done deal.

A few weeks later, Harpootlian called his client's parents to check on whether they'd heard anything more, because the plea meant they might face civil penalties. They said, oh, yes, they'd already been sued and settled. The Murdaugh firm had filed a wrongful death suit a few days after the plea and their insurance had paid out $1 million in coverage.

Harpootlian's clients were happy. Their son was free. The dead man's family was compensated $700,000 for their loss and the Murdaugh firm got paid $300,000 for a few hours' work.

"Was it unethical as hell?" Harpootlian would say as he recounted the story. "Sure. But it was also a win-win-win."

OUT OF FONDNESS for the Murdaugh family and the lure of a big fee, Harpootlian had agreed to represent Paul on the criminal charges in the boat wreck. He'd stayed on to represent Alex on the financial and homicide charges for reasons including a sizable retainer left over from the boat case, a low opinion of SLED, and a deep love for the limelight. As a Democratic state senator, Harpootlian had no affection for Attorney General Alan Wilson, either, the Republican foil he'd taken on over everything from alleged cronyism to the pandemic's mask mandates.

Harpootlian demanded a speedy trial to call SLED's bluff and deny them another year or more to build a case against his client.

"He believes that the killer or killers are still at large," Harpootlian told the judge at Alex's arraignment. "This would allow SLED to put this behind them and go look for the real killers."

Within days of the charges being filed, the prosecution and defense clashed over how best to share evidence without running the risk of leaks. Creighton Waters insisted they agree on guardrails to protect the autopsy photos in particular, which could fetch millions of dollars in the wrong hands. Harpootlian countered that any leaks were coming from the state, not the defense, since so far Alex's lawyers had not seen any of the evidence.

In August 2022, Harpootlian held a press conference outside his office, a historic mansion in downtown Columbia. He harangued prosecutors for a "trial by ambush," in a senatorial voice raised to make himself heard over traffic noise and drizzling rain.

"I don't have a shred of paper, I don't have an email, I don't have an exhibit," he yelled. "Give us the stuff!"

Harpootlian later joked that he should have been careful what he wished for. The prosecution promptly buried him in paper, delivering thousands of pages of documents and hundreds of photos. When he saw the kennel video, Harpootlian found himself at a rare loss for words. For months he and his co-counsel, Jim Griffin, had been insisting that Alex never went down to the kennels before going to check on his mother, a story Griffin recounted in detail in a documentary streaming on HBO Max that fall. The kennel video obliterated their claims and Alex's alibi. They had planned to build a case on the lack of motive for Alex to kill his wife and son, but had to pivot to why he lied about being with them in the moments before they died.

Harpootlian was on a first-name basis with reporters at every major news outlet in the state and the nation. He knew that the best way to deal with bad news was to get it out before your opposition and frame it in the best light possible. He let it be known that the state had found a video showing Alex was at the kennels, but what it demonstrated was devastating to the state's case, as it showed a loving father having a joking conversation, not a man minutes away from flying into a homicidal rage.

Harpootlian and Griffin were particularly eager to draw attention to Curtis Eddie Smith's failed polygraph. A video of the interview had been turned over to the defense as part of discovery. The lawyers filed a motion forcing the state to turn over the examiner's notes and quality control reviews, too. In a sly maneuver, they made sure their motion was accompanied by a partial transcript of Cousin Eddie's disastrous interview with SLED. As veteran defense attorneys, Harpootlian and Griffin were well aware that no court in the state would allow polygraph results to be entered into evidence. But they also knew that dozens of news outlets would publish the transcript. In the court of public opinion, the cherry-picked responses the lawyers shared provided just the right diversion at the right time.

"The state is apparently turning a blind eye to the obvious," the defense attorneys argued in the filing. "The reason Smith failed the polygraph when asked if he murdered Maggie and Paul is because he committed these heinous crimes."

THROUGH ALL THE skirmishing, Alex remained in the Richland County jail. At times he seemed hyperaware and almost fond of his growing notoriety, but also oblivious to its implications for his son, friends, and family members. He was shocked when Buster told him he'd been recognized at a casino in Las Vegas. He asked his son to brief him on what was being published about him, because he only caught glimpses on TV news broadcasts, like a snippet of his brother John Marvin talking on what appeared to be an episode of ABC's *20/20*.

"Was it the same old stuff with a bunch of innuendo and false stuff?" he asked Buster.

"I would assume it was the same old thing," Buster said, adding that he tried to tune the coverage out.

"Are they still trying to say like there's some mystery around Gloria's death?"

"I don't know," Buster said.

"Are they saying anything about Stephen Smith?" he said. "Did SLED ever come out and say there's no connection?"

"Personally, I would not count on SLED to help in any way," Buster said.

Liz, John Marvin's wife, spent her time on the phone trying to nudge Alex toward reflection. She often talked about her faith in Jesus and encouraged him to pray, or at least try.

"I feel like faith is going to be the thing to get you through this," she said.

"I guess that's the thing to do," he said. "I don't want to talk about it right now. I still have a hard time."

Liz had been the one to welcome Paul into her home while he worked his summer job. She had eulogized Maggie and had taken to calling SLED on the seventh day of every month, an homage to June 7, the day Maggie and Paul died. She told Alex that if he put his trust in God, he would see them both again in heaven. Liz asked whether he'd had any near-death experience after he got shot in the head.

Alex said he couldn't see for a minute, maybe two.

"Were you seeing the light?" she asked.

"No," he said. "I wasn't seeing light. I was seeing dark."

IT TOOK WEEKS for the defense to sort through the discovery, which was more than a terabyte of information. There were no indexes or explanatory reports to use as guideposts. Even with all that data, Harpootlian had the feeling there was still evidence missing and filed a fiery motion asking the judge to compel the state to turn over any handwritten notes from the autopsy; the results of DNA and gunshot residue testing on Maggie's and Paul's clothes; copies of any of Alex's phone calls from jail expected to be used as evidence; any SLED interoffice emails about the case; geofencing data showing what phones were pinging off towers near Moselle around the time of the homicides; and recordings of interviews with Cousin Eddie, as well as the results of any other polygraph tests.

Harpootlian had two main worries: explaining why Alex had lied about being at the kennels, and refuting a report that the T-shirt Alex had been wearing was stained with blood, probably Paul's.

"That's not good evidence when you've got the dead kid's blood on your shirt," he grumbled.

One of Harpootlian's longtime paralegals researched the prosecution's claim that the bloodstain was high-velocity blood impact spatter, or blowback from the shotgun blasts to Paul. Among the tens of thousands of documents shared by the prosecution, the paralegal found the final report from an outside expert stating there were more than a hundred tiny droplets of blood. But she could not find any data to support that claim. When she searched the database by the expert's name, the paralegal discovered another bombshell buried in an attachment to the emailed evidence. It was a report from SLED's lab that concluded the preliminary report had been wrong. There was no human blood on the shirt after all.

Sensing a huge opening, the defense asked if their own expert could examine the shirt at SLED's forensics lab. The prosecution hemmed and hawed for a few days, then finally replied that the shirt was no longer in a condition to be tested. SLED, it turned out, had sprayed the shirt with chemicals that over time had caused the white shirt to turn a blue so deep it bordered on black.

The defense filed nearly two hundred pages of motions and exhibits seeking to get the shirt thrown out as evidence. They also asked that SLED's outside expert be sanctioned for acting in bad faith. They accused the expert of conducting "science fair" experiments at home with expired blood in a failed effort to defend his sloppy work.

Creighton Waters was furious to learn that one of his key pieces of evidence had been debunked by the state's own testing. SLED was scrambling to figure out what had gone wrong. Agent Owen tried to reconstruct how he had never learned of the new finding from SLED. Owen pored through his old email, rifling through his inbox until nearly midnight, checking to see if he had missed the automated notification. But there was no notification. It had not been sent his way.

Alex's team made the most of the debacle. Not only had the prosecution claimed they had a shirt stained with Paul's blood, they had also neglected to admit their mistake and withdraw the evidence. Harpootlian and Griffin responded with a strategy known in legal circles as "PR by motion," filing one explosive allegation after another to paint SLED as a bungling outfit hellbent on framing their client.

The prosecution's case, never a slam dunk, now appeared barely capable of standing up in court.

IN THE MIDST of these reports damaging to the prosecution, Alex's former colleagues at the firm began emerging from the bunker. The Parker Law Group had collectively paid millions of dollars back to Alex's victims, with each of the partners chipping in. They had withstood initial scrutiny by accountants, as no evidence emerged that members of the staff or any of the partners had been aware that Alex had been stealing from firm clients. A year after the homicides, the firm started by Alex's great-grandfather looked as though it would survive, an outcome that had not always been certain.

The restoration of the firm's reputation was boosted when Johnny Parker, the managing partner, won a $50 million verdict for a client in a defamation case. As in days of old, the firm celebrated by throwing a dinner on the eve of the trial lawyers' convention, a once again coveted invite. Randy Murdaugh was there, along with young Buster. Their collective appearance at the convention was seen as rebranding, not just for the firm but the family. Alex was still in jail, shackled to all his charges. But the rest of the Murdaugh men were stepping back into the spotlight.

The state's trial lawyers were not ready to sweep Alex's many sins under the carpet. In acknowledgment of the shame he had brought down upon them all, they excised his name from the program's roll of distinguished past presidents. In a keynote session on legal ethics, held in a ballroom, one speaker put Alex's smirking headshot up on a big screen and pointed to their former leader as an object lesson in bad behavior.

In their chairs, under the ballroom lights, the lawyers in the Parker Law Group sipped coffee and said nothing.

CHAPTER THIRTY-SIX

Four years after the boat wreck, Anthony Cook was still having nightmares. That January, in the weeks leading up to the trial, his mother was having trouble sleeping, too. Beverly's days were filled with reminders of all that Alex Murdaugh had taken from her family and Mallory Beach's family and so many others. Beverly now stayed in the truck while her husband went inside Piggly Wiggly. She couldn't face being stopped on every aisle and asked for her take on the upcoming trial.

The case would not leave her alone, visiting her at night in her own dark and amorphous dreams. One morning she awoke with Mallory's voice in her head. She had known Mallory through all the nineteen years of her life, long before she became Anthony's girlfriend. Now Mallory was telling her something, and when Beverly awoke, she jotted it down.

They all think the dark, black waters took me. But I need them to see . . . the dark, black secrets needed me. To set them all free . . . it took me.

. . .

THE STATE OF *South Carolina v. Richard Alexander Murdaugh* was already being called the trial of the century. There were a thousand details to be dealt with before jury selection began, and first and foremost was the removal of Old Buster's portrait. Judge Newman didn't want to risk influencing jurors one way or another with Buster staring them down. Not everyone in town revered the Murdaugh name, but nearly all the locals knew enough to fear it, and the judge did not want jurors cowed by the family's influence or tempted to seek payback by convicting Buster's grandson.

For months, the clerk of court, the sheriff, and other town officials met weekly to prepare for the trial. They'd arranged for food trucks to set up outside the courthouse, reserved space for media tents, and arranged parking for satellite trucks, mobile police stations, and a Taj-Ma-Stall port-a-potty. Next to the old jail where Old Buster had forced his son Randolph to hear a murderer's confession, the officials set up a media workspace in a new wildlife sanctuary. Reporters worked alongside plexiglass containers housing snakes, turtles, and a small alligator.

One of the most delicate questions was how to handle the Murdaugh family. The Murdaughs were simultaneously the people closest to the accused and to the victims. A maelstrom of attention followed them everywhere, with paparazzi stalking young Buster as he took out the garbage or bought hamburgers and hot dogs at Costco. An army of Redditors, growing by the hour, parsed the family's handling of everything from Maggie's estate to their removal of guns from Moselle. The courthouse staff bent over backward to accommodate the Murdaughs. Yes, they could have a private room where they could retreat at meals or breaks. Yes, they could have access to a separate bathroom and their own security detail to escort them in and out of the courthouse. But the clerk could not grant their unprecedented request to sit in the middle of the courtroom, in chairs placed in the center aisle, so they could show allegiance to both Alex on the defense side and deference to the memories of Maggie and Paul on the prosecution side. The fire marshal said no, he would not allow them to block the aisle. The family would have to pick a side.

The Colleton County sheriff's office worked out an elaborate plan to escort Alex from the county detention center to the courthouse. The transport team planned to pick him up every morning at the jail in a van outfitted with a small cell known as the cage. Alex would be handcuffed and locked in the cage for the quarter-mile journey. Once they pulled up behind the courthouse, armed deputies would lead him out of the van, one on each side, one behind, and one in front. His lawyers had asked that he be allowed to wear business attire. The deputies agreed to their additional request that he be allowed to drape his sports coat over his shackled hands, to avoid photographs of him being led into the courthouse in chains.

One of the leads on the security detail, a deputy named 'Nette Grant who typically served as a victim's advocate, urged her colleagues to be careful. She'd known Alex for years and remembered how jovial he'd always been, stopping to speak to every lawyer, bailiff, and passer-by in the courthouse.

"It's the nice ones you have to look out for most," she said.

She reminded the deputies to keep their guns as far as possible from Alex's hands, and not to let him carry papers, which could hold paper clips, or loose pencils, which could be used to jab someone's eye or ear. If that happened, she said, Alex might take advantage of the distraction to run.

"Be careful," she said. "He's got nothing to lose."

THE NIGHT BEFORE the trial started, Creighton Waters went to the courthouse in shorts, a T-shirt, and a baseball cap to get a better feel for the room where he'd be prosecuting Alex Murdaugh. The courtroom had been designed in 1820, and it showed. It had a stately formality that felt spacious, but when the prosecutor walked around, he discovered that the quarters were surprisingly tight. The jury box was barely an arm's length from the prosecution table. There would be no hiding here. Waters and his team would have to be mindful of their facial expressions, their body language, any exasperated sighs. If one of them so much as raised an eyebrow, the jury would notice. Millions of view-ers might notice, too, given that every minute of the trial would be streamed to news sites around the country.

In his career, Waters had never experienced a case that attracted so much rabid attention. That night, when he left the courthouse, the surrounding square was lined with barriers and ringed by satellite news trucks. A nearby stand, he noticed, was selling elephant ears. It looked like a carnival, he thought. It felt like a carnival, too, operating on the edge of light and dark, ready to turn on a dime. The only thing missing was a Ferris wheel.

JURY SELECTION BEGAN on a cold and brilliant Monday. The clerk had sent out nine hundred jury summonses, five times the normal number, knowing that nearly everyone in Colleton County had some connection to the Murdaughs and the ones who didn't were likely to have followed the case in the media. One in twenty eligible voters got a summons, meaning if there were a hundred people at a country church on the Sunday before the trial, five of them had gotten a sum-mons. Everyone in town knew someone who had been chosen.

That Monday, the first of three batches of prospective jurors ar-rived in a surreal cattle call, filling the 120 seats in the back half of the courtroom. There were married couples and divorced couples, people who knew each other from high school or church, people who recog-nized one another from the Ford dealership or the Walmart bakery counter or the car detailing shop. Among them all there was a thrum of anticipation, a nervous murmur that it was finally go-time.

Alex had already entered the courtroom. The bailiffs had removed his shackles beforehand, and he strode forward holding a brown accor-dion file of papers, then took his seat between Jim Griffin and Dick Harpootlian. He wore a strangely affable smile and was quiet and al-most still, except for his chewing of the stem of his glasses and the clenching and unclenching of his jaw. He seemed to barely blink. Dressed in a white button-down shirt, gray slacks, and a blue blazer with shiny gold buttons, he looked like just another member of his defense team. He was so gaunt, it didn't seem possible the clothes he wore belonged to him. After an earlier court appearance, he had been ridiculed on social media for what some characterized as flirting with a woman on the defense team. On this morning, he did not speak to the young lawyer or even look in her direction. She was experienced and respected but had been relegated to the far end of the table.

On the bench, Judge Clifton Newman was an oasis of calm. In his seventy-one years, he had seen the best and worst the state had to offer. He had grown up in a segregated farm town a hundred thirty miles north of Hampton, and when he left to study law in the Midwest, it was the first time he'd been in class with white students. In his twenty years on the bench, he had overseen all manner of cases, most notably the trial of a white police officer accused of shooting an unarmed Black man in the back five times as he ran away. Newman had been handpicked by the chief justice of South Carolina's supreme court to oversee the Murdaugh trial, a national spectacle that would also test the state's judicial system. With less than a year until retirement, the judge knew this was the case he would be remembered for.

Judge Newman had been a steady and measured presence in the flurry of pretrial hearings. But two weeks before the trial began, tragedy struck. His forty-year-old son had suffered a fatal heart attack. Newman had asked the state's chief justice, a close friend, to assign the Murdaugh case to someone else to allow him time to mourn. But the chief justice said no. This was Newman's case. As he presided, the judge knew he would need to draw on his experience, both to control his emotions and to make sure the trial was impeccably run. He wanted no mistrial, no hung jury, no appellate court telling him he'd deprived the accused of any of his rights.

Flanked by the flags of South Carolina and the United States, Newman gazed out across the courtroom at the potential jurors. He asked the clerk to begin questioning them. When she asked who among them knew anything about the Murdaugh case, all 120 stood. Among this first group was the clerk's own daughter, along with the fiancée of the second deputy on the scene of the murders and the brother of the third deputy to arrive.

The clerk ran through a set of standard questions, inquiring as to the prospective jurors' occupations and marital status.

"Divorced, happily," said one man, prompting laughter. "I'm single, but I'm looking."

One woman stood with her hand on her hip. When asked where she worked, she said, "The Monkey Farm."

Another round of laughter. All the locals in the room understood that the Monkey Farm was a nickname for a medical testing facility on the outskirts of town. "I bet you could tell some stories," the clerk said.

Monkey Farm was Harpootlian's type of juror. He tended to pick women in middle age, ones who made eye contact when he talked and who seemed they might laugh at his jokes. If the juror liked him, they might also like his client. This woman had offered a glimpse of her own sense of humor. Harpootlian already felt a budding rapport.

Nearly all of the potential jurors had some connection to someone involved in the case, leaving Judge Newman to decide how close was too close. Mallory Beach's first cousin was not excused. Neither was Eddie Smith's friend from the dart league or the paramedic who went skeet shooting with one of Alex's brothers. The judge excused the postmaster from the tiny town of Islandton, where Moselle is located, as well as a young man who had been friends with Paul and had several other friends on the witness list. The first cousin of the sergeant who tested Alex's hands for gunshot residue was not disqualified until she shared that she worked at the wedding venue where the defense was staying for the duration of the trial.

Next the pool was asked whether anyone had a criminal background. Suddenly people were making confessions among strangers, as if they questioned who they were to stand in judgment of another.

"I shoplifted when I was a teenager."

"I sold pot in 1971."

"I had a domestic violence charge in the nineties."

When asked about any hardships that might result from serving on a weeks-long trial, at least a dozen of the potential jurors said they would lose their home if they missed even a week of work.

Alex followed these exchanges closely, whispering to his lawyers who he would keep and who he would strike.

By Wednesday morning, the pool had been winnowed from the 900 people who'd received a summons, to the 360 who showed up for voir dire, to the 120 without significant hardships or conflicts of interest, to the final 80 deemed eligible to serve. The clerk began pulling juror numbers at random, each potential juror coming to the front of the courtroom to face the prosecution and defense. The lawyers would check the notes they'd made on each juror, then quietly consult. For the defense, Alex always had the last word.

The first juror picked was the woman who worked at the Monkey Farm. As she took her seat in the jury box, the clerk called the next candidate. It was clear the defense preferred to seat middle-aged white men. The defense used six strikes, most of them on Blacks, including two Black females. The prosecution used three strikes, all on white candidates, including a male defense lawyer who was friends with some members of the Murdaugh firm. In the end, the jury consisted of two Black women, six white women, and four white men. The alternates included two Black women, one Black man, and three white men, including the younger brother of one of the first deputies on the scene. Many of the jurors were acquainted with one another. A bailiff escorting them had to resist the urge to talk to the ones he knew by name, including the Monkey Farm juror, a cousin by marriage, and the deputy's brother, whom he'd babysat years ago.

The clerk swore them in. Then the judge addressed them, saying they had been chosen for a sacred duty. "Out of all the people who live here in Colleton County, out of all the people who live here in the state of South Carolina or anyplace else," said Newman, "only the twelve of you who will deliberate can decide the facts of this case."

With that, he said it was time for opening statements.

. . .

CREIGHTON WATERS WAS itching to begin. For months, he had been working twelve-hour days, preparing for this moment. In his room at the Hampton Inn, he had practiced his opening again and again, pacing back and forth. Now his nerves settled into something approaching calm or at least resolution. He was as ready as he'd ever be.

When the judge signaled him, Waters stood up and began by telling the jury how on the evening of June 7, 2021, Alex Murdaugh had murdered his son Paul.

"The defendant over there"—the prosecutor pointed to Alex—"took a twelve-gauge shotgun and shot him in the chest and the shoulder with buckshot."

Miraculously, though, Waters said, the first blast did not kill Paul. Alex fired the shotgun again, this time from an angle below his son's chin, wreaking catastrophic damage to the young man's brain and head. The evidence would show, Waters said, that Alex had then picked up the .300 Blackout and opened fire on his wife, Maggie, at close range.

"Pow pow!" Waters yelled, slapping his hand on the prosecution desk. "Two shots! To the abdomen and in the leg, they took her down."

Then Alex, he said, had walked over to his wife and shot her in the wrist, then finished her off with two shots to the head.

At the defense table, Alex was glowering at the prosecutor, his pupils so wide they blotted out the whites of his eyes.

Waters told the jurors about how Alex had spent more than a year telling anyone who would listen that he was never down at the kennels with his wife and son. But then a video had been discovered, he said, that proved he was with Maggie and Paul just before the shooting began.

"He was there just minutes before their cellphones go silent forever," Waters said.

Waters took the jury through the evidence that would be presented over the course of what would be a long and complex trial. They would hear forensic evidence, including that shell cases found at the firing range and near the house at Moselle were fired from the same gun as those surrounding Maggie's body. They would hear how Alex had carried what looked like a balled-up blue tarp over to his mother's house a few days after the murders. He'd carried it upstairs, to a part of the house his aging parents had not used in years. They'd hear how investigators later found a massive blue raincoat, covered in gunshot residue on the inside.

As the prosecutor spoke, the light coming through the shaded windows dimmed, and from a distance came the rumble of thunder.

"You're going to reach the inescapable conclusion that Alex murdered Maggie and Paul," Waters told the jury.

He pointed to Alex again. He was the storm, the prosecutor said, and on that night in June the storm had been coming for Maggie and Paul, just like the storm the jurors could hear outside the courtroom.

DICK HARPOOTLIAN WAS grumpy. An early riser by nature, he had been awakened well before his standard 5 A.M. by wild geese squawking overhead at Eden at Gracefield, the estate where the defense team was staying. He was still trying to slough off the tail end of a bout of Covid, and he did not feel himself.

Even on an off day, Harpootlian was better than most lawyers on their best. He had prosecuted or defended more than fifty murder cases, honing a reputation as lovably gruff and mercurially brilliant. He was an attack dog in Democratic presidential primaries and in the state senate and loved nothing more than the gamesmanship afforded the man in the center of the ring, part of the reason why he'd stuck with the Murdaugh case even when his client ran short of money to pay him. He'd made no secret that in whatever movie was made from this case, he wanted to be played by Billy Bob Thornton.

For his opening statement, in the biggest trial of a career full of big trials, he wore an emerald-green and sapphire-blue print tie by Charvet, the Parisian purveyor of $300 silk ties. As he stood to make his opening statement, he conducted the same ritual he had for the past fifty years. He'd learned the hard way as a young solicitor that you wanted the jury smiling with you, not at you. He checked to make sure his fly was up.

Harpootlian approached the jury box without a script or even notes, a crutch he despised. His mantra was "You've got to become the case." A lawyer that memorizes or, worse, reads an opening statement has not become the case, and has no strategy to connect with the jury. If the prosecutor had sold a story, Dick Harpootlian was selling himself.

"Ladies and gentlemen of the jury," he began, enunciating each syllable as he introduced himself and the rest of the defense team.

"It is our honor to represent Alex Murdaugh," he said, more slowly still. "I say it's our honor because I submit to you that what you have heard from the attorney general as 'facts' are not. They are not. They're his theories. His conjecture."

He asked Alex to stand up.

"This is Alex Murdaugh," he said. "Alex was the loving father of Paul and the loving husband of Maggie."

The state had no evidence that Alex Murdaugh committed these horrendous crimes, he said. They had never found the guns that killed Maggie and Paul, he said. "There's no camera, there's no fingerprints, there's no forensics tying him to the crime," he said, his voice rising. "None! I say that without any fear of contradiction whatsoever. None!"

He asked the jurors to look again at Alex, who had chosen each of them to judge the case because he trusted them to be fair.

"You have agreed to follow the law, and here's the law," Harpootlian said. "He . . ." A pause. "Didn't . . ." Another. "Do it.

"He is presumed innocent. As you sit there right now, when you look at him, you have to believe he is innocent. He didn't do it."

THE STATE'S FIRST witnesses were the first officers on the scene. Sgt. Daniel Greene told how Alex pressed him on getting paramedics there quickly, though it was clear that Maggie and Paul were dead. The prosecution played video from Greene's body camera while the members of the jury craned forward for their first look at Alex on the night of the murders. He was pacing and sniffling.

"His immediate reaction was to tell me about an incident that had happened with his son with a boating accident," Greene said. "He did not appear to be crying. He was upset, but I did not see any visible tears."

Captain Jason Chapman, Greene's supervisor, testified that he initially took Alex's decision to get a shotgun from the house as a sign that there might still be shooters nearby. He said he was flummoxed, though, by subtle changes in Alex's demeanor when they asked questions that posed even the slightest challenge to his version of events. Chapman said that when he asked about what appeared to be multiple sets of tire tracks in the grass near the kennels, Alex's "breathing slowed and he began to watch us more closely, out of the corner of his eye."

During Detective Laura Rutland's testimony, prosecutors played the video of law enforcement's first official interview with Alex. It had been recorded just before 1 A.M., with Alex in the passenger seat of David Owen's car and Detective Rutland seated in the back seat, directly behind Alex. During the course of the forty-minute video, Alex stared straight ahead while telling how he'd come home from his mom's house and found Maggie's and Paul's bodies by the kennels. He said he had checked both of them for a pulse, then fiddled with Paul's phone before placing it on his backside and calling 911.

"How would you describe the defendant's hands when you saw him?" assistant prosecutor John Meadors asked.

"They were clean," Rutland said.

"How would you describe his arms?"

"They were clean."

His T-shirt, shorts, and shoes—all of them had been clean.

"And is the individual you described as clean from head to toe in this courtroom?"

"Yes," the detective said, pointing to Alex, who nodded and gazed back at her with a smile.

. . .

DURING THE BREAKS, Alex was led through the back door of the courtroom into the hallway behind the judge's bench, where he was shackled and taken into the elevator. There he rode the two floors down to the basement holding cells collectively known as the dungeon. One of the holding cells contained the rolling cart carrying the hundreds of exhibits, including the sealed autopsy photos. The other cell was Alex's. The cell had a low metal toilet without a lid and a long metal bench. The walls were painted a sickly yellow and the interior of the metal door was marred by graffiti, with the names of gangs and epithets against the police scratched into the backside of the door with any sharp implement available, as pencils and pens were not allowed inside.

Alex was allowed some privileges, including ordering lunch from the same takeout menus used by jurors. He had fried chicken and field peas from the Olde House buffet and Italian subs from down the block at Carmine's. But his lawyers complained mightily about the lack of privacy in their conversations with him. They could not sit in the cell for safety reasons and had to conduct their strategy sessions out in the open, on opposite sides of a plexiglass divider like the ones at movie ticket booths.

When his lawyers left and he was alone, Alex would often lie on the bench with his eyes closed and his hands steepled on his chest. Sometimes he would sit with his head bowed toward his knees and his hands clasped. Court personnel watched him on security cameras, not just because they had to but because they wanted to. Opinion was almost evenly divided on whether he was praying, or, since he knew he was being watched, pretending to.

THAT NIGHT, BLANCA was watching a recording of the first day of testimony when she caught a small detail no one had mentioned.

"Pause it!" she said to her husband. "Back it up!"

The state was playing the video from Daniel Greene's body cam the night of the murders. As he approached the open door of Alex's black Suburban and glanced briefly inside, the video showed a blue beach towel with an exotic leaf print wadded in the driver's seat.

A terrible feeling came over Blanca. She'd always understood Alex's flaws but overlooked them because he'd treated her kindly, like a baby sister. When he hung up the phone, he'd say, "'Bye, B, talk to you later, love you." At first it had surprised her, but soon she'd found herself saying it back: "Love you too."

Blanca had not wanted to accept that Alex could've killed Maggie and Paul. But as she and her husband watched the three-second snippet over and over, something changed. She'd cleaned out the Suburban all the time, dumping out spit cups and taking stray cash inside the house for safekeeping. Not once had she found a stray beach towel.

"He did it," she told her husband. "He did it."

Blanca knew that towel. She had washed it and put it on the top shelf in the laundry room for Maggie to take back to Edisto. Alex, she realized now, must have grabbed the towel from the laundry room at the same time he grabbed the Black Sheep T-shirt from the drying rack.

Suddenly the pieces clicked into place. The pajamas in the laundry room door, laid out to look as though Maggie left them there. The fact that Maggie had left all her stuff in the Mercedes, not just the Louis Vuitton tote and matching suitcase but her purse, too. Maggie must've changed her mind about staying over. It was then that Blanca's heart sank even lower. She remembered putting two of Alex's empty pill baggies in the trash can beside Maggie's bathroom sink. She'd meant to empty the trash but got distracted.

Blanca felt certain Maggie must have parked the Mercedes, come inside to use the bathroom, and seen the baggies right away. Had the baggies triggered an argument that had led Alex to finally snap? With a sick feeling in her stomach, she wondered if Alex had killed Maggie and Paul because she forgot to take out the trash.

CHAPTER THIRTY-SEVEN

The first week of the trial passed in fits and starts, with the prosecution methodically working through law enforcement witnesses and the defense poking holes in the witnesses' missed calls. That stalemate changed on the fifth day of testimony, when the prosecution finally played the kennel video. The jurors were instantly transported into that night, with the crickets buzzing in the woods, the glowing eyes of Cash the puppy, and Maggie in the background, somewhere behind Paul, exclaiming that Bubba had caught a guinea. Paul corrected her with perhaps the last words he would ever say.

"It's a chicken," he said.

Then the jurors could hear Alex somewhere nearby.

"C'mere, Bubba, c'mere."

Watching and listening along, Alex's face turned red. At the sound of his son's voice, he began puffing air from his lips and nodding rapidly.

The jurors did not look at him. But a woman seated in the front row of the jury box closed her eyes and crossed her arms at the sound of Maggie's voice.

The defense tried to undo the damage with their cross-examination of the next witness, Paul's longtime friend Rogan Gibson. Rogan,

Cash's owner, testified he'd been waiting anxiously the night of June 7 for Paul to send him that video. But it had never come. Rogan said there was no doubt in his mind that it was Alex's voice he heard in the background. The Murdaughs had been his second parents.

"They were loving to each other and to Paul and Buster and their friends, correct?" Griffin said.

"That's correct," Rogan said.

"Can you think of any circumstance that you can envision, knowing them as you do, where Alex would brutally murder Paul and Maggie?"

"Not that I can think of," Rogan said.

The defense had been arguing for weeks, including in filings before the trial began, that the jury should not hear evidence of what was happening in Alex's life at the time of the homicides, particularly the confrontation at the law firm over the missing $792,000 fee. They said he was on trial for murder, not financial crimes. In the short break after Rogan Gibson's testimony, Creighton Waters said the defense had opened the trial to precisely that kind of evidence by asking whether he knew any reason Alex might murder his wife and son.

"We've gone through the looking glass," Waters said.

The prosecution was not legally required to establish a motive for the murders. But juries typically like having a context for whatever criminal charges come before them. Knowing why completes the story. If the jurors in this case were allowed to hear about the pressures building on Alex in the days leading up to the murders, that would be a crucial win for the state.

Judge Newman said he was not prepared to announce a definitive ruling on the financial evidence. But with the next witness, Waters pressed his advantage. He asked Will Loving, Paul's roommate in Columbia, about guns and Snapchat videos and other minutiae before launching into a half dozen questions about Alex's finances.

"Did you know anything about what his bank account balances were?"

Loving said he had no clue.

Harpootlian, who had been checking his phone, looked up and leaned toward his co-counsel. It was Griffin's job to raise objections, since this was his witness to cross-examine. But at this crucial moment, the defense attorney seemed loath to antagonize the judge, who'd chastised him already for frequent and repetitive objections. Griffin stayed silent.

On the stand, the witness said no, he didn't know anything about how much money Alex had in the bank.

Having heard no protest from the defense, Waters blazed forward with a rapid-fire sequence of related questions.

"Did you know the specific things that were going on in the boat case the week that Paul and Maggie were murdered?" Waters asked. "You know anything about civil discovery and how it can expose financial information? Do you know anything at all about him being confronted on June seventh, 2021?"

Will Loving knew nothing of these matters. But that wasn't the point. Just by asking the questions, Waters was suggesting to the jury why Alex might have killed Paul and Maggie.

Finally Griffin stood up and objected. But it was too late. The judge allowed the prosecutor to ask the witness his next question.

"Did you know anything about him being confronted on the morning of June seventh, 2021, about $792,000 of missing fees from his law firm?"

Harpootlian threw his phone down on the table with a *thwack* that could be heard from the back of the courtroom.

"Objection, Your Honor," Griffin said. "That's totally improper."

Overruled, said the judge.

That was it. The way was now clear for the prosecution to explore Alex's finances with the witnesses. By asking about his life with Maggie and Paul, the defense attorneys had made a strategic error. By not objecting the second the prosecution began firing off questions about a possible financial motive, they had compounded one mistake with another.

They had accidentally opened the door, then stood by while the prosecution kicked it wide open.

. . .

THE STATE BEGAN making its financial case with Jeanne Seckinger, the chief financial officer of the family law firm. She described how she and Alex's paralegal Annette Griswold came to suspect Alex was hiding money and how Jeanne had confronted him about it on the afternoon of the homicides.

Jan Malinowski, the acting head of Palmetto State Bank, walked the jurors through the ways Alex siphoned money from client accounts and spent it from his own almost as quickly as it came in. He was frequently overdrawn, sometimes by hundreds of thousands of dollars. The bank charged him a $5 overdraft fee, though it was not always enforced.

"Perhaps the most generous overdraft policy ever seen?" Waters asked.

Malinowski, who'd married into the Laffitte family but was not from Hampton County, smiled wryly.

"Quite possibly," he said.

The state had dozens of Alex's financial victims to choose from, but they put only one on the stand: Tony Satterfield, Gloria's older son. Harpootlian fought hard to prevent it, saying the state was trying to damage Alex's character by putting a child on the stand.

"I believe he's an adult," the judge said. Tony was boyish-looking but was in his early thirties.

"I apologize," Harpootlian said. "He looks young to me."

The judge allowed Tony to testify on the basis of the magnitude of the theft from his family, and the fact that Alex had previously admitted to it in a filing in the boys' civil lawsuit.

Tony had not seen Alex since his mother's funeral. As he stood up to take the stand, his lawyer, Eric Bland, gave him a hug. "They're scared of you for a reason," Bland whispered.

Tony told the jury he was an emergency room technician who took care of his brother, a vulnerable adult. His voice was soft and hesitant, his eyes wide behind his glasses. He told the jury his mother had worked for the Murdaughs for twenty years and had regarded Alex as family. He said he was relieved when Alex tried to get some money to pay her funeral bills and help him and his brother keep her mobile home. He read aloud a letter he had faxed over to Alex in the spring of 2021 along with a bill from the hospital and the trailer company.

"What does this mean?" he'd asked. "And do I need to do anything?"

Harpootlian objected repeatedly, trying to unnerve the prosecutor and the witness, a strategy he called the kidney punch. It didn't work. On cross-examination, the defense attorney suggested that the Satterfield brothers had benefited from Alex's lying about the cause of his mother's injuries.

"I mean, if she just fell down the stairs, there'd be no lawsuit, right?" Harpootlian asked.

"I guess," Tony said.

Harpootlian also noted that Tony's lawyer had ended up recovering $6.5 million after filing a lawsuit over the missing money.

"That's two million more than you would have gotten had he not taken your money?"

"Okay," said Tony.

At that question, a male juror on the front row lowered his chin and raised his eyes. A female juror shook her head. Most of the jurors' eyes followed Tony as he left the stand and went to retrieve his hoodie from his seat beside Eric Bland. They were close enough to hear what Tony said about Harpootlian:

"That man is not a nice man."

MARK TINSLEY WALKED into the courtroom, armored in his gray suit.

He had watched Tony Satterfield's wrenching testimony from a hacienda in western Mexico, where he'd been hunting mule deer in the Sonoran Desert. When the prosecution called and asked him to testify, he cut his trip short and hurried back home.

Tinsley was key to understanding why Alex had been under such pressure in the hours before the murders. He had exerted much of that pressure himself, filing motions demanding that Alex turn over his financials in the boat case. The hearing at which Alex was supposed to hand over those records—and thereby expose himself as a thief—had been set for Thursday, June 10. But that hearing had been canceled because Paul and Maggie Murdaugh had been murdered the previous Monday night. If the jury needed a motive, they would hear it from Tinsley. It was Tinsley who had pieced together Alex's cover-up of the boat crash. He'd gone to SLED and to the attorney general's office, showing them exactly what Alex had done.

As Tinsley arrived in court, Dick Harpootlian walked over to greet him. The two of them had worked a big case together several years back, resulting in a $10.5 million settlement against a methadone clinic. Dick had been impressed with Mark's doggedness, and Mark had been impressed with Dick's ballsiness. After the boat wreck, when Paul needed a criminal defense lawyer, one of Alex's law partners asked Tinsley who the Murdaughs should hire. Tinsley had recommended Harpootlian.

Now that Tinsley was here to strike a blow against the defense, Harpootlian told him he was wasting his time. Long before the trial began, the defense had hired a firm to test how the financial evidence would play with mock juries across the state. Not one of the juries, Harpootlian said, bought the financials as a motive.

Tinsley smiled.

"We-ell," he said, stretching the word into two syllables, as he often did before delivering a blow, "I hope you can get your money back."

Once he was sworn in, he stepped up to the witness stand, lowered himself into the creaky wooden chair, and surveyed the packed courtroom. The faces were inert and silent, reminding him of the cardboard cutouts that were staples in baseball stands during the pandemic.

When asked to state his name for the record, he leaned extra close to the microphone so his voice would be louder than necessary. He'd been waiting a long time for this moment. He might as well make some noise.

"Mark Tinsley," he said.

He looked across the room at Alex, whom he'd not seen in person since the two of them had locked horns years before. Alex was looking back at him, tautly focused on his former friend, no more rocking, no tears, no Tic Tacs.

The energy in the courtroom was electric, almost breathless. Tinsley was charged with a barely contained rage. Alex had created Paul, nurturing his recklessness even after he'd killed Mallory. Alex had then killed what he'd created, the son whose rot was the inevitable outcome of his father's own. Maggie had been collateral damage.

Creighton Waters asked Tinsley about his first phone conversation with Renee Beach, when she'd described seeing the Murdaughs waved past the crime scene tape at Archers Creek.

"Did she give you any particular instructions about proceeding forward based on that experience?" Waters asked.

"No," Tinsley said. He paused, knowing he should be diplomatic but unable to stop himself. "Nobody really gives me instructions."

He walked the jurors through the history of the wrongful death suit and his attempts to compel Alex to hand over his financials. He told them about running into Alex at the trial lawyers' convention, the way Alex had confronted him.

"He gets up close in my face," Tinsley said, holding his palm three inches from his nose. He recalled Alex saying he thought they were friends, and how he'd replied that they were friends but that he was ready to burn Alex's house down if he didn't settle the case.

The prosecutor asked Tinsley what he'd made of their encounter that day at the convention. Tinsley looked over at Alex, who was staring at him.

"I took it as he tried to intimidate me," Tinsley said. "He didn't intimidate me."

The two of them kept their eyes locked for another fifteen seconds. Finally, Alex looked down.

During cross-examination, a junior member of Alex's defense team prodded Tinsley on whether the June 10 hearing was truly a day of reckoning.

"Maybe you've never tried a civil case," Tinsley said.

The defense lawyer pressed on, paying no heed to the warning the witness had just given him. As a practical matter, the young lawyer noted, the boat crash hearing had been canceled because of the murders. He flipped through a stack of papers, ticking off the items Tinsley had been requesting. The judge had never granted Tinsley's motion to compel the financials, correct?

"You thought wrong," Tinsley said.

This was the moment Tinsley had been waiting for. He'd had a hunch that Alex's lawyers had overlooked an email sent by the judge that October while Alex was in rehab, saying he expected the defense to hand over the documents.

Tinsley reached into his suit pocket and pulled out a copy of the order.

"There's a lot of papers, so maybe you got confused."

YOUNG BUSTER HAD greeted Tinsley when he first walked into the courtroom. But once the lawyer began to testify, Buster's veneer of politeness fell away. Watching from a few rows behind his father, the young man raised his middle finger to his lips, covering the insult by chewing his nail.

The more Tinsley talked, the more devastating it became for Alex and his son. At one point, a bailiff looked over and saw Buster appearing to use his hands as pistols. He kept the motions near his lap, where almost no one could see. But the bailiff was standing close, at an angle that afforded a clear view. Buster, he would later say, was cocking each thumb and firing away with index fingers aimed directly at the witness.

CHAPTER THIRTY-EIGHT

The Murdaughs had ended up sitting directly behind Alex, not in the aisle. But they'd continued testing the courtroom's limits. Social media was awash with criticism that Alex was being afforded privileges not available to other defendants. From their prime seats Alex's family could almost touch the defense table, and he was speaking with them every morning and even exchanging fist bumps. The judge soon ordered the removal of a bailiff, a high school friend of Alex's, for allowing these violations of the rules. The clerk of court, meanwhile, had asked the defense team to stop letting Alex suck on mints and hard candy. When the clerk's request was ignored, she'd repeated it in an email.

The last straw came when someone called in a bomb threat. In the chaos of evacuation, Alex's sister had passed a hardcover book to the defense team's paralegal, who gave it to Alex. Books were contraband for most prisoners, and at the very least had to be examined to ensure they did not conceal weapons, drugs, or other dangerous items. The book the family sent was *The Judge's List* by John Grisham.

As the evacuation ended and people filed back into the courthouse, the Murdaughs were informed that the judge wanted them moved from their perch directly behind Alex to several rows back. Disgusted, Buster Murdaugh kicked over a water bottle.

It was around this time that the bailiffs minding the dungeon noticed that Alex seemed to be taking advantage of his lunch perk, writing his name on the daily takeout menu and ordering double meals. They started having the jail send over lunch for Alex in a brown paper bag. From then on, he'd be treated like any other prisoner.

A TRIAL IS inherently unpredictable and frequently dull. Shaky witnesses soar and big names flail. Functionaries testify for hours on end, identifying their signature on the seal of an evidence envelope. Sometimes it feels as though the prosecution has to build the clock before telling the jury what time it is. In Alex Murdaugh's trial, some of the most powerful testimony was sandwiched between technical testimony, delivered at inauspicious moments by unfamiliar names.

Marian Proctor, Maggie's older sister, was the state's fifty-fifth witness. Unlike other witnesses, who were scrutinized by the press corps as they waited to be called from the back row of the gallery, Marian was led into the courtroom from the hallway, flanked by a victim's advocate on one side and her husband on the other. She wore a crisp white blouse under a pale gold sweater, her blond hair pulled back and framing her dark eyes. It was as if the ghost of Maggie Murdaugh had swept into the room.

Neither Marian nor her parents had spoken publicly about their loss. Not one of Maggie's friends and family had been a visible presence during the trial. Now the jurors leaned forward to hear Marian's soft voice. She told them she was five years older than Maggie, a difference in age that was significant when the two were children but melted away once they became empty-nesters. She said she spoke to Maggie almost every day, including on June 7, when Maggie called her that afternoon to say Randolph III was declining rapidly. Maggie said she had planned to stay the night in Edisto because she had men working on the beach house, but Alex said Paul was coming home and he needed her there, too.

"Well, Maggie," she remembered saying, "that's probably what you should do. Go be with him if he needs you."

"You encouraged her to go to Moselle?" Waters asked.

Marian sucked in her breath. "I did," she said.

"Was that the last time you talked to her?"

"Yes," she said, her voice breaking.

Pained expressions marked the faces of several female jurors. Waters passed the witness a box of tissues, and Marian took two and folded them in her hand. Waters asked if she was all right, and when she nodded, he pressed on.

Marian said that after the murders, Alex seemed focused on getting Buster back into law school and clearing Paul's name in the boat case.

"I thought that was so strange because my number one goal was to find out who killed my sister and Paul."

"Did he ever act scared or afraid that the real killers were out there somewhere?" Waters asked.

Her family had been afraid, Marian said. "We didn't know what was going on . . . I was scared for Alex and Buster. I felt like they needed protection. I think everybody was afraid, and um . . ."

For fifteen seconds, she sat quietly, shaking her head slightly from side to side. It was unclear whether she had completed her thought until finally, she spoke softly.

"Alex didn't seem to be afraid."

At the defense table, Alex's face hardened, and he turned toward Jim Griffin with a shocked look. His lawyer nodded and said nothing.

On Griffin's cross-examination, he asked whether Marian was criticizing Alex for trying to clear Paul's name after the murders, and she said she was not, she just thought it was odd that he was not trying to find out who had killed Paul and Maggie.

"We thought this horrible person was out there," she said. "We thought that up until September . . ."

"Right," Griffin said.

"And then"—she paused—"things started to change a little bit."

Griffin flipped back and forth through the pages of notes in his hands, as though he did not know what to say or do next. His questions to the witness, he realized, had inadvertently opened the door to another set of facts the defense did not want the jury to hear about, namely the roadside shooting. Marian hadn't referred explicitly to the shooting, but her allusion to things changing in September had taken her in that direction. If she were allowed to testify about the roadside shooting, it would give the jury more evidence of Alex's pattern of lies.

The judge sent the jury out so he could hear whatever Marian had to say before deciding whether to let the jury hear it, too. The witness described getting a call in the hours after the roadside shooting and being told that Alex had been fired from his law firm for stealing client money. She said the call was from Jim Griffin, who'd represented Paul and become close to Alex.

"That's hearsay," Griffin said. "Absolute hearsay."

The courtroom erupted with laughter. The judge smiled.

"What kind of quandary does that put you in?" he said. "You're going to be a witness as well?"

The judge denied the state's request to ask Marian about whether Maggie had thrown Alex out of the house for having an affair. He narrowly limited what she could testify to about the roadside shooting, agreeing with the defense that it was a "bridge too far" in terms of potential damage to the jury's understanding of Alex's character. But he warned Harpootlian and Griffin to be careful with their questions. Alex's life was a minefield of misdeeds, and it was proving impossible for the defense not to step on bomb after bomb.

LIKE MARIAN, SOME of the most powerful witnesses were the women who knew the Murdaughs best, including those who worked for the family.

Shelley Smith, Miss Libby's night nurse, was visibly shaking when she testified about Alex seeking her out after his father's funeral reception. She recalled how he had asked her about her job at the school cafeteria, then said he had a friend who could help her get better hours. He told her he'd heard she was getting married and offered to help with wedding expenses—all while hinting she should tell the police he'd stayed longer at Almeda than she knew he had.

Shelley was crying softly.

"Why are you crying, Miss Smith?" prosecutor John Meadors asked.

"Because it's a good family, and I love working there," she said. "I'm sorry all this happened. Good people, you know."

"He wasn't there no thirty to forty minutes, was he?" Meadors asked.

"No," she said.

Blanca was nervous about testifying. She'd just gotten braces on her teeth and felt self-conscious; she was worried about the bags under her eyes because she couldn't seem to stop crying. As she approached the witness stand, she could sense Alex watching her, but she wasn't ready to meet his eye. She hadn't seen or talked to him for more than a year. When she took the stand, though, she did her best to project calm. Like Shelley Smith, Blanca said she, too, had felt pressured by Alex to lie to the police. He wanted her to say he had been wearing the loose-fitting Vineyard Vines–type shirt on his way to work that morning. But she clearly remembered fixing his collar on a different shirt, a blue polo underneath a sport coat.

Meadors asked Blanca if Maggie had been anxious about anything in the months leading up to the murders. Blanca recounted the story of the day Maggie had made them both a cup of coffee, led her into the gun room, and closed the door.

"Was she anxious about money issues?" Meadors asked.

Harpootlian threw a stack of papers on the table and leaped to his feet.

"Your Honor," he said, "I object." It was hearsay, he said, and completely inappropriate.

Again the judge sent the jury from the courtroom. In the interminable silence while they filed out, Blanca sat motionless on the witness stand, looking down, pursing her lips. She'd been startled by the sound of the papers hitting the desk and the anger of Dick Harpootlian, whom she'd met at Moselle after the funeral. She worried, irrationally or not, that she'd said something so wrong that she was going to jail.

Once the judge called the room back to order, Harpootlian immediately asked for a mistrial. It was outrageously prejudicial, he said, to
let Blanca say that Maggie was worried about money after the jury had
heard witness after witness talk about Alex's financial misdeeds.

"You can't unring the bell," he said. "You can't correct that."

The judge overruled him, saying he'd allowed the defense to question witnesses about Alex and Maggie's loving relationship, and he was
going to allow Blanca to answer this question.

With the jury back in the room, Blanca confirmed that Maggie had
been worried about money. "She felt that Alex was not being truthful
to her about what was going on in that lawsuit," she said.

Meadors then asked her about how Maggie felt about being at Moselle at night, particularly down at the kennels.

"She was scared," Blanca said. "It got dark out there."

As Blanca made her way out of the courtroom, a reporter pushed a
tape recorder in her face, prompting a SLED agent to take her by the
elbow and whisk her out the back of the courtroom.

From the safety of her truck, she called her husband, who told her
that reporters had come by the house as well. She decided to spend the
night at her daughter's house in Bluffton and stopped at Walmart on
the way. A woman recognized her and asked, "Excuse me, are you
Blanca?" Another approached her in the bread aisle and said, "You did
so good."

Blanca barely knew what to say. She felt desperately alone. She'd lost
her best friend and her sweet Paul. She'd been abandoned by the
Murdaughs, including Buster, whom she'd known since he was a boy.
The family had been angry that when she left Moselle in the frantic
hours after the roadside shooting, she'd turned the keys over to Agent
Owen and not to John Marvin. Blanca also felt shunned by lawyers at the
firm, many of whom she'd known for years. One lawyer she knew particularly well had stayed late on the night of the funeral to help her
straighten up. He'd complimented her singing of "Amazing Grace" and
poured her a glass of Alex's best bourbon, a high-end Woodford Reserve.

When he testified, he had referred to her simply as "the maid."

By the third week, the trial had developed its own rhythm and rules. The courtroom was kept at 67 degrees, prompting some in the audience to wear puffy coats. The two dozen journalists who attended every day self-policed a seating arrangement roughly based on how long and how frequently they'd covered the story. Over time, more and more recognizable faces popped up among them, as network news anchors and hosts of prime-time TV news magazines made appearances in hopes of landing interviews with key players. The jurors were not supposed to follow any news coverage of the case, but it was not lost on them that the outside world was obviously watching every minute of the trial. One barometer of the trial's popularity was the increasingly frequent presence of Nancy Grace, who sauntered into the courtroom between broadcasts in full makeup and teased hair. Most days she wore a silk blouse and sport coat over black workout pants and her signature cowboy boots, dark sunglasses tucked into the inner side of one boot.

As the prosecution had entered the second week of presenting its case, Attorney General Alan Wilson drove over from Columbia and took a seat every morning at the state's table. Wilson was a seasoned politician, and his decision to plant himself at the trial, in full view of the courtroom cameras, was taken as a sign of his confidence in the prosecution's case. Creighton Waters appreciated the show of faith from his boss. But Waters was wary of reading too much into what he saw in the jurors' eyes. Like most lawyers, he studied his jurors to see when they were with him and when they turned cold. He'd been right more often than he'd been wrong over the years, but the times he'd been wrong had been devastating. This trial was far from over.

The kennel video was a huge problem for the defense, especially since Alex had told everyone, even his own lawyers, that he'd not gone down to the kennels that night. The Big Lie, Harpootlian and Griffin called it, and if they had any hope of an acquittal, they would have to find a way to account for their client's deception. But the defense had also tripped itself, inadvertently opening the door to the evidence of the roadside shooting and Alex's string of financial crimes.

Making matters worse, Harpootlian and Griffin were running out of money. In addition to the $500,000 retainer from the boat wreck case, they'd gotten a judge to award them $600,000 from Alex's rapidly depleting assets. They had burned through most of it halfway through the trial. By then, the grueling weeks in the courtroom had taken a toll as well. Harpootlian, who'd turned seventy-four on the first day of jury selection, was still feeling fatigued from having Covid. In the middle of testimony, he sometimes wandered out of the courtroom to stretch his legs. During breaks he liked to kibitz with the press corps, railing against the weakness of the state's case and the sloppiness of the investigation.

"If they're trying to win this thing, it certainly is not showing," he said. "No testing for fingerprints, no examining the tire tracks, no footprint analysis."

Harpootlian promised that the defense was ready to demolish the state's case.

"Just wait," he said, "until we get David Owen on the stand."

THE TRIAL HAD been a personal ordeal for Agent Owen from the beginning. His mother had been in a nursing home for years and had been hospitalized on the first day of testimony with double pneumonia. She had died on Valentine's Day, the day her son was scheduled to testify. To allow him time to be with her, the state had postponed his appearance until the next day. When he took the stand, he wore his glasses instead of his contact lenses, his eyes irritated from lack of sleep and crying.

He described how he'd gone up to the house at Moselle to take Alex's clothes the night of the murders, lingering long enough to note that nothing seemed out of place. He enumerated the inconsistencies in Alex's stories that nagged at him, particularly about the shifting amount of time he said he spent riding the property with Paul or napping or visiting his mother. The prosecution played the pivotal third interview with Alex that took place two months after the homicides, where Owen told Alex he was the only suspect.

"Were there any other credible leads that you investigated that led you to anybody else beside Alex Murdaugh?" John Meadors asked.

"Not credible," Owen said. "No, sir."

Alex despised the SLED agent. He believed Owen had double-crossed him by pretending to be friendly and caring while in reality considering him a suspect. This view was both baffling and revealing. After his family's many decades in law enforcement, Alex must have understood that detectives often were required to hide their suspicions until they had enough evidence to back them up. Maybe he simply believed, as with so many other things, that a Murdaugh should be exempt from such realities.

His loathing of Agent Owen manifested itself in his lawyers' treatment of the witness. As cross-examination began, Jim Griffin set out to paint a picture of Owen as not just sloppy but duplicitous. Griffin noted that in that third interview, Owen had wrongly told Alex that SLED had found other weapons at Moselle loaded with the same combination of birdshot and buckshot that killed Paul.

"Was that an investigative tool," Griffin said, "or were you just under the misimpression that that was the case?"

"Investigative tool," Owen said.

"So you lied to him?"

"I'm allowed to use trickery to elicit a response," Owen said. This was correct, as the courts have long allowed police to deceive suspects during questioning.

But Owen had told the same lie to the grand jury a few months later, Griffin pointed out. "Were you mistaken then, or were you trying to trick the state grand jury?"

"I was not trying to trick the state grand jury," Owen said, but he acknowledged he'd said something in his testimony that turned out not to be true.

"I mean, people do make mistakes, do they not?" Griffin asked.

"Yes," Owen said. "They do make mistakes."

Griffin cornered Owen on another falsehood he'd shared with the grand jury, when he said blood spatter had been found on Alex's white T-shirt. Owen explained he had been relying on SLED's initial test results, and he had never seen the follow-up results showing there was no blood on the shirt.

"How is it," Griffin said, "the lead case agent is left out of the information channel on something so significant?"

"I did not see that report," Owen said. "I was not made aware of its existence."

The defense attorney forced Owen to acknowledge other ways Owen and his team had stumbled: the failure to conduct a thorough search of the house at Moselle on the night of the murders, the failure to have Maggie's and Paul's clothes tested for DNA, the failure to preserve tire tracks at the crime scene.

Griffin was raising his voice now, sometimes even yelling. He pressed Owen on whether they'd sufficiently investigated members of the Cowboys, a local drug gang that was supplying Cousin Eddie Smith with drugs for Alex. Had SLED searched gang members' phone records to find out if they'd been near Moselle, or compared their DNA to an unidentified sample under Maggie's fingernails? No, Owen said, they had not.

. . .

WHEN HE HAD the chance to question Owen again on redirect examination, prosecutor John Meadors clutched a stack of yellow Post-it
notes from his colleagues. They were individual pieces of evidence the
defense had sought to dismiss; Meadors needed Owen to put the pieces
back together.

Meadors started with the defense assertion that there had been no
indication Alex had washed anything down that night, as demonstrated
by investigators finding nothing wet in the back of the Suburban.

"Are you familiar with what's known as a cooler?" Meadors asked.

"Yes," Owen said.

"A good old cooler?"

"Yes, sir."

"Could you put wet garments in a cooler?"

"You can, yes."

Owen said he'd seen an overturned cooler at a skinning shed
near the kennels in the wee hours after the murders. Groundskeeper
C. B. Rowe had told him the cooler wasn't there when he left the Friday before.

Meadors asked again about the SUV's interior. "Was there blood on
the steering wheel of the Suburban, that car?"

"There was blood found on that steering wheel, yes."

"And that DNA from that blood came back to whom?"

"Maggie Murdaugh."

What about the shotgun Alex had when deputies arrived that night,
what gauge was it? Meadors asked.

Owen said it was a twelve-gauge shotgun.

"As a result of swabs, was blood identified on that gun?"

"Yes, sir."

"And whose blood, whose DNA was that?"

"Maggie Murdaugh," Owen said.

How about Shelley Smith, whose testimony indicated Alex had
parked out back eight to ten minutes before he came inside the house?

Alex's lawyer had questioned whether those minutes mattered, Meadors said.

"But would it take time to go hide guns?"

"Five minutes, ten minutes, yes," Owen said, if somebody knew the property.

At last, Meadors turned to the blue raincoat.

"Was there a whole bunch of GSR found on that inside of that rain jacket?"

Yes, Owen said.

And Shelley said she saw Alex with it?

"Yes, she said it was balled up in his arms," Owen said.

The prosecution could not come out and assert their theory outright, but Meadors hoped the jury understood. It was entirely possible that Alex had wadded up his wet clothes and thrown them in the cooler, wrapped up the guns in the raincoat, and loaded it all on the golf cart and hightailed it up to the house at Moselle. Then he could have thrown the cooler and guns in the back of the Suburban, driven to Almeda, and hidden them out back at Randolph III's smokehouse until it was safe to get rid of them for good.

Owen left the stand after five grueling hours. The prosecution had done its best to piece some things together. But the defense had still notched by far their best day yet in their attempt to discredit SLED's work.

Any momentum Alex's team gained was short-lived, though.

In an effort to toss out an alternative motive, Griffin had brought up Alex's relationship with Cousin Eddie Smith and implied he was a possible suspect. The next morning, the judge ruled that the defense's questioning had opened the door to more testimony about the roadside shooting. No longer was it a bridge too far, he said.

"The defense decided to build a road over that bridge," Newman said. "They decided to just go right there as if they could dance through fire without getting burned."

. . .

ON THE MONDAY morning after the Super Bowl, while the lawyers were settling in at their tables, Creighton Waters came over and whispered in Dick Harpootlian's ear.

"Fuck!" the defense lawyer yelled, loud enough to turn heads.

Two jurors had tested positive for Covid over the weekend. A doctor was in the jury room testing the others. The clerk of court, who typically sat feet away, was out with the virus, too. One alternate juror had already been dismissed due to a separate medical issue, leaving just three alternates in reserve. The lawyers understood that the fate of the trial rested on the vagaries of the human body and whether fifteen people sitting in a box together could avoid contracting a highly contagious disease. The state and defense were in agreement. They needed to delay the trial.

When the judge came in, they made their case.

"Trust me, it would be an economic disaster for us," Harpootlian said. "What I don't want is to run the risk that we have a mistrial because they all get Covid."

Waters said he wanted a delay, too, or barring that, a mask mandate and some social distancing, maybe clearing the gallery of spectators.

Judge Newman said no. The jurors would be retested in two days' time. He would encourage them to wear masks, as he believed everyone should. His decision pressed some buttons in the courtroom. Masks were a fraught issue in South Carolina, and two of the officials who had debated the issue were sitting in front of the judge. Harpootlian, a Democratic state senator when he wasn't practicing law, had sued Alan Wilson, the Republican attorney general, in an attempt to allow the University of South Carolina to impose a mask mandate.

The courtroom staff passed around a box of masks. A few people in the gallery took one but virtually no one put them on. Someone in the back of the room coughed. Six of the jurors put on masks, but only for an hour or two.

"This is terrifying," one television producer whispered to her seatmate. "We're definitely all getting Covid."

The jurors were tested again that Wednesday. When the judge announced they all had tested negative, there was an audible sigh.

THE COURTROOM DRAMA made for riveting viewing. One of the
millions who tuned in was someone at General Motors, who watched
an FBI agent testifying about how they had tried and failed to extract
the data from the black box inside Alex's Suburban. Months before,
GM had informed investigators that the data was unreachable. But
whoever was watching knew better. Within seventy-two hours of the
FBI agent's testimony, GM sent the prosecution an email with the
black box's contents attached.

It was an immense amount of information, including 4,820 GPS
points with time stamps and the speed Alex had been traveling at each
of those points. Suddenly it was possible to track his precise movements on the night of the murders.

Both the prosecution and the defense spent the weekend poring
over that data, assessing what it meant for their respective cases. Harpootlian felt blindsided.

To explain what all the data showed, the state called on a rookie
SLED agent named Peter Rudofski. For the better part of a year, Rudofski had been gathering details from two dozen sources—phones,
cell towers, automated license plate readers—to build a minute-by-
minute timeline of what Alex and Paul and Maggie had been doing
that night. The timeline tracked not just their movements, but their
phone calls and texts and videos. After the stunning email from GM,
handing over the long-sought information, Rudofski had updated the
timeline with the data points from the Suburban's black box. Now his
job was to explain to the jury what it all meant.

On the stand, Rudofski displayed a Midwesterner's matter-of-
factness and a millennial's fluency with devices. The data he'd gathered
did not lie, he said. The jurors had already heard Alex's voice on the
kennel video. Now, with a detailed PowerPoint presentation, Rudofski

laid out how the kennel video had ended at exactly 8:45:45 P.M., and how Paul's phone had locked for good three minutes and sixteen seconds later, and how Maggie's phone had locked thirty seconds after that. The state argued that this was when they were killed. Through test drives, SLED had already established that it would have taken Alex roughly ninety seconds to drive the golf cart back to the house from the kennels. Even if Alex had left immediately at the end of the kennel video, he would barely have made it to the front door by 8:49 P.M. The state had conducted audio tests to prove a person at the house, either inside or out, would almost certainly have heard the seven gunshots piercing the quiet.

One of the bailiffs was assigned to keep a close watch on the jurors. By now, he knew their quirks and habits. He knew who needed a blanket on days when the courtroom was particularly chilly. He knew the kinds of cookies they liked to have on hand back in the jury room. As Rudofski testified, the bailiff watched the testimony registering on the jurors' faces. He could see the tumblers in their minds falling into place.

After Rudofski's methodical reconstruction of the timeline, the state rested its case. At the next break, the Murdaugh family left the courtroom in silence. Most were in tears.

IN FRONT OF the cameras and the jury, the Murdaughs had maintained stoic expressions. But 'Nette Grant, the deputy in charge of escorting them through the halls outside, saw the toll the testimony and constant scrutiny had taken on them.

One morning 'Nette was called down to escort Liz Murdaugh, Alex's sister-in-law, into the building. Liz was running late because her child had left a science project at home that needed retrieving. The deputy and Liz were riding the elevator up to the courtroom when Liz broke down. The pressure was overwhelming, she said. Her children were getting teased at school. They couldn't turn on the TV without seeing news of the case. She started to hyperventilate.

'Nette stopped the elevator and pulled Liz in for a hug.

"It's okay, it's gonna be okay," she said. "We all go through shit. Everybody has a battle in their life. This too shall pass."

ONE OF THE first witnesses called by the defense was Buster Murdaugh. The twenty-six-year-old entered the courtroom dressed in the style of the modern-day Southern gentleman—a navy sport coat, white button-down, and khakis. The only flashy touch, peeking out from under his cuff, was the occasional glint of a large watch. On social media, Reddit-ors who'd frozen the livestream and zoomed in on his wrist, quickly identified the watch as a steel-and-gold Rolex Submariner.

Buster testified that Paul had left guns lying around everywhere, bolstering the defense theory that Maggie and Paul were killed by family weapons because they were readily available to anyone who stumbled upon the kennels. He softened the blow of Shelley Smith's testimony by saying it wasn't unusual for his father to go to Almeda at night. The prosecution had attached great weight to the fact that Alex had parked behind his parents' house near the woodshed, suggesting that he had chosen that location to hide evidence, possibly the guns. But Buster said it was customary for the family to park out back, not in the driveway.

Most important, he attested to Alex as a doting father. "My father coached every Little League team I played on," he said.

Buster's presence on the stand was meant to demonstrate that Alex was a human being, not a monster, and that his love for his family was real. When it was time for cross-examination, Meadors asked only a few questions and released him from the stand in a matter of minutes.

"I'm sorry about your mother," Meadors said. "And I'm sorry about your brother. And I'm sorry about your grandfather."

FROM THE START, Alex had insisted he should take the stand. Har-pootlian and Griffin had spent weeks trying to talk him out of it, going so far as to call other defense lawyers who Alex respected so they could tell him that every good lawyer in South Carolina thought it would be a mistake. But as the trial entered a second month, Alex's lawyers could see the case was not going their way. Harpootlian grumbled that the judge was letting the state build a murder case by "putting up widows and orphans," but he understood that all the financial testimony had assassinated his client's character in the eyes of the jury. Griffin, who tended to bond with his clients, felt haunted by the ghosts of defendants past who'd decided not to testify and been convicted anyway. They'd spent the rest of their lives regretting the decision.

On the evening of Wednesday, February 22, the lawyers met with their client and let themselves be persuaded that the only person who could demonstrate that Alex was not a bad man was the man himself. Even more crucial, he was the only one who could address why he had lied about being at the kennels.

The next morning, out of the presence of the jury, Harpootlian and Griffin made an audacious proposal: They would encourage their client to testify if Judge Newman allowed the prosecution to ask questions only about the murders, not about the financial crimes.

"This isn't a murder trial," Harpootlian said. "This is a Bernie Madoff trial."

The judge shut down the request immediately. Alex, he said, would be treated like any other defendant. He had no right to tell the jury only what he wanted them to hear.

Newman asked Alex to stand up at the defense table and reminded him that he alone should decide whether he took the stand.

"No one can make you testify," he said. "Whether or not you testify is a personal right."

But he warned Alex that if he testified, he forfeited the right to plead the Fifth Amendment, meaning he had to answer any and all questions from the state.

"What is your decision?" the judge said.

"I am going to testify," Alex said. "I want to testify."

CHAPTER FORTY

"Call your next witness," the judge said.

Defense lawyer Jim Griffin stood up. "Thank you, Your Honor," he said, speaking more loudly and deliberately than normal. "The defendant, Richard Alexander Murdaugh, wishes to take the stand."

One juror's chin dropped. Another crossed her arms and lowered her chin. All the jurors and alternates watched Alex rise from the defense table to his full height and walk over to be sworn in.

"You'll place your left hand on the Bible and raise your right," the clerk of court said. She'd known Alex for more than twenty years; she noticed that he met her eyes but seemed to be looking straight through her. "You swear or affirm that the testimony you give today will be the truth, the whole truth, and nothing but the truth?"

"Yes, ma'am," Alex said.

He settled into the chair, angling his body toward the jury box. He looked over at the jurors. He was so close, they could almost touch him.

"Good morning," he said.

"Good morning," several jurors said back.

The lawyer quickly got to the point. Like a father coaxing a child to come clean, Griffin asked his client why he'd lied about being down at the kennels.

It was the answer they had all been waiting for, the why of the Big Lie.

"As my addiction evolved over time," Alex said, "I would get in these situations or circumstances where I would get paranoid thinking. It . . . it . . . it . . . and it and it could be anything that triggered it. It might be a look somebody gave me. It might be a reaction somebody had to something I did. It might be a policeman following me in a car."

The night he found Maggie and Paul, he was in shock, he said. He became even more agitated when his partners told him not to talk to law enforcement without a lawyer. It became impossible to rein in his anxiety when police swabbed his hands for gunshot residue and questioned the status of his marriage.

"Normally, when these paranoid thoughts would hit me, I could take a deep breath real quick and just think about it," he said. He demonstrated by drawing in air and holding it a moment. "Reason my way through it, and just get past it."

"But you continued lying after that night, did you not?" Griffin said.

"Once I lied, I continued to lie, yes, sir," Alex said.

AS ALEX TOLD the jury about finding his wife's and son's bodies, he began referring to them repeatedly as "Mags" and "Pau Pau." The nickname for Maggie was obvious enough, but inside the formal trappings of a courtroom, the other nickname sounded jarring. Paul had been twenty-two when he died, a young man, no longer a child.

"Who's Pau Pau?" Griffin asked.

Alex smiled.

"That's Paul," he said. "My son—Pau Pau."

The lawyer paused.

"Your name for him was Pau Pau?"

The intended message—the reason his lawyer had lingered on this detail, giving the jury time to absorb it—was clear enough. Anyone who called his wife and son by such sweet pet names couldn't possibly have gunned them down so cruelly.

Alex described how he and Paul rode around Moselle the evening of June 7, checking sunflower and corn plots for deer and doves and checking on the fruit tree that refused to stand straight.

"And were you and Paul having a good time, at that point?" Griffin asked.

"You could not be around Pau Pau"—Alex paused, sniffling—"you could not be around him and not have a good time."

Alex went on to describe himself and Paul fiddling around at the hangar until Maggie pulled in to the driveway by the kennels around 8 P.M. They all went up to the house together, he said. He was hot and sweaty, since it was muggy out and he was on the heavy side at the time, about 265 pounds. At the house, he said, he took a shower and changed out of the khaki pants, blue button-up shirt, and brown loafers he'd worn to work.

"What did you change into?" Griffin asked.

"I changed into the clothes that you've seen in this trial," he said—the green cargo shorts and white T-shirt with the Black Sheep logo.

By the time he was out of the shower, Paul was finishing his dinner. Alex said Maggie fixed plates for the two of them and they ate in front of the TV. When they were done, Maggie asked him to come down to the kennels, but Alex said he begged off because he did not want to get sweaty again. Besides, he said, dealing with the dogs was always chaotic.

Alex said he'd lain back on the couch and put his feet up, but as he had done many times in the past when he'd refused to do something Maggie asked of him, he quickly changed his mind. He got up and took the golf cart to the kennels. Grady and Bubba, the two dogs that were more like pets than hunting dogs, were running along the tree line in the dark. "Bubba had to mark every tree," he said. A male juror on the front row smiled, hearing a country boy state a universal truth.

Paul was in the kennel fooling with Cash, Alex said. Then Bubba caught the chicken.

"He was proud that he had caught it," he said. "That chicken wasn't dead, but a lot of times, they would be stunned. And they would just be real lethargic. So you had to take the chicken and you had to put it up somewhere where the chicken could be by itself for a minute."

"Did you get the chicken out of Bubba's mouth?" Griffin asked.

"I did," Alex said. He had a method, which was to press Bubba's lip against his teeth and force him to release his jaw. "Ultimately, that chicken did die," he noted.

"And what did you do after you got the chicken out of Bubba's mouth?" Griffin asked.

"I got out of there," he said. "I . . . I . . . I . . . I left, and I went back to the house."

He'd lain on the couch, maybe dozed off, and then decided to go visit his mother. His mother's caretaker had called earlier that day and asked him to come by because his mom was agitated, he said. He knew his mom got fussy when his dad was in the hospital, crying like she knew he was gone. Alex said he drove over to the house at Almeda and parked around back.

The caretaker, Shelley Smith, let him in. He went into his mother's room and sat on her hospital bed, he said. He held her hand, relieved that she wasn't as agitated as he feared. He tried to say a few reassuring things. He said he and Shelley made small talk and watched TV.

Griffin moved on to Alex's departure from Almeda. The lawyer needed to blunt the impact of the data recently recovered from the OnStar system on Alex's Suburban, which showed him stopping at the head of his mother's driveway for roughly a minute.

"What were you doing when you stopped?" Griffin asked. "Do you recall?"

Alex said his phone had slipped between his seat and the Suburban's center console. He had stopped to retrieve it.

"Were you, during that minute or however long it was, were you disposing of murder weapons, Alex?"

"No."

"Were you disposing of bloody clothes?"

"No."

When he reached Moselle, he said, the lights were on at the house. He went in, but he couldn't find anyone. He checked in the gun room, because that room was warmer than the rest of the house, and sometimes Maggie retreated there to watch TV without shivering. He checked the bathroom to see if she was taking a bath. But he couldn't find either Maggie or Paul. He thought they might still be down at the kennels, so he drove there in his Suburban to check.

"And what'd you see?" Griffin asked.

Alex was nodding, coughing and bobbing his chin toward his chest. For five seconds he was silent, then five seconds more. Then he answered, looking up at the jury.

"I saw what y'all have seen pictures of," he said.

"Did you see them on the ground when you were pulling up in your Suburban?"

"A bit."

"And what did you do when you came to a stop, Alex?"

The defense needed to explain why it took less than twenty seconds from the time Alex put the Suburban in park until he called 911, especially since Alex had said repeatedly that he'd checked on both Maggie and Paul before placing the call. It was the tensest moment so far in a trial filled with them. Someone dropped a water bottle, and the whole room flinched.

The answer, Alex told the jury, was that he was in such a state of shock and horror, he wasn't sure exactly what he'd done.

"I think I jumped out of my car," Alex said, nodding. "I know I got out of my car. I know I ran back to my car, called 911. I called 911. I was on the phone with 911. And I was trying to tend to Pau Pau. I was trying to tend to Maggie."

He drew in a deep breath and described going back and forth between his wife and son. He checked Paul for a pulse and tried to turn him over.

"Why were you trying to turn him over?" Griffin asked.

"I don't know, I don't know, I don't know why I tried to turn him over," Alex said. "I mean, my boy's laying facedown. And he's done the way he's done . . . the way his head was."

He didn't know what to do, he said. He could see Paul's brains on the sidewalk. So he grabbed one of the belt loops of Paul's shorts and started to lift him, he said, and that's when Paul's phone popped out.

The prosecution had made much of the fact that Paul had been texting and talking with his friend Rogan in the minutes before Paul was shot. Rogan had continued to try to reach Paul thereafter, so there would have been multiple notifications of missed calls and texts visible on his home screen. There was even a missed call at 10:08 P.M., which would have been the same time Alex said he was trying to tend to his dead son.

"What did you do with the phone?" Griffin asked.

"I put it back on Pau Pau," Alex said. He said he didn't see any messages on the phone.

Griffin asked whether he had also checked on Maggie. Alex said he believed he had touched her body at the waist, but he wasn't sure.

"Oh, man," he said, sniffling again, struggling to speak. "Excuse me."

Griffin asked a tech to play the 911 recording. Together, the lawyer and his client and the jury listened to Alex's voice that night, asking for help.

> *You said it's your wife and your son?*
> *My wife and my son.*

On the stand, Alex had begun to rock.

> *He's shot in the head. And he's shot really, really bad. He's . . .*
> *Okay. Where is it? Where is he shot at?*
> *Ma'am, I don't know. But he had blood everywhere. It—his brain—*
> *I can see his brain.*

It was disorienting, listening to that disembodied voice as Alex rocked in his chair. It was like two versions of the same man, both coming apart. On the tape, he was the hysterical father and husband, begging for help for his wife and son, surrounded by blood. In the chair, he was the weeping defendant, refuting the prosecution's insistence that he was the one who had spilled all that blood in the first place.

Okay. Is he breathing at all?
No. No.
Do you see anything? Do you see anyone in the area?
No, ma'am. No.
Is there any guns near them at all?
No. The—are—are. Here.

On the tape, the dispatcher asked for the exterior color of Alex's house, so the emergency crews could recognize it. But Alex wanted to return to her question, which had been asked and answered ninety seconds before, about whether he had seen any guns.

If that's what you're asking, they didn't shoot themselves, ma'am.
What—

Griffin asked the tech to pause the tape. He noted that in the middle of that exchange, Alex had said the word "here."

"Are you calling anybody or anything?" Griffin asked.

No, Alex said. He wasn't calling one of the dogs. He wasn't speaking to another person. He was talking only to the dispatcher, he said, trying to make her understand that Paul and Maggie had not committed suicide.

"Where were the dogs?" Griffin said.

"The dogs were in the kennels."

The jurors had heard about pools of water gathered on the cement pad in front of the kennels. They'd heard about the haphazardly rolled-up hose. Had Alex been the one to roll it up? No, he said.

"Did you do anything down there at the kennels when you got there, other than call 911 and attend to Maggie and Paul?"

"I was trying to find a flashlight," Alex said. "I was trying to find a gun. Other than those things, no, I didn't do— I didn't do anything . . . I didn't do anything with any hose. I didn't do anything with any dogs."

"Was there anybody with you?"

"No."

Griffin asked the tech to hit play again on the 911 tape. The dispatcher was asking Alex if he'd heard anything at the time of the shootings.

I've been gone. I—I just came back.

Okay. And was anyone else supposed to be at your house?

No ma'am.

On the tape, the sound of barking mixed with Alex's voice.

Oh. Oh. Should have known.

Griffin interrupted the tape again to ask what Alex had meant by those last words. What should he have known? Alex said he had been talking to his dead son, saying he should have known Paul was in danger after all the threats he'd received in the months after the boat wreck.

When was the last time Alex had seen Maggie and Paul? the lawyer asked. After dinner, Alex said, when he'd joined Paul and Maggie in the kennels, just before Paul had shot the video.

"The video we've seen is time-stamped 8:44 P.M.," Griffin said. "Is that correct?"

Alex said that was right. The last time he'd seen Maggie and Paul was a few moments after that, when he took the chicken from Bubba's mouth and then left.

AFTER NINETY MINUTES of Alex walking the high wire, the judge called a ten-minute break. The defense had wanted white men on the jury, and with the trailing off of alternates, they now had a jury with five of them. Someone told Harpootlian they'd noticed a white male juror on the front row actually had tears in his eyes. Harpootlian worked the courtroom like a post-debate spin doctor, hanging out by reporters' row and talking about the crying juror. Putting his client on the stand was a gamble, he said, but it was paying off so far.

"The guy's been a trial lawyer for twenty-five years," Harpootlian said of Alex. "If anybody could pull this off, it's him."

WHEN COURT WAS back in session, Jim Griffin circled back to Alex's description of how he'd touched the bodies. Did he recall getting blood on his hands or anywhere else on his body?

"I know I got blood on my fingertips," said Alex.

He didn't know if it was Paul's blood or Maggie's. Probably both. Traces of Maggie's blood had been recovered from the steering wheel of the Suburban. He said he assumed he had left it there when he drove up to the house after discovering the bodies. If there had been any blood found on the shotgun he brought down from the house, the one he had near him when the first deputy arrived on the scene, he said he assumed it had brushed off his fingers, too.

"Just to be clear," said Griffin, "were you anywhere in the vicinity when Paul and Maggie were shot?"

"I was nowhere near Paul and Maggie when they got shot."

Griffin was moving faster now, nailing down the specifics that could prove his client innocent. He prompted Alex to confirm that he had been with Buster and other members of the family the day after the murders. The unspoken point: He was not alone and would have had no chance to dispose of the murder weapons.

Griffin walked Alex through the ways he'd tried to help police, consenting to a search of the property, giving SLED the passcode to Maggie's phone and computer, and pressing to get the GPS data from the Suburban. The black box data was extremely important, Alex said. He said he had known from the start he would be a suspect, simply because he had discovered the bodies. He needed the GM data to confirm he went where he said he did, when he said he did.

"I knew that my Suburban, and my phone and Maggie's phone never crossed paths," he said. "And that was extremely important to me."

DAVID OWEN WAS sitting barely fifteen feet from Alex, behind the prosecution table. Alex stared at Owen whenever he mentioned the agent's name, describing how he felt deceived by his friendly approach and betrayed by his handling of the so-called bloody shirt. Owen tended to look down or jot notes when his name came up, keeping his expression neutral, a skill he'd cultivated until it became second nature. It wasn't about him, he told himself. It was about Maggie and Paul.

Owen's seat was on the aisle, close to the jury box, and he allowed himself the occasional glance to gauge whether the jurors saw what he saw. He'd started out believing every word Alex had said that rainy night, a grieving father giving a disjointed account because he was in shock. Would the jury believe him, too?

Owen believed, rightly or wrongly, this case would make or break his career. Alex's family ran a powerful law firm. If Alex was acquitted, he feared they would come after him in civil court and make his life a living hell. He'd spent every waking moment for almost two years thinking about the evil acts of a depraved man, which was hell enough for a lifetime.

GRIFFIN TURNED TO his next bit of clean-up work: having Alex refute the testimony of some of the trial's most powerful witnesses. It was a delicate task. Griffin had watched enough faces on enough juries to know when a witness's testimony landed.

He asked first about Shelley Smith, Alex's mother's night caretaker, who said he'd wanted her to say he'd stayed longer at Almeda than he actually had. Alex said he didn't remember talking about the length of the visit, just that he gave her a heads-up that SLED would want to talk with her and she should be sure to tell the truth.

What about Shelley saying you carried something that looked like a blue tarp into the house a few days later?

"I mean, Shelley's got something in her mind about that," Alex said. "I certainly don't remember it."

By this time, half of the jurors had dropped eye contact with Alex.

Griffin pressed on. He asked Alex about Blanca, who said she'd felt pressured to say he was wearing a different shirt to work than the one she remembered. Alex said he had simply wanted to know whether she'd seen the blue button-up shirt from the video in the weeks after the homicide.

Alex used the question to take a dig at SLED's botched testing of his Black Sheep T-shirt. He said the state had never cared what he'd been wearing until his lawyers proved them wrong about the blood spatter on his T-shirt.

Griffin moved to another damning witness, Mark Tinsley. *Was your financial house,* Griffin asked, *about to come tumbling down?*

"No," Alex said, turning to the jury. "I've been a plaintiff's lawyer like Mr. Tinsley that sat here. We do the same exact thing."

Alex said in his twenty-seven years of experience, no defendant had been forced to turn over the kind of detailed financial information Tinsley was seeking.

Griffin turned to the testimony about Alex's financial misdeeds that had dominated the trial's early weeks. Had Alex really stolen from his clients? Alex said yes, he had, and from his law firm, too, though he struggled to articulate why.

"You know, I'm not quite sure how I let myself get where I got," he said. "But it came from, you know, I battled addiction for so many years. I was spending so much money on pills."

Alex kept his addiction from his law partners, he said, until they confronted him about stealing from the firm. He said his older brother, Randy IV, took most of his stash, leaving him just enough to avoid withdrawals until he could get into detox. By the next morning, the Saturday of Labor Day weekend in 2021, he was jonesing for pills and arranged to meet up with his dealer.

"But the time I met with him," Alex said, "I changed my plans."

"And what was the change in plans?"

"Not to get pills from him anymore and instead I asked him to shoot me."

"Did you ask him to shoot you as a sympathy ploy?"

"As a sympathy ploy?"

"Why did you ask him to shoot you? What was the end goal that you wanted to accomplish?"

"I meant for him to shoot me so I'd be gone."

"And who was this? Who did you ask to do this?"

It was Eddie Smith, Alex said. He tried to explain his thinking at the time, however muddled it may have been.

"I mean, I knew all this was coming to a head. I knew how humiliating it was gonna be for my son. I mean, I'd been through so much. At the time, in the bad place that I was, it seemed like the better thing to do."

The defense had spent roughly three hours walking through Alex's reasons for all the lies he'd told, with one goal in mind: to show that despite his other deceptions, he'd loved his wife and son too much to ever lie about their deaths.

"Alex, will you tell this jury about Maggie?"

She was beautiful inside and out, he said, a loving mother and a giving wife with a laugh so contagious, you had to laugh when you heard it, even if you didn't know what was funny.

"I would never hurt Maggie. Ever."

"Would you tell the jury about Paul, please?"

Paul had a sweetness to him, Alex said. He doted on his grandparents and took care of his friends.

"To be such a tough person, he would get all his buddies and get on a boat and go watch a sunset," he said, sniffling. "Any twenty-two-year-old people you know do stuff like that? I mean, he was such a special boy."

Aware that his testimony was being beamed out to the world, he leaned into the microphone.

"I would challenge you right now," he said. "Go find somebody, somebody that knew Pau Pau, and really knew him, that did not have an ulterior motive, that would say something negative about him. And I challenge everybody who can hear me now to do that.

"It hurt Paul so bad when Mallory died," he said. "But how many twenty-two-year-olds do you know that think that way? 'Be present. Appreciate things around you.' At twenty-two years old."

Griffin cut in, trying to avoid further lionization of a troubled young man. Paul had been the victim of a violent senseless death, but so had Mallory Beach.

"Alex," the lawyer said, "do you love Paul?"

"Did I love him? Like no other. He and Buster."

"Do you love Maggie?"

"More than anything."

"Did you kill Maggie?"

"No. I did not kill Maggie. I did not kill Paul. I would never hurt Maggie. And I would never hurt Paul ever. Under any circumstances."

CHAPTER FORTY-ONE

Creighton Waters had spent two years becoming the world's foremost student of Alex Murdaugh, starting long before the homicides, ever since he'd first heard the phrase "the boat case."

The defense lawyers could say whatever they wanted: that it was a game-time decision, that they'd advised against it, that they hadn't been sure Alex would go through with it. But Waters had always known Alex would take the stand. He wouldn't have been able to help himself, not with the lure of a jury at his knees and a microphone to the world.

The direct examination of Alex by the defense had stretched into midafternoon, making for an unusually late 2:30 P.M. lunch break. That meant the biggest cross-examination of Waters's career would begin in the late afternoon. Waters ate two Kind energy bars as he finalized his opening questions in the attorney general's makeshift headquarters in a trailer next to the food trucks. It had been weeks since he'd sat down for a proper meal. His colleagues would often walk to the Cracker Barrel for fried chicken and Bud Light, but every minute spent waiting for food or making small talk was time better spent preparing for this cross. He had lost ten pounds over the course of the trial, lost most of his voice to a cold, and slept four or five hours on a good night.

He'd be getting Alex on the witness stand just before 4 P.M. Waters didn't want to get too confrontational too fast, since he'd inevitably have to continue his questions the next morning. Waters, as tactical a lawyer as Alex was an intuitive one, opted to start out as the good cop, seeking Alex's buy-in on key facts of the state's case, a legal strategy known as the constructive cross.

WATERS COULD FEEL Alex's eyes on him as he put his papers on the lectern. He spoke for the first time to a man he felt he knew very well.

"Mr. Murdaugh," he said. "Let's start with a few things we agree on."

"All right, sir."

"You agree that the most important part of your testimony here today is explaining your lie for a year and a half that you were never down at those kennels at eight-forty-four. Would you agree with that?"

"I, I think all of my testimony is important, Mr. Waters."

Waters asked whether it was accurate to say that the first time prosecutors or law enforcement heard Alex admit he was at the kennels was earlier that day on the witness stand.

"Yes, sir."

"All right. All this time later, this is the first time you've ever said that?"

"Yes, sir."

"And you would agree with me that for years you were stealing money from clients?"

"Yes, sir, I agree with that."

"And that you were stealing from your law firm."

"Yes, sir, I agree with that."

Waters moved on. "Let's talk first about your family's legacy here in the legal profession, okay?"

"Talk about anything you want to."

"Tell me about your great-grandfather."

Alex said his great-grandfather was Randolph Murdaugh Sr., who'd served as solicitor for twenty years.

"Did you ever get to know him?"

"Oh, no, sir. He got killed in 1940."

What about your grandfather, Waters asked.

Alex said his grandfather's name was Randolph Murdaugh Jr., though he went by Buster. He told how his grandfather took over as solicitor after his great-grandfather died and then served from 1940 to 1986, the longest-serving prosecutor in the country.

"I knew him extremely well and loved him dearly," Alex said.

Waters knew Alex had not just loved Old Buster but had wanted to be him. Alex had told colleagues he was born a generation too late because he would have thrived in Buster's era.

"Idolized him, did you not?"

"Yes."

Alex said his grandfather had retired because you weren't allowed to be solicitor after age seventy-two. His father, Randolph Murdaugh III, took over and filled Buster's unexpired term, serving from 1986 to 2006.

"I actually worked a case with him," Waters said.

"He's a fine, fine, fine man," Alex said. "An excellent lawyer."

"That's a big part of your family legacy and your heritage that's so ingrained around here," Waters said, "that history of being the chief prosecutor and being a central part of the legal community, is that correct? Would you agree with that?"

"That my family's been a central part of the legal community? Yes, sir, I agree with that."

"And not only just a central part of the legal community, but the chief prosecutor for this area since 1910, I think? Up until 2006."

Alex corrected him. "1920," he said. "1910 is when my great-grandfather started the law firm."

Waters was not just establishing the dominance of the Murdaugh family. He was inviting Alex to showcase the precision of Alex's memory. Other witnesses had described it as almost photographic. Waters needed the jury to see how keen the witness's recall was, so perhaps they'd question why he was so fuzzy on details from the night of the murder.

Alex went on to say he had gone to law school, just like the Murdaugh men before him. He graduated in 1994 and worked in Beaufort for a few years before coming home to the family firm in Hampton.

"And then you went to the law firm that doesn't exist anymore," Waters said, "that started in 1910, but it doesn't exist anymore because of your activities, correct?"

Alex scowled. "That's correct."

"You were a trial lawyer, correct?" Waters asked. "Successful trial lawyer."

"I—I don't know about your adjective. But—I was, you know—I—I guess so, yes, sir."

"Did you make millions of dollars in legal fees?"

"Yes, sir."

"But you won't tell this jury that's successful?"

If the criterion was money, Alex allowed he'd been successful.

Waters asked whether Alex had done jury trials, looking jurors in the eyes and making arguments. Alex said yes, he'd worked a lot of jury trials as a plaintiffs' lawyer, primarily representing people involved in wrecks. He'd even served as head of the state trial lawyers' association.

"So can we agree now on successful?" Waters asked.

They parried over the degree to which Alex was successful, a surreal argument in a place where Alex made more money in a year than most people earned in a lifetime and where Murdaugh was a household name. Then they haggled over whether he and his family were prominent.

"I never thought of myself as prominent."

Waters said he wasn't asking what Alex thought. Did others see him and his family as prominent?

"I mean, like a big shot? No, sir, I don't think that."

"What about your family?"

"That my family thought we were big shots? No, sir."

"That people viewed . . ."

"I definitely don't think that."

". . . your family as prominent in this community."

"Prominent?"

"Yeah."

"As in . . ."

"It's not a hard question."

"Well, I—I'm just not sure, you know, I think my family was very well thought of. I think my family was respected. I think my family helped a lot of people."

"I'm not challenging you on any of that. I'm just getting you to agree with what seems to be a basic fact."

Waters had to rein in his impulse to go harder at Alex. He also made a point of slipping back and forth in the chronology, circling with one line of questions and then shifting to another to make it harder for the witness to settle into a rhythm. All of the prosecutor's questions were designed to expose Alex's capacity for lying about every aspect of his life. Waters needed to harness Alex's desire to explain himself, knowing that once Alex started talking, he wouldn't stop. And the more he talked, the more his ego would trip him up, and the more he would reveal himself.

The prosecutor turned to the Murdaugh family's ties to law enforcement. Would it be fair to say the Murdaughs had close relationships, given their dual roles in the solicitor's office and their civil practice specializing in wrecks? Alex said he supposed so. Would it be fair to say the family cultivated friendships with law enforcement officers, too? Well, Alex said, *it's not like the firm sponsored events for law enforcement, more like the lawyers themselves may have had friends they hung out with.*

"It's a simple point," Waters said. "You had a lot of friends in law enforcement. Your family and you had a long association with the law enforcement community in this circuit. Is that correct?"

"Association being friendships and working relationships? Absolutely."

As for Alex's own experiences in the solicitor's office, Alex said he took five cases to trial over the years, mostly as a way to spend time with his father. He'd had a badge since 1998.

"You actually had two badges, right?"

Yes, Alex said, he'd inherited his grandfather's badge when Old Buster died.

Waters picked up what looked like a brown paper lunch bag tucked in a stack of file folders. Alex worked his jaw forward and back while Waters walked over to the defense table and pulled out two thin leather wallets for Jim Griffin to inspect. He then brought the bag to the witness stand and asked Alex to identify the badge tucked in the first wallet. Alex donned his reading glasses and said the first badge was #571, the one he was given when he joined the solicitor's office. The second was badge #570, which had belonged to his grandfather Buster near the end of his career, after he retired as the solicitor and kept working as an assistant prosecutor.

Waters asked where he typically kept his grandfather's badge, and Alex said no particular place.

"Would you dispute if it was recovered out of the Mercedes you were driving on September fourth, the day of the side of the road incident?"

"No, I believe that."

Waters took the wallet back from him and placed it faceup on the overhead projector, where the jury could see the brass badge against the black leather. There was an eagle, arms outstretched, clutching a banner with the words ASS'T SOLICITOR. Below was the glossy enamel of the state seal, with South Carolina's dual mottos in Latin: ANIMIS OPIBUSQUE PARATI ("Prepared in mind and resources") and DUM SPIRO SPERO ("While I breathe, I hope").

Waters asked where he kept his own badge, #570. Again, Alex said nowhere in particular, sometimes on the front seat, sometimes in the cupholder, and occasionally on the dashboard.

Really? Waters said. There was no rhyme or reason to where Alex kept the badge?

Alex said he might occasionally put it in the cupholder or on the dash if he got pulled over so an officer could see it. He said it so matter-of-factly, it wasn't clear whether his legendary power to read jurors' minds momentarily failed or he simply had no choice but to cop to this shocking display of privilege.

"Now why would you do that?" Waters asked. "Why would you have it in the cupholder? You're not sayin' you were on official business, are you?"

No, Alex said.

Well, why, then? Waters asked.

Alex's face became hard. He looked at Waters out of the side of his eye. "Because," he said. "I found that law enforcement oftentimes is friendlier when you're in law enforcement."

"When you're law enforcement," Waters said. "So you considered yourself law enforcement?"

"No, sir. I, I can't say that I considered myself law enforcement."

Waters took a beat. He repeated Alex's words back to him. *So you'd sometimes drive with the badge faceup on the dashboard?* Yes, Alex said. *And you don't consider yourself law enforcement?* Correct, he said.

"All right, so you were just using this badge to your advantage and taking license with it. Is that correct?"

"I—I guess in some circumstances, that is accurate."

To get better treatment, right?

That was probably fair to say, Alex said.

At the defense table, Harpootlian held his mouth in a thin line for most of the exchange, then pulled at his ear like a third base coach signaling his runner not to try to steal.

Waters put Alex's badge on the overhead alongside his grandfather's. The contrast was clear, the badge of a fake lawman beside the badge of a real one. Buster, in spite of his subversion of his role, had been a public servant. He'd put in the work. Alex hadn't even pretended. The previous generations had gathered entitlements to themselves by virtue of carrying this badge, but Alex took the spoils without the sacrifice.

"Did you ever have lights in your vehicle?"

"Yes, sir, I did."

Alex said he'd had them installed in the SUV provided by his law firm, the one he'd had for five years prior to the Suburban. Alex said he sought permission from three sheriffs in the Fourteenth Circuit, including Andy Strickland, the former sheriff in Colleton County.

Waters knew all about Strickland. He'd run him out of office on public corruption charges less than a year before the homicides.

"You said, 'Hey, I'm going to get some blue lights installed in my vehicle.' And he said, 'That's cool.' Or words to that effect?"

"I mean, that doesn't sound like the words that he would've used or I would've used. But I certainly asked him and he certainly said it was okay."

Waters showed Alex a picture taken on the night of the homicides with Alex's badge facing up on the dashboard of the Suburban. Alex said he didn't remember putting it there but didn't dispute that he might have.

Waters said he wanted to change the subject a bit and talk about the boat case. Alex asked whether he meant the civil lawsuit or the criminal charges the state brought against Pau Pau.

"Pau Pau," Waters said. "That was your nickname for Paul?"

"Yeah, I called him Pau Pau. Maggie called him Pau Pau. Bus calls him Pau Pau."

Alex had given three lengthy statements to police about the homicides, all of which had been played for the jury. Waters pointed out that in all those hours of interviews, Alex had never referred to his son as Pau Pau. Alex said he'd call him Paul if that's what the prosecutor wanted.

"No, you can call him whatever you want. I'm just asking you if you ever called him that during the course of that entire investigation. Or is that also the first time today, at least publicly?"

Alex said he commonly called his son Pau Pau, similar to the way he used Ro Ro as the nickname for his neighbor Rogan Gibson. Waters turned back to the boat case.

"And we've talked a little bit about your badge. Did you have your badge with you on the night of the boat wreck?"

Alex's eyes widened and he lifted his chin—whether in surprise or recognition wasn't clear. He repeated the prosecutor's question out loud, buying time, then said he didn't believe he'd had the badge at Beaufort Memorial. When Waters asked whether he was acting in any official capacity that night, Alex again repeated the question, then said no, he hadn't been.

Waters walked over to the prosecution table, picked up a picture, and handed it to Alex. He asked him to identify the man on the right, standing in the emergency room hallway, the tall man in the white fishing tournament T-shirt.

"Is that you?" the prosecutor asked.

"Yeah, it looks like me."

"All right. What's hanging out of your pocket in plain view?"

"Looks like a badge."

"Did you generally walk around with your badge hanging out your pocket?"

"Generally speaking, no, sir, I did not."

"Or only when you wanted some advantage from it?"

"Did I . . . did I . . ."

"Did you want some advantage from wearing it like that?"

"Did I hang it out my pocket when I wanted an advantage?"

"Yes."

"I certainly may have."

Waters walked back to the lectern a few paces in front of Alex and leaned over it, his weight on his crossed arms. Alex was staring him down, no longer the sniffling and crying defendant of earlier that afternoon but the Alex of old, nice until he was not. Waters stared back over the top of his glasses.

"What advantage did you want?"

"When?" Alex said, an edge in his voice.

That night in the picture, Waters said, when Alex walked inside the emergency room after the boat wreck.

"I don't even recall this, Mr. Waters," Alex said. "I guess I would want—you know, as I said—a badge has a warming effect with other law enforcement. And so if I was seeking any advantage, as you say, then I guess that would be what it was."

The prosecutor looked down at his notes, letting Alex's words hang in the air for ten long ticks of the clock. Alex was staring at him with black eyes.

Waters had spent months investigating Alex's every move that night. He'd watched and rewatched the hospital security footage as Alex had gone from room to room, trying to get all the witnesses under his control.

"Do you remember going around, talking to the kids? The other kids that were on the boat?"

"Yeah. I talked to some of them."

Waters asked whether it was just instinct for Alex to put on his badge, but Alex demurred, repeating that he didn't even remember having it. He said it was possible when he'd shoved the wallet in his pocket, the badge side got stuck open on the outside, since as the prosecutor could see, it wasn't like it was sealed shut with Velcro or anything.

"So you're saying it might be an accident that your badge was hanging out there."

"I'm saying that I have no memory of that whatsoever."

Was Alex telling the jury he had no intention behind carrying the badge? Alex said he certainly didn't flash it to gain access to the other kids' rooms.

Waters asked whether Alex told any of Paul's friends to keep their mouths shut.

"I never told anybody not to cooperate with law enforcement, whether I had a badge hangin' out my pants, didn't have a badge."

Waters asked whether Alex found out just before the homicides that there was a state investigation into his actions that night.

Yes, Alex said, he'd heard about the investigation sometime that spring. Waters was trying to show that Alex knew that Mark Tinsley was not the only tiger on his tail. The attorney general's office was after him, too.

"I understood there was an investigation into whether or not I was acting in a public manner or whatever," Alex said. "Whatever it was y'all were investigating. Public corruption."

Jim Griffin stood up. "Objection, Your Honor," he said. He didn't see how any of this was relevant to the murders of Maggie and Paul. Judge Newman agreed.

Waters changed tacks.

"You testified that you've had a pill addiction for approximately twenty years, correct?"

Alex said that sounded about right.

"So when did you start stealing money from clients? How long did it take before you started doing that?"

Alex said he wasn't sure.

"You don't know?"

Alex said he couldn't pinpoint when the thefts began. He had been in rehab and in jail, he said, and hadn't had much time to review the files.

Waters paused, allowing the jurors a moment to absorb this answer. The indifference of the man. The excuses he was using to paper over that indifference.

ALANIA PLYLER WAS watching Alex's testimony. She had not seen him in years, though rarely a day passed by lately without her thinking about him. She remembered the first time she met him, riding in the car he'd sent for her.

When Alania heard about the shooting on the side of the road, she'd texted banker Russell Laffitte in a panic, worried someone was out to kill Alex, too, after he'd already lost his wife and son. The intervening year had shown Alania that everything she thought she knew about Alex was a lie. She'd been so broke in her teen years, she'd felt like a homeless person begging for change, asking family members for money for food and clothes, not knowing that she and her sister had more money than they could ever need. Alex had been too busy spending to even tell them about the settlement money parked in Palmetto State Bank.

She did not need to work but she chose to, putting in twelve-hour shifts as a patrol deputy at the sheriff's office in Lexington County, a suburb of Columbia. She was applying to be a detective in hopes of living out her mantra: Healed people are the best people to help hurting people. The trial had taken a toll she hadn't seen coming, as she relived all her loss, remembering the crash over and over and the painful years that followed. "Mr. Alex" had promised he'd take care of her. *Lainey,* he'd told her, *we're going to make this right.*

She wanted to hear what he had to say on the witness stand. By then she had learned so much about him that she had come to believe he might actually have been capable of gunning down his own wife and son.

THE PROSECUTOR TURNED to the subject of Alex's opioid addiction. Was that the cause of his financial problems?

"It was certainly a cause," Alex said. "Yes, sir."

"A cause," said Waters. "Not the only cause, though, correct?"

Waters reminded Alex of his land deals that went bad as the recession hit in 2008, and the big settlements he'd won in the years that followed. Those big cases, Alex said, had not ended his financial woes.

"Let's go with the Pinckney case . . . Hakeem Pinckney. Do you remember him?"

Alex did remember Hakeem, the crash on the highway, his head injury and paralysis. But he said he did not recall the amount of the settlement.

Waters handed the witness a document that reported the settlement as $10.2 million, paid out in 2011. Alex collected just over $4 million as his legal fee.

But that $4 million had not been enough, Waters said. Hadn't Alex stolen hundreds of thousands of dollars more? The witness said he did not remember exactly, but if that was what the records showed, then he did not dispute the amount.

Waters asked if it was correct that Hakeem's injuries had rendered him paraplegic.

"No, sir," said Alex. "He was a quadriplegic, unfortunately."

Waters looked at the witness.

"Quadriplegic," he said. "Thank you for correcting me."

Alex admitted he'd also stolen from Hakeem's mother and from Hakeem's teenage cousin, Natarsha Thomas, who had been paid a settlement of $2 million.

How old was Natarsha, Waters asked, when she became Alex's client?

"I'm not sure. She was young."

Waters asked about when Alex had sat down with the teenager and gone over the case with her—much as he was sitting down now with the jury. Had he looked this underage girl in the eye as he stole from her? Alex avoided saying yes. Instead, he said it would not have been unusual for him to look his clients in the eye while discussing their cases.

"While you were doing some fast-talking to a teenager, correct?"

"I don't know if I was talking fast or slow," Alex said. "But I wasn't telling the truth."

"All right," said Waters. "Well, you ultimately convinced her that there was nothing amiss here, right, while you were stealing her money, correct?"

Alex looked back at the prosecutor.

"I admit candidly in all of these cases, Mr. Waters, that I took money that was not mine and I shouldn't have done it. I hate the fact that I did it. I'm embarrassed by it. I'm embarrassed for my son. I'm embarrassed for my family. And I don't dispute that I did it."

. . .

HAKEEM'S MOTHER WAS not in the courtroom to hear Alex's eva-sions. She was home recovering from yet another surgery.

Justin Bamberg was there representing Pamela and her family. Bamberg was the rare young Black plaintiff's lawyer in the area, a thirty-four-year-old wunderkind and state House member who'd made a name for himself representing Black men shot by police. He had no love lost for Alex Murdaugh. An ambitious and young Black lawyer hanging out a shingle in a predominantly Black community had posed an existential threat to established white law firms, especially one like the Murdaugh firm, which had never had a Black law partner in its 113-year history. When he first set up shop, Bamberg remembered hearing that Alex was telling contacts in law enforcement not to deal with the new lawyer, saying Justin had a thing against the police. In fact, Bamberg's father was a county sheriff and his mother had been a longtime detective. He had good relationships with the cops and needed to preserve them. He confronted Alex, who denied ever saying anything. The man had always been such a smooth liar.

When Bamberg arrived at the trial, he wore his gold legislative pin on his lapel. He seethed as he watched Alex on the stand. Hakeem had died in a cut-rate nursing home paid for by Medicaid. He'd suffo-cated, unable to sign for help because he was paralyzed and unable to cry out because he had a tube in his throat. Miss P had needed that money to bring her son home. And Alex was up there trying to say he cared about the Pinckneys, when Bamberg had discovered the documents he'd backdated so he could steal even more money after Hakeem died.

He hoped the jury wasn't buying Alex's story. *All those tears, all that snot dripping from his nose, all that fake emotion,* he thought. *It's just a show.*

WATERS WANTED ALEX to talk some more about all the clients he'd stolen from. So far, he had described the thefts in an almost academic way, as though the details were only a matter of paperwork. Waters wanted Alex to talk about Arthur Badger, the man whose wife had been killed when the UPS truck crashed into their car. Alex had stolen more than $1.3 million from him. Had Alex looked Mr. Badger in the eye as he stole all that money from him and his children? Almost certainly, Alex said.

Why, the prosecutor asked, had Alex needed so much money?

"Were you living a wealthy lifestyle?"

"Probably."

Waters didn't want to let him wiggle around the question. Alex had been making more than $1 million a year at the firm, not counting what he stole.

"Can we at least agree that that's a lot of money?"

Alex agreed it was a great deal of money. If the prosecutor wanted to say he'd been living a wealthy lifestyle, he said, that was fine.

Turning to another case, the prosecutor asked the witness if he remembered Alania and Hannah Plyler.

"They were two young girls," Alex said.

"What loss did they suffer? Who died?"

"Their mother," Alex said. "Their mother did."

ALANIA PLYLER WAS still following the testimony. When she heard this answer from her former lawyer, she was furious.

Her brother. Alex had completely skipped over the fact that Alania's fourteen-year-old brother had also been killed in the crash.

Mr. Alex had made millions of dollars off the deaths of her mother and brother. How could he have forgotten Justin, who had been sitting in the front seat of their Explorer when the tire exploded? The last time Alania had seen him was when the paramedics zipped him into a body bag. Alania still thought of Justin every time she looked at her son, who was now almost the same age her brother had been when he died. She had named him Justin after her older brother.

And now Alex Murdaugh had erased him.

To Alania, the settlement from their crash had been blood money, a measure of her mother's and brother's worth. In the eyes of the law, that money had been the only way to show that their lives and deaths mattered. And Alex Murdaugh had stolen it and spent it like it was nothing. So much of nothing, he had forgotten her brother even existed. And now he wanted the jury to believe he was sorry.

ALEX WANTED TO move past this slow recounting of the Plylers and the Pinckneys and the Badgers and all the other vulnerable people he'd stolen from. But Waters would not skip any of it. Again and again, he grilled the witness on whether he had looked these victims in the eye as he lied to them and told them everything was fine, even as he maneuvered to take millions of dollars of their money.

"I remember stealing from people," Alex said. "I remember lying to people. And I remember misleading people."

He repeated himself so often the words sounded rote.

"How many times," Waters asked, "have you practiced that answer before your testimony today?"

Never, Alex said.

"I'm asking you to tell me about just one conversation," the prosecutor said, "one time where you recall looking somebody in the eye and convincing them with your lies that nothing was amiss. One conversation."

Alex said it was hard for him to recall sitting down with a specific client and lying to them that way.

Waters stared at the witness.

"They certainly remember it, don't they, Mr. Murdaugh?"

Waters paused long enough to let the blow reverberate.

"These were real people you were dealing with, right?"

"They're very real people," Alex said.

One of the saddest things, he added, was that all these years after his betrayals, he still cared about those people. Once again, he was sniffing, his face clouding with emotion, on the edge of tears.

"There's no question that the actions that I did, the things that I did wrong, hurt a lot of the people that I care about the most," he said, his voice catching. "And I did a lot of damage. And I wreaked a lot of havoc that I'm—"

The prosecutor cut him off.

"You did a lot of damage and wreaked a lot of havoc," he said. "I hear you."

FINALLY, JUST PAST 5:30 P.M., Judge Newman sent the jury home for the night. The cross-examination would continue the next morning.

Once the jurors had left, Dick Harpootlian complained to Judge Newman about all the time the state was devoting to Alex Murdaugh's financial crimes.

"I could've sworn this was a murder case," the defense attorney said. "For two hours now, we haven't heard the word 'murder' once."

Newman cut him off.

"The credibility is an issue," said the judge.

Of course Alex had looked into his victims' faces as he deceived his clients. Every time Creighton Waters hammered at this point, he was reminding the jury that the accused was a master of deception, someone who had looked into the eyes of not just his vulnerable clients but also the detectives and his law partners and even his own family as he lied to them all. Now, on that witness stand, he was looking into the eyes of the jurors and swearing to them he was an innocent man.

CHAPTER FORTY-TWO

Mark Tinsley was not in the courtroom during Alex's testimony. It was agonizing enough to watch from home. During the questioning from his own lawyer, Alex had sniffled and shaken in near-perfect mimicry of a grieving man. It reminded Tinsley of the Alex of old, who could turn the tears on and off during a closing argument. He stopped watching the testimony when he felt Alex getting into a rhythm, like a boxer finding his legs. He could see that Alex was acting, but could the jury?

In the nights leading up to Alex's testimony, Tinsley tossed and turned. The case was inescapably personal to him. He'd known Alex and his family for more than twenty years. He'd kissed Maggie's cheek countless times and had lain on the floor with Paul playing video games. Now he was seeing Alex's dark eyes in his dreams.

The stakes seemed impossibly high. Tinsley had lost his friendships with Alex's law partners, his only peers for fifty miles. He had poured years into this case, allowing it to eclipse other work. Tinsley was the product of a blue-collar family, his father a machinist, his mother a trucking dispatcher. The way the Murdaughs perverted their power offended him to the bone. A guilty verdict would mean justice for

Maggie and Paul and, to some degree, Mallory. It would mean that the host had rejected the virus infecting it for a century.

He was afraid he was too close to the trial to see it clearly. He checked an online poll predicting the outcome. He was alarmed by how many people predicted a hung jury, or worse, a verdict of "not guilty."

CREIGHTON WATERS PROWLED the courtroom. As the prosecutor resumed his cross-examination, he leaned over the lectern, fixing the witness with a stare of disbelief. Again and again, he walked up to Alex Murdaugh and handed him a document to review and then stood slightly behind, arms folded, hovering in Alex's blind spot. He wanted the man to be uncomfortable.

After the endless circling of the afternoon before, Waters launched into a series of tightly focused questions designed to expose Alex as not just a liar but a murderer, too.

"Let's see if we can move forward with this a little bit," the prosecutor said. "See if we can go back to some things we may be able to agree on."

Waters turned his attention to Alex's addiction. It wasn't the cause of Alex's behavior, he would argue. It was an excuse.

He pointed out that Alex had been able to function as a lawyer despite the pills, and that he had convinced his staff that nothing was amiss, and that he had carried off his elaborate thefts. Alex confirmed it all.

In those weeks before the murders, Waters asked, had Maggie and Paul been watching him closely to keep him away from the pills? Alex said they had been watching him for years. The tensions created by his addiction, he said, were nothing new.

Alex said he and his lawyers had tried repeatedly to tell prosecutors about the specifics of his addiction and his financial crimes. But the state had never listened.

It galled Waters that Alex was trying to say he'd been eager to supply law enforcement with information. Had Alex ever told anyone in law enforcement that in fact he had been down at the kennels that night with Maggie and Paul?

"No," said Alex. "I didn't have the opportunity to, Mr. Waters, because you would not respond to my invitations to reach out and tell you about all the things that I'd done wrong."

A hint of a smile played at the sides of Waters's mouth.

Had Alex ever told his law partners the truth about him at the kennels? Had he told his brother Randy? Had he told his friends or family?

No, Alex said. No. And no.

The discovery of the kennel video had forced Alex to change his story, Waters said. "Isn't that true?"

"No, sir."

Waters painted the kennel lie as part of a long pattern: lie until the evidence forces a correction, then lie some more. Only a few months before, one of his lawyers had appeared on national TV and repeated Alex's story that he'd been napping in the house when the murders occurred. Alex said he hadn't seen that segment. He'd been in jail.

Griffin was on his feet, arguing that these questions violated attorney-client privilege.

The judge overruled the objection. "There's no attorney-client privilege," he said, "to national television interviews."

In the gallery, people were covering their mouths with their hands, trying not to laugh.

Now Waters turned to the pressures that had been building on Alex in the days leading to the murders. The prosecutor reminded him that Jeanne Seckinger had confronted him about the missing check earlier that day.

"I didn't take it as a confrontation," Alex said.

Later that week, Waters pointed out, Alex was supposed to finally hand over all his financials in the boat crash case.

"I wasn't overly concerned about it," Alex said.

The jury had already heard from Mark Tinsley about how Alex had confronted him over the case at the trial lawyers' conference. Hadn't Alex asked Tinsley, "What's this I'm hearing, Bo?"

"No," Alex said. "Absolutely, unequivocally, never happened."

TINSLEY, STILL WATCHING from his farmhouse, was in disbelief. Alex was actually arguing that he wasn't feeling pressure from him or from Jeanne Seckinger?

On the days he was in the courtroom, Tinsley had taken to passing notes with pointed questions up to the prosecution table. That morning, he texted Waters from home. "He was paranoid about cars on the road but he wasn't paranoid about me or Jeanne?!"

Tinsley had chided the prosecution for pulling punches when they opted against seeking the death penalty. In Tinsley's mind, prison was too good for Alex Murdaugh, just another hustle for him to run.

Tinsley saw Alex's decision not to protect Maggie and her assets in the civil suit as evidence he'd planned to kill her all along. He also believed Alex never meant to kill himself for life insurance because he had no life insurance to begin with. The court-appointed receivers in the Beach case couldn't find any evidence of a policy, and Alex's lawyers hadn't produced one. Besides, life insurance was for cautious men. Alex was anything but.

Tinsley wanted Waters to push those two points, because in his mind, they showed premeditation and a pattern of deceit. Several of Tinsley and Alex's mutual friends had accepted that Alex was capable of theft but not of murdering his wife and son. Once Tinsley told them he had no life insurance, he saw something click in their minds. If he had no policy, why had he concocted a story about trying to arrange his own murder on the side of the road? What other possible reason except he was trying to gain sympathy and buy time, just as he did with the homicides?

It's possible Tinsley was so stuck on prodding Waters because it was easier than accepting that the case was out of his hands. He'd done all he could do in the four years since the boat wreck and four hours on the witness stand. All he could do now was watch and wait.

WATERS KEPT PRESSING, showing all the stressors bearing down on the accused just before the murders. Hadn't he been suffering from opiate withdrawal that weekend? Yes, Alex said. Hadn't both Maggie and Paul been pushing him to get off the pills? Alex quibbled with that, but anyone who'd read the family text messages the state had introduced as evidence knew it was true.

The prosecutor returned to Alex's lie about not joining Maggie and Paul at the kennels after dinner. In all his desire to help the police, had the witness not deemed it important to tell the truth about where he'd been just before the murders? Alex had told the jury he'd tried his best to be cooperative and forthcoming.

"But you left out the most important parts, didn't you?"

"I left out that," Alex said. "I sure did."

When he went down to the kennels, what did he and Maggie talk about? Alex said he wasn't sure. Had he been suffering withdrawal symptoms at that moment? No, Alex said, because he was back on the pills.

What about the dogs? When Alex joined his wife and son at the kennels, had the dogs been acting as though they sensed any strangers in the vicinity? No, Alex said.

"There was nobody—"

Waters cut him off. "There was nobody?"

"—around that the dogs didn't know. There was nobody else around for them to . . . sense."

"All right," said Waters. "Good."

Over at the defense table, Jim Griffin had gone quiet.

Waters reminded Alex that he'd testified to leaving the kennels shortly after Paul finished recording the video.

"Why'd you get out of there so quick, Mr. Murdaugh?"

"Because it was chaotic. It was hot. And I was getting ready to do exactly what I didn't want to do."

The prosecutor paused, staring at the witness.

"You were getting ready to do what you didn't want to do?" he said.

A frisson swept across the courtroom.

"That's correct," Alex said, trying to recover. "I was getting ready to sweat. I was getting ready to work. I went back to the air-conditioning."

Well, the prosecutor asked, did he say goodbye to his wife and son? Or did he just take off?

"I mean, I would have said, 'I'm leaving.' "

The prosecutor reminded Alex of the state's detailed timeline, placing Alex with his wife and son only minutes before they were murdered. The kennel video had ended at 8:45:45. Would it have taken Alex a couple of minutes more to return to the house? Yes, Alex agreed. And according to his story, he had taken a nap back at the house? A short one, Alex said.

"Are these also convenient facts in your new story that have to fit with the timeline now that that evidence has been thrown in your face?"

"No, sir."

"Does that sound like real life to you," asked Waters, "that you jet down there and jet back, Mr. Murdaugh?"

On the stand, Alex struggled to answer. He didn't agree that he had "jetted" anywhere. He didn't agree that he was changing elements of his story to account for the kennel video.

"Just a second, Mr. Waters. Hang on."

In his original account, shared on the night of the murders, Alex had said he had napped for approximately an hour, during the period when Paul and Maggie had been murdered. Now he was saying he had been at the kennels with them, then returned to the house around 8:49 P.M., taken a nap, and left at 9:02 to go see his mother.

"Did you hear anything at all, Mr. Murdaugh, during that time period?"

"No, I did not."

Alex wanted the jury to believe he'd done his best to help the police with the case, correct?

"Other than lying to them about going to the kennel, I was cooperative in every aspect of this investigation."

"Very cooperative," Waters said, "except for maybe the most important fact of all—that you were at the murder scene with the victims just minutes before they died. Right?"

Another murmur stirred among the audience.

Judge Newman called a break. For the next twenty minutes, Alex stood alone in the doorway behind the witness stand, unable to return to the defense table and consult with his lawyers. He stared out at the circus his actions had created, the journalists comparing notes on the high-wire fall they'd just witnessed, the defense lawyers consulting on how, if it was even possible, to put the lions back in the cage. If Alex was the ringmaster, he was losing control. When the break ended and the jurors returned, they did not meet his gaze.

During the break, the prosecution had put a timeline of that evening on a screen. Waters asked Alex to confirm that the cellphone tower showed no activity on his phone between 6:52 P.M. and 9:04 P.M. The jury by now knew Alex almost always carried his phone and was constantly calling and texting. Confronted with this unusual silence of more than two hours, Alex said he didn't always carry the phone around Moselle, especially because the reception was terrible.

The pedometer in Alex's phone recorded no steps between 8:09 P.M. and 9:02. Given that Alex had admitted to being at the kennels during that window, he obviously had set down his phone. Alex said he wasn't sure where he had put the phone. Maybe near the couch, maybe in the bathroom.

Maggie's phone data showed her taking steps at 8:30, after dinner. Paul's phone showed him at the kennels at 8:38. Six minutes later, Paul had pressed Record on the kennel video. Both Paul's and Maggie's phones had locked at 8:49. Four minutes later, someone was holding Maggie's phone and walking with it.

"That's what the data shows," Alex said. "Yes, sir."

Then, at 9:02 P.M., Alex's phone came to life. Suddenly he was making calls and walking around. What had he been doing? Getting ready, he said, to check on his mother at Almeda.

In the next four minutes, the phone showed him taking 283 steps, the distance of two football fields.

"Did you get on a treadmill?" Waters asked.

"No, I didn't get on a treadmill."

"Jog in place?"

"No, I didn't jog in place."

"Do jumping jacks?"

"No, sir. I did not do jumping jacks."

Then what was he doing in those four minutes? the prosecutor asked.

"Preparing to leave for my mom's house."

Waters stifled a laugh. Alex had testified he'd been sleeping on the couch in the front room, woken up and then gone straight outside to his Suburban. How could those actions have resulted in so much walking around?

"I don't know if I got up and went to my room, went to the gun room, went back in the . . ."

"Doing what?" said Waters. "You've been so clear in your new story about everything. What were you doing during these four minutes?"

Alex bristled.

"I know what I wasn't doing, Mr. Waters. And what I wasn't doing is doing anything—as I believe you've implied, that I was cleaning off, or washing off, or washing off guns, or putting guns in a raincoat. And I can promise you that I wasn't doing any of that."

During those four minutes, the data showed, Alex had called his father and called Maggie's phone. But when the police had downloaded the contents of his phone a few days later, they discovered that dozens of phone calls and texts from the night of the murder had been deleted. They included calls to his father and to Maggie and Paul.

"Did you delete them, Mr. Murdaugh?"

"Not intentionally," Alex said. "I can tell you, this jury, and everybody who's listening that I did not intentionally delete phone calls from my phone."

It was a classic non-denial denial, and it reflected Alex's awareness that he was testifying not just for the jury, but for the viewers following the trial around the world.

Waters returned to the 283 steps between 9:02 and 9:06 P.M., and all the phone calls Alex had made.

"You're a busy bee on that phone right out of the gate at 9:02, right?"

Jim Griffin objected to the prosecutor's sarcasm.

"Objection is overruled," said the judge.

"Am I a busy bee?" Alex asked.

"Yeah," said Waters.

Alex did not admit to that characterization. But he did acknowledge he'd made some phone calls.

About those calls to Maggie, Waters said. As the first deputies arrived at the scene, Alex made a point of telling law enforcement about his calls to Maggie and even encouraged them to check his phone records. That was all part of manufacturing his alibi, correct?

"Absolutely incorrect," Alex said. "I never, ever, ever created an alibi."

Alex had arrived at Almeda at 9:22 P.M. Twenty-six minutes later, the records showed him leaving. And yet he had originally told the investigators he'd stayed at Almeda for between forty-five minutes and an hour, wasn't that correct? Alex said he'd been unsure of the time and had always known that the data from his phone and from his Suburban would nail down the exact length of his visit.

There was no question that Creighton Waters was landing blow after blow against Alex's credibility. But as the cross-examination stretched into the hours, Alex never veered far from his folksy calm. He took issue with some of Waters's questions. But he did not lose his temper. Even when he was cornered, he maintained a steady drumbeat of denial, acting as though he was doing his level best to tell the truth.

The jurors had heard Jeanne Seckinger describe her confrontation with Alex about the missing money earlier on the day of the murders. Alex said there had been no confrontation. Blanca had testified that Alex had grilled her on what she would tell the detectives about his clothes. Alex ignored the gist of her testimony and confirmed that the two of them talked about his clothes. Shelley Smith had described Alex pressuring her to overstate the time he spent at Almeda. Alex had expressed respect for Shelley but said she was mistaken.

For more than a century, the Murdaughs had practiced the art of putting a polished sheen over the mess of reality. Alex was asking the jurors to hold incompatible thoughts at the same time. He insisted he was telling them the truth even as he admitted to lying to every other person in his life. And they should accept that his version was right even when the women who knew him best swore otherwise.

WATERS CONTINUED TO play snippets from Alex's interviews with David Owen, calling out discrepancies. He pointed out that when Owen asked him to confirm that the last time he'd seen Paul and Maggie was at supper, Alex had said, "Yes, sir."

"So, I mean, again, you repeated the same lies over and over again."

"I did."

"Effortlessly and convincingly."

"I don't know about that."

What about the day in September when his law partners had confronted him with evidence of his thefts?

"This time they had unassailable evidence, correct?" Waters said. "No wiggling out of this one?"

Waters recounted how Alex had lied to the 911 dispatcher about being attacked by an unknown man, then to the paramedic in the ambulance, then to SLED at the hospital, even going so far as sitting down with a sketch artist and describing the face of the supposed assailant. All of it was a lie, correct?

"It was."

"When accountability is at your door, Mr. Murdaugh, bad things happen."

Alex disputed that characterization. Waters ignored him.

"For the first time in your life of privilege and prominence and wealth, when you're facing accountability, each time, suddenly you became a victim and everyone ran to your aid. Isn't that true?"

"I disagree with that."

"Shame, for you," Waters asked, "is an extraordinary provocation, isn't it, Mr. Murdaugh?"

"I don't like to be shamed," Alex admitted.

"The prospect of humiliating the legacy is an extraordinary provocation to you, isn't it, Mr. Murdaugh?"

They were peers in some respects, the prosecutor and the defendant. They had been contemporaries in law school, though they never knew each other. Both were the sons of successful lawyers. Both had sons of their own. But that's where the similarity ended. Waters had spent his career prosecuting white-collar crimes, a role that made him unpopular in the state's chummy ruling class. Alex, on the other hand, used the members-only elevator at the State House and had bought drinks at one time or another for virtually every lawyer in the state. Alex was tall and redheaded and earned well over a million dollars a year. Waters was five foot eight and prematurely gray, making less than Alex's guaranteed minimum salary of $125,000 for most of his career.

"I was actually a couple years behind you in law school," Waters said. "But we never knew each other, did we?"

"I never knew you. No, sir."

Waters pressed Alex on the magnitude of his success and influence. There was an absurdity to Alex's disputing something so plainly true, as if he were so accustomed to swimming in the water of privilege, he forgot it was water at all.

"Mr. Murdaugh, are you a family annihilator?"

"You mean, like, did I shoot my wife and my son?"

"Yes."

"No. I would never hurt Maggie Murdaugh. I would never hurt Paul Murdaugh, under any circumstances."

"You say that, but you lied to Maggie, didn't you?"

"I did lie to Maggie."

"You lied to Paul."

"Sometimes."

"You lied to your father."

"I'm sure I did at some point."

"Did you tell him all the stuff you'd been up to over the years before he died?"

"No, I didn't tell him."

"Did you lie to your brothers?"

"About the financial things?"

"Yes," Waters said.

"I would've lied to Randy at some point, I'm sure."

"Did you lie to him about the last time you saw your wife and son alive?"

"I did."

"Did you lie to their wives?"

"I'm sure I did."

"Did you lie to Marian Proctor?"

"Yes."

His brother-in-law? Maggie's parents? His best friends? His law partners? His paralegals? Yes, Alex said, yes, he'd lied to all of them. What about his clients?

"Did you lie to Pamela Pinckney?"

"I did."

"Hakeem Pinckney?"

"Again, I don't know that I talked to Hakeem, but I certainly lied about that."

"Arthur Badger?"

"I did."

"The Plyler girls?"

"That's— I—I'm not sure that I talked specifically to them, but I lied about that."

What about Tony Satterfield, Waters asked. Didn't you tell him just five weeks before the homicides that you were working hard on the case?

"And you stole millions from those boys?"

"I, I stole those funds."

Waters wanted the jury to see that nobody knew who Alex really was. He lied all the time, about everything. Only when backed into a corner did he come up with a new version of events.

"And you've been able to lie quickly and easily and convincingly if you think it'll save your skin for well over a decade. Isn't that true?"

"I have lied well over a decade."

Yet now, the attorney pointed out, Alex wanted the jury to believe his new story, manufactured to explain his presence at the kennels.

No, sir, Alex said.

Waters reminded Alex that he had testified he hadn't decided to lie about the kennels until Agent Owen had interviewed him in his car. Now the prosecutor showed Alex the footage from more than an hour earlier that night, when he had talked to Sgt. Daniel Greene, the first officer on the scene.

Watching the bodycam video, the whole courtroom saw the lie. There was Greene, asking Alex when he last saw his wife and son. There was Alex, saying he'd been gone an hour and a half and hadn't seen them since around 8:15 P.M.

Waters froze the video.

Alex had just testified he'd lied to Owen because the drugs had made him paranoid. Because his law partners had encouraged him to have a lawyer during questioning. Because he didn't trust SLED. Because Agent Owen had questioned him about the state of his marriage.

But on the video, Alex and Sgt. Greene had been alone.

"At that point in time, SLED was not there," Waters pointed out.

No one had yet collected any gunshot residue. Alex's law partners hadn't had time to caution him.

"That's correct," Alex said.

"No one had asked you about your relationships. David Owen was not there."

"That's correct."

"But you still told the same lie," Waters said. By now his voice was rising, crackling with contempt. "And all those reasons that you just gave this jury about the most important part of your testimony was a lie, too. Isn't that true, Mr. Murdaugh?"

Alex suddenly grew smaller. His shoulders were hunched, his body bent.

"I disagree with that," he said quietly.

Waters walked away, still bristling, turning his back toward the witness.

"Nothing further."

PART SEVEN

THE RUINS

At the end of the trial testimony, the jurors were taken to Moselle. The twelve of them, along with the two remaining alternates, were loaded into two transport vans with tinted windows.

After all this time, their identities were strangely anonymous and wildly public. The cameras in the courtroom went to great lengths to avoid showing their faces, but the courtroom denizens studied them every day, gauging their reactions to witnesses, some observers even jotting down notes about their reactions, using their juror numbers or nicknames. Some names were based on the professions they had provided at voir dire, such as "postman" or "surgical assistant." Others were based on a descriptive trait, such as Dip Can, the man on the front row who kept his tobacco tin perched on the jury rail. They had not been sequestered, so when they weren't in the courtroom, they were local celebrities. Everyone knew exactly who they were, and often where they lived and went to church. Yes, it was a big case, but it was also a small town.

Dick Harpootlian had been pushing to bring the jurors to Moselle since opening arguments. He wanted them to get a sense for the vastness of the property and how a person might not know what was going on at the kennels from up at the house. Conversely, he wanted them to see the tight confines where Paul and Maggie had been killed, so they could understand that whoever shot Paul in particular would have been drenched in blood. Alex's clothes had been clean.

As the vans of jurors left the courthouse, they joined a motorcade of black and gray vehicles. To some, the twenty-two-mile journey felt like a surreal school field trip, not to the state capital or a museum but to a place of intense fascination, bearing a beautiful name inextricable from a hideous act.

The weather was sunny and warm, with puffy white clouds dotting the bright blue sky. The somber line of vehicles took the main drag out of Walterboro, then continued westward past the Dairy-Land drive-in and the motels lining the I-95 exit, past small farms and a country church, past an old metal trailer that served as the local post office. The landmarks were deeply familiar to many of the jurors. Many of their families had lived there for generations.

The sky had darkened since they'd left the courthouse. Some of the jurors wondered if it might rain.

After twenty minutes, they turned onto the long and narrow road to Moselle. They passed the cow field where Maggie's phone had been tossed. They rolled past the curving brick gates that marked the formal entrance to the big house, a decorative touch added by Maggie when they moved in a decade prior. A smattering of TV trucks lined the far side of the road, with reporters filming the jury vans' arrival. The vans proceeded another 500 feet before turning left into the second entrance to Moselle, the one primarily used by the family. The black mailbox at the head of the driveway was covered in spiderwebs and topped by a No Trespassing sign. The caretaker's cabin appeared deserted, the shrubs out front bushy and overgrown.

The vans rolled slowly up the dirt drive and parked on the far side of the hangar. The jurors were warned to watch out for snakes. They climbed out of the vans and walked wordlessly toward the deserted kennels. They were not clustered in a group but spread out, alone with their own thoughts, having been told they could not talk with one another or anyone other than the judge while on the property. Tall pines towered overhead. A deep quiet held sway in every direction, interrupted only by birdsong.

The property had stood vacant for twenty months now. Random items seemed to have been left where they fell: a tube of sanitizing wipes, a deflated football. A small dog bed lay inside one of the kennels, along with a discarded dog toy, a stuffed chicken.

One juror checked out a yellow hose on the mount where a hose had been wrapped haphazardly the night of the shootings; the state was saying that it indicated someone had cleaned up in a hurry. Another juror rubbed his finger in the bullet hole in the side of the quail house; the defense was arguing that this bullet had been fired at an angle that suggested the presence of two shooters. A juror balanced on the edge of the concrete pad running alongside the kennels, proving to himself that the shooter could've easily tripped backward, stunned by the blowback from the first blast of the shotgun and explaining the acute upward angle of the second shot.

Nearly all the jurors took turns standing in the center of the feed room, facing out as Paul would have been when the first shot hit him. The feed room was six feet wide and ten feet deep, with a door that was slightly offset right of center and a wooden shelf at waist height to the left, extending from the doorjamb to the wall. Standing in the center of the room, it seemed clear Paul would not have been able to see a shooter who was crouching just outside on the left, as the state argued the killer had been. Paul had survived that first shot and stumbled forward, walking slowly toward the door. He almost certainly would have seen who fired the second shot, the force of which severed his brainstem, leaving traces of his blood and red hair on the top of the doorframe.

The state's forensic expert Kenny Kinsey had told them he believed Paul had been shot first. Maggie had been on the far side of the hangar and had come running toward her son when she heard the shots. Several jurors counted off the twelve paces from where Paul died to the spot where Maggie fell. They'd seen the photos of the prints her flip-flops had made as she ran. They had heard how she'd been shot first in the leg and abdomen, knocking her down but not killing her. She had been on the ground, her body canted forward, her dark blond hair falling around her face, when the killer had shot her from behind with the assault rifle, the bullet opening her skull. Then, when she was already dead, her assailant had shot her once more in the head for good measure.

There were no visible markings where Maggie had fallen, just a dusty patch where grass refused to grow. Likewise, there were no bloodstains remaining on the cement where Paul had bled out. The jurors could see the holes in the back of the window where the large buckshot pellets had blown through and the dings in the metal door left by dozens of tiny bits of birdshot. But the clearest sign that something wicked had happened there was the feel of the place itself.

The visit to Moselle brought out visceral responses that were not available in the cold courtroom, the same way a song can spark a sense of longing and a smell can summon the past. No amount of words, no stack of crime scene pictures, could convey the feeling of the place. Asked later, almost to a person, everyone repeated the same word. It was the same one David Owen had used a year earlier. They felt a sense of heaviness, though they varied whether they said it was in the air or in the ground itself.

As the jury lingered, the air cooled and the wind picked up, billowing skirts and mussing hair. One juror stood with her back to the kennels and looked off toward the house, two football fields away, and saw its shiny tin roof in the distance. Another juror walked toward the nearby tree line, convincing herself no intruder could have approached without the dogs barking. Another juror stood on the spot where Maggie had died.

A dominant impression, shared by many, was that Moselle felt like a place where the barrier between the living and the dead was very thin.

Captain Jason Chapman, one of the first officers on the scene after the 911 call, watched the jurors' movements, how they seemed to be measuring distances, which were far more compact than a diagram could show. Chapman had overseen courthouse security and watched nearly every minute of the trial on a TV in the command post a few steps away from the back entrance. He'd heard the defense ask, loudly and more than once, for the jury to make this trip. He could not say for sure, but based on what he saw in the jurors' faces, he did not think it was going as planned.

The clerk of court, Becky Hill, was also studying the jurors, several of whom she'd known for years. She read the sadness in their eyes. It mirrored her own. She was eager to leave, to return to the courthouse and see the case to its conclusion. Her grandmother and grandfather had run a still in Old Buster's bootlegging ring. They'd been criminally charged, as had her uncle, still a teenager at the time. She knew the Murdaughs' capacity to ruin lives.

After about forty minutes, the jurors began walking toward the main house. They were offered a ride but declined, one after another, preferring to walk along the grassy former runway. They were quiet, listening to the wrens in the trees, swatting the occasional gnat. After a few minutes, they reached the big white house. It looked much smaller than its 5,000 square feet, placed as it was in such a vast expanse of land. A long and wide porch stretched in front of the house, with planters on both sides of the doors, as well as small dog beds on decorative wicker frames. On a table tucked between two rocking chairs was a small blue flowerpot with a snowman painted on it, along with the name Buster.

Leading up to the porch was the flight of brick steps where Gloria Satterfield had fallen. To the side of the steps was a green bicycle with a weathered wicker basket, like the one witnesses had testified Maggie would sometimes ride to check on the dogs. On the right side of the house was a separate entrance to the gun room.

Dick Harpootlian had been chauffeured to the crime scene in his black Mercedes sedan by a junior member of the defense team. Over the years, Harpootlian had been to Moselle many times, sometimes for political fundraisers. It had always been a showplace. But on the day of the jury visit, he was the first to leave, ducking out while the jurors still wandered the property.

"This place gives me the creeps," he said. "It's like it's fucking haunted."

CHAPTER FORTY-FOUR

By the time the jury returned from Moselle, the sun had come back out. Bright light was streaming through the courtroom's windows, but as the jurors filed back toward their seats, their expressions were subdued.

Judge Newman called on Creighton Waters, and the prosecutor walked over to the jury rail.

"It's been a long trial, hasn't it," he said.

They'd been in the courtroom together for six weeks, through seventy-five witnesses and more than eight hundred exhibits, from mundane bank records to gruesome autopsy photos.

"Yes, it has," one juror said.

Waters did not tell them he was exhausted. Going to trial was like waging a war, and as the lead prosecutor, the battle had been entirely his responsibility. He had led his team in preparing for the dozens of witnesses and had strategized over what to ask those witnesses and what not to ask them, when to introduce the body cam videos and the kennel video and all the other exhibits, how to build a case that would make sense to the jury. When the courtroom's sound system had failed, he'd gone to Best Buy and bought a karaoke machine. When the lectern wobbled, he had tracked down a screwdriver and stretched out on the courtroom carpet to tighten the screws at the lectern's base.

Preparing for this day, Waters had pulled his first all-nighter since college, printing out draft after draft of what he would say. Now the time for practicing was over.

Waters thanked the jurors for sticking with him. He promised he would try to distill the case down to its essence.

Alex Murdaugh, the prosecutor said, was a person of singular prominence who had never been questioned about anything his entire life. When he stumbled into a series of bad land deals and was pinched for cash to fund his extravagant lifestyle, Waters argued, it had been easy enough to start stealing. Alex was addicted, yes, but his addiction was to money, and he stole millions of dollars over the course of a decade to maintain the illusion of his own image.

His thievery had gone unchecked until the boat crash. Then Mark Tinsley had pushed for his financials and Jeanne Seckinger had asked for answers about the missing check. That evening, Waters said, Alex had killed Maggie and Paul to buy himself time. He had valued his family name more than his family itself.

"In the wake of this, everything changes," Waters said. "All those things that were coming to a head immediately go away. It's a different world now."

The law firm stopped asking about the missing money, giving Alex time to borrow more money to pay it back. The pressure from the boat case evaporated. Tinsley had thought his lawsuit against Alex was over, given the sympathy the public would feel for a grieving husband and father.

"Who would better understand that than Alex Murdaugh, who does the same work?"

Waters told the jury he was aware that the story he was telling was hard for most people to wrap their heads around, but that was because most people don't think like Alex Murdaugh. The prosecutor asked the jury to remember his ticking through dozens of victims' names, with

Alex unable to recall a single time he sat down with any of them individually and lied to their face.

"He couldn't name one conversation, and didn't want to talk about any of those individuals who trusted him as he looked you in the eye and asked you to do the same."

Waters walked the jury through the elements of the state's case: motive, means, opportunity, and evidence of consciousness of guilt.

The motive, he said, was staving off the gathering storm—the mounting questions from the boat crash case and from his own firm about the missing money. The means were the family-owned weapons used in the killings, the .300 Blackout rifle that killed Maggie and the Benelli Super Black Eagle shotgun that killed Paul. Investigators had never found the missing weapons, but at the scene they had found the shotgun's wadding and pellets as well as shell casings from the assault rifle. The shotgun, the testimony had shown, had been Alex's favorite firearm.

The opportunity had arisen when Alex found Paul and Maggie at the kennels that night. Waters reminded the jury that Alex had lied for months about his whereabouts, telling anyone who asked he was never down at the kennels.

"Why would he lie about that, ladies and gentlemen? Why would he even think to lie about that if he were an innocent man?"

Alex had testified to taking a nap when he returned to the house that night sometime between 8:50 and 9:02 P.M.

"The shortest nap," Waters said, "in the history of the South."

Now Alex was asking the jurors to believe that some intruder or intruders had appeared just after Alex left the kennels and had known they'd find a shotgun and an assault rifle conveniently waiting for them there. The lack of any defensive wounds on Paul's or Maggie's hands or arms showed that they had not been approached that night by a stranger.

At the defense table, Alex pursed his lips and jotted down notes.

As for consciousness of guilt, Alex's behavior had proven that repeatedly. He had convinced both Paul and Maggie to return home that evening, even though neither had planned to be at Moselle. He had leaned on Blanca Simpson about the clothes he was wearing the day of the murders and leaned on Shelley Smith about the length of his visit to Almeda. He had used his phone to create an alibi, proof that he knew what he was going to do and tried to cover it up. Waters said he believed Alex was telling the truth about two things: whoever did this had anger in their heart, and they had planned the murders for a long time.

Waters paused, walking back over to the lectern, steady now, and shuffled through the notes he'd spent all night revising. When he spoke again, his tone was one of bewilderment.

No one, he said, had known the real Alex Murdaugh.

"He avoided accountability his whole life. He relied on his family name. He carried a badge and authority. He lived a wealthy life. But now, finally, he was facing complete ruin."

Waters looked into the jurors' faces.

"His father who he idolized . . . was dying. His son was facing charges for the boat case. He was facing a civil action that not only could potentially ruin him but expose the reality of what he'd been doing for years. He had an opiate addiction. The entire illusion of his life was about to be altered.

"Shame is an extraordinary provocation. His ego couldn't stand that, and he became a family annihilator."

Waters concluded by holding up two pictures. One showed Maggie and Paul smiling at a family get-together just a few days before they died. The other was a graphic image of their dead bodies.

"This is what he did," Waters said, nodding toward Alex. "This defendant has fooled everyone. Everyone who thought they were close to him, everyone who thought they knew who he was. He's fooled them all. And he fooled Maggie and Paul, too, and they paid for it with their lives. Don't let him fool you, too."

. . .

THE DEFENSE TEAM had asked to split their closing argument, with Jim Griffin addressing the technical elements and Dick Harpootlian dealing with the emotions at the heart of their case. They argued that the evidence was so voluminous, it was only fair to allow them to share the workload. The judge considered their request for several days before denying it, saying he knew of no precedent and wasn't about to set one.

The decision put the defense in a tough spot. Harpootlian was a living legend among trial attorneys, known for his power to convince jurors to see things his way.

"The jury wants a story," he'd say. "You've got to work the jury."

But Harpootlian was worn down by the sustained concentration required for a long trial. For days, he had been sitting at the defense table, motionless as a sphinx.

That left Jim Griffin to go it alone. Griffin had litigated mammoth white-collar cases but lacked Harpootlian's experience with the visceral realities of violent crime. He approached the lectern clutching a stack of papers.

"Wow," he said.

He began with a set piece borrowed from Harpootlian, saying his co-counsel had attended a trial in Scotland at which jurors were given three options: guilty, not guilty, or not proven. He told the jury to consider "not guilty" and "not proven" as combined in the American criminal justice system; therefore, if any of them believed the state had not fully proved its case, they had to find Alex not guilty.

Griffin then turned to how little the state had done to meet its heavy burden of proof.

SLED had focused solely on Alex from the beginning, he said. He held up a posterboard sign with the SLED statement from shortly after the murders, reassuring the public there was no danger.

"They had decided that unless we find somebody else, it's going to be Alex."

Investigators had bungled the physical evidence in astonishing ways, Griffin said. They'd ignored tire tracks in the wet grass. They'd failed to take impressions of a footprint in the feed room or test Maggie's and Paul's clothing for DNA. They didn't protect the information on Maggie's phone, so her location data the night of the murders got rewritten. And somehow, Griffin said, Agent Owen had missed an email from SLED's own lab that Alex's shirt showed no human blood.

"Did the dog eat his email? I mean, how's the lead investigator in the case not get the lab report that says there's no blood on the shirt?"

Griffin mocked the prosecution's inference that Alex had cleaned himself off at the kennels. "After brutally murdering Maggie and Paul, he takes a hose and washes himself off," Griffin said. "He gets in a golf cart, butt-naked I guess, and drives to the house."

The only reason Alex was on trial at all was the kennel video, Griffin said. He played the video one last time, asking the jurors to listen to the light tone of Maggie's, Paul's, and Alex's voices.

"This is a family down at the dog kennels doing what families do," he said. "There's nothing on that tape that indicates there's any strife, any conflict, any anger, any planning, anybody being afraid, anybody running, anybody scurrying. Nothing."

Why then, four minutes later, would Alex Murdaugh kill his wife and son? The state had tried to paper over that question with the shock of the kennel video.

"We are back to the lie," Griffin said. "Because that's all they have in this case, is that Alex lied to them, when he last saw them. And he shouldn't have."

The defense attorney paused.

"He lied because that's what addicts do."

Griffin choked up, his closing words racked with emotion.

"On behalf of Alex, on behalf of Buster, on behalf of Maggie, and on behalf of my friend Paul, I respectfully request that you do not compound a family tragedy with another. Thank you."

. . .

THE LAW GAVE the state the final word, a brief rebuttal to the defense's closing argument. After Griffin wrapped up, Judge Newman asked the state if it was prepared to begin.

John Meadors rose sheepishly. "I just need to go to the bathroom," he said.

The courtroom filled with laughter. The judge called a brief recess and Meadors joined the scrum spilling out into the hallway and downstairs to the lone set of public restrooms.

Mark Tinsley had come to court to watch the closing. During the break, he ran downstairs to the men's room and found himself standing at the urinals next to Meadors. The prosecutor did not ask advice on the closing he was about to deliver. Tinsley offered it anyway.

"You can make this really quick," Tinsley said. "Stand up and say, 'Three people went down there, one came back, and he lied about everything.'"

MEADORS HAD SPENT his career trying murder cases, a preacher's son who could have passed for a preacher himself, with a voice that soared and fell, then soared again.

He began by telling the jury that years ago, his mother had given him a copy of *The Velveteen Rabbit,* the childhood classic about a stuffed animal who became real. That had been his mother's advice to him: Always be real.

"This case," Meadors said, "is about the defendant never being real."

He asked them to call to mind the witnesses who had shown genuine emotion, like Blanca Simpson, who'd dropped the phone when Alex told her Maggie and Paul were dead, and Shelley Smith, who'd cried when she testified that Alex pushed her to lie about how long he'd been at Almeda.

"That's real," the prosecutor said. "Shelley's real."

Alex Murdaugh was a living, breathing lie, he said. "I think he loved Maggie. I think he loved Paul. But you know who he loved more than that?"

He leaned toward the jurors.

"Alex."

Meadors chastised the defense for beating up on law enforcement. It was Alex who had impeded the investigation, he said, cleaning up the scene and lying about the single most important fact of the case: the last time he saw his wife and son alive.

"I find it offensive that a family with a great-grandfather, a grandfather, and a father, Solicitor Randolph Murdaugh, who was good to me when I was a young prosecutor," he said—"I find it offensive that the defense, through the defendant, who is also a part-time solicitor, claims that law enforcement didn't do their job."

Alex had blamed others to avoid getting caught. He thought he could get away with killing his wife and son, Meadors said, because he had gotten away with everything his entire life.

"It stops here. We respectfully request, it stops here today."

CHAPTER FORTY-FIVE

Before deliberations could begin, the judge had to handle a problem with the jury. He had been investigating allegations that a juror was talking publicly about her opinion of the case, which was forbidden.

The juror had been the first one chosen, which had meant she'd had the catbird seat in the front row of the jury box. She'd been among the most memorable prospective jurors during jury selection, the one who had referred to her workplace as the Monkey Farm.

Judge Newman said he had interviewed the juror and the people she had allegedly spoken with during a hearing in his chambers. He had also reviewed affidavits taken by SLED. Though the juror's conversations did not appear to be extensive, he'd concluded she had discussed the case with at least three people. She had to go.

This was devastating news for the defense. The Monkey Farm woman had smiled at Alex throughout the trial. She had listened closely when Griffin talked and had laughed at Harpootlian's jokes. The defense had considered her their strongest chance for a "not guilty" voice in the jury room.

The judge's announcement was met with stunned silence. Tinsley waited for the defense to move for a mistrial on the grounds of improper removal of a juror. He knew the motion would not have been granted, but it would have preserved an avenue for a potential appeal. But the defense made no such motion.

The judge asked the bailiff to bring out the juror. She shuffled into the courtroom and stood alone in the jury box, smiling as she always did, though warily. To some of the core group of journalists, lawyers, and court staff, it felt like watching a classmate get kicked out of school on the last day.

The judge told the juror that he'd determined that, intentionally or unintentionally, she'd discussed the case with other people.

"You have been, by all accounts, a great juror," he said. "You've smiled consistently and performed well. I'm not suggesting that you intentionally did anything wrong, but in order to preserve the integrity of the process, we're going to replace you with one of the other jurors."

He asked the juror if she'd left anything in the jury room.

"A dozen eggs," she said.

"Say it again?"

"A dozen eggs," she said. Another juror had brought farm eggs for anyone who wanted them, she said, so she needed her eggs, her purse, and her bottle of water.

The judge asked the bailiff to fetch them for her, and then she left the courtroom. The remaining jurors and final two alternates filed in. One alternate had taken to covering her face with a blanket during tedious testimony, even stuffing tissue in her ears. She had a tendency to turn toward the audience and wink or roll her eyes. The other alternate was the brother of one of the first deputies on the scene, who'd been chosen only after being questioned in the judge's chambers about his ability to be impartial.

The deputy clerk put two slips of paper in a small cardboard box and shook them around. She drew the slip for the deputy's brother. He was a recent Clemson graduate working as a construction manager. He always wore a coat and tie; in the jury room he was known as Suits.

. . .

THE JURORS BEGAN their deliberations at close to 4 P.M. The first thing they did was form a circle in the jury room to pray together.

Many of the jurors had been acquaintances beforehand. The newest juror, Suits, whose real name was James McDowell, had known several of the others by name before the trial even began. But after weeks together at the trial, they had all come to know one another well. On some days, when they'd heard no testimony, they had just sat back there together without screens of any kind to distract them. Sometimes they read or played cards but mostly they talked about weekend plans or local gossip or problems at home, the ups and downs of daily life. They wore pink and red on Valentine's Day, a signal to all that they had bonded. They had held group meetings a couple of times over the course of six weeks, to talk and pray together when one or another of them was feeling overwhelmed. Juror Amie Williams, a payroll specialist with the water company, led them in prayer that afternoon, asking for clarity, wisdom, and that the truth would be revealed.

The jurors sat down and wrote their initial votes on slips of paper. They had decided to take an anonymous vote so they could express their opinions freely. Some jurors thought they already knew what the others were thinking based on their body language. But they didn't know for sure until the forewoman read the tally: nine "guilty," two "not guilty," and one "not sure."

They'd each been given a notebook to keep in the jury room so they could jot down questions for deliberations. They started talking, the words coming out in a rush after so long of not being able to discuss everything they'd heard.

One of the first questions was about Alex's white shirt. Laura Rutland had testified it was completely clean, as though it had just come out of the dryer. The SLED technician who'd processed the shirt had testified that it had smelled like laundry detergent. But how was that possible? The jurors had seen footage of Alex sweating and wiping his face. They asked the bailiff to bring them the evidence bag to examine. Once they realized it did not identify the contents as belonging to Alex Murdaugh, they reached a consensus that the SLED tech who opened the bag would have had no reason to say she smelled laundry detergent unless she actually had. Maybe the smell of the fabric softener had been activated by the friction from Alex moving around. Maybe the scent was preserved when the shirt was sealed in an evidence bag.

They moved on to a bigger question: the credibility of law enforcement. They worked through the defense's various raps against Agent Owen, especially the fact that he'd told the grand jury the white shirt had human blood on it when it didn't. They found Owen's error understandable, given the information he had at the time. Several of the jurors who fished wondered whether the shirt could have initially tested positive for blood because there were remnants from gaffing a fish at some point in the past. After all, it was a fishing boat T-shirt.

They agreed that law enforcement could have done some things differently, like searching the house more thoroughly or checking out Almeda right away. But they did not see any big error that tainted an overall solid job, especially since at the time, the Murdaughs were a prominent family and no one knew about the other crimes Alex was hiding.

Then they talked about Alex taking the stand. How could he have said he didn't know his badge was hanging off his pocket at the hospital? Or that he'd gotten official permission to put blue lights in his car? Or that he wasn't wealthy when he made a million dollars a year? They debated his many displays of emotion and whether there had been any real tears in them. One juror, a carpenter named Craig Moyer, had been sitting about six feet from Alex. He saw no tears, just snot.

They all had smaller, more nitpicky questions, too, like what was the deal with Alex and his taste for Capri Suns? Someone wondered if Alex had left the empty pouch in the gun room as he reached for the shotgun and the rifle.

The more the jurors talked, the closer they came to a consensus. The timeline was tight, but they thought sixteen minutes would have been enough time after the shootings for Alex to clean up before leaving for Almeda, especially since he had another nineteen minutes when he got back between the time he called 911 and when the first officer arrived.

They didn't know when he showered or what had happened to the guns or his clothes. They could not answer every question. In the end, their decision came down to one inescapable piece of evidence: the kennel video.

"If he didn't do it," McDowell said, "how did he know what time to lie about not being there?"

Juror Gwen Generette said as soon as she heard Alex speak on the witness stand, she knew that had truly been his voice on the video. *Okay,* she told herself. *It really was him down at the kennels.*

By now it was close to six o'clock. The bailiff tapped on the door to see if they wanted to place an order for dinner. They looked at one another. Nobody was yelling or arguing. They still had more they wanted to discuss, but it didn't seem likely that any of their remaining questions would add up to reasonable doubt. They told the bailiff they wanted just a little while longer but they wouldn't be needing dinner.

CHAPTER FORTY-SIX

At 6:41 P.M., the lawyers hustled back to the courtroom. The major networks cut into their regular programming. The jurors had sent word: They had a verdict.

Five hundred miles away, Mallory Beach's mother, Renee, was sitting in the sand at Santa Rosa Beach in Florida, watching the sun slip into the water, when her surviving daughter called.

"Mama, you've got to get back to the TV. The jury's come back."

Anthony Cook watched live with his parents, sitting in the same living room where he'd spent so many nights after the boat wreck, plagued with nightmares in which he searched for Mallory under the dark water. Beside him, his mother braced for an acquittal. Beverly figured Alex had fixed the jury.

JUDGE NEWMAN GAVELED the court to order.

As the jurors filed back to their seats, Jim Griffin looked at each of them, but no one looked back. Alex stared straight ahead. There was no longer any point in trying to win them over.

The judge asked the forewoman to stand.

"Have you reached a verdict?" he asked.

"Yes, sir. We have."

"Is it unanimous?"

"Yes, sir. It is."

She passed the paperwork to the judge, who scanned each page slowly before handing them to the clerk of court.

"The defendant will rise," he said.

Hill read the full indictment, a long series of docket and statute numbers that took a full minute to get through. No one spoke or even seemed to move.

"Guilty verdict," the clerk said, "signed by the forelady."

Guilty on all four charges—two for the murders, two for weapons.

Alex stood still. His face showed nothing. The deputy charged with guarding him touched his elbow and turned him to place the handcuffs on his narrow wrists. In the silent courtroom, the metal cuffs clicked loudly. By now Alex was facing his family. He mouthed "I love you" to Buster. But Buster just stared ahead with his chin in his hand.

David Owen, sitting behind the prosecution, surprised himself by bursting into tears. *Why am I crying,* he wondered, *but not Alex?*

The Murdaughs' security detail whisked the family downstairs into the private office that had become their sanctuary. Once the door closed, some of them started to cry. Buster fell to his knees.

Harpootlian and Griffin gathered their files and swept out of the courthouse, past the media.

"No comment. No comment."

Outside, a hundred people gathered on the courthouse lawn, some having walked up from surrounding neighborhoods and downtown bars, some holding insulated cups of beer. The prosecution team and investigators stepped outside into the hot lights and stood before a bank of microphones. Waters stepped up to speak, and the crowd cheered.

"Justice was done today," the prosecutor said. "It doesn't matter who your family is."

Drops of rain began to fall, smearing Waters's words in the notebooks of reporters almost as fast as they could jot them down.

"It doesn't matter how much money you have, or how much money people think you have. It doesn't matter how prominent you are. If you do wrong, if you break the law, if you murder, justice will be done in South Carolina."

A street preacher in long robes shouted blessings, saying earthly justice had been done.

Blanca was spending the night at her daughter's house in Bluffton. She'd been having trouble sleeping ever since she testified and was on edge with the inescapable news of the trial. She turned off notifications on her phone and spent the evening playing with her grandchildren, whose sweet chaos soothed her. That night, she went to bed early and got the best sleep she had in ages. She missed the verdict altogether; her husband told her the next morning. She took no joy in the news. It hurt her to know that the man she thought she knew was a fiction.

Tony Satterfield tried to describe his feelings on his Facebook page, but his words were a jumble. He was grateful for earthly justice, he said, but intended to forgive Alex and pray for him.

Judas betrayed Jesus too, he wrote. *But Jesus still fed him and washed his feet.*

At the rented condo down in Florida, Mallory's mother broke into tears. Renee had never wished any harm on Paul. She'd just wanted him to apologize and become a better person. Now that Alex had been found guilty, Renee felt an abiding satisfaction. The man had gotten away with so much for so long.

The news shows blew up with analysis of the verdict and what it meant. By then, viewers around the world had watched more than five million hours of trial coverage on Court TV alone. For decades, the Murdaugh family had operated in secret, in an almost forgotten corner of the South. Those days were over.

The hollow man, the vessel who'd poured out so much chaos, sat inside the Colleton County jail, spending his last night among the drunk drivers and petty thieves before being transferred to state prison. A television was mounted in the jail's common room, but it was too far away for Alex to hear what everyone was saying about him.

CHAPTER FORTY-SEVEN

In court the next morning, Judge Newman told Alex to step forward. Three deputies stood nearby, their eyes trained on their prisoner and their hands crossed in front of their bulletproof vests.

"This has been perhaps one of the most troubling cases," Newman said, "not just for me as a judge, for the state, for the defense team, but for all of the citizens in this community and state."

Alex listened quietly.

"You have a wife who's been killed, murdered. A son, savagely murdered. A lawyer, a person from a respected family who has controlled justice in this community for over a century. A person whose grandfather's portrait hangs at the back of the courthouse that I had to have ordered removed in order to ensure that a fair trial was had by both the state and the defense."

In the gallery, young Buster had begun clenching and unclenching his jaw, just as his father had done throughout the trial.

The judge pointed toward the portraits of the judges on the courtroom walls. He said he couldn't help remembering that Alex's family had prosecuted men in this very room, sending them to death row for lesser conduct. Newman had a reputation for harsh sentences, and for a moment, several lawyers in the room wondered whether he might sentence Alex to execution.

Mark Tinsley, seated in the second row behind the prosecution, was holding his breath. When he looked around the room, he realized everybody else was, too.

In the end, the judge said he would not challenge the state's decision not to seek the death penalty. Instead, he asked Alex a question.

"Remind me of the expression you gave on the witness stand, 'Oh, what a tangled web we weave.' What did you mean by that?"

"It meant when I lied, I continued to lie," Alex said.

"The question is when will it end? It's ended already for the jury. They've concluded that you continued to lie and lie."

The judge looked at Alex.

"Where will it end?" he asked again. "Within your own soul, you have to deal with that. I know you have to see Paul and Maggie during the nighttime when you're attempting to go to sleep. I'm sure they come and visit you."

Alex nodded.

"All day and every night," he said.

Newman said he could not imagine the pressures bearing down on Alex in the days leading up to the murders: his father on his deathbed, the law firm cornering Alex about the missing check for $792,000, Mark Tinsley pursuing him to hand over his financials. Tinsley, the judge said, had been a tiger on his tail.

Alex had clearly understood that his reckoning was at hand, the judge said, and yet in front of the jury he'd had the audacity to insist that he'd been under no particular pressure on June 7, 2021.

"To have you come and testify that it was just another ordinary day, that 'my wife and son and I were just out enjoying life'?" Newman said. "Not credible. Not believable."

The judge paused.

"In the murder of your wife, Maggie Murdaugh," he said, "I sentence you for a term of the rest of your natural life."

The judge paused again. He, too, was a father who'd lost a beloved son.

"For the murder of Paul Murdaugh," he said, "whom you probably love so much, I sentence you to prison for murdering him for the rest of your natural life."

PHILLIP BEACH, MALLORY'S father, watched from the courtroom's back row. He had come to the sentencing to remind people that some measure of justice had finally come from his daughter's death. That morning was the fourth anniversary of the day when Mallory's body had been recovered from the wilderness of the marshes.

For Phillip, those years had been made longer by the Murdaughs' inescapable presence in Hampton County. He was tired of the family's phony show of caring even as they sought to avoid accountability. Every time Phillip turned around, it seemed, he'd see Alex on the street or at the Piggly Wiggly, and Alex would hurry over.

"Hey, Bo, how you doing?" Alex would say. "I'm thinking of you and praying for you."

Phillip had moved to the next county over, away from Hampton and the Murdaughs, to find some peace.

Once the sentencing was over, Phillip saw John Marvin heading his way. In his mind, Phillip could still visualize Alex's younger brother working the causeway at Archers Creek, schmoozing with his friends at DNR just minutes after he'd cried alongside Paul in prayer. The man had been politicking then and he was politicking now. Once a Murdaugh, always a Murdaugh.

"I didn't see you back here," John Marvin said, extending his hand.

Phillip held his hands up in the air.

WHEN COURT WAS dismissed, Mark Tinsley went to pay his respects to Judge Newman. Tinsley worked his way back to the private hallway behind the courtroom and saw John Meadors crying outside the judge's chambers. Tinsley hugged the prosecutor, then walked inside to greet Newman, who was taking off his robe.

"Judge," Tinsley said, "that was the most powerful and articulate statement that I've ever heard anyone utter. Thank you."

To Tinsley's surprise, his cheeks were suddenly wet. A wave of emotion had been building inside him for months. Now it broke.

"Why are you crying?" asked the judge.

Tinsley said he wasn't sure. Somehow, he said, he felt responsible for Maggie's and Paul's murders.

Newman stood in front of him, at six foot one, taller than Tinsley had remembered. The judge took both of Tinsley's hands in his own. Tinsley was struck by how big those hands were, and how warm. Newman asked why the lawyer felt he had anything to do with the murders.

Tinsley told the judge he knew, rationally, he had not caused the violence of that summer night. Still, he felt guilty about what had happened to Maggie and Paul. He had intentionally made life difficult for Alex, pressuring him to settle the boat case. But he had never imagined that his intense pursuit of the lawsuit would end in a double homicide.

For months, Tinsley had felt a frantic worry that Alex was going to get away with murder. When the verdict was read, he had felt relief for a few fleeting moments. But what remained inside him afterward was something awful. He told Newman that people kept asking if the verdict made him happy. He didn't feel that way at all.

"I feel dirty," he told the judge. "Dirty is the only word I can think of."

Newman offered what comfort he could. Still clasping Tinsley's hands, the judge assured him the murders had not been his fault. He said the lawyer had done good work, representing the Beaches as they sought justice for Mallory's death and following his instinct that something was terribly wrong with Alex's finances. He told Tinsley he could not have known, nor could he have controlled, the mind of a madman.

Alex Murdaugh remained a mystery to them all.

NOVEMBER 28, 2023

They say a spider's web is an extension of its mind. Every spider has eight glittering eyes; Robert Penn Warren compared them to mirrors in the sun, "like God's eye." Even so, the creature is nearly blind. The silken threads that spin out of its body extend its understanding, a lacy brain suspended in thin air. The spider can sense when prey is ensnared and can read its web like a map, leading it to unfortunate insects, a lesser order. The spider then poisons its prey and spins more gauze to envelop them. The spider understands the web on a level deeper than thought, or even memory, because the web is itself.

If a spider is removed from its web, it is irrevocably diminished—still menacing and unpredictable, but, separated from its world, no longer beguiling.

Nearly nine months after he was convicted of the murders, on the Tuesday after Thanksgiving, Alex Murdaugh stood in court before Judge Newman one more time to be sentenced for his financial crimes. Alex looked almost like a different person—thinner, with his hair gone blondish gray. He was like a ghost. The bailiffs didn't bother to make eye contact, and his family was nowhere to be seen. The only smiles he got were from his lawyers, who, truth be told, were annoyed to have to be in court at the tail end of a holiday weekend.

The prosecution was there, along with Agent Owen. They had years of work yet ahead to untangle the remaining loose ends of the mess Alex had left behind. They were searching for his clients' missing money, chasing leads that as much as $6 million was tied up in a captive insurance scheme or sequestered offshore or lost in seized drug shipments or buried at Moselle. They were trying to nail down whether someone had helped Alex clean up the murder scene, moving vehicles and dismantling and disposing of guns. Investigators were still trying to prove who had killed Stephen Smith and what, if anything, the Murdaughs had to do with his death. They also were still investigating the death of Gloria Satterfield. Gloria's family had stated publicly they do not believe anyone pushed her down the steps, though they were angered by how cruelly Alex exploited her death.

At that day's hearing, Alex was pleading guilty to stealing from Gloria Satterfield's sons and Pamela Pinckney and every other financial victim the state had identified. The plea deal his lawyers had reached with the state resolved roughly a hundred charges and called for Alex to receive twenty-seven years in prison.

As they waited for the sentencing to begin, Creighton Waters and Dick Harpootlian made small talk. They had recently been dueling speakers at CrimeCon, a true crime convention in Orlando. Waters's band, Sole Purpose, had performed at the opening night concert, with Creighton slaying the solo on his guitar during "Sympathy for the Devil." Waters did not point out that the line at his meet-and-greet was three times as long as his rival's. Harpootlian had realized as soon as he set foot in the convention center that he was there to play the villain. The crowd had catcalled him during their Q&A, but Harpootlian had given as good as he got, yelling back that he had an oath to uphold.

"I suggest you read the Constitution!"

Jim Griffin had started a podcast about criminal defense law. For better or worse, his name was forever linked with his infamous client. Griffin had been chastised by the South Carolina Department of Corrections for secretly recording Alex reading aloud from a diary he was keeping behind bars. The recordings were broadcast in a Fox News documentary showcasing the Murdaugh family's side of the case. Alex's team had sought $600,000 for their participation, with half going to Buster and half to the lawyers. When state officials heard that Alex's defense team was skirting prison rules by helping him record the diary, they revoked Alex's phone privileges and sent a nasty email to Griffin, who responded with a shrug.

Now the defense team and the prosecution were back in court again. A reporter had recently asked Dick Harpootlian if the Murdaugh saga would ever end.

Harpootlian shook his head.

"The Murdaugh case is like a sexually transmitted disease. It's never gonna be over."

As part of the plea agreement for the financial crimes, Alex had waived his right to appeal. He would have to serve at least eighty-five percent of the sentence, meaning he would be at least seventy-eight years old when his sentence was up, a few years shy of the age his father had been when he died. The prosecution viewed the deal as insurance that Alex would spend the rest of his life in state prison no matter what happened with his murder convictions. Alex's team was requesting a new trial on the grounds of alleged jury tampering by Becky Hill, Colleton County's clerk of court. The defense alleged that Hill had coached jurors, many of whom she knew, to disregard Alex's testimony. The primary witness against her was the Monkey Farm lady, who claimed that Hill had engineered her last-minute removal from the jury. Hill had denied the allegations, but her credibility was in question. She was the subject of a state ethics investigation related to a memoir she'd written about the trial. Her son, the county's technology director, had been arrested two days before Thanksgiving on charges he'd tapped an administrator's phone to suss out the case against his mother.

The request for a new murder trial was expected to take months, if not years, to work its way through the system. Hill's actions had kicked up a mess of tabloid headlines, but it was not clear whether the clerk had done anything to affect the jurors' decisions enough to merit a retrial. Judges in general and South Carolina judges in particular give great deference to their peers' decisions in big cases, especially a veteran judge like Clifton Newman. After watching him preside over the Murdaugh trial, fans had made T-shirts and coffee mugs proclaiming him AMERICA'S JUDGE. Only a month from retirement, Newman had agreed to let another judge take over the Murdaugh murder appeal, which meant that this sentencing would be his swan song.

The hearing was held in the Beaufort County Courthouse, in a courtroom just off the hallway where a boyish Paul Murdaugh had stood for his mug shot nearly four years before. On the wall behind Alex was a painting of a Murdaugh protégé, the judge who'd signed off on the secret settlement in the Satterfield case.

Judge Newman called the proceedings to order.

Creighton Waters began by reminding the judge that the case against Alex Murdaugh almost hadn't happened. Waters said that when he first sought out Alex's suspected victims, many were too scared to talk. People told him over and over again nothing would ever change in Hampton County. *You don't understand how things work,* they'd told him. *You don't understand that we have to live in this place under the influence of this family.*

The victims showed true courage, Waters said. "I told them we would see this through to its conclusion."

The prosecutor invited the victims to tell the judge how Alex's actions had affected them. A dozen had driven over from Hampton County.

Ginger Hadwin, Gloria Satterfield's sister, asked the judge's permission to face her old classmate directly. She'd known Alex since they were children.

"I just don't understand," she said. "Did you not have a soul?"

When it was her turn, Pamela Pinckney reminded Alex that when they first met, she'd been in the hospital. Her body was broken in a half dozen places. Her son Hakeem was paralyzed.

"I never thought you would betray me and my family," she said. "At a vulnerable time at our life. At our lowest state."

Ronnie Richter, a lawyer for the Satterfield family and the Plyler sisters, told the judge that Alex's true nature had finally been revealed. The only question that remained was why. How had Alex become so devoid of empathy or conscience?

"It doesn't matter," Richter said. "Because the only person who can answer that question is Alex Murdaugh."

Most of the victims and their lawyers spoke in favor of the twenty-seven-year sentence. Almost to a person, they said it would spare their poor communities the pain and expense of a long trial. Almost to a person, they said they were satisfied.

The sole exception was Mark Tinsley.

Tinsley had told himself, even the night before, that he wasn't going to attend the sentencing. He knew that in a negotiated plea deal, the judge could only say yes or no, and had no ability to change the terms. But it galled him to see Alex still gaming the system. The receivers in the Beaches' civil case had just recently realized that tens of thousands of dollars' worth of Maggie's jewelry was unaccounted for, including her wedding ring. Alex could've told them where everything was, but he wouldn't.

At the lectern, Tinsley stood ten yards from his adversary. Again, he was wearing a gray suit. He told the judge he would respect his decision, but he didn't think the punishment fitted the crime.

Tinsley turned to the defendant.

"Alex, you're a broken person," he said.

All the victims in the courtroom didn't matter, Tinsley said, because the only person that mattered to Alex was Alex himself.

Tinsley turned back to Judge Newman.

"If he wants to be accountable, he wants to be contrite, he ought to tell these people where their money is," he said. "That's not going to happen. The same as he's not going to lay in bed at night and think about the wrongs and feel sorry for what he did."

Tinsley did not share all of his thoughts with the judge. Ever the hunter, he believed Alex should be put down. Tinsley would have been glad to do it himself. He'd already picked out the bullet. It was a .22, which rolls around inside the skull, inflicting maximum damage. It costs three cents, worthless just like Alex.

JIM GRIFFIN TOLD the judge Alex wanted to speak. The lawyer said he expected him to talk ten minutes at most, but even after representing Alex for nearly five years, he underestimated his client.

Alex rose at the defense table and the bailiff unfastened his handcuffs from each other so Alex could hold his reading glasses. He juggled his shoulders, then sucked in air and blew it out.

"Ooh boy."

When he spoke, it was with an exaggerated drawl. He apologized to all his victims and told them that he understood their pain and that it was important to him that they knew how bothered he was by his crimes. Then he apologized to Buster, wherever he was. In the Fox News documentary, Buster acknowledged that his father had done many bad things and had the characteristics of a psychopath, but he said he did not believe his dad had killed his mother and brother. Buster and his fiancée had just bought a house in nearby Bluffton. He was trying to put some distance between himself and his father, but it was hard with that hair and that name. On Halloween, someone had sneaked an iPhone photo of him dressed as a hunter and his fiancée dressed as a deer. She was passing out candy to trick-or-treaters and Buster was offering Jell-O shots to their parents.

Alex advised Buster to tune out the noise.

"I am so proud of you. Mom is proud of you. Pau Pau is proud of you."

On and on Alex went. He apologized to his brothers, his law partners, and Maggie's parents. He said he was sorry for humiliating them and disgracing the law firm he had loved. Then he stared at the reporters taking notes and said he was sorry his actions had made the media think it was okay to disparage his father and grandfather: "Two men who spent their life in service helping others, two men fully and wholly committed to justice, two men who were most honest and most decent and if they were here today, two men that would be devastated by what I have done."

Alex next trained his eyes on David Owen.

"I now apologize to every single person who cares about Maggie and about Paul," he said. "Because I know that things that I did, that I'm pleading guilty to here today, allowed SLED and the attorney general's office to focus on me and not to pursue the person or the people who hurt and killed Maggie and Paul."

Owen stared back, unblinking. He'd heard it all before.

After close to an hour, Alex finally stopped talking. At the end of his speech, the judge called a recess.

Joe McCulloch, the lawyer representing the Monkey Farm juror and an ally of the defense team, looked dazed.

"Narcissistic fucking sociopathy," he said.

Harpootlian and Griffin huddled in the hallway.

"I don't even know what to say," Harpootlian said.

Waters was not surprised by the arrogance of Alex's meanderings. He clearly thought he had been delivering a soliloquy plumbing the deepest corners of his soul. Instead, he had bored everyone with his epic self-absorption, revealing who he was to everyone but himself.

When the hearing resumed, the judge sentenced Alex to the twenty-seven years that had been agreed upon. Staring down at the prisoner in his shackles, Newman said he vividly remembered Alex standing poolside at the trial lawyer's convention, just after Maggie and Paul were killed, seemingly having the time of his life, a friend to all. He said he could not reconcile the man he thought he knew with the man standing before him. Alex, he said, had become a void, unknowable even to himself.

"You are empty."

THE CONVICT WAS loaded into a cage for the long drive back to McCormick Correctional Institution, the maximum security prison where he had already begun serving the two life sentences for Maggie's and Paul's murders. His exalted former self had vanished. No matter what happened, even if he was granted a new trial in the murder charges, he could never reclaim any semblance of his former standing. The spider had been removed from his web.

In Hampton County, when his name popped up in conversation, people would nervously laugh and make a cross with their fingers, as though warding off the undead.

During his first months inside McCormick, Alex sought to become the master of another small world. Even though he had been disbarred, he endeared himself to other violent criminals by helping draft appeals when the warden rescinded their privileges. He received dozens of emails from lovesick strangers, some offering to replenish his commissary account, others with breathless descriptions of what they'd like to do to him. He sweet-talked older women on the prison staff and was rewarded with small perks; it was not lost on other inmates when he was issued a brand-new tablet, not a janky used one. When his phone privileges were taken away for recording the forbidden diary entries, he cajoled another inmate into sharing his PIN and was back on the phone the next day. When that deception was discovered and he was disciplined again, Alex had another inmate, a serial pedophile, call Griffin's office to relay the message that Alex needed more money in his canteen account.

He had left behind the ruins of one empire. Now he was building another.

ACKNOWLEDGMENTS

My heart is so full of gratitude, I don't know where to start. So I'll start at the beginning.

In June of 2021, the top editor of *The Wall Street Journal* called to ask if I was following this crazy case in South Carolina. Of course I was. I love South Carolina with all my heart and the case was bananas. We talked a while and then I asked a classic question: "So, what's *The Wall Street Journal* version of this story?" And to his credit, he sighed, and said, "Damn it, sometimes a good fricking story is just a good fricking story." Thank you, Matt Murray. You were right.

That summer, I reported on the Murdaugh case in fits and starts, as I was also covering the tragic condo collapse in Surfside, Florida. By the time my story ran, it was a few weeks after Labor Day and the Murdaugh saga had reached whole other levels of crazy. It was clear there was more to say, not just about the case but the place where it happened. My dear friend Tripp Mickle introduced me to his literary agent, Daniel Greenberg. Daniel helped me shape the idea for this book and has been a steady hand and trusted partner ever since. Daniel led me to Jennifer Hershey and Mary Reynics, brilliant editors at Ballantine who saw the possibility in this project long before Alex was charged. Thank you all for believing in this story and in me. Mary, thank you for pushing me to write this book like the epic American saga it was. Your instincts have been right time and again and I have been so fortunate to work with you.

A few months after I started working on this book, I heard Hampton native Sara Holstein Graves on my friend Seton Tucker's podcast talking about the collapse of the local economy in the 1920s, a subject that I happened to be obsessed with. I reached out and asked her to help with research. Thank you, Sara, for your relentless pursuit of hard-to-find facts. I am grateful for your organizational skills, your intricate family trees, and your constant good cheer.

For the first year or so, I focused on the history, since we knew very little about what happened to Maggie and Paul. After Alex was charged, we went from an absence of knowledge to an abundance, particularly during the six-week murder trial. I drove home from Walterboro in a panic, because I knew I needed to reimagine the book. My friends Bill Adair and Stephen Buckley urged me to call their former colleague Tom French, a Pulitzer Prize–winning journalist and professor who had coached many writers on their books. I am forever grateful that Tom said yes. Tom is a narrative architect, who not only can see how stories are built but teach others how to build them. Tom is wonderfully positive and freakishly energetic. He put me on a writing schedule that seemed superhuman, until I'd open a shared document at 6 A.M. to find he'd already been working for an hour. A bonus was getting to work with Kelley Benham French, a writing and editing force, and getting to know Tom and Kelley's girls, Juniper, Brookie, and Greysi. My day was made many times by hearing a chorus of "Hi, Val!" from the carpool line. I love you guys.

At the trial, I was embedded in the courtroom with some crackerjack journalists, including John Monk, who I've known and admired for more than twenty years. Thanks to Carol Gable and Haylee Barber, my seat mates and running buddies, and Craig "Craig Cam" Melvin, a pro's pro. Thanks to Michael DeWitt Jr. and Jason Ryan, my companions on Authors' Row. Thanks to my friends in the press corps, including Will Folks, Jenn Wood, Dylan Nolan, Thad Moore, Ted Clifford, Drew

Tripp, Seton Tucker, Matt Harris, Arthur Cerf, and the one and only Kathleen Parker. A special shout-out to Avery Wilks, whose daily Twitter Megathread was a feat of reporting and analysis. Thanks to Jay Bender for your leadership in the courtroom and to Andrew Whitaker and Steven Gresham for your deft work at Moselle. Thanks to Mike Gasparro and the Cinemart team for making two great documentaries and inviting me to be part of them. Thanks to Joe McCulloch for being Joe McCulloch. And thanks to Meg Kinnard Hardee for being an inspiration and the dean of the South Carolina press corps—a worthy successor to my mentor, the late great Lee Bandy.

I'm grateful for the news judgment and smarts of my former and current *Journal* editors, including Emily Nelson, Ashby Jones, Tedra Meyer, Matthew Rose, Tamara Audi, Karen Pensiero, Kate Ortega, Christine Glancey, Josh Jamerson, Miguel Bustillo, and Bruce Orwall. Thanks to former editors I now count as close friends, especially Ken Otterbourg, Brian Tolley, John Drescher, and Rick Brooks.

Many authors offered their time and advice, especially early on, when I had no idea what I was doing. They include Tripp Mickle, Erich Schwartzel, Jennifer Berry Hawes, Amy Argetsinger, Jennifer Levitz, Laura Meckler, and Bryan Gruley. A special thanks to Cam McWhirter, who told me that writing a book is all about laying bricks, then checked on me every few days to make sure I had laid some. Thanks to Bronwen Dickey for being a badass from the word go.

I'm grateful to all the people who spoke with me for this book, too many to name and some who might prefer not to be. Many of the subjects are people I feel privileged to know and hope to continue to know for years to come. Thanks to Aubrey Dempsey, Danielle Corbin, Laurin Manning Gandy, and Susanne Andrews. Thanks to Patrick and Starr Carr, Michael Gunn, Eric Bland, and Justin Bamberg. So many South Carolinians enriched my understanding of the themes and history at play, especially Alex Sanders, Fred Carter, Jim Hodges, Henry McMaster, Bryan P. Stirling, Colden Battey, Bill Nettles, Winston Holliday, and Gregory P. Harris. A special thanks to Larry Rowland, whose curiosity about the world is as wondrous as his research.

I am very grateful for the talent and expertise of Julie Tate, who fact-checked this manuscript. You were right, Julie, about so many things. You are also tireless and kind and I am glad to know you.

I feel so fortunate for the *Devil* team at Ballantine, including Kara Welsh, Kim Hovey, Jennifer Garza, Brianna Kusilek, Quinne Rogers, Allison Schuster, and Ivanka Perez. Thanks to Scott Biel for the gorgeous cover. Thank you to the production team of Pam Alders, Ted Allen, Debbie Glasserman, Linnea Knollmueller, and Mark Maguire. Thanks to Dan Novack and Ojasvinee Singh for their careful legal review.

My friends have stuck with me in spite of years of canceled plans. Thanks to Catherine George, Mary Davila, Creecy Johnson, Meghan Stark, Lynn Castle, Megan Hughes Hemmerlein, and Jennifer Emmett. Thanks to Nell Jorgensen, my heart friend since childhood, and all the Jorgensens and Knopfs, my second family. Thanks to Jackie Gibson and Megan Courtney (from your chief). Thanks to Gareth Palmer, Jack Morton, and Katherine Bird Poole. Thanks to Michael Schoenfeld and all my friends at Duke, especially the students and faculty of the DeWitt Wallace Center for Media and Democracy. Thanks to Joyce Fitzpatrick, Liza Roberts, Wade Smith, and our many shared friends, including Francie Keenan, the rare person willing to fly to hear me talk. Thanks to the mothers and daughters of the National Charity League's Dogwood Chapter. Girls, dreams do come true. Sometimes it just takes a minute. I am forever grateful for my friends in the Certain Women Bible Study, whose fellowship and prayers have enriched my life for a decade: Linda Berry, Hayden Constance, Beth Grace, Charlotte Griffin, Lee Hayden, Amanda Martin, and Susan Rountree. Thanks to Greg Jones and the staff, vestry, and congregation at St. Michael's Episcopal, our church home, and to Church of the Servant in Wilmington, where I grew up.

My parents, Rose and John Bauerlein, gave us two lasting gifts: roots and wings. Mom and Dad, I love you both so much. You have been steadfast your entire lives in your word and example. Thank you for encouraging us to try new things, and for not rushing to fix them when we fell short. I didn't know how hard that was until I was a parent. Thanks, Mom, for the joy and kindness you bring to every conversation, which has helped me be a better listener. Thanks, Dad, for your wonderful writing, which has inspired my own. Thank you, too, for being RoRo and Papa, the lovingest grandparents imaginable. I want to thank my sisters, Lisa Bauerlein and Jessica Bauerlein Widener, who have been obsessed with this story from the beginning. At first Lisa, Jess, and our bonus sister, Carolyn Ponte, were mostly glad that I finally made it on *Dateline*! But they showed their support constantly by checking on me, loaning me clothes so I wouldn't repeat outfits on Court TV, and passing around tattered printouts of early versions of the book. It is a gift to count your sisters as your best friends. Thanks, too, to Jessica's husband, Warren, and their boys, Gus and George, my angels. I love you like my own. Thanks to Barbara "BB" Widener and our sweet Pop. Thanks to our cousins and extended family. I am grateful, too, to my late grandparents, who each, in their own way, encouraged me to be a writer: Pearl and George Bauerlein and Louise and Walter Raleigh Hunnicutt Jr.

I am thankful to have been a Jackson for almost twenty years. Thanks to Betty Jackson, my mother-in-law, and Cliff, my late father-in-law, for their abundant love and for raising such fine sons. Thanks to my brother-in-law Allen and his wife, Felicia. I love being the favorite (only) aunt to their four girls, who I've watched grow up and start families of their own. Thanks to Allison, Josh, and Maddie Kaufman; Emily and Jacob Bassil; Molly and Daniel Miramontes; and Baily, Harrison, and Samuel Kossover.

I am as unsure how to end these acknowledgments as I was how to start them. It means putting into words my love and gratitude for my husband, Scott, and our children, Amelia and Luke. Scott, thank you for having faith in me even when I was sure I would never finish one chapter, much less a whole book. You took on so much of the life of the family, particularly while I was on the road. You made us laugh every day. You made sure we had food, went outside, and learned to drive(!), all while managing your own career. The day I met you was the luckiest of my life. Yes, we can finally get a second dog!

Amelia, I dreamed of being a mom since I was a little girl, but I never could have imagined how strong, talented, and generous in spirit my daughter would grow up to be. Thank you for the Jar O' Love, and for always keeping it filled. Luke, you make me feel like I can do anything. You have that effect on people, with your kind heart and keen intelligence. Thanks for always walking on the beach with me and continuing to pretend that I'm good at hoops.

I love all three of you fiercely. This book is for you. It feels like we did it together.

—Valerie Bauerlein Jackson

A NOTE ON SOURCES

This book is based on hundreds of hours of interviews and includes scenes witnessed over four months of reporting on the ground in South Carolina. I was in the courtroom for every major moment in Alex's legal saga, from his initial bond hearing in October 2021 to his sentencing on federal fraud charges in April 2024. I visited all the sites described in the book, including the train crossing where Randolph Sr. was killed, the rural road where the body of Stephen Smith was found, and the roadside where Alex tried to fake his own murder. I also traveled by boat to re-create the route taken the night Mallory Beach was killed. The reader may infer that scenes and descriptions are based on interviews with the main players and my own observations.

The reader may also infer that sensitive quotes or details not ascribed to a specific person or cited in the endnotes were provided on a background basis. An independent fact-checker vetted this book and is aware of the identity of each source. She checked my representation of all sources' accounts against my notes.

The chapters on the history of the Murdaugh family relied on property records and century-old legal filings at the Hampton County courthouse; genealogical records, including Reconstruction-era slave registries, military service records, and birth and death certificates; 900

pages of federal court filings and transcripts maintained at the National Archives in Atlanta; and back issues of *The Hampton County Guardian,* which are available on microfilm at the Hampton County library and the South Caroliniana Library at USC. I also relied on several indispensable histories of the region: *Railroads and Sawmills* by Rose-Marie Eltzroth Williams; *Both Sides of the Swamp* by the Hampton County Tricentennial Commission; and *The History of Beaufort County,* a three-volume set co-authored by Larry Rowland, whose scholarship on the Lowcountry is unmatched. I will cite these and other helpful books in the bibliography.

Additional material about the modern-day Murdaugh family came from family members' posts on social media, real estate listings, and multiple volumes of *The Rebel,* the Wade Hampton High School yearbook. The details of Alex and Maggie's spending, including ten years of transactions from their main checking account, came from exhibits filed in *U.S. v. Laffitte,* the federal fraud case against Russell Laffitte. I will provide supplemental sources for each chapter in the endnotes, particularly the many podcast episodes, YouTube streams, documentaries, and news magazine stories devoted to this incredible tale.

BIBLIOGRAPHY

Bass, Jack, and W. S. Poole. 2009. *The Palmetto State: The Making of Modern South Carolina*. Columbia: University of South Carolina Press.

Berendt, John. 1994. *Midnight in the Garden of Good and Evil*. New York: Vintage Books Edition.

Boling, Katherine. 1972. *A Piece of the Fox's Hide*. Orangeburg, S.C.: Sandlapper Publishing.

Carter, Luther F., and David S. Mann. 1992. *Government in the Palmetto State: Toward the 21st Century*. Columbia: University of South Carolina Press.

Cerf, Arthur. 2023. *Les Meurtres du Low-Country*. Paris: Editions 10/18.

Conroy, Pat. 2010. *The Death of Santini: The Story of a Father and His Son*. New York: Nan A. Talese / Doubleday.

———. 1986. *The Prince of Tides*. Boston: Houghton Mifflin.

Danielson, Michael N. 1995. *Profits and Politics in Paradise: The Development of Hilton Head*. Columbia: University of South Carolina Press.

DeWitt, Michael M., Jr. 2024. *The Fall of the House of Murdaugh: Moonshine, Manipulation and Murder in South Carolina*. Charleston, S.C.: Evening Post Books.

———. 2015. *Images of America: Hampton County*. Charleston, S.C.: Arcadia Publishing.

———. 2023. *Wicked Hampton County*. Charleston, S.C.: History Press.

Ethridge, Mark. 2006. *Grievances: A Novel*. Montgomery, Ala.: New South Books.

Foote, Shelby. 1958–1974. *The Civil War: A Narrative*. New York: First Vintage Books Edition.

Gergel, Richard. 2019. *Unexampled Courage: The Blinding of Sgt. Isaac Woodard and the Awakening of President Harry S. Truman and Judge J. Waties Waring*. New York: Sarah Crichton Books.

Glatt, John. 2023. *Tangled Vines: Power, Privilege, and the Murdaugh Family Murders.* New York: St. Martin's Press.

Graham, Cole Blease, Jr., and William V. Moore. 1994. *South Carolina Politics and Government.* Lincoln: University of Nebraska Press.

Greene, Melissa F. 1991. *Praying for Sheetrock.* Cambridge, Mass.: Da Capo Press.

Hampton County Tricentennial Commission. 1970. *Both Sides of the Swamp.* Columbia, S.C.: R. L. Bryan Company.

Harr, Jonathan. 1995. *A Civil Action.* New York: Vintage Books.

Harriott, Michael. 2023. *Black AF History: The Un-Whitewashed History of America.* New York: Deyst.

Harvey, W. Brantley, Jr. 2015. *Palmetto Patriot: W. Brantley Harvey, Jr., A Memoir.* Beaufort: Murr Manufacturing and Printing.

Hawes, Jennifer B. 2019. *Grace Will Lead Us Home: The Charleston Church Tragedy and the Hard, Inspiring Journey to Forgiveness.* New York: St. Martin's Griffin.

Helsey, Alexia J. 2005. *Beaufort: A History.* Charleston, S.C.: History Press.

Hewtson, Kathleen M. 2022–2023. *Murdaugh, She Wrote.* Kathleen M. Hewtson.

Horwitz, Tony. 1998. *Confederates in the Attic: Dispatches from the Unfinished Civil War.* New York: Vintage Departures.

Keyserling, Harriet. 1998. *Against the Tide: One Woman's Political Struggle.* Columbia: University of South Carolina Press.

Kilgo, James. 1998. *Daughter of My People.* Athens: University of Georgia Press.

Marrs, Aaron W. 2009. *Railroads in the Old South: Pursuing Progress in a Slave Society.* Baltimore: Johns Hopkins University Press.

Marscher, Fran. 2007. *Remembering the Way It Was,* vol. 2, *More Stories from Hilton Head, Bluffton and Daufuskie.* Charleston, S.C.: History Press.

McCurry, Stephanie. 1995. *Masters of Small Worlds: Yeoman Households, Gender Relations & the Political Culture of the Antebellum South Carolina Low Country.* Oxford: Oxford University Press.

McKinley, Shepherd W. 1998. *Stinking Stones and Rocks of Gold: Phosphate, Fertilizer, and Industrialization in Postbellum South Carolina.* Gainesville: University Press of Florida.

McTeer, J. E. 1976. *Fifty Years As A Low Country Witch Doctor.* New York: Beaufort Book Co.

———. 1970. *High Sheriff of the Low Country.* Bloomington, Ind.: IUniverse.

Pittman, Rebecca F. 2023. *Countdown to Murder: Alex Murdaugh: Money, Murder and Deception in South Carolina.* Wonderland Productions LLC.

Rivers, Mildred B. 1983. *Prison War Camp World War II, Hampton S.C.* Bluffton, S.C.: Accurate Lithograph Printing Company.

Rogers, George P. 1992. *Generations of Lawyers: A History of the South Carolina Bar.* Columbia, S.C.: South Carolina Bar Foundation.

Rossignol, Rosalyn. 2018. *My Ghost Has a Name: Memoir of a Murder*. Columbia: University of South Carolina Press.

Rowland, Lawrence S., Alexander Moore, and George C. Rogers Jr. 1996. *The History of Beaufort County, South Carolina*, vol. 1, *1514–1861*. Columbia: University of South Carolina Press.

Rowland, Lawrence S., and Stephen R. Wise. 2015. *The History of Beaufort County, South Carolina*, vol. 3, *Bridging the Sea Islands' Past and Present, 1893–2006*. Charleston, S.C.: University of South Carolina Press.

Ryan, Jason. 2011. *Jackpot: High Times, High Seas and the Sting that Launched the War on Drugs*. Guilford, Conn.: Lyons Press.

———. 2024. *Swamp Kings: The Story of the Murdaugh Family of South Carolina & a Century of Backwoods Power*. New York: Pegasus Crime.

Stone, H. David, Jr. 2008. *Vital Rails: The Charleston & Savannah Railroad and the Civil War in Coastal South Carolina*. Columbia: University of South Carolina Press.

Theroux, Paul. 2015. *Deep South*. Boston: Houghton Mifflin Harcourt.

Tyson, Timothy B. 2004. *Blood Done Sign My Name*. New York: Three Rivers Press.

Warren, Robert Penn. 1996. *All the King's Men*. San Diego: Harcourt Brace.

Williams, Rose-Marie E. 1998. *Railroads and Sawmills: Varnville, S.C., 1872–1997*. Columbia, S.C.: R. L. Bryan Company.

Wise, Stephen R., and Lawrence S. Rowland. 2015. *The History of Beaufort County, South Carolina*, vol. 2, *Rebellion, Reconstruction, and Redemption, 1861–1893*. Columbia: University of South Carolina Press.

Zucchino, David. 2020. *Wilmington's Lie: The Murderous Coup of 1898 and the Rise of White Supremacy*. New York: Grove.

NOTES

EPIGRAPH

vii. Cormac McCarthy, *Blood Meridian* (New York: Vintage Books, 1985). p. 20.

PART ONE: THE PRINCE OF HAMPTON COUNTY

CHAPTER ONE

3. **It had been designed** Native Charlestonian Robert Mills designed sixteen courthouses in the state, according to *The South Carolina Encyclopedia*, edited by Walter Edgar.

CHAPTER TWO

10. **Hampton County** My account of Hampton County history draws on interviews with Larry Rowland and his and his co-authors' three-volume *History of Beaufort County*, which spans 1514–2006.

10. **Hampton had been founded** Rowland has a "The Secession of Hampton County" section in volume 2 of *The History of Beaufort County*. Local author Michael DeWitt also describes the explicit intent to form a white county in his book *The Fall of the House of Murdaugh*.

11. **In those 3,300 square miles** The Fourteenth Judicial Circuit is composed of five counties, whose boundaries have remained fairly consistent for more than a hundred years. They are Allendale (408 square miles), Beaufort (576), Colleton (1,056), Hampton (560), and Jasper (655). Square mileage is taken from the federal census.

CHAPTER THREE

12. **When she left the hospital** Alania Plyler Spohn's story is based on her testimony in Laffitte's trial on Nov. 14, 2022, and the amended complaint against Laffitte and the bank filed Sept. 8, 2022, *Hannah Plyler and Alania (Plyler) Spohn v. Russell Lucius Laffitte and Palmetto State Bank*. Alania declined interview requests. She discussed her case previously in "'I Trusted Him': Alex Murdaugh's $1M Theft Victim Speaks Out Against Disgraced Lawyer, Banker," *Law & Crime Sidebar* podcast, March 15, 2023, and "The Magic Men," *The Murdaugh Murders Podcast*, season 1, episode 56, Nov. 11, 2022.

16. **They were wed** The description of Alex and Maggie's relationship is based on interviews, a eulogy delivered by Maggie's sister-in-law Liz Murdaugh, and the couple's wedding announcements published Aug. 15, 1993, in *The State* and *The* (Charleston) *Post and Courier*.

17. **The one state trooper** Woody Gooding represented Alex on the open container charge and recounted the story to me.

18. **Every summer** I attended the Watermelon Festival in 2022 and talked with locals about prior years.

19. **Alex was one of the biggest individual donors** Kacen Bayless of the *The Island Packet* analyzed Alex's political spending in "Murdaugh Family Donated This Money," July 2, 2021.

19. *The Hampton County Guardian* Alex's stint as a jury boy was featured on Oct. 10, 1973.

20. **"That's my daddy,"** he'd say Alex's habit of pointing out his family's portraits was described to me by several lawyers, including Mark Tinsley. It was also mentioned by an unnamed source in the HBO Max documentary *Low Country: The Murdaugh Dynasty*, episode 1, "Kings of the Low Country," Nov. 3, 2022.

20. **In the words of another South Carolina lawyer** Jay Bender, who practiced statewide for more than forty years.

CHAPTER FOUR

22. **Pamela Pinckney woke up** The account of the Pinckneys' lives before, during, and after the wreck was based on lengthy interviews with Pamela Pinckney. Financial details came from interviews with Justin Bamberg, the family's lawyer, and exhibits in *U.S. v. Laffitte*. Pamela and Justin gave other helpful interviews to *Dateline NBC*'s "Alex Murdaugh Vowed to Help Her," Nov. 4, 2022, and to *The Murdaugh Murders Podcast*'s episode 28, "What Happened to Hakeem Pinckney? Part One," Jan. 19, 2022, and episode 55, "What Happened . . . Part Two," Aug. 3, 2022.

23. **The wreck shut down the interstate** The wreck was described in "4 Injured in I-95 Accident," *Bluffton Today*, Aug. 25, 2009.

25. **The big oak** *The* (Sumter) *Watchman and Southron* reported on Dec. 19, 1914, that the inquest after one lynching was conducted by local doctor J. B. Harvey and "acting coroner Murdaugh." The acting coroner was almost certainly Randolph Sr., given his prominence in the community and ties to Dr. Harvey, his father-in-law.

25. **The office on Mulberry Street** Legendary reporter John Monk was among the first to use the moniker "the house that CSX built" in print in his prescient feature "Powerful SC Family Faces Scrutiny . . . ," *The State,* April 5, 2019.

26. **The Murdaughs almost always won** Hampton County's reputation for generous verdicts was memorialized in "Judicial Hellholes 2004," a publication of the American Tort Reform Foundation, and "Home Court Advantage," *Forbes,* June 10, 2002.

26. **His standard fee** Law firm administrator Jeanne Seckinger testified that Alex's standard fee was 35 percent, though it would rise to 40 percent in complicated cases.

27. **For years he had been hiding pills** Law firm treasurer Mark Ball testified that Alex had misused his company credit card "since the beginning." Alex joined the firm in 1998.

29. **He'd been prescribed hydrocodone** Alex described his drug use on the witness stand and in his fourth recorded interview with SLED on Sept. 13, 2021.

30. **Paul kept crashing his F-150** Several wrecks are documented in an affidavit submitted May 4, 2022, by Morgan Doughty in the Beach lawsuit. Beverly Cook told me about an additional wreck involving her son Anthony.

31. **When Maggie found out** Marian Proctor testified about her sister's worries about infidelity, saying Maggie made Alex move out over messages with a woman he knew in college. "It was an affair that happened, or Maggie thought it was an affair that happened, many years ago. They were able to resolve the issues but Maggie still brought it up," she said.

31. **One summer morning in 2009** The arson was described in *Bluffton Today,* including in articles headlined "Local Attorney Victim of Attempted Arson," July 9, 2009, and "Arrests Made in Arson . . . ," July 16, 2009. The description of the charges was based on public filings and the recollection of Blanca Simpson, who helped Maggie tally the damage.

32. **The disconnect between appearance and reality** The description of the interior of Holly Street was based on Maggie's Facebook photos, the recollection of friends, and the inventory at the auction of the Murdaughs' household items on March 23, 2023, at Liberty Auctions in Pembroke, Georgia. The framed poem was an edited version of *The Man in the Glass,* published in 1934 by Peter Dale Wimbrow Sr. It sold for $650.

PART TWO: MURDAUGH ISLAND
CHAPTER FIVE: RANDOLPH MURDAUGH SR. (1887–1940)

35. **Past midnight, at a crossing** The account of the crash relied heavily on "Randolph Murdaugh Sr Killed by Train" in *The Hampton County Guardian* on July 24, 1940, and "Our Solicitor Dies in Wreck" in *The* (Walterboro) *Press and Standard* on July 25, 1940. *The Press and Standard* was a key historical source, as it closely tracked the Murdaughs' comings and goings.

35. **At age fifty-three, he'd been sick for years** Randolph Sr.'s decline was chronicled in *The Hampton County Guardian,* including in "Solicitor Stricken as Court Opens" on Feb. 22, 1949, and "Two Announce for Solicitor" on July 24, 1940. In his run for solicitor after his father's death, Buster Murdaugh boasted that he had already been doing the job for two years because of his father's illness, according to *The Press and Standard* on Aug. 15, 1940. Randolph Sr.'s lengthy illness was also disclosed in an announcement of the court term in Allendale in *The State* on April 3, 1940.

35. **Earlier in the day, the temperature had climbed** Randolph died during the hottest stretch of summer, according to historic data from the National Weather Service. The temperature was in the nineties and a few days later hit that summer's high of 101 degrees, according to *The Press and Standard*'s year-end review on Jan. 9, 1941.

36. **There is no dark like a country backroad** Kenny Kinsey, the state's forensic expert, said nighttime in rural Hampton County is "a new definition of dark," in Netflix's *Murdaugh Murders: A Southern Scandal,* season 2, episode 2.

37. **Randolph's body was found beside the tracks** His death certificate lists cause of death as "crushed skull" and "macerated brain."

37. **At the inquest, the engineer** In his book *Swamp Kings,* author Jason Ryan cites testimony from the inquest, with the train engineer saying, "The right of way was perfectly clear and he could have seen the train." The engineer also testified that the car surged onto the track at the last minute, noting, "I had no idea they were going to drive up on the track." The fireman testified that "if [Randolph Sr.] had any intent on getting out of the car, he could have done it."

37. **The Charleston & Western Carolina Railway** The significance of the railroad to the development of the backcountry is described in multiple books, including H. David Stone Jr.'s *Vital Rails.* In an interview, Larry Rowland said, "Without the railroad, there wouldn't be a Hampton County."

38. **The founding families intermarried** It was Walter Edgar who described South Carolina's white elite as "a vast cousinage" in his definitive *South Carolina: A History.* Rowland, whose family is from Hampton County, said, "Hampton County is more of a tribe than a community."

38. **Some plantations thrived** There were 25 slave-owning planters in 1860 in

the parish that would eventually form much of Hampton County, according to *Both Sides*.

38. **Randolph Sr.'s grandfather** Josiah Murdaugh owned 23 slaves in 1850 in the U.S. Federal Census Slave Schedules. Twelve of them were under age 18.

38. **Randolph's father, Josiah, was a Confederate veteran** The obituary ran in *The State* on Oct. 6, 1912.

38. **Hampton County was an inland frontier** Rowland writes about the fence around Hampton in *The History of Beaufort County*, volume 2.

39. **Randolph was the only student in his class from Hampton** USC has digitized back issues of the *Garnet & Black* yearbook, which lists the hometowns of the roughly 30 members of his class. Other details of Randolph Sr.'s college days come from *The Gamecock* student newspaper.

39. **The university was all white** USC admitted Black students for a brief period after the Civil War, but that ended with the collapse of Reconstruction, according to a history of the university on its official website.

40. **Randolph had started his practice at a fortuitous moment** The changes in railroad law were laid out in "The Federal Railroad Safety Program: 100 Years of Safer Railroads," published in August 1993 by the U.S. Department of Transportation, and "A Brief History of Workers' Compensation," an academic study by Gregory P. Guyton in 1999.

43. **A rumor persists** The lore about the prisoner's drowning was shared by Sam Crews III, whose mother, Betty Ruth Crews, was the unofficial town historian, and whose great-grandfather was the longtime undertaker and a contemporary of Randolph Sr.

43. **At trial, the man was acquitted** Coverage was breathless and voluminous, including "Marshall Trial Near Jury Stage," in *The* (Charleston) *News and Courier*, Feb. 8, 1933.

44. **He took two cases against the railroad** The case of the demoted foreman was *Youmans v. Charleston W.C. Railway Co.* The case involving the porter was *Marshall v. Charleston & Western Carolina*.

46. **The family sued the railroad** The lawsuit was *Randolph Murdaugh Jr. v. Charleston & Western Carolina Railway Co.*, on file with the Hampton County Clerk of Court.

CHAPTER SIX

50. **Arthur Badger Jr. was a widower** The narrative of Arthur Badger's case was built on his testimony in Laffitte's federal trial, interviews with Badger family lawyer Mark Tinsley, and filings in *Arthur Badger v. Russell Laffitte et al.* The description of Arthur's financial straits also relied on reporter David Weissman's excellent exposé "Murdaugh Stole His Money . . . ," *The* (Myrtle Beach) *Sun News*, Sept. 9, 2022.

55. **At 1,700 acres** The attributes of the Moselle property are laid out in a six-page sales pamphlet published in 2022 by Crosby Land Company of Walterboro. The property was sold under the new name Cross Swamp Farm.

56. **It was not uncommon for shrimpers to be middlemen** Author Jason Ryan detailed the mechanics of Lowcountry shrimp boat smuggling in *Jackpot: High Times, High Seas and the Sting that Launched the War on Drugs*.

CHAPTER SEVEN

59. **Deep into a summer night** The accounts of Stephen Smith's death and subsequent investigation are built on a 110-page report by the S.C. Highway Patrol's Multi-Disciplinary Active Investigation Team. The report includes troopers' notes, photos, maps, 911 records, and other documents. Other details come from Sandy Smith's letter to the FBI on Sept. 28, 2016. Sandy spent years championing her son's case and has told her story dozens of times, including on Netflix's *Murdaugh Murders,* season 1, episode 3, "No Secrets Are Safe," and HBO Max's *Low Country,* season 1, episode 2, "Something in the Road." The details vary slightly in some accounts, so when there were discrepancies, I relied on the FBI letter. Randy Murdaugh disputes some aspects of her accounts, telling HBO that he only heard that Stephen died after the funeral. Also helpful was "Who Killed Stephen Smith?" a six-episode arc on Mandy Matney's *The Murdaugh Murders Podcast,* with the first episode streaming June 30, 2021. Sandy spoke with Mandy multiple times and credits her for drawing attention to Stephen's case, which was cold for years.

61. **A few minutes later** Randy Murdaugh issued a statement to CBS's *48 Hours* that he learned of Stephen's death from Joel, who asked him to get involved. He said he met with Joel, then went to the scene with a private investigator. The episode, "Stephen Smith: A Death in Murdaugh Country," ran Nov. 25, 2023.

61. **Stephanie could not stop thinking** The descriptions of Stephen's childhood and teen years are based on interviews with Sandy and Stephanie Smith in HBO Max's *Low Country* as well as a Q&A with Sandy in Rebecca Pittman's book *Countdown to Murder: Alex Murdaugh: Money, Murder and Deception*.

65. **Dozens of leads pointed to the Murdaugh family** The description of the fits and starts in the investigation and the cloudiness of Randy Murdaugh's involvement are also based on documentary and news magazine episodes devoted almost entirely to Stephen Smith's case: HBO Max's *Low Country,* "Something in the Road," and Netflix's *Murdaugh Murders,* "No Secrets Are Safe."

66. **A lieutenant even went** Lt. Tommy Moore said he took the file to the sheriff's office but was turned away, in "Stephen Smith: State Trooper Who . . . ," on Savannah station WJCL, March 22, 2023.

CHAPTER EIGHT: RANDOLPH "BUSTER" MURDAUGH JR. (1915–1998)

67. **The bootlegger's wife** The accounts of the bootleg conspiracy and trial are based on more than 900 pages of the *United States v. Haskell Thompson* file at the National Archives in Atlanta. The file includes transcripts of the testimony of key witnesses, including Edith Freeman, as well as the indictment of Buster and other conspirators. The case also relies on news articles, particularly news of busts and arrests in *The* (Walterboro) *Press and Standard* and the daily trial coverage by legendary reporter Jack Leland of *The* (Charleston) *News and Courier.*

69. **In opening arguments, the U.S. attorney** Longtime journalist David Lauderdale quoted the prosecutor in "Decades Ago, a Murdaugh Patriarch Was the 'Brains' Behind a Lowcountry Criminal Enterprise," *The Island Packet,* May 18, 2022.

69. **Like a preacher's kid** Buster's exploits were told frequently in news stories, particularly at milestone moments. Particularly helpful were "A Heritage in the Law: Randolph Murdaugh '38," *Carolina Lawyer,* vol. IX, 1989; "Career of Prosecutor Spans Four Decades," *The Island Packet,* Jan. 14, 1982; "Legendary Murdaugh to Retire," *The Beaufort Gazette,* Oct. 31, 1986; and "Longtime Lowcountry Solicitor 'Buster' Murdaugh Dies at 84," *The Beaufort Gazette,* Feb. 6, 1998.

70. **"It was the only time"** Several lawyers told me the story of the garden hose during the 1979 murder trial of John Plath and John Arnold, though none more colorfully than Beaufort defense lawyer Colden Battey.

70. **In one high-profile murder case** Michael Linder was convicted in the 1979 fatal shooting of a highway patrolman and acquitted in a 1981 retrial, where he was represented by David Bruck, a South Carolina native and leading death penalty lawyer. There is a primer on the case at *The National Registry of Exonerations.*

71. **She and Buster were married** They married at Mackay Point Plantation, where her father held the prestigious job of year-round caretaker for the owner, George Widener Jr., famous for his dedication to thoroughbred racing. In "Mr. Widener's Quail," an Oct. 6, 1958, feature for *Sports Illustrated,* Widener demonstrated his technique for roasting the fowl he harvested at Mackay Point.

72. **Ruthven Vaux came from one of the nation's first families** Several friends and associates of the Murdaughs were featured in John Berendt's *Midnight*

in the Garden of Good and Evil, the true-crime classic set just over the state line in Savannah, Georgia. They include Ruth's ex-husband, Harry Cram, who attended one of Jim Williams's black-tie Christmas parties just before Williams's murder trial. "His family sends him monthly checks from Philadelphia with the understanding he'll never go back there," Williams said to Berendt. "He leads a life of high style—traveling around the world, hunting, drinking, and playing polo. He's a wild man, completely charming."

72. **One day, when Buster was not home** Jason Ryan reports in *Swamp Kings* that Buster skipped town with a handle of liquor when he heard that Ruth was coming to confront Gladys. He drank as he drove south to the state line, which was the Savannah River, and stared out at the water, contemplating the ruin the revelation could make of his life. Ryan interviewed a friend of Buster's, who said Buster eventually decided to go back and deal with the fallout. "The drunker I got, the braver I got," Buster said, according to this friend.

72. **That professional relationship blew up** The dispute was covered extensively, including in "Hot Words Are Exchanged . . ." in *The* (Charleston) *News and Courier,* Feb. 8, 1949.

73. **Once, when a lawyer in Columbia** Joe McCulloch has recounted the "if you ever need anybody killed" anecdote to me and others, including the makers of the HBO Max documentary *Low Country.*

74. **The judge determined that Buster had been "grossly negligent"** The case of *Murdaugh v. Commissioner,* filed Aug. 31, 1955, said Buster's civil practice was "of a general nature and includes the preparation of Federal income tax returns. He handled many injury and workmen's compensation cases on a contingent fee basis which was usually 50 per cent of the settlement."

CHAPTER NINE

82. **He took Maggie on a private plane** Alex and Maggie flew with friends to the wedding of Michael Gunn, a principal of Forge Consulting. The wedding was featured in a front-page story in *The New York Times,* Jan. 25, 2016, "New York Weddings Blanketed in White."

82. **His closest friends knew he'd had sex** Former sex worker Lindsey Edwards described four violent encounters with Alex in an hour-long video interview with Will Folks of FITSNews.com, Aug. 2, 2022.

83. **Michael DeWitt, the editor** DeWitt published a plea to the community for information about Stephen's death in "Mother of Slain H.C. Teen . . . ," *The Hampton County Guardian,* Nov. 24, 2015. DeWitt writes about the decision to publish the Thanksgiving article in his book *The Fall of the House of Murdaugh.*

CHAPTER TEN

85. **One winter morning** The account of Gloria's demise relies on the 911 recording; exhibits in *Nautilus v. Murdaugh,* a federal lawsuit by the carrier of Alex's umbrella policy, including a recorded interview with Alex by independent investigator Bryant McGowan; a civil lawsuit filed by Gloria's sons, *Estate of Satterfield v. Alexander Murdaugh,* including the 12-page second comprehensive report by insurance investigator R. Scott Wallinger; Tony Satterfield's testimony in Alex's murder trial; Tony's Facebook posts; and interviews with Tony, Blanca Simpson, and Eric Bland.

87. **Once, when Paul was little** Several people close to Gloria have shared stories of Paul's violent childish antics with the media, including Linda Hiers, who grew up with Gloria, and Kim Brant, who told the story about Paul wielding the knife in the documentary *Murdaugh Murders: Deadly Dynasty,* episode 2, "Something Wicked . . . ," which began streaming June 19, 2022.

91. **It was a big Christmas** The description of the Murdaughs' activities over the 2018 holidays is based on interviews with people close to the family, social media posts, and filings in the Beach case, including depositions, affidavits, and Morgan Doughty's photos and videos of Paul's drinking.

91. **In a matter of weeks, Alex had burned through** Alex's frenetic spending and correspondence around the time of the first Satterfield payments is outlined in exhibits in the double murder trial and the Laffitte federal trial.

CHAPTER ELEVEN: RANDOLPH MURDAUGH III, (1939–2021)

93. **The boy did as he was told** The account of the "Pig Pen Slaying" and jailhouse confession is based on articles and photos in *The* (Walterboro) *Press and Standard,* particularly "Woman Found Buried in Hog Pen . . . ," April 14, 1949, and "Jury Convicts Wyman Hiott in Pig Pen Slaying," Sept. 21, 1949. Buster and Randolph III discuss their memories of the case in the aforementioned *Carolina Lawyer* feature "A Heritage in the Law."

96. **A judge who'd watched him in court** Retired Fourteenth Circuit Court judge Perry Buckner eulogized Randolph III and was quoted in *The Island Packet's* "Joyful Celebration Commemorates Life" on June 13, 2021. Buckner was close to the Murdaughs and hired Becky Hill as his court reporter, bringing her into the Murdaughs' orbit.

96. **He was a Murdaugh, after all** Nancy Head Thode recounts the story of Randolph III's hit-and-run in a forthcoming memoir about her mother, Ann Christensen Head. Nancy Head was there when Randolph III and Buster came to visit her mother and has a draft of the civil lawsuit against the Murdaughs. Ann Head published four novels and was a mentor to many Lowcountry writers, including Pat Conroy. In an interview, Nancy

said her mother believed in giving second chances, especially to young people.

97. **To borrow a term** The historian is Stephanie McCurry, who wrote *Masters of Small Worlds: Yeoman Households, Gender Relations & the Political Culture of the Antebellum South Carolina Low Country.*

99. **At the family's homestead** Several high school friends of Alex's described the raucous parties at Almeda. Michael DeWitt, a contemporary of the Murdaugh sons, also described them in *The Fall of the House of Murdaugh.*

99. **His circuit consistently had one of the lowest** According to *The Beaufort Gazette*'s "Area's DUI Conviction Rate Among Lowest," on July 29, 1994, the Fourteenth Circuit had a 55 percent conviction rate on DUI charges, compared to an average of 69 percent statewide.

99. **When the first strip club** Randolph III relished his rakish image, saying, "I promise you, I'll keep a close eye on their activities," at the Gold Club, according to *The Wicked South* podcast, episode 1, "The History of the Murdaugh Family," June 29, 2023.

100. **A week or so later** Libby Murdaugh's fake obituary was widely covered, including on the front page of *The Beaufort Gazette* in "Murdaugh Obit a Cruel Hoax," Nov. 18, 1976.

101. **In 1998, John Marvin** The description of the 1998 boat wreck is based on hundreds of pages of records from the Department of Natural Resources, including the title history of the boat showing that it belonged to the solicitor's office; interview transcripts with the driver and passengers, many of which were corrected over time as they changed their stories; and a 16-page summary by the sergeant brought in to oversee the investigation.

103. **He had survived one heart attack** Heart problems bedevil the Murdaugh men. Randolph III had a heart attack while visiting his mother, Gladys, in the hospital on the day she died, June 10, 1997. He was fifty-seven years old, a few months younger than his father, Buster, had been when he had a serious heart attack.

103. **His doctor caught him one day** Dr. Glenn Welcker of Hampton recounted the story to Becky Hill for her memoir, *Behind the Doors of Justice: The Murdaugh Murders,* self-published in August 2023 by Wind River Media LLC. She and her co-author, Neil R. Gordon, halted sales of the book in December 2023 after Hill admitted plagiarizing passages of the preface from a newspaper article.

PART THREE: THE WILDERNESS

CHAPTER TWELVE

107. **That Saturday evening** The crash re-creation is based on the DNR investigative file released after Paul's death, including hundreds of pages of law

enforcement reports, affidavits, timelines, atmospheric data, maps, body and dashcam videos, and other information. It is also based on filings and exhibits in the wrongful death lawsuit *Renee S. Beach v. Gregory Parker et al.* The description is also based on my interviews with the players as well as interviews in other media, especially Netflix's *Murdaugh Murders,* season 1, episode 1, "Where Is Mallory?"

109. **Earlier in the evening** The Beach family and the other boat passengers reached an $18.5 million settlement in July 2023 with Greg Parker, owner of the Parker's Kitchen store where Paul bought alcohol. The Beaches have filed a separate lawsuit against Parker, alleging that he inflicted intentional emotional distress with an overly aggressive defense in the wrongful death case. I wrote about that lawsuit for *The Wall Street Journal,* "A Convenience-Store Magnate, Teen Drinking and a Fatal Boat Crash," Aug. 13, 2022.

CHAPTER THIRTEEN

116. **Alex Murdaugh got the call** The emergency-room scene is based on interviews, non-public cellphone and medical records, hospital surveillance video, DNR investigative filings including interview notes and affidavits from hospital staff, filings in the Beach civil suit, exhibits in the double murder trial, and Alex's testimony on cross-examination. It also draws from other published accounts, including HBO Max's *Low Country,* episode 1, "Kings of the Low Country."

118. **The boy had never been able to sit still** Alex testified that Paul had been diagnosed with ADHD and would "jump around from thing to thing."

CHAPTER FOURTEEN

129. **The road passed the ruins** Legend held for more than a century that Old Sheldon Church was burned by troops under the command of General Sherman. More recent scholarship, including in Rowland's *History of Beaufort County,* volume 2, posits that the church was somewhat damaged after the war but left in ruins by later cannibalization for building material.

CHAPTER FIFTEEN

136. **Even though he and Alex had drifted apart** The account of Marty Cook's charges is based on interviews and public records. Marty has talked frequently about how Alex used their shared past to intimidate him, including in an interview for *Dateline NBC*'s "Dark Waters," which aired Nov. 4, 2022.

138. **Hours after the crash, they'd insisted** The disappearance of evidence in the boat wreck is documented in numerous court filings, including a request by Connor Cook's lawyer Joe McCulloch filed July 7, 2021, to take

additional depositions in the Beach wrongful death suit. The filing, called a Rule 24 petition, alleges a possible civil conspiracy to cover up the wreck.

CHAPTER SIXTEEN

146. **The following Sunday, one week after the crash** Keith and Kenny Campbell's discovery of Mallory's body was described in their 911 call, written statements to law enforcement, and Kenny Campbell's interview for Oxygen's *Alex Murdaugh: Death. Deception. Power,* one of the earliest documentaries to air about the saga in late 2021.

PART FOUR: SEVEN SHOTS IN THE DARK

CHAPTER SEVENTEEN

153. **The hunter pursued his prey** Tinsley described his hunting adventures, and their relation to his day job, in interviews, and shared videos and photos of his experiences in the wild.

159. **Paul was flanked** John Heilemann and Mark Halperin describe Harpootlian as "a human IED" in *Game Change: Obama and the Clintons, McCain and Palin, and the Race of a Lifetime.* In South Carolina's 2008 Democratic primary, Harpootlian deliberately played a head game with Bill Clinton to make him lose his cool over the Clintons' record on race, which Bill did in a devastating televised rant. Barack Obama credited Harpootlian with shifting the momentum his way at a rally just on the eve of the vote: "Obama wrapped a bear hug around Bill Clinton's tormentor, then laughed approvingly and marveled, "You're a *crazy* son of a bitch.""

CHAPTER EIGHTEEN

163. **He had an aptitude for isolation** Tinsley completed a master's degree in forestry at Clemson University before starting law school at USC. The singer-songwriter Darrell Scott says a career in forestry requires an "aptitude for isolation" in the song "And the River Is Me" on his album *The Invisible Man,* 2006.

167. **The other side wasn't having it** A petition started by Connie Whitehead had 149 signatures on Change.org as of April 14, 2019. The organizer said she'd been pressured to remove the petition from other social media sites.

CHAPTER NINETEEN

177. **She'd told Morgan Doughty a more sinister interpretation** Morgan said in Netflix's *Murdaugh Murders,* season 2, episode 1: "Maggie and I used to talk a lot. We'd just sit in the kitchen and talk. She told me that one time,

Mr. Randolph's wife, Mrs. Libby, wanted a divorce, and he published her obituary . . . I think it was kind of like a gesture to kind of scare her into staying. I think that was her way of just letting me know what I was signing myself up for. I think it was kind of like a warning."

CHAPTERS TWENTY AND TWENTY-ONE

184. **The end of May blurred into the beginning of June** The descriptions of the weeks leading up to the homicides and 911 call are based on interviews and testimony and exhibits from the double murder trial.

CHAPTERS TWENTY-TWO THROUGH TWENTY-FOUR

193. **Sergeant Daniel Greene was four hours into** The events of June 7–8, 2021, are re-created beat by beat in the testimony in the murder trial and the exhibits, including the timeline created by SLED agent Peter Rudofski and the body and dashcam videos recorded by law enforcement. I also interviewed many of the players.

PART FIVE: **BLACK BOX**

CHAPTER TWENTY-SEVEN

229. **Two Murdaugh podcasts sprang up** *The Impact of Influence* podcast hosted by Seton Tucker and Matt Harris and *The Murdaugh Murders Podcast* hosted by Mandy Matney debuted on June 22, 2021.

CHAPTER TWENTY-EIGHT

240. **Her son Tony was surprised** Gloria Satterfield's family members say they first heard about the $505,000 settlement after Mandy Matney of FITSNews.com published court filings in Gloria's case in "Murdaugh Murders: Unanswered Questions About Multiple Suspicious Deaths." The story posted June 10, 2021, three days after the murders.

CHAPTER THIRTY

259. **The medevac helicopter** The online news outlet FITSNews.com raised numerous questions about the Sept. 4, 2021, roadside shooting while Alex was still in rehab, including in Mandy Matney's "Murdaugh Murders: Helicopter Dispatched to Alex Murdaugh Shooting Before Sheriff's Office" on Sept. 10, 2021.

CHAPTER THIRTY-ONE

262. **SLED had discovered** Agent Ryan Kelly, the lead investigator on the roadside shooting, testified that Alex's brother Randy called SLED on Sept. 6 to report Alex's illicit cellphone use.

264. **Via a publicist** Amanda Loveday, a longtime colleague of Harpootlian's, released Alex's statement to the *Guardian* on Sept. 6, 2021.

266. **Two days after the shooting** The *New York Times* reporter Nicholas Bogel-Burroughs quoted an anonymous member of the firm as saying the missing amount was in the millions in "Lawyer Shot After Wife and Son Were Killed Had Been Pushed Out of Law Firm," Sept. 7, 2021.

268. **His younger brother shared the news** Reporter Liz Farrell was the first to file a FOIA for Alex's phone calls. She used them as the basis of "Incoming Call from Alex Murdaugh," a three-episode series that began streaming Feb. 23, 2022, on *The Murdaugh Murders Podcast*. Harpootlian and Griffin filed a lawsuit to block the release of further recordings on the grounds that it violated Alex's privacy. Though they did not prevail, the calls dried up nonetheless. No calls have been released since Alex went into state custody in March 2023.

CHAPTER THIRTY-FOUR

280. **Alex had chosen to wear** Jason Ryan was the first to report that the clothes Alex was wearing belonged to his lawyer's college-age son in "Alex Murdaugh Borrows Clothes . . ." for *The Daily Beast*, July 20, 2022.

PART SIX: RAIN

CHAPTER THIRTY-FIVE

288. **A Highway Patrol lieutenant** Alex was indicted for stealing $125,000 from Lt. Tommy Moore, who, coincidentally, investigated the Stephen Smith case.

291. **"He believes that the killer or killers are still at large"** I covered Murdaugh's arraignment for *The Wall Street Journal* in "Alex Murdaugh Pleads Not Guilty . . . ," July 20, 2022.

293. **She had eulogized Maggie** Liz Murdaugh described her rituals honoring her late sister-in-law and nephew in an interview with *The* (Charleston) *Post and Courier* for "Murdaugh Family Hopes for Answers," March 27, 2022.

294. **One of Harpootlian's longtime paralegals** Harpootlian described paralegal Holli Miller's discovery in an interview with his fellow senator Stephen Goldfinch the day after the sentencing for his podcast *Trilogy Outdoors*. "Senator Dick Harpootlian" aired March 4, 2023, season 2, episode 50.

295. **The restoration of the firm's reputation was boosted** Johnny Parker and Danny Henderson represented the mayor of Bluffton in a defamation case, described in *The Island Packet*'s "Jury Awards $50 Million to Bluffton Mayor," Feb. 1, 2022.

CHAPTER THIRTY-SIX

301. **In his seventy-one years, he had seen** Jennifer Berry Hawes described Judge Newman's early life in a definitive profile for *The* (Charleston) *Post and Courier,* "Murdaugh Cases Overseen by SC Judge Clifton Newman . . . ," Sept. 4, 2022.

301. **As he presided, the judge knew he would need** Judge Newman talked in general about his approach in a Q&A on March 28, 2023, at Cleveland State University School of Law, his alma mater.

302. **If the juror liked him** Harpootlian talked about jury selection and trial strategy with me and others, including Reuben Guttman for a post on the Whistleblowers Blog, saying, "Pick a jury not based only on your client's profile, but also yours. If the jury hates you, they usually won't like your client. This has caused me to gravitate towards unattractive people on juries. They don't feel threatened by me and aren't disdainful like attractive people."

305. **As he stood to make his opening statement** Harpootlian has frequently described his trial rituals, including on "Tips and Tales, with Legal Legend Dick Harpootlian," episode 24 of *May the Record Reflect,* a podcast by the National Institute for Trial Advocacy, released on Nov. 2, 2021.

308. **During the breaks** The description of Alex's cell is based on my inspection in the weeks after the trial. Alex's habit of reading and resting during the breaks is based on interviews with bailiffs and the clerk.

CHAPTER THIRTY-SEVEN

317. **Watching from a few rows behind his father** A Murdaugh spokesman said Buster chewed his nails as a nervous habit and did not intend to make an insulting gesture. The question was hotly debated, including in a panel discussion on Court TV, "Did Buster Murdaugh Flip the Bird?" Feb. 10, 2023.

CHAPTER THIRTY-EIGHT

318. **The Murdaughs had ended up sitting** Jim Griffin said the Murdaughs did not know the rules against mouthing words or handing up books. "It's bullshit, to be honest with you," Griffin said in an interview on episode 177 of *Impact of Influence: The Murdaugh Family Murders,* a podcast co-hosted by Seton Tucker and Matt Harris.

CHAPTER THIRTY-NINE

324. **The two dozen journalists who attended every day** There were an equal number of journalists across the street in the overflow space at the Wildlife Center, where they were allowed to use electronic devices. Among them was *The* (Charleston) *Post and Courier's* Avery Wilks, whose daily Mega-

thread of tweets logged each major testimony or argument in real time in what amounted to a first draft of the first draft of history.

333. **The only flashy touch** There were many subreddits, or forums on a specific topic on the social media network Reddit, devoted to the Murdaugh case. At the time of the trial, the biggest of these was r/MurdaughFamilyMurders with more than 60,000 members.

333. **Harpootlian and Griffin had spent weeks trying to talk him out of it** Alex's lawyers talked about why they allowed their client to take the stand in interviews with me and at the *"20/20* Presents: The Murdaugh Defense Team" panel at CrimeCon, Sept. 23, 2023.

CHAPTER FORTY-ONE

348. **Creighton Waters had spent two years** Waters talked about his cross-examination strategy in interviews with me and at "Fall of a Southern Giant: Inside the Prosecution of Alex Murdaugh" at CrimeCon, Sept. 22, 2023.

358. **Alania Plyler was watching Alex's testimony** Alania testified about the impact of Alex's deception at the sentencing of Russell Laffitte in federal court in Charleston on Nov. 14, 2022. The description of her reaction to Alex's testimony is based on her twitter feed (@alaniaspohn) and interviews, including "I Trusted Him" on Law & Crime Network's online *Sidebar* program, March 15, 2023.

362. **Alania Plyler was still following** Alania tweeted her response in real time: "Mr Alex Murdaugh you just highly disrespected my brother who died in the wreck along with my mother. you represented them . . . you made millions . . . and you couldn't remember he also died."

PART SEVEN: THE RUINS

CHAPTER FORTY-THREE

384. **Captain Jason Chapman, one of the first officers on the scene** Chapman, Rutland, and Greene discussed the jury visit and the case in a two-part, two-hour interview with Charleston-based ABC News 4 called "Murdaugh Murder Investigators Speak Candidly After Trial."

385. **They'd been criminally charged** Becky Hill describes her family's bootlegging history in interviews with me and in *Behind the Doors of Justice*. Her grandparents' arrest was big news at the time, with the seizure of a state-of-the-art still, 270 gallons of corn liquor, and 4,000 pounds of sugar documented in *The* (Walterboro) *Press and Standard*'s "Large Whiskey Still Was Raided by Federal Men" on Oct. 8, 1953.

CHAPTER FORTY-FOUR

387. **When the lectern wobbled** Waters (@creightonwaters) tweeted out behind-the-scenes pictures from the trial after its conclusion, including one of him crouching on the carpet fixing the lectern.

CHAPTER FORTY-FIVE

395. **Before deliberations could begin** This chapter relies on my observations in court and extensive interviews with juror James McDowell. It also includes accounts from a televised interview with McDowell, Amie Williams, and Gwen Generette, "Murdaugh Jurors Speak Out," NBC's *Today* show, March 6, 2023. Jim Griffin talked about losing the Monkey Farm juror in an interview with me, on episode 19 of his podcast *The Presumption*, which aired Oct. 17, 2023, and also during "*20/20* Presents: The Murdaugh Defense Team," at CrimeCon.

398. **One juror, a carpenter** Craig Moyer spoke with *Good Morning America* hours after the verdict was reached for the segment "Murdaugh Juror Says Cellphone Video Sealed Disgraced Attorney's Fate."

399. **Juror Gwen Generette** She described hearing Alex's voice on the video for the first time on *Murdaugh Murders: A Southern Scandal*, season 2, episode 3.

CHAPTERS FORTY-SIX AND FORTY-SEVEN

400. **At 6:41 P.M.** The account of the reading of the verdict and the reactions of some of Alex's victims is based on my observation in the courtroom and my interviews with the main players. Juror James McDowell spoke with me at length about how Alex's testimony played with the jury.

401. **"Guilty verdict"** I covered the jury's decision for *The Wall Street Journal*, including "Alex Murdaugh's Trial Lasted Six Weeks. Two Days Mattered Most," published March 3, 2023.

401. **He mouthed "I love you"** Will Folks, who was sitting beside me when the verdict was read, saw Alex mouth "I'm sorry" and "I love you" to Buster, which he wrote about in "*Murdaugh Murders* Trial: Alex Murdaugh Guilty On All Counts," published March 2, 2022, on FITSNews.com

402. **By then, viewers around the world** The viewership numbers were shared in "Court TV Gets Big Bounce from Alex Murdaugh Verdict" on *Broadcasting+Cable*.

EPILOGUE

407. **Every spider has eight glittering eyes** I had this quote from Robert Penn Warren's *All the King's Men* taped to my wall for the entirety of this project: "The world is like an enormous spider web and if you touch it, however lightly, at any point, the vibration ripples to the remotest perimeter and the

drowsy spider feels the tingle and is drowsy no more but springs out to fling the gossamer coils about you who have touched the web and then inject the black, numbing poison under your hide. It does not matter whether or not you meant to brush the web of things. Your happy foot or your gay wing may have brushed it ever so lightly, but what happens always happens and there is the spider, bearded black and with his great faceted eyes glittering like mirrors in the sun, or like God's eye, and the fangs dripping."

407. **The silken threads that spin out of its body** Joshua Sokol surveys research on spider cognition in "The Thoughts of a Spiderweb," published in *Quanta Magazine* on May 23, 2017.

407. **Nearly nine months after he was convicted** The epilogue is based on scenes and dialogue I witnessed at a defense press conference in Columbia, S.C., on Sept. 4, 2023; at CrimeCon, a true crime convention held in Orlando from Sept. 21–24, 2023; and at Alex's sentencing on the financial crimes in Beaufort, S.C., on Nov. 28, 2023. It also draws on legal filings in Alex's appeal for a new trial.

408. **Jim Griffin had started a podcast** The first episode of Griffin's podcast with co-host Sara Azari, a Los Angeles–based defense lawyer, aired in June 2023: "001—Welcome to the Presumption," *The Presumption* podcast.

408. **Griffin had been chastised** Griffin defended recording Alex's trial diary on multiple occasions, including on his podcast. The reprimand was included in the South Carolina Department of Corrections' "Murdaugh Disciplinary" press release on Aug. 30, 2023.

409. **The recordings were broadcast** The snippets from Alex's trial diary were broadcast in a documentary *The Fall of the House of Murdaugh*, which began streaming on *Fox Nation* on Sept. 25, 2023. The documentary has no relation to the book by the same name written by Michael DeWitt.

409. **A reporter had recently asked** Michael DeWitt (@mmdewittjr) tweeted out Harpootlian's "sexually transmitted disease" remark on Nov. 17, 2023.

409. **As part of the plea agreement** Alex agreed to serve a minimum of twenty-three years and would be at least seventy-eight years old when his sentence was up. Randolph III was eighty-one years old when he died, according to his obituary, published by Parker-Rhoden Funeral Home.

409. **She was the subject of a state ethics investigation** Becky Hill's memoir, *Behind the Doors of Justice,* was removed from circulation in December 2023.

INDEX

PHOTO CREDITS

ABOUT THE AUTHOR

VALERIE BAUERLEIN is a national reporter for *The Wall Street Journal* who writes about small-town America and Southern politics, economics, and culture. She has covered the South her entire career, including nineteen years at the *Journal* and four years at *The State* in Columbia, South Carolina. Ms. Bauerlein graduated from Duke University. She lives in Raleigh with her husband and their two children.

X: @vbauerlein